Inflation Expectations

Inflation is widely regarded as a menace that damages business, and can only make life worse for households. Keeping it low depends critically on ensuring that firms and workers expect it to be low, and expectations of falling prices are dangerous, too, in other ways. So expectations of inflation are a key influence on national economic welfare. This collection pulls together a galaxy of international experts on inflation expectations, to debate different aspects of the issues involved. The main focus of the volume is how to get as much information as possible from surveys of inflation expectations, how best to study it and summarize it, react to it, and what the evidence tells us about the main factors that make people's varying, and often erroneous, inflation forecasts evolve over time.

A number of factors have led practitioners and observers of monetary policy to place increasing emphasis recently on inflation expectations. One is the spread of inflation targeting, invented in New Zealand over 15 years ago, but now encompassing another 25 countries, across all five continents, including Brazil, Canada and the UK. Still more significantly, the European Central Bank, the Federal Reserve System in the United States, and the Bank of Japan are among leading monetary institutions now contemplating some move, or a further move, in the same direction. A second factor is the large reduction in actual rates of inflation that has been observed in most countries over the last 15 years.

These considerations underscore the critical – and largely under-recognized – importance of inflation expectations. They emphasize the importance of the issues, and the great need for a volume that offers a clear, systematic treatment of them. This book, edited by Peter Sinclair, should prove very important for policy makers and monetary economists alike.

Peter Sinclair is Professor of Economics at the University of Birmingham and a former director of the Centre for Central Banking Studies at the Bank of England.

Routledge international studies in money and banking

1 **Private Banking in Europe**
Lynn Bicker

2 **Bank Deregulation and Monetary Order**
George Selgin

3 **Money in Islam**
A study in Islamic political economy
Masudul Alam Choudhury

4 **The Future of European Financial Centres**
Kirsten Bindemann

5 **Payment Systems in Global Perspective**
Maxwell J. Fry, Isaak Kilato, Sandra Roger, Krzysztof Senderowicz, David Sheppard, Francisco Solis and John Trundle

6 **What is Money?**
John Smithin

7 **Finance**
A characteristics approach
Edited by David Blake

8 **Organizational Change and Retail Finance**
An ethnographic perspective
Richard Harper, Dave Randall and Mark Rouncefield

9 **The History of the Bundesbank**
Lessons for the European Central Bank
Jakob de Haan

10 **The Euro**
A challenge and opportunity for financial markets
Published on behalf of Société Universitaire Européenne de Recherches Financières (SUERF)
Edited by Michael Artis, Axel Weber and Elizabeth Hennessy

11 **Central Banking in Eastern Europe**
Edited by Nigel Healey and Barry Harrison

12 **Money, Credit and Prices Stability**
Paul Dalziel

13 **Monetary Policy, Capital Flows and Exchange Rates**
Essays in memory of Maxwell Fry
Edited by William Allen and David Dickinson

14 **Adapting to Financial Globalization**
Published on behalf of Société Universitaire Européenne de Recherches Financières (SUERF)
Edited by Morten Balling, Eduard H. Hochreiter and Elizabeth Hennessy

15 **Monetary Macroeconomics**
A new approach
Alvaro Cencini

16 **Monetary Stability in Europe**
Stefan Collignon

17 **Technology and Finance**
Challenges for financial markets, business strategies and policy makers
Published on behalf of Société Universitaire Européenne de Recherches Financières (SUERF)
Edited by Morten Balling, Frank Lierman, and Andrew Mullineux

18 **Monetary Unions**
Theory, history, public choice
Edited by Forrest H. Capie and Geoffrey E. Wood

19 **HRM and Occupational Health and Safety**
Carol Boyd

20 **Central Banking Systems Compared**
The ECB, the pre-Euro Bundesbank and the Federal Reserve System
Emmanuel Apel

21 **A History of Monetary Unions**
John Chown

22 **Dollarization**
Lessons from Europe and the Americas
Edited by Louis-Philippe Rochon and Mario Seccareccia

23 **Islamic Economics and Finance: A Glossary, 2nd Edition**
Muhammad Akram Khan

24 **Financial Market Risk**
Measurement and analysis
Cornelis A. Los

25 **Financial Geography**
A Banker's view
Risto Laulajainen

26 **Money Doctors**
The experience of international financial advising 1850–2000
Edited by Marc Flandreau

27 **Exchange Rate Dynamics**
A new open economy macroeconomics perspective
Edited by Jean-Oliver Hairault and Thepthida Sopraseuth

28 **Fixing Financial Crises in the 21st Century**
Edited by Andrew G. Haldane

29 **Monetary Policy and Unemployment**
The US, Euro-area and Japan
Edited by Willi Semmler

30 **Exchange Rates, Capital Flows and Policy**
Edited by Peter Sinclair, Rebecca Driver and Christoph Thoenissen

31 **Great Architects of International Finance**
The Bretton Woods era
Anthony M. Endres

32 **The Means to Prosperity**
Fiscal policy reconsidered
Edited by Per Gunnar Berglund and Matias Vernengo

33 **Competition and Profitability in European Financial Services**
Strategic, systemic and policy issues
Edited by Morten Balling, Frank Lierman and Andy Mullineux

34 **Tax Systems and Tax Reforms in South and East Asia**
Edited by Luigi Bernardi, Angela Fraschini and Parthasarathi Shome

35 **Institutional Change in the Payments System and Monetary Policy**
Edited by Stefan W. Schmitz and Geoffrey E. Wood

36 **The Lender of Last Resort**
Edited by F.H. Capie and G.E. Wood

37 **The Structure of Financial Regulation**
Edited by David G. Mayes and Geoffrey E. Wood

38 **Monetary Policy in Central Europe**
Miroslav Beblavý

39 **Money and Payments in Theory and Practice**
Sergio Rossi

40 **Open Market Operations and Financial Markets**
Edited by David G. Mayes and Jan Toporowski

41 **Banking in Central and Eastern Europe 1980–2006**
A comprehensive analysis of banking sector transformation in the former Soviet Union, Czechoslovakia, East Germany, Yugoslavia, Belarus, Bulgaria, Croatia, the Czech Republic, Hungary, Kazakhstan, Poland, Romania, the Russian Federation, Serbia and Montenegro, Slovakia, Ukraine and Uzbekistan.
Stephan Barisitz

42 **Debt, Risk and Liquidity in Futures Markets**
Edited by Barry A. Goss

43 **The Future of Payment Systems**
Edited by Stephen Millard, Andrew G. Haldane and Victoria Saporta

44 **Credit and Collateral**
Vania Sena

45 **Tax Systems and Tax Reforms in Latin America**
Edited by Luigi Bernardi, Alberto Barreix, Anna Marenzi and Paola Profeta

46 **The Dynamics of Organizational Collapse**
The case of Barings Bank
Helga Drummond

47 **International Financial Co-operation**
Political economics of compliance with the 1988 Basel Accord
Bryce Quillin

48 Bank Performance
A theoretical and empirical framework for the analysis of profitability, competition and efficiency
Jacob Bikker and Jaap W.B. Bos

49 Monetary Growth Theory
Money, interest, prices, capital, knowledge and economic structure over time and space
Wei-Bin Zhang

50 Money, Uncertainty and Time
Giuseppe Fontana

51 Central Banking, Asset Prices and Financial Fragility
Éric Tymoigne

52 Financial Markets and the Macroeconomy
Willi Semmler, Peter Flaschel, Carl Chiarella and Reiner Franke

53 Inflation Theory in Economics
Welfare, velocity, growth and business cycles
Max Gillman

54 Monetary Policy Over Fifty Years
Heinz Herrman (Deutsche Bundesbank)

55 Designing Central Banks
David Mayes and Geoffrey Wood

56 Inflation Expectations
Edited by Peter Sinclair

Inflation Expectations

Edited by Peter Sinclair

Routledge
Taylor & Francis Group

LONDON AND NEW YORK

First published 2010
by Routledge
2 Park Square, Milton Park, Abingdon, Oxon OX14 4RN

Simultaneously published in the USA and Canada
by Routledge
270 Madison Ave, New York, NY 10016

Routledge is an imprint of the Taylor & Francis Group, an informa business

Typeset in Times by Wearset Ltd, Boldon, Tyne and Wear

British Library Cataloguing in Publication Data
A catalogue record for this book is available from the British Library

Library of Congress Cataloging in Publication Data
Inflation expectations/edited by Peter Sinclair.
p. cm. – (Routledge international studies in money and banking; 56)

1. Inflation (Finance) 2. Rational expectations (Economic theory)
I. Sinclair, P.J.N.

HG229.I45153 2009
332.4′1–dc22

2009023556

ISBN10: 0-415-56174-4 (hbk)
ISBN10: 0-203-86371-2 (ebk)

ISBN13: 978-0-415-56174-7 (hbk)
ISBN13: 978-0-203-86371-8 (ebk)

Contents

List of illustrations   xi
List of contributors   xvii

1 **Inflation expectations: an introduction**   1
   PETER SINCLAIR

2 **How robust are quantified survey data?: evidence from
   the United States**   8
   ROY BATCHELOR

3 **Inflation expectations and empirical tests: theoretical
   models and empirical tests**   34
   RICHARD CURTIN

4 **Heterogeneous expectations, adaptive learning, and
   forward-looking monetary policy**   62
   MARTIN FUKAČ

5 **Consumer inflation expectations: usefulness of survey-
   based measures – a cross-country study**   76
   RYSZARD KOKOSZCZYŃSKI, TOMASZ ŁYZIAK AND
   EWA STANISŁAWSKA

6 **Further evidence on the properties of consumers'
   inflation expectations in the euro area**   101
   MAGNUS FORSELLS AND GEOFF KENNY

7 **Household versus expert forecasts of inflation: new
   evidence from the European survey data**   118
   CHRISTINA GERBERDING

8   **The role of expectations in the inflation process in the
    euro area**   140
    MARITTA PALOVIITA AND MATTI VIRÉN

9   **The European consumer and monetary policy**   158
    JAN MARC BERK AND GERBERT HEBBINK

10 **Testing near-rationality using survey data**   177
    MICHAEL F. BRYAN AND STEFAN PALMQVIST

11 **400,000 observations on inflation perceptions and
    expectations in the EU: what do they tell us?**   196
    STAFFAN LINDÉN

12 **Finding the optimal method of quantifying inflation
    expectations on the basis of qualitative survey data**   219
    FABIEN CURTO MILLET

    Index   250

Illustrations

Figures

2.1	Individual expectations and survey responses	13–14
2.2	US inflation expectations: quantitative Michigan SRC data	18–19
2.3	Alternative estimators of mean expectations	21–22
2.4	Alternative estimators of standard deviation of expectations	25–26
2.5	Michigan SRC inflation expectations versus quantified expectations	27
3.1	Year-ahead inflation expectations: distributions of responses, 1978–2005	43
3.2	Year-ahead inflation expectations: distributions of responses, 1980	44
3.3	Year-ahead inflation expectations: distributions of responses, 2001	44
3.4	Median and mean inflation expectations (monthly data, 1978–2005)	46
3.5	Inflation expectations: twenty-fifth, fiftieth, and seventy-fifth percentiles	47
3.6	Inflation expectations: interquartile range.	47
4.1	The impulse response value at time $t = \{4, 8, 16, 40\}$	71
5.1	Speed of convergence of expectations towards actual inflation	86
5.2	Measures of consumer inflation expectations in the Czech Republic	92
5.3	Measures of consumer inflation expectations in Hungary	92
5.4	Measures of consumer inflation expectations in Poland	93
5.5	Measures of consumer inflation expectations in Slovakia	93
6.1	Perceived, actual and expected inflation	103
6.2	Expectation errors: autocorrelations	107
6.3	Hybrid Phillips curve – recursive parameter estimates (γ_f)	114
7.1	Actual and perceived inflation	121
7.2	Expected inflation according to EC Consumer Survey	122–123

7.3	Consensus forecasts of inflation	124
8.1	Time series with aggregate euro area data	144
8.2	Time series with pooled euro area data	145
8.3	OECD inflation forecasts for the following year	145
8.4	Evolution of inflation and inflation expectations	146
8.5	Impulse responses for aggregate euro area data	152
8.6	Impulse responses for pooled euro area data	153
9.1	Euro-effect and indicator of "visible" inflation	171
10.1	Long-run Phillips curve under near-rationality	177
10.2	Coefficients on expected inflation for alternative Phillips curve specifications in high- and low-inflation samples	180
10.3	Inflation regimes in the United States and Sweden	182
10.4	Aggregate expectations errors and inflation in the United States	185
10.5	Aggregate expectations errors and inflation in Sweden	186
10.6	Share of US households expecting no inflation and inflation	190
10.7	Share of Swedish households expecting no inflation and inflation	190
10.8	Share of US Households underpredicting inflation and inflation	191
10.9	Share of Swedish households underpredicting inflation and inflation	191
11.1	The Balance Statistic for perceived (Per BS) and 12 months lagged expected inflation (Exp BS) in the euro area, and the actual rate of inflation	201
11.2	Perceived inflation rates for the euro area, quantified by using the Carlson–Parkin (C–P) and the Anderson methods, and the actual inflation rate	202
11.3	Expected inflation rates for the euro area lagged 12 months, quantified by using the Carlson–Parkin (C–P) and the Anderson methods, and the actual inflation rate	202
11.4	Perceived (Per And + Dum) and 12 month lagged expected (Exp And + Dum) inflation for the euro area, quantified by using the Anderson method adjusted for the structural break in 1 January 2002, and the actual inflation rate	204
11.5	Quantitative perceived and expected inflation in the euro area (left) and Sweden (right) – depending on income of household, education, gender, and age	207
11.6	Quantitative perceived and 12 month lagged expected inflation rates for the euro area, and the actual inflation rate	208
11.7	Perceived inflation rates depending on respondents' likelihood to buy a car, a house, or spend a large amount of money on home improvements	212
11.8	Expected inflation rates depending on respondents'	

	likelihood to buy a car, a house, or spend a large amount of money on home improvements	212
11.9	Perceived inflation rates depending on respondents' likelihood to buy a car, a house, or spend a large amount of money on home improvements	214
11.10	Expected inflation rates depending on respondents' likelihood to buy a car, a house, or spend a large amount of money on home improvements	215
12.1	Quantitative Gallup data and actual CPI inflation, United Kingdom	227
12.2	HIP perceptions versus actual inflation, Sweden, 1979q1–2005q3	228
12.3	HIP expectations versus actual inflation, Sweden, 1979q1–2005q3	228

Tables

2.1	Selected questions from the University of Michigan Survey Research Center survey of consumers	11
2.2	Estimates of threshold models	24
2.3	Explanatory equations for expected business conditions and expected financial position	30
3.1	Change in inflation expectations over the six-month interval within selected demographic subgroups, panel data 1993–2005	50
3.2	Impact of lagged changes in actual inflation rate on change in inflation expectations, 1993 to 2005	52
3.3	Tests of rational expectations hypothesis based on university of michigan's inflation expectations data, quarterly data 1978–2005	56–57
4.1	Dynamics under rational expectations, and the contrast between adaptive learning and rational expectations	68
5.1	Survey data on perceived price changes	78
5.2	Survey data on expected price changes	80
5.3	Estimates of parameters of the regression model	81
5.4	Dispersion of inflation expectations measures versus inflation volatility	82
5.5	Usefulness of different measures of expectations in economies considered	84
5.6	Unbiasedness test – Czech Republic	85
5.7	Unbiasedness test – Poland	86
5.8	Long-run convergence of expectations towards actual inflation – Czech Republic	87
5.9	Long-run convergence of expectations towards actual inflation – Poland	87

5.10	Estimates of the hybrid Phillips curve – Poland	90
5.11	Estimates of the hybrid Phillips curve – Czech Republic	91
5.12	Overall degree of uncertainty	94
5.13	Usefulness of objectified probability measures of inflation expectations	94
5.14	Usefulness of subjectified probability measures of inflation expectations	95
5.15	Usefulness of regression measures of inflation expectations	95
5.16	Estimates of the hybrid Phillips curve – pooled Poland and Czech Republic data	97
6.1a	Mean error: alternative measures of expected inflation	104
6.1b	Root mean squared error: Alternative measures of expected inflation	105
6.2	Test for unbiasedness, sub-periods, $(\pi_t = \alpha + \beta\pi_t^e + u_t)$	106
6.3	Unit root tests	108
6.4	Error correction coefficients	109
6.5a	Test for efficiency, euro area sub-periods, $(\pi_t - \pi_t^e = \delta + \varphi\Omega_{t-12} + u_t)$	110
6.5b	Test for efficiency, euro area countries $(\pi_t - \pi_t^e = \delta + \varphi\Omega_{t-12} + u_t)$	111
6.6a	Estimates of hybrid Phillips curve	113
6.6b	Restricted estimates of hybrid Phillips curve	113
7.1	Questions and response categories of the EU consumer survey on price developments (question 5 and 6)	119
7.2	Comparison of RMSEs of alternative scaling procedures	123
7.3	Structure of quarterly consensus forecasts for consumer prices	124
7.4	Comparison of predictive power	126
7.5	Are the forecasts unbiased?	127
7.6	Are the forecast errors orthogonal to selected information variables?	128
7.7	Survey forecasts und subsequently realized inflation rates $(e_{t-4}\pi_t, \pi_t)$	130–131
7.8	Inflation, inflation expectations and output	133–134
8.1	Estimation results with aggregate euro area and pooled (stacked) cross-country data	147
8.2	Estimation results with pooled cross-country data	148
8.3	Variance decompositions for time horizons 1, 2 and 20	149
8.4	Comparison of variance decompositions using different specifications	150
8.5	Variance decompositions with pooled cross-country data for the euro area	150
8.6	Variance decompositions with individual country data	151
8.7	Wald tests for unbiasedness of inflation expectations	154

8.8	Pooled cross-country results with a VECM (2) model	155
9.1	Testing for causality between expected and actual future inflation	164
9.2	Effect on expected inflation of change in actual inflation	166
9.3	Effect on expected inflation of change in	167
9.4	Effects on perceived inflation of euro introduction	170
10.1	Household inflation expectations errors and inflation in the United States and Sweden	183
10.2	Expectations errors as a nonlinear function of inflation in the United States and Sweden	185
10.3	Fraction of households expecting no inflation, fraction of households underpredicting inflation, and inflation in the United States and Sweden	188
10.4	Proportion of households expecting no inflation and proportion of households underpredicting inflation as a nonlinear function of inflation in the United States and Sweden	189
11.1	Quantified inflation rates of perceived and expected inflation in the euro area using qualitative answers from question 5 and 6	200
11.2	Correlations between perceived and expected inflation and the actual euro-area inflation rate, for the total sample and two sub-samples split 1 January 2002, the introduction of the euro	203
11.3	Balance statistic for perceived and expected inflation in the euro area for different demographic groups	205
11.4	Quantitative perceived and expected inflation in the euro area and the balance statistic for different demographic groups (averages for May 2003 to October 2005)	206
11.5	Correlations between quantitative perceived and expected inflation and the actual euro-area inflation rate, and between quantitative perceived and expected inflation and the qualitative data	209
12.1	Expectations measures selected for comparison	220
12.2	RMSE results for predicting actual inflation	222
12.3	Average rank and RMSE for predictive success	223
12.4	MSE decomposition, details	224
12.5	MSE decomposition, averages by measure	225
12.6	Correctly predicted turning points (%)	226
12.7	Average rank, success in turning point prediction	227
12.8	HIP Survey, quantitative questions	227
12.9	Predictive performance of quantitative measures	229
12.10	Correlations with quantitative measures	229
12.11	Ability to match quantitative data	230

12.12	Correctly indicated turning points (%)	231
12.13	Non-nested testing results, United Kingdom	232
12.14	Non-nested testing results, Sweden	232
12.15	Wage equation structure	233
12.16	Empirical wage equation, sign priors	235
12.17	Wage equations, retained lags of expectations	238
12.18	Results from the Swedish wage equation	239

Contributors

Roy Batchelor is Professor of Banking and Finance at the Cass Business School, City of London.

Jan Marc Berk is Director of the Statistics and Information Division, and former Head of the Monetary and Economic Policy Department, and Research Department, at de Nederlandsche Bank, in Amsterdam.

Michael F. Bryan is a Vice President and Economist in the Reseach Department of the Federal Reserve Bank of Atlanta.

Richard Curtin is Research Professor and Director of the Surveys of Consumers, at the University of Michigan

Fabien Curto Millet is a Senior Consultant at NERA Economic Consulting in Brussels, London and Paris, and former Lecturer in Economics at Balliol College, Oxford

Magnus Forsells works in the DG-Economic at the European Central Bank, in Frankfurt.

Martin Fukač is a Senior Research Analyst at the Reserve Bank of New Zealand, and previously a Senior Economist with the Czech National Bank.

Christina Gerberding works in the central office of the Economics Department of the Deutsche Bundesbank, in Frankfurt.

Gerbert Hebbink is a Senior Economist with the Economics and Research Division at de Nederlandsche Bank, in Amsterdam.

Geoff Kenny works in the DG-Research at the European Central Bank, in Frankfurt.

Ryszard Kokoszczyński is Director of the Bureau of Macroeconomic Research at the National Bank of Poland, and Professor of Economics at the University of Warsaw.

Staffan Lindén works in the Directorate General of Economic and Financial Affairs at the European Commission in Brussels.

Tomasz Łyziak works with the Bureau of Macroeconomic Research at the National Bank of Poland, in Warsaw.

Stefan Palmqvist works at the Monetary Policy Department of the Riksbank, in Stockholm.

Maritta Paloviita is an economist working at the Bank of Finland, in Helsinki.

Peter Sinclair is Professor of Economics at the University of Birmingham, United Kingdom.

Ewa Stanisławska works with the Bureau of Macroeconomic Research at the National Bank of Poland, in Warsaw.

Matti Virén is Professor of Economics at the University of Turku, Finland, and Scientific Advisor to the Bank of Finland.

1 Inflation expectations

An introduction

Peter Sinclair[1]

On 10 July 2007, the Chairman of the Federal Reserve Board, Ben Bernanke, (Bernanke 2007), gave a major speech at the National Bureau of Economic Research, in Cambridge, Massachusetts. He chose to devote it to the topic of Inflation Expectations.

That choice may have been motivated by the fascinating debate on the role that inflation expectations had played in the Great Moderation – the remarkable decline in the average level and variability of inflation that the world's leading economies have witnessed since the early 1990s. It may also have been prompted by a small but growing sense of alarm that, with recent rises in inflation, this phase might be drawing to a close. The issue of what tethers inflation expectations to a target, declared or implicit, is now uppermost in many central bankers' and economists' minds: that, and fears that, in the wake of the explosion of many primary commodity prices from 2004, they might start to get detached from it.

The Bernanke speech followed close upon an important conference in Warsaw, organized by the National Bank of Poland in 2006. That conference was devoted, too, to inflation expectations. This volume presents newly finalized versions of papers that were presented there. Why are inflation expectations so important?

Part of the answer runs like this. Beyond some pretty modest levels, both unemployment and inflation are invariably thought of as social ills. They are the classic two ingredients of "economic misery". It is the monetary authorities' task to try to minimize them – or more properly, in most approaches, the discounted future stream of the weighted sum of the squares of their deviations from optimal or equilibrium values. There is one thing that everyone agrees *must* increase at least one of these two sources of misery, and often both. That is the expected rate of inflation. Expectations of higher inflation shift up the short-term trade-off (the Phillips curve) between actual inflation on the one side, and unemployment (or some measure of lost output, which will accompany the unemployment: the difference between actual real GDP and its trend value, the output gap, should betray this) on the other. That must entail higher actual inflation at a given rate of unemployment (or higher unemployment at a given rate of inflation).

This is the unambiguously sinister side of inflation expectations. Sometimes a rise in them could appear more benign. All else equal, it should lead to higher consumption and investment spending, in response to the lower expected real interest rate. This will not occur, however, if the rise in expected inflation is more than offset by an accompanying (or staggered) jump in nominal (policy) interest rates. The Taylor Rule[2] will advise just that, since anything less can only cause instability. Assume that the central bank is believed to follow the precepts of the Taylor Rule.[3] In this case, a rise in near-future inflation expectations will make agents anticipate higher real interest rates; they will then see that that should squeeze output and jobs later on; and the end result will be a fall in the current expectations of inflation at or a little beyond that horizon. When prices are expected to decline, on the other hand, the zero lower bound to nominal policy rates means that real aggregate demand will be boosted (depressed) by expectations of slower (faster) decline in the rate of inflation. Recent Japanese experiences have shown that this threat is no laughing matter.

With this one exception, then, we learn two things: first, that higher (lower) inflation expectations have the potential, typically, to create major economic damage (benefit); and second, that the size and character of those effects will depend critically on how agents think the central bank will react. At its best, a fully credible central bank, committed to fighting inflation as a first priority, should succeed in keeping inflation expectations steady, at least on average over time. Departures from any explicit or inferred target should then be brief – and small.

So inflation expectations are of enormous practical importance, a point stressed forcefully recently by Mishkin (2007). If expectations were fully rational, all they would do would be to reflect (presumably the latest) information and knowledge. They would simply be consistent with "the" model, whatever that might be.[4] They would not really have any life of their own. And presumably we would observe them only indirectly. There would be an element of circularity: it would be rather like using consumption spending to infer the income expectations upon which they were assumed to be based.

True, inflation expectations can be inferred from an estimated model, under the assumption of rational expectations. But we have two other potential sources for them, both of them effectively independent of the model in which we formalize their influence upon the course of actual inflation and output. One is financial data, such as those on the prices and relative yields of both indexed and unindexed bonds. The second is surveys. This volume is devoted to the latter.

Why study surveys? One practical answer is provided by Ang *et al.* (2007). US evidence, they find, shows that inflation expectations culled from surveys actually turn out to be better predictors of subsequent actual inflation than either statistical macroeconomic models, or financial asset price data. A second argument turns on the fact that the size and character of macroeconomic models are disputed: model-based expectations require the investigator to preselect the model. Third, there is the point that financial market data may be contaminated by transaction costs, risk premia, tax treatment questions, and, above all, data paucity. In many countries, indexed bonds are comparatively recent, if they exist at all, and the range of maturities on which they are offered, if any, is invariably very limited. Of course one need not confine oneself to any one source: Fu

(2007) shows that there are interesting lessons to be learnt from combining surveys and financial market data. Nonetheless, survey data are remarkably rich and extensive, and surely merit close attention. And, like Mount Everest, they exist.[5]

All sorts of questions arise, to which survey data can enable us to obtain some answers. For example, to what extent do survey-based inflation forecasts in fact qualify as *rational*? How big are the departures from rationality – trivial, appreciable, or really pronounced? How long do such departures, if any, tend to persist? Does actual inflation betray good links with, and/or strong influences from, prior expectations of inflation in the relevant period? Are economic experts better or worse at predicting inflation than sampled households? Are there any other differences between the two groups? Do survey expectations show evidence of learning? Are they adaptive, and if so to what, when, and how quickly? What can be learnt about lags, and the serial correlation patterns? Is there evidence, from the massive survey evidence accumulated in the United States, for example, that the answer to these questions has been changing over time? Does the evidence actually vary across countries? Does the United States differ from West European countries in such respects? Is Western Europe homogeneous or diverse? Do the transition countries of Central and Eastern Europe manifest similar or different behaviour in their inflation – inflation expectations relationships? And other narrower but intriguing questions: are some countries' households better at predicting inflation than others', for example?

Then there are prior questions. Typically, most survey questions have been qualitative or comparative; and some can be tantalizingly vague. For example: Do you think prices will increase in the coming year? Will the rate of inflation increase? Will prices stay roughly the same? The interrogators will attempt to collate the respondents' varying answers, which will be distributed between various ranges or buckets. Moving from this coarse partitioning towards a continuous distribution is a journey fraught with hazard. Assuming a particular class of distribution will help, but is this not rather arbitrary? The goal will be to try to capture some quantitative estimate of the centre of the distribution of inflation expectations from the survey data. But which? The mean? Might not the median provide a safer measure of "average opinion", particularly if tails are long, large, and, above all, asymmetric? And what about the standard deviation (or variance) to inform us of the degree of dispersion? Or some other measure, such as the 95 per cent confidence limits, or the range between the first and third quartiles? More generally, what are the pros and cons of different ways of converting answers to qualitative questions into quantitative form? And can we use evidence to tell us which method is best?

Furthermore, what is the statistical relationship between *perceptions* of inflation, and either expectations of future inflation or actual inflation outturns? Have perceptions and actual inflation converged? What are the lessons learnt from the adoption of euro notes and coins in 2002 in this regard?

If agents differ in their inflation expectations, that is itself prima facie evidence against rational expectations in its purest form. Heterogeneous answers to survey questions may point to irrationality, but they might also reflect differences in people's spending patterns at a time when relative prices had diverged, or were thought likely to. But heterogeneity of expectations would have to be accepted as a fact. Could it be reconciled, though, with a less restrictive form of rational expectations, which made some allowance for the costs of gathering, updating and processing information? Is information actually "sticky" in the way we assume many goods and factor prices are? And what might it imply for monetary policy if expectations were heterogeneous – would it reinforce or modify the case for fighting inflation vigorously?

It is in the labour market that inflation expectations probably play the biggest role. Money wage rates are renegotiated at discrete intervals. Employers' and employees' expectations of inflation over the upcoming interval will be key in determining the size of nominal pay rises agreed upon. Can we therefore use labour markets as a test bed for our different methods of quantifying inflation expectations from survey data? And if we do, what do we find?

Some of these questions have been explored before. There are valuable survey papers, for example, by Thomas (1999) on US inflation expectations survey evidence. There are interesting discussions, for instance by Mankiw *et al.*, (2003) on sticky information and the dispersal of inflation expectations. We have a really magisterial analytical survey on the general issue of measuring expectations by Manski (2004). And the distinguished contributors to this volume have themselves, between them, a remarkable corpus of publications touching on several of these questions. But, many of the questions posed here have not been addressed before; and even the more familiar questions attract somewhat different or more nuanced answers, particularly in the context of a broad group of papers studying several different countries.

Let me now attempt a brief sketch of the chapters that follow this introduction. I shall not spoil the reader's appetite by attempting a summary of them; all chapters are accompanied by carefully written introductions and conclusions that perform this task well. Rather, I shall describe some of the key issues they address.

The first chapter is by Roy Batchelor, whose pioneering contributions to the study of expectations surveys stretch back over two decades. Here, Batchelor develops and compares different methods of translating qualitative survey response data into quantitative statistics. He focuses on US data for expectations of three big-player variables noted above: for inflation, for interest rates, and for unemployment.

Next comes a chapter by Richard Curtin. Curtin asks how far, and in what ways, households' inflation expectations data appears to deviate from the principles of strict rationality. He identifies key characteristics of heterogeneities in expectations, the extent, of and lag structures, in adaptation, asymmetries in speeds, and, *inter alia*, causal patterns in the crucial relationship between expectations of inflation and actual inflation rates.

Martin Fukač picks up the baton next. He runs with the two concepts of expectational diversity and adaptation that Curtin illuminates. Fukač asks what difference it may make if central bankers do not share the inflation expectations of the populace at large. In particular, would this reinforce the case for strictly anti-inflationary monetary policy, or weaken it?

The volume now moves to a group of chapters that make European inflation expectations survey data their primary or sole focus. Ryszard Kokoszczyński, Tomasz Łyziak and Ewa Stanisławska, organizers of the Warsaw conference, probe inflation expectations in four central European countries: the Czech Republic, Hungary, Poland, and Slovakia. They are concerned above all with the role of inflation *expectations* as a potential driver of *actual* inflation. They use data on the former to identify the forward-looking term in the "hybrid" Phillips curve to gauge, *inter alia*, the extent of bias, and convergence character, for the two countries – the Czech Republic and Poland – for which data are good enough to yield successful tests.

From central Europe, we now travel west. Magnus Forsells and Geoff Kenny also look at the hybrid Phillips curve to ascertain the role of expectations of inflation in the dynamics of subsequent actual inflation, in the biggest five Euroland economies. They update their previous work on European Commission survey data into the new century, up to 2004, importantly across the point (January 2002) when euro notes and coins first appeared. Like Curtin, they ask whether the implications of strict rational expectations are confirmed by data.

Christina Gerberding follows, by retaining their focus on EC survey data for France, Germany and Italy, but swapping the Netherlands and Spain for the United Kingdom. Do *perceived* or *experienced* inflation statistics scale the surveys answers best, she asks? Do experts outperform households in their predictions? Do inflation predictors prove to look forward or back, how biased are they, and what causal inferences can be drawn from them?

EC survey and Consensus Forecast data are probed in the next chapter, by Maritta Paloviita and Matti Virén. They explore data for the Euroland aggregate, and its 12 original member countries, to run vector autoregressions (VARs) linking the output gap, actual inflation, and expected inflation. Just what role do inflation expectations play? How important are they? How do they react to the other variables, and how long do they persist?

Jan Marc Berk and Gerbert Hebbink provide the next chapter, and continue this econometric theme. Among other things, they explore vector error correction models (VARs amended to allow phased adaptation to temporary deviations from the long run) to probe the causality issue for 11 EU countries and two aggregates. How do inflation and interest rate *surprises* affect inflation expectations? Do household reactions vary with impressions of central bank credibility? And what did the euro's advent do to perceptions of inflation?

We now go to Sweden, and also back briefly to the United States. Michael F. Bryan and Stefan Palmqvist compare survey data on perceptions and expectations of inflation for these two countries. Do perceptions match actual inflation well, they ask? Which set of households predicts inflation better? And to what extent does evidence support the claim of Akerlof *et al.* (2000) that while appreciable rates of inflation should get perceived and predicted (more) accurately on average, small positive inflation gets ignored?

The gap between inflation perceptions and inflation outturns is mysterious. The next contribution, by Staffan Lindén, seeks to see whether consumers' purchasing intentions appear to be related to it (and to the expectations-outturn gap). Lindén also gives us a valuable first look at a new European Commission dataset which quantifies expectations and perceptions of inflation directly, rather than leaving others to try to derive them from qualitative survey responses, as previous studies have tried to do.

The final contribution to the volume is very wide ranging. It is by Fabien Curto Millet. He starts by asking what is the *best* method of making that crucial derivation (when, as almost always, only qualitative response summaries are available). He explores three main types of method, with a number of variants (some of his own creation), and tests them all on Swedish and UK data. The various methods are then contrasted in the context where inflation expectations are generally thought to matter most – the determination of money wage increases, in these two and six other EU countries.

With the Great Moderation era seemingly drawing to a close, inflation now at decade-plus record highs in many economies, and increasing concern about whether inflation expectations are remaining at anchor or casting adrift from their recent moorings, this volume brings much new light to a subject of both topical and enduring importance.

Notes

1 Professor of Economics, Department of Economics, University of Birmingham, Edgbaston, Birmingham, B15 2TT, United Kingdom. Email: p.j.n.sinclair@bham.ac.uk.
2 Traditionally, this stipulates that policy rates should change in the direction of (*a*) the gap between actual and presumed trend output, and (*b*) the gap between the actual and the desired rate of inflation, but with a bigger coefficient, greater than unity, on (*b*).
3 And that might change if the policy regime can change, as emphasized by Davig and Leeper (2007).
4 If there is a single model, but with structural parameters which are unknown, Weitzman (2007) shows that Bayesian updating of parameter estimates will tend to spread some of the mass of the probability distribution out towards its tails; and, in contrast to the traditional approach, that this can help to remove a number of seeming anomalies in macroeconomic and financial relationships. "Exceptional" events will be less surprising. There may also be uncertainty about which model describes reality best: Sargent (2008) has much to say on that issue, and also earlier, in Sargent (1999), in what really best explains the Great Moderation in the first place.
5 This was a mountaineer's famous answer to the question, why climb it?

References

Akerlof, G., W. Dickens and G. Perry (2000), Near-rational wage and price setting and the long-run Phillips curve, *Brookings Papers on Economic Activity*, 1: 1–60.
Ang, A., G. Bekaert and M. Wei (2007), Do macro variables, asset markets or surveys forecast inflation better? *Journal of Monetary Economics*, 54: 1163–1212.
Bernanke, B. (2007), *Inflation Expectations and Inflation Forecasting*, speech to the National Bureau of Economic Research, 10 July.

Davig, T. and E.M. Leeper (2007), Generalizing the Taylor Principle, *American Economic Review*, 97: 607–635.

Fu, D. (2007), Inflation expectations, real interest rates and risk premiums – evidence from bond market and consumer survey data, *Federal Reserve Board of Dallas Working Paper*, 0705.

Mankiw, N.G., R. Reis and J. Wolfers (2003), Disagreement about inflation expectations, *National Bureau Economic Research Working Paper*, 9796.

Manski, C.F. (2004), Measuring expectations, *Econometrica*, 72: 1329–1376.

Mishkin, F. (2007), Inflation dynamics, *National Bureau of Economic Research Working Paper*, 13147.

Sargent, T.J. (1999), *The Conquest of American Inflation*, Princeton, NJ: Princeton University Press.

Sargent, T.J. (2008), Evolution and Intelligent Design, *John Flemming Lecture*, Bank of England, and *American Economic Review*.

Thomas, L.B. (1999), Survey measures of expected US inflation, *Journal of Economic Perspectives*, 13: 125–144.

Weitzman, M.L. (2007), Subjective expectations and asset-return puzzles, *American Economic Review*, 97: 1102–1130.

2 How robust are quantified survey data?

Evidence from the United States

Roy Batchelor

1 Introduction

In the monthly surveys of US consumers conducted in the United States by the Survey Research Center of the University of Michigan, individuals are asked questions about their perceptions and expectations of general business conditions, their perceptions and expectations about their own household's financial situation, and their expectations about a range of economic indicators, including unemployment, borrowing costs, and prices. One aim of this chapter is to determine which of these general economic indicators really matters to consumers, and whether uncertainties about unemployment, interest rates and inflation are as important as their expected values. Parallel to this, we are interested in the reliability of the survey data, and in particular the robustness of estimates of the mean and dispersion of expectations derived in different ways from qualitative survey questions.

For the most part, the surveys do ask qualitative questions. For example the Michigan SRC survey asks: during the next 12 months, do you think that prices in general will go up, or go down, or stay where they are now? The questions asked about unemployment, interest rates, past and future general business conditions, and the past and future financial situation of the respondent's household are similar. Responses are reported in the form of balance statistics – the difference between the percentages of respondents expecting prices to go up, and to go down, suggesting that this gives information about the inflation expectations of a typical consumer. Balance statistics enter press reports, broader indices of consumer confidence, and in some cases indices of leading economic indicators.

Under strong assumptions, it is possible to translate the qualitative survey responses into quantitative estimates of the mean and standard deviation of the distribution of expectations across survey respondents. The pioneering paper is the Carlson and Parkin (1975) study of UK Gallup poll data. Their key assumptions are that the distribution of expectations is normal, that the range of price changes which elicit a no-change response is constant over time and symmetric around zero, and that expectations are unbiased. As it happens, the Michigan SRC also asks for quantitative estimates of future inflation, so for this variable it is possible to obtain direct measures of the mean and standard deviation of the expectations distribution, and test the reasonableness of the Carlson–Parkin assumptions.

Quantified mean expectations have been used to test whether consumer expectations are efficient or technically rational, and as inputs into econometric models. The standard deviation of individual expectations looks as if it should contain information about the degree of uncertainty of a typical respondent, and uncertainty about employment, interest rates and inflation should in turn affect consumer decisions. However, the conditions under which the dispersion of individual expectations correlates with subjective uncertainty prove to be quite restrictive, and, perhaps because of this, less use has been made of data on the dispersion of expectations in economic modelling. An exception is Batchelor and Dua (1992) where the dispersion of expectations about inflation and household financial position are found to be significant in the US consumption function.

This chapter sets out in Section 2 a framework for analysing qualitative survey responses and clarifying the relationship between dispersion and uncertainty; then in Section 3 examines how this framework can be used to interpret aggregate survey responses, and discusses the statistical properties of quantified expectations and dispersion measures from the SRC surveys; and finally in Section 4 assesses which expectations and uncertainties really matter for economic well-being, as perceived by US consumers. We also, crucially, test whether the inflation expectations obtained from qualitative data lead to the same inferences as the directly measured inflation expectations.

We find that mean expectations of unemployment, interest rates and inflation are all statistically significant determinants of consumer expectations about general business conditions. Unemployment and inflation also impact significantly on expectations about households' own financial position. Consumers seem subject to some fallacy of composition in framing these expectations, however, with general business conditions expected to behave in a regressive way (with bad times expected to follow good times), while their own financial situation is simply extrapolated (with bad times followed by more bad times). Regarding the quality of the survey-based expectations, measures of mean inflation expectations are fairly robust, with similar results obtained for both qualitative and quantitative measures. The same is not true of the dispersion of expectations. Measures of the standard deviation of inflation expectations differ significantly between quantitative and qualitative surveys, and produce contradictory and counterintuitive results in our models of consumer expectations formation.

2 A model of individual survey responses

The Michigan SRC Surveys of Consumers started in 1946, and were conducted two or three times per year until 1960, when (with a few interruptions) they moved to a quarterly cycle with surveys in February, May, August and November each year. Starting from January 1978 the survey has been run monthly. The early surveys were based on quota samples of around 1,000 to 3,000 individuals, but by 1980 the sample size had been reduced to around 500. The survey is currently conducted by telephone, with a rotating sample consisting of around 60 per cent new randomly selected households, and 40 per cent re-interviews of respondents from the survey six months earlier. Individuals within each household are selected to obtain a representative age and gender profile.

Table 2.1 sets out selected questions currently asked in the survey. The first two, labelled PFP and PFE, ask about changes in the past and expected financial position of the respondent's family. The next two (BCP, BCE) ask about the respondent's perceptions of changes in past "business conditions" in general, and expected future business conditions. The final three sets of questions (UE, RE, PE) ask more specifically about the expected direction of change in unemployment, interest rates and prices. Supplementary to the price question, respondents are asked to provide a quantitative estimate the rate of inflation over the next 12 months (QE). The PFP and PFE questions, the BCP and BCE questions, and the qualitative price expectations question PE, have all been present in the survey from its early days. The unemployment and interest rate questions start in November 1960 and February 1969 respectively. Quantitative information on inflation expectations QE was initially gathered in the form of range information, starting in May 1966, and the current form of the question was introduced in August 1977.

For the qualitative questions, our data consist of the percentage responses in each category. For the quantitative inflation expectations question PE, the SRC publish data on the mean and variance of the individual expectations, and the percentages of responses lying in various ranges (<0, 0, 1–2, 3–4, 5, 5–10, over 10).

To interpret these figures, it is helpful to have some model of the respondent's mental process when answering the survey questions. First we define the information environment of the individual respondent, and develop an expression describing the mean and variance of the subjective probability distribution for the surveyed variable. Then we ask how this might translate into a qualitative (up/same/down) response to the survey question. Finally we consider the aggregate distribution of responses across individuals, and the conditions under which its mean and variance might provide information about the subjective probability distributions of individual respondents.

2.1 Information environment

The framework used to interpret unemployment, interest rate and inflation expectations, and by implication general business conditions, is similar to that developed in Batchelor (1986a) and Batchelor and Orr (1991). We suppose that at the time of survey t individual respondent i accesses three kinds of information relevant to the forecasting of variable y_t, say:

- an estimate y_{it} based on individual-specific information
- an estimate y_{ht} based on the time series history of the target variable
- a government policy target y_{gt}

Table 2.1 Selected questions from the University of Michigan Survey Research Center survey of consumers

Variable	Survey question
FPP	We are interested in how people are getting along financially these days. Would you say that you (and your family living there) are better off or worse off financially than you were a year ago? Better Now/Same/Worse/Don't Know
FPE	Now looking ahead – do you think that a year from now you (and your family living there) will be better off financially, or worse off, or just about the same as now? Will be Better Off/Same/Will be Worse Off/Don't Know
BCP	Would you say that at the present time business conditions are better or worse than they were a year ago? Better Now/About the Same/Worse Now/Don't Know
BCE	And how about a year from now, do you expect that in the country as a whole business conditions will be better, or worse than they are at present, or just about the same? Better a Year from Now/About the Same/Worse a Year from Now
UE	How about people out of work during the coming 12 months – do you think that there will be more unemployment than now, about the same, or less? More Unemployment/About the Same/Less Unemployment
RE	No one can say for sure, but what do you think will happen to interest rates for borrowing money during the next 12 months – will they go up, stay the same, or go down? Go Up/Stay the Same/Go Down/Don't Know
PE	During the next 12 months, do you think that prices in general will go up, or go down, or stay where they are now? Go Up/Stay the Same/Go Down/Don't Know If Stay the Same: Do you mean that prices will go up at the same rate as now, or that prices in general will not go up during the next 12 months?
QE	By about what percent do you expect prices to go(up/down) on the average, during the next 12 months? Per Cent/Don't Know If Per Cent > 5%: Let me make sure I have that correct. You said that you expect prices to go (up/down) during the next 12 months by (X) percent. Is that correct? If Don't Know: How many cents on the dollar do you expect prices to go (up/down) on the average, during the next 12 months?

Source: University of Michigan Survey research Center web site www.sca.isr.umich.edu/main.php.

In the case of inflation expectations, the individual-specific data might depend on the individual's shopping basket. In the case of unemployment expectations, it might depend on the individual's own situation, or on the unemployment rate among friends or in the local community. In the case of interest rate expectations it might depend on the individual's debt position and credit rating. Respondents also have some selective information from news media.

The precision of these estimates is likely to vary across individuals, as

$$y_{it} = y_t + u_{it}, \; u_{it} \sim N(0, \tau_{it}^2)$$

where τ_{it}^2 is a measure of the variance of individual experiences of the target variable, and for simplicity of exposition the distribution is assumed normal. Fishe and Idson (1990) use micro-data from the SRC survey to show that the size of the forecast errors (and the number of "don't know" responses) in inflation expectations are correlated negatively with factors like age, education and income, which are associated with greater economic activity, and hence with superior information acquisition and processing. *Ceteris paribus*, they find errors are negatively correlated with gender, where male = 1, female = 0.

We assume that the target variable follows the process:

$$\begin{aligned}
y_t &= y_{gt} \text{ with probability } \pi_{it} \\
&= y_{ht} + u_{ht}, \; u_{it} \sim N(0, \tau_{ht}^2) \text{ with probability } 1 - \pi_{it}
\end{aligned} \quad (1)$$

where π_{it} is the probability that the government target will be enforced, an index of the credibility of policy. Differences in individual political affiliations are liable to induce differences in π_{it} and hence more optimistic expectations among the supporters of the incumbent government. Absent the policy, y_{ht} is the time series prediction of y, and τ_{ht}^2 is a measure of the volatility of the target variable over time. Many macroeconomic variables follow near unit root processes, so that the time series prediction can be proxied by the lagged observed value y_{t-1}, possibly with added drift.

From observations on y_{it}, y_{gt}, and y_{ht} the respondent can form a subjective probability distribution for the target variable. If the individual is rational in the sense of Muth (1961) this will coincide with the statistically optimal conditional distribution. Following DeGroot (1970: 167) this distribution will be $N(\mu_{it}, \sigma_{it}^2)$ where

$$\mu_{it} = w_{it} \, y_{it} + (1 - w_{it}) \, \{\pi_{it}.y_{gt} + (1 - \pi_{it}).y_{ht}\} \quad (2)$$

$$\sigma_{it}^2 = \frac{\tau_{it}^2 (1 - \pi_{it}) \{\pi_{ht}(y_{ht} - y_{gt})^2 + \tau_{ht}^2\}}{\tau_{it}^2 + (1 - \pi_{it}) \{\pi_{ht}(y_{ht} - y_{gt})^2 + \tau_{ht}^2\}} \quad (3)$$

and the weight w_{it} assigned to individual-specific as opposed to general information is

$$w_{it} = \sigma_{it}^2 / \tau_{it}^2 \quad (4)$$

Figure 2.1a shows the distribution of expectations for a typical individual.

The estimate μ_{it} is the individual's estimate of the value of the target variable, and the variance σ_{it}^2 is a measure of individual subjective uncertainty. The mean expectation is a weighted average of the individual-specific estimate, the time series estimate and the government target, with weights that reflect the relative precisions of these estimates and the credibility of the target.

Uncertainty similarly depends positively on the variance of the individual-specific information, the volatility of the variable over time, the credibility of the government target, and the gap $y_{ht} - y_{gt}$ between the time series estimate of the underlying variable, and the government target for that variable. Batchelor and Orr (1991) explore the analytics of the inflation uncertainty expression (3). Among other things, it implies that uncertainty is raised by deviations of inflation from target rates, and that increased policy credibility will decrease uncertainty only if credibility is already above a certain minimum threshold. Otherwise the announcement of a target far from the current rate of inflation increases uncertainty by widening the range of possible future outcomes for inflation.

2.2 Survey responses

Given this subjective probability distribution, how will a survey respondent answer the question: do you expect the value of y to fall, remain unchanged, or rise? Following Batchelor (1986b) and consistent with the above model of rational information processing, we assume that the respondent implicitly conducts a hypothesis test of the null of no change H0: $m_{it} = y_{t-1}$ against the alternatives H1: $m_{it} > y_{t-1}$ or $m_{it} < y_{t-1}$, where m_{it} is the true mean of individual i's subjective probability distribution. One way of viewing the no-change null is that it implies that individual specific information has no value ($w_{it} = 0$), and

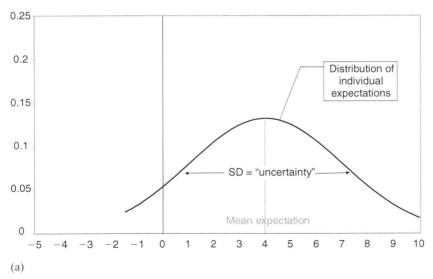

(a)

Figure 2.1 Individual expectations and survey responses.

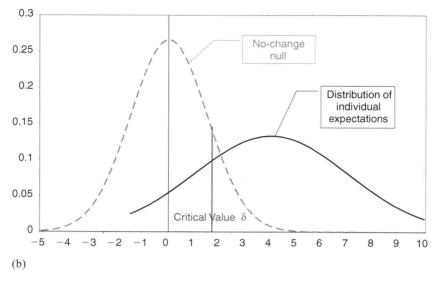

(b)

Figure 2.1 continued

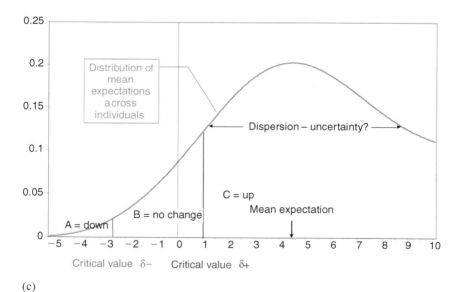

(c)

Figure 2.1 continued

either $\pi_{it} = 0$ (no policy effectiveness), or that $y_{gt} = y_{ht} = y_{t-1}$ say, so that the variable y is already at its target level. In this case, the subjective variance in (3) reduces to τ_{ht}^2, the time series volatility measure.

The form of the test is to reject the null if

$$\mu_{it} - y_{t-1} > \delta_{it}^+$$

or

$$\mu_{it} - y_{t-1} < -\delta_{it}^- \tag{5}$$

where the δ_{it} are critical values chosen so as to minimize the expected disutility of Type I and Type II errors. Figure 2.1b shows the distributions of an individual's expectations under null and alternative hypotheses, the areas measuring the probabilities of Type I and Type II error, and the critical values δ_{it}. All else equal, the δ_{it} will depend positively on the gap between the estimated mean μ_{it} and the benchmark no-change value of the variable y_{t-1}. If the variance under the null depends only on τ_{ht}^2, the δ_{it} will also depend positively on the time series variance, since an increase in τ_{ht}^2 reduces the relative probability of a Type I error.

For at least some of the variables in the SRC survey, the critical values are likely to be asymmetric. For the questions relating to unemployment, interest rates and inflation, and even general business conditions, the individual respondents have no stake in the outcome. They are likely to treat positive and negative Type II errors (i.e. missed signals of change in the economy) symmetrically. However, when thinking about their own financial position, the conventional assumption is that individuals have concave utility functions. Potentially damaging events such as an increased probability of unemployment, increased interest costs on debt, and increased inflation, would be treated as more serious than potentially beneficial events. For variables FPP and FPE, the critical value δ_{it}^+ applied to adverse events is therefore likely to be smaller than the critical value δ_{it}^- for beneficial events.

Recently, some direct evidence on the properties of individual thresholds has become available. In the quarterly IFO World Economic Survey, experts are asked about whether 6-month-ahead inflation rates (in 90 countries!) will be higher, lower, or remain unchanged. In July 2004, participants were also asked to state the percentage by which inflation would have to rise/fall for them to make a positive response to the survey question. From pooled data for major economies, Henzel and Wollmershauser (2005) confirm that these thresholds vary directly with the average expected inflation rate, directly with the past volatility of inflation, and are higher for increases in inflation than for falls. This is encouragingly consistent with the signal detection theory of survey responses outlined above.

3 Interpreting aggregate survey data

Suppose the survey conducted at t has n_t respondents. Of these, some number, say n_t^A report that they expect variable y to fall, since for these individuals, $\mu_{it} - y_{t-1} < -\delta_{it}^-$. Similarly n_t^C will report that they expect y to rise since for them $\mu_{it} - y_{t-1} < \delta_{it}^+$. The survey responses are the reported to users in the form of the proportions A_t, B_t and C_t of the sample expecting a fall, no change and a rise, where for example $A_t = n_t^A/n_t$ and $C_t = n_t^C/n_t$. We have seen that individuals have expectations drawn from heterogeneous distributions, and will in general use different decision rules to frame their answers. Can these response proportions be used to make inferences about the average and standard deviation of the expectations μ_{it} across individuals? Can the responses be used to make inferences about average subjective uncertainty σ_{it}^2?

We start by setting out the theory of "quantification" of aggregated survey responses, then look at the results of quantifying the Michigan SRC surveys.

3.1 Quantification

In order to make progress, some assumption must be made about the form of the distribution of μ_{it} across individuals, shown in Figure 2.1c. Responses to a qualitative survey are conventionally summarized in the form of a "balance statistic", $C_t - A_t$, measuring the difference between the proportion expecting a rise in the underlying variable, and the proportion expecting a fall. The conventional understanding is that this is proportionate to, or is at least strongly informative about, the average individual expectation. However, the balance statistic is a sufficient statistic for the average individual expectation μ_t only under a very unrealistic assumption about the distribution of the individual expectations. As shown in some early work on the quantification of tendency surveys (Pfanzagl 1952; Theil 1958), the μ_{it} must follow a discrete signum distribution, of the form

$\mu_{it} = -\theta$ with probability A

0 with probability B

$+\theta$ with probability C

For any critical values δ_{it}^- and $\delta_{it}^+ < \theta$, the expected value and variance of the distribution can be estimated from the survey responses by the Balance and Disconformity statistics

$$BAL_t = \theta\,(C_t - A_t) \tag{6}$$

$$DIS_t = \theta^2\{(C_t + A_t)^2 - (C_t - A_t)^2\} \tag{7}$$

In press reports, θ is set to 1, but it could be chosen to ensure that the Balance statistic had the same average value as the target variable over a run of surveys, in which case (6) would yield a series of quantitative estimates of the average expectations μ_t of individuals, and the square root of the disconformity statistic in (7) would estimate the standard deviation of expectations across individuals.

Carlson and Parkin (1975) instead assume that the distribution of mean expectations across individuals is normal, and that the critical values δ_{it}^- and δ_{it}^+ are symmetric, equal for all individuals, and constant over time, so that $\delta_{it}^- = \delta_{it}^+ = \delta$, say. Then the mean and standard deviation of expectations across individuals can be estimated as:

$$CPMEAN_t = \delta\,(a_t + b_t)/(a_t - b_t) \qquad (8)$$

$$CPSD_t = \delta. - 2/(a_t - b_t) \qquad (9)$$

Where a_t and b_t are percentiles of the cumulative normal distribution corresponding to the sample proportions A_t and $(A_t + B_t)$. Again, these can be turned into quantitative estimates by choosing δ to ensure that mean expectations are unbiased.

While the use of a continuous distribution is more realistic, the conditions under which the mean individual expectations will be normally distributed are very restrictive. Specifically, μ_{it} will be normal only if all individuals are sampling from the same distribution of individual-specific information (so all are equally well informed) and that all individuals hold the same beliefs about the credibility of policy targets. In this case, the μ_{it} will effectively be drawn from the same sampling distribution for the mean, and will indeed be normally distributed in large samples.

Under these conditions, the standard deviation of mean expectations across individuals is proportionate to the common subjective standard deviation of individual expectations (see for example Batchelor 1986a), so that the dispersion of mean expectations can be used as a proxy for individual uncertainty about the target variable. In the US Survey of Professional Forecasters, respondents are asked to provide a probability distribution for inflation and growth forecasts, so one can test directly whether forecaster disagreement over the mean inflation rate is correlated with average subjective uncertainty. For this group of forecasters at least, the evidence is encouraging. For example, Giordani and Soderlind (2003) report a correlation of +0.83 for inflation expectations. Some studies (for example, Rich *et al.* 1992) have tried to measure this correlation indirectly, by testing whether dispersion in the Michigan SRC consumer inflation expectations data is higher at times when forecasts are particularly inaccurate, with negative results. However, this indirect approach assumes that subjective uncertainty about inflation is rational. Batchelor and Zarkesh (2000) show that "variance rationality" is rejected by the professional forecasters in the Survey of Professional Forecasters, so it is unlikely to hold for the lay respondents to the Michigan SRC surveys.

On the other hand, theory and evidence are strongly against homogeneity in individual probability distributions. Under our model, the distribution of mean expectations can be characterized as a mixture of normal distributions. If individuals differ only in the precision with which they gather economic information, this would argue for the use of a symmetric fat-tailed distribution rather than a normal curve, since mixtures of normals with the same expected values show positive kurtosis (see, for example, Titterington *et al.* 1985). If individuals also differ in beliefs about policy effectiveness, say, the mixture distribution will become asymmetric.

Responses to the Michigan SRC quantitative inflation expectations question QE can be used to generate direct estimates of the mean, standard deviation, skewness and kurtosis of the US consumer inflation expectations. Results are shown in Figure 2.2. The two series for the mean and standard deviation correspond to alternative estimates computed from the individual data, and from grouped data. The distribution is consistently mildly positively skewed, and is highly leptokurtic. This is in line with earlier evidence from Carlson (1975), Batchelor (1981, 1982) and Lahiri and Teigland (1987), and with the theory above. Some caution must be exercised in interpreting the SRC quantitative data, however. Curtin (1996) notes that the individual expectations distribution in any month is heavily influenced by outliers – individuals forecasting inflation of 50 per cent or 100 per cent for example. Although these may not be too influential on the mean, they do induce much volatility in month to month estimates of the

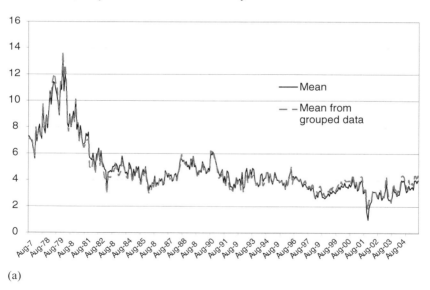

(a)

Figure 2.2 US inflation expectations: quantitative Michigan SRC data.

Notes
Top panel shows mean calculated from individual data (MSRC) and grouped data. Middle panel shows standard deviations from individual (SSRC) and grouped data. Bottom panel shows skewness and excess kurtosis from grouped data.

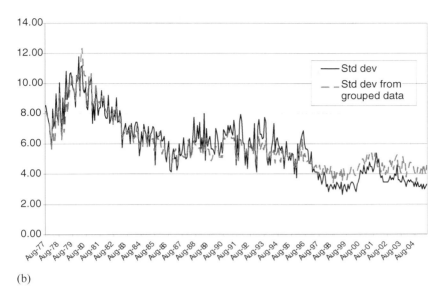

(b)

Figure 2.2 continued

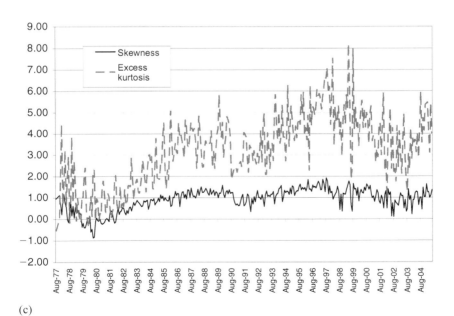

(c)

Figure 2.2 continued

standard deviation of expectations across individuals, even after trimming or winsorizing the data. These outliers also make the distributions look fat-tailed, and explain the erratic month to month movements in the kurtosis figures in Figure 2.2c.

Some studies have applied mildly non-normal, fat-tailed distributions such as the logistic and t-distributions to the estimation of a_t and b_t in (8) and (9), and there have been some recent applications of asymmetric distributions in the quantification of tendency surveys, notably Balcombe (1996) on New Zealand data, and Berk (1999) and Nielsen (2003) on Europe-wide inflation expectations. Encouragingly, these papers find little practical difference between the series for mean expectations generated from balance statistics, normal curves, and non-normal distributions such as non-central *t*- and scaled chi-squared distributions. However, these results do not carry over into comparisons of standard deviations. Batchelor (1986c) shows that for plausible patterns of responses, the disconformity measure of dispersion (7) will be *negatively* correlated with the Carlson–Parkin variance measure based on (9). And for the SRC data there is only a weak correlation between the Carlson–Parkin standard deviation (9) and the standard deviations directly estimated from the quantitative survey question.

None of the above studies addresses the problem of time variation and asymmetry in the response thresholds. This matters because any systematic movement in δ will mapped directly into mean expectations through (8). With different thresholds $-\delta^-$ and δ^+ the mean and standard deviation of expectations are estimated by

$$\text{ASMEAN}_t = (a_t\delta^+ + b_t\delta^-)/(a_t - b_t) \tag{8$'$}$$

$$\text{ASSD}_t = -2(\delta^+ + \delta^-)/(a_t - b_t) \tag{9$'$}$$

This will change the average value and volatility of the expectations estimates. However, the asymmetric threshold estimates (8$'$) and (9$'$) are linear transforms of the Carlson–Parkin estimates (8) and (9), so their use will not affect any inferences from linear models using the quantified expectations data.

Some studies have used variable thresholds. Seitz (1988) uses a time-varying parameter model, in which the δ follow a random walk. Batchelor (1986b) and Batchelor and Orr (1988) implement a variant of the Carlson–Parkin model in which thresholds are symmetric but vary systematically with the mean and variance of inflation expectations, and with past volatility in inflation. Their model is

$$\text{TVMEAN}_t = \delta_t\,(a_t + b_t)/(a_t - b_t) \tag{8$''$}$$

$$\text{TVSD}_t = \delta_t \cdot -2/(a_t - b_t) \tag{9$''$}$$

where

$$\delta_t = \delta_0 + \delta_1\,(a_t + b_t)/(a_t - b_t) + \delta_2 \cdot -2/(a_t - b_t) + \delta_3\,VOL_t + v_t \tag{10}$$

Here, the first two regressors are the unscaled mean and standard deviation from the survey data, proxies for the mean and standard deviation of individual expectations, and VOL_t is the standard deviation of the target variable over the past year, proxying the time series volatility τ_{ht} in (1).

3.2 Application to SRC data

The data used in this study start in February 1969, and are quarterly up to January 1978, when the monthly surveys begin. For the questions about past and future business conditions, and past and future financial situation, there is no single "actual" variable against which the survey responses can be benchmarked. Variables FPP, FPE, BCP, BCE have therefore been quantified using the formulae (8) and (9) with the threshold $\delta = 1$. Time series for the expectations variables FPE and BCE are shown on Figure 2.3.

Interest rate, unemployment and inflation expectations have been quantified using, respectively, the 3-month US Treasury Bill yield, the seasonally adjusted US civilian unemployment rate, and the consumer price index. The T-bill yield is not a consumer borrowing rate, but is available for a long period, and is highly correlated with consumer loan rates. For each variable, three sets of mean and dispersion estimates are calculated from the survey responses, corresponding to the constant threshold, constant asymmetric threshold and time-varying threshold models above.

The thresholds, and the parameters of the model of thresholds in (10), are chosen to minimize the mean (over time) squared error in the mean (over individuals) expectation. This is not exactly the same as the "unbiasedness"

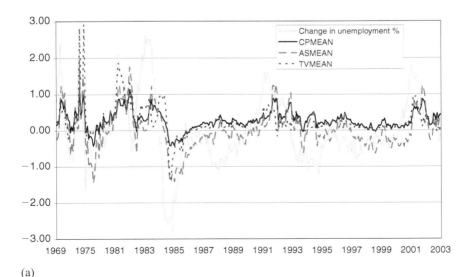

(a)

Figure 2.3 Alternative estimators of mean expectations.

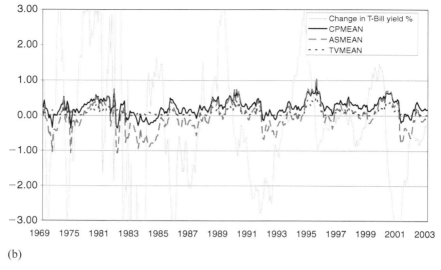

(b)

Figure 2.3 continued

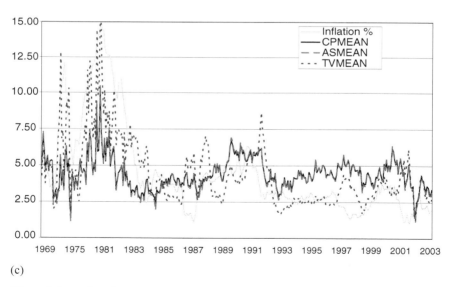

(c)

Figure 2.3 continued

assumption of Carlson and Parkin (1975), who set δ to make average mean inflation expectations equal to average actual inflation rates. Whether reasonable for
price expectations or not, this is not a sensible procedure for variables like
changes in unemployment and interest rates that have average values in our
sample close to zero. For inflation also we have the possibility of relaxing the
assumption that expectations are unbiased with respect to actual inflation, and
assuming instead that expectations are unbiased with respect to the mean expectations revealed by the quantitative question in the SRC survey. So we generate
three additional sets of inflation expectation measures, with the thresholds
selected to minimize the mean square deviation between the mean expectations
derived from responses to the qualitative PE and quantitative QE survey
questions.

Table 2.2 summarizes the results of estimating these thresholds and threshold
models. The procedure works well for unemployment and inflation, but quantifying interest rate expectations proves difficult. Our least squared error criterion
leads to implausibly low values of the symmetric threshold (around 0.10 per
cent) and a negative value for the upper threshold in the asymmetric model. To
make the figures more realistic we have set the symmetric threshold = 0.25 per
cent, the typical minimum move in official interest rates, and constrained the
upper threshold in the asymmetric model to 0. The time varying parameter
model produces implausibly large negative coefficients δ_2 and δ_3 on dispersion
and time series volatility, and these have been set to zero. This does not significantly affect the error in mean interest rate forecasts, and does not affect linear
inferences from the data.

Figure 2.3 compares resulting mean expectations of unemployment, interest
rates and inflation. The asymmetric threshold estimates of mean unemployment
and interest rate expectations tend to be lower than those from the symmetric
Carlson–Parkin model. For inflation, the two estimates are almost identical. The
time varying threshold estimates of mean unemployment and interest rate expectations are very close to the Carlson–Parkin means. However, for inflation they
are systematically different, giving higher expectations figures in the early part
of the data period, up to about 1981, and lower figures later in the sample, from
1991 onwards. The time varying threshold means are much closer to actual inflation, since the Carlson–Parkin estimates tend consistently to underestimate inflation in the 1970s, and overestimate it in the 1990s. The models for thresholds
estimated by minimizing the error between qualitative survey means and SRC
means are very similar to those from the method matching survey means with
actual inflation, and hence the resulting estimates for the mean and standard
deviation of inflation are also very close. In what follows we use the figures
scaled to actual inflation.

Figure 2.4 compares estimates of the standard deviation of expectations
across survey respondents. The asymmetric threshold estimates of standard deviations tend to be higher than the symmetric estimates for unemployment and
interest rates, but again very close for inflation. For unemployment and inflation,
the time varying threshold models produces standard deviation estimates which

Table 2.2 Estimates of threshold models

Model	Notation	Parameters	Unemployment	Interest rate	Inflation v actual	Inflation v SRC
Constant threshold	CP	δ	0.58	0.25	1.82	1.96
		Fit (RMSE)	0.89	1.98	2.73	1.86
Asymmetric threshold	AS	$\delta-$	-1.76	-0.89	-2.61	-0.04
		$\delta+$	0.63	0.00	1.47	2.81
		Fit (RMSE)	0.80	1.95	2.73	1.83
Time varying threshold	TV	d0	1.30	-0.02	0.64	1.68
		d1	0.01	0.07	-0.11	-0.42
		d2	-1.64	0.00	0.35	0.66
		d3	1.65	0.00	1.77	1.17
		Fit (RMSE)	0.84	1.97	1.98	1.34

Note
Table shows estimated values of thresholds used in quantifying unemployment, interest rate and inflation expectations, using text equations (8) and (9), (8″) and (9′), and (8″) and (9″). Fit (RMSE) is the root mean square errors in the mean expectations relative to the appropriate target variable. In the Inflation v. Actual column parameters have been chosen to minimise mean square error of inflation expectations. In the Inflation v. SRC column, parameters have been chosen to minimise differences between quantified mean expectations and the SRC survey means. The thresholds δ and $\delta+$ for the interest rate have been constrained to 0.25 per cent and 0 per cent respectively.

are correlated with time series volatility. However, for unemployment, these estimates sometimes become negative. For interest rates no significant effect of volatility or dispersion on threshold could be found. Even so, the time varying threshold models for interest rates produce estimates of the standard deviation which are often negative. In the case of inflation, the Carlson–Parkin and asymmetric threshold models suggest that the dispersion of individual expectations is much greater than the time series standard deviation of inflation. In addition the Carlson–Parkin and asymmetric threshold models suggest that the standard deviation of expectations across individuals has remained more or less constant since 1981, in spite of several subsequent episodes of increased variability in inflation. The time varying threshold model tracks changes in the volatility of inflation more closely, falling in the 1990s as inflation became more stable. Overall the impression is that allowing the response threshold to vary with the standard deviation of expectations and with time series volatility produces more realistic inflation expectations estimates, but is of less value in quantifying unemployment rates and interest rates.

Figure 2.5 compares the mean and standard deviations from the quantified inflation expectations with the directly computed means and standard deviations from the quantitative question in the SRC survey. The means are fairly closely correlated. The time varying threshold model fits better in the volatile 1970s, when the Carlson–Parkin models underestimate both actual inflation and the SRC mean expectation of inflation. In the mid-1990s, however, the time varying threshold model, while closer to actual inflation, understates the mean expectation in the SRC survey. In this period – when inflation expectations seem to have

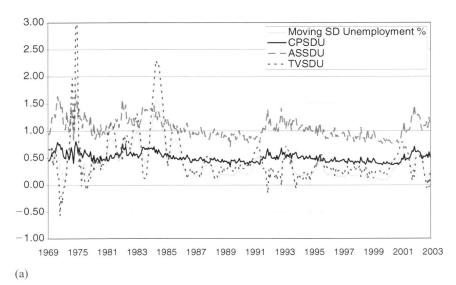

(a)

Figure 2.4 Alternative estimators of standard deviation of expectations.

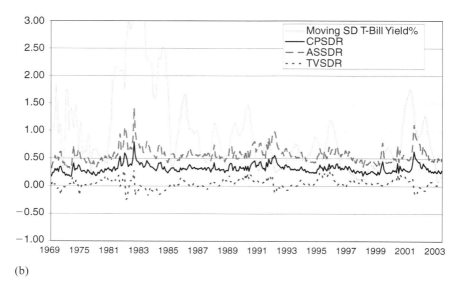

(b)

Figure 2.4 continued

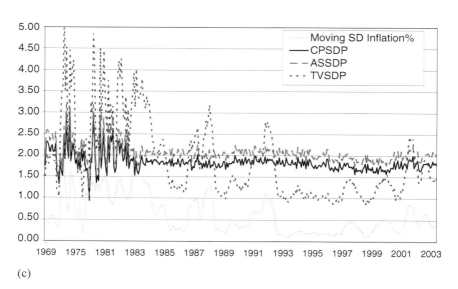

(c)

Figure 2.4 continued

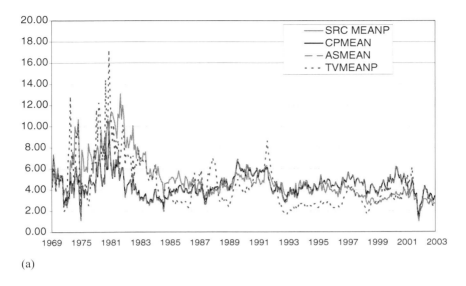

(a)

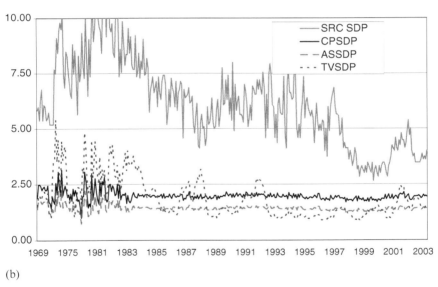

(b)

Figure 2.5 Michigan SRC inflation expectations versus quantified expectations.

been biased upwards – the Carlson–Parkin models do a better job in mimicking the SRC quantitative means.

The lower panel of Figure 2.5 compares standard deviations. This picture is more worrying. All the quantified expectations series have standard deviation estimates well below the standard deviation of responses to the SRC quantitative survey question. Moreover, the patterns of movement over time are quite different. The constant threshold and asymmetric threshold models produce very stable standard deviation estimates. However, the SRC quantitative data show dispersion that starts high in the 1970s, and falls markedly in the early 1980s, and again in the late 1990s. The time varying threshold model does fall between the 1970s and 1980s. But its average level then remains flat, with a couple of idiosyncratic peaks, one in 1987 when the SRC data shows a local trough. While mean expectations from qualitative survey data seem to be informative, corresponding estimates of the dispersion of expectations across respondents seem to tell us little.

4 Impact of uncertainty on expectations

These differences between qualitative and quantitative measures of dispersion matter only if they are misleading when used in modelling and decision making. This final section of the chapter estimates simple models of the formation of consumers' expectations about general business conditions and their own financial situation. Inputs to these models are the mean and standard deviation of unemployment, interest rate and inflation expectations. We then test whether the quantified inflation expectations yield results similar to the directly measured inflation expectations.

The models are:

$$\begin{aligned}
\mathrm{BCEMEAN}_t &= a_o + a_1\mathrm{BCEMEAN}_{t-1} + a_2\,\mathrm{QDUM}_t\,\mathrm{BCEMEAN}_{t-1} \\
&\quad + a_3\,\mathrm{BCPMEAN}_t + a_4\mathrm{UEMEAN}_t + a_5\mathrm{REMEAN}_t + a_6\mathrm{PEMEAN}_t \\
&\quad + a_7\mathrm{BCPSD}_t + a_8\mathrm{UESD}_{t+}a_9\mathrm{RESD}_t + a_{10}\mathrm{PESD}_t + u_t
\end{aligned} \tag{11}$$

$$\begin{aligned}
\mathrm{FPEMEAN}_t &= b_o + b_1\mathrm{FPEMEAN}_{t-1} + b_2\,\mathrm{QDUM}_t\,\mathrm{FPEMEAN}_{t-1} \\
&\quad + b_3\,\mathrm{FPPMEAN}_t + b_4\mathrm{UEMEAN}_t + b_5\mathrm{REMEAN}_t + b_6\mathrm{PEMEAN}_t \\
&\quad + b_7\mathrm{FPPSD}_t + b_8\mathrm{UESD}_t + b_9\mathrm{RESD}_t + b_{10}\mathrm{PESD}_t + v_t
\end{aligned} \tag{12}$$

where BCEMEAN is the mean quantified response to the question BCE on expectations about changes in expected business conditions, BCPMEAN is the mean perceived change in past business conditions, FPEMEAN is the mean expected change in own household financial situation, and FPPMEAN the perceived past change in financial situation. BCPSD and FPPSD are the standard deviations of perceived past changes in business conditions and financial situation. The lagged dependent variables allow expectations to adjust gradually to changes in economic variables. QDUM is a dummy taking the value 1 in the period February 1969–November 1977, when our data are quarterly rather than monthly, and the dynamics of adjustment of expectations are therefore different.

UEMEAN is the quantified mean expected change in unemployment, REMEAN the expected change in interest rates, and PEMEAN the expected inflation rate. UESD, RESD and PESD are their respective standard deviations. For each of these variables there are three possible measures – based on the constant threshold Carlson–Parkin model, the asymmetric threshold model, and the time varying threshold model. In the case of inflation expectations PEMEAN and PESD can also be measured directly from the quantitative SRC survey question. Since the asymmetric threshold measures are perfectly correlated with the constant threshold measures, they will give identical results for significance levels in the regressions (11) and (12), so we do not consider them here. The time varying threshold models for unemployment and interest rates are also unsatisfactory, producing negative values for standard deviations in some months, so we use only the constant threshold measures for these variables.

We therefore estimate three variants of each equation, one using the Carlson–Parkin estimator for PEMEAN and PESD, the second using the time varying threshold model for PEMEAN and PESD, and the third using the estimates from the quantitative survey question.

Two factors complicate the estimation of (10) and (11). The current values of the unemployment, interest rate and inflation expectations in (10) and (11) cannot be considered exogenous, since unexpected shocks u_t and v_t to business conditions and personal financial situation respectively might induce changes in the mean or dispersion of expectations about other economic variables. Ordinary least squares would then lead to biased coefficients on the endogenous regressors. The second econometric issue is that, because the forecast horizon of expectations (say 12 months) is greater than the sampling frequency (one month), the shocks u_t and v_t will be serially correlated. Any event that causes a downward revision in expectations in month t is liable also to cause downward revisions in 12-month ahead expectations formed in months $t + 1, t + 2, \ldots t + 11$. The errors in (10) and (11) can therefore be expected to follow an eleventh order moving average process. The parameters of the equations have therefore been estimated by instrumental variables, using lagged values of all variables in the system as instruments, and an MA(11) error process has been estimated for the error terms. Coefficient standard errors have been corrected for bias due to the moving average error terms using the Newey–West adjustment to the conventional variance covariance matrix. The results are shown in Table 2.3.

The upper panel shows the models for the determinants of expectations of future business conditions. Interestingly, all models show some kind of mean reversion in expectations, with a negative relation between perceptions of past changes in business conditions and expected future changes. Mean expectations of unemployment, interest rates and inflation all impact significantly and negatively on consumers' expectations for future business conditions. As scaled here, the coefficients on unemployment are similar to the coefficients on interest rate expectations, suggesting that a 1 per cent rise in the expected unemployment rate is treated as equivalent to a 1 per cent rise in T-bill yields. However, because of uncertainty about the scaling of interest rate expectations, this should not be taken too literally.

The coefficients on inflation expectations are very similar across the different measures of mean expectations, which is encouraging for the use of survey-based inflation expectations measures. All suggest that increased inflation

Table 2.3 Explanatory equations for expected business conditions and expected financial position

Variable	Inflation expectations measure					
	Carlson–Parkin constant threshold		Time-varying threshold		SRC quantitative survey question	
	coefficient	t-stat	coefficient	t-stat	coefficient	t-stat
Constant	0.5384	3.27	0.4862	3.32	0.2815	2.42
BCEMEANt-t	0.1731	2.90	0.2052	3.86	0.2210	2.87
QDUMt BCEMEANt-1	−0.1514	−1.17	−0.1935	−1.44	−0.1387	−1.50
BCPMEANt	−0.0150	1.53	−0.0150	−1.48	−0.0295	−3.34
UEMEANt	−0.9259	−8.53	−0.8945	−8.54	−0.9554	−7.10
REMEANt	−1.1810	−5.55	−1.2887	−7.21	−0.7297	−3.92
PEMEANt	−0.0493	−2.27	−0.0346	−2.99	−0.0606	−6.28
UESDt	0.5100	2.00	0.5439	2.02	0.9208	4.22
RESDt	−1.1398	−1.82	−1.0460	−1.82	0.1760	0.33
PESDt	0.0680	0.98	0.0414	2.39	0.0044	0.46
RS	0.8760		0.8768		0.8830	
Durbin Watson	2.0104		2.0167		1.9939	

Note
Dependent variable = Mean Expected Business Conditions BCEM.

Variable	Inflation expectations measure					
	Carlson–Parkin constant threshold		Time-varying threshold		SRC quantitative survey question	
	coefficient	t-stat	coefficient	t-stat	coefficient	t-stat
Constant	0.2798	2.42	0.3076	2.62	0.4478	3.92
BCEMEANt-t	0.3833	4.39	0.3875	4.08	0.2282	2.47
QDUMt BCEMEANt-1	−0.1156	−1.96	−0.1066	−1.66	−0.0537	−1.06
BCPMEANt	0.2609	5.86	0.2314	5.38	0.1747	3.65
UEMEANt	−0.1352	−3.45	−0.1053	−2.45	−0.1950	−5.76
REMEANt	−1.1681	−1.23	−1.2154	−7.21	−0.1172	−0.98
PEMEANt	−0.0478	−4.65	−0.0364	−4.78	−0.0446	−6.13
UESDt	0.2510	1.68	0.2288	1.51	0.3667	2.68
RESDt	−0.1318	−0.53	−0.2837	−1.15	0.5425	1.89
PESDt	0.0730	1.86	0.0485	2.75	−0.0081	−0.93
RS	0.8610		0.8642		0.8760	
Durbin Watson	1.9871		21.9871		1.9979	

Notes
Dependent variable = Mean Expected Financial Position FPEM.
Text equations (11) and (12) estimated by instrumental variables on data quarterly from February 1969 to November 1977, and monthly from January 1978 to October 2004. t-statistics in italics alongside the estimated coefficients are calculated from Newey–West standard errors robust to the assumed MA(11) process in the regression residuals.

impacts negatively on consumer expectations about business conditions – and that inflation is treated as a far less serious problem than interest rates and unemployment. Roughly, a 1 per cent increase in expected unemployment or a 1 per cent in the general level of interest rates is (not very plausibly) estimated to be as serious as a jump in inflation from 2 per cent to 20 per cent. However, problems in the scaling of the unemployment and interest rate measures may be distorting this result.

In all specification, the dispersion of expectations about unemployment is, curiously, associated with a significantly lower assessment of future business conditions. The dispersion of interest rate expectations does not seem to impact on expected business conditions. Whether the dispersion of inflation expectations appears significant depends on the measure used. The standard deviation of quantitative survey responses is not significant, nor is the standard deviation derived from the Carlson–Parkin constant threshold method. However, the time varying threshold estimate suggests that a rise in the dispersion in inflation expectations is significantly associated with an expected improvement in business conditions.

The lower panel of Table 2.3 reports results for the parallel regression (12) explaining mean expectations about households' own financial situation. In these models, expectations seem extrapolative, not regressive, with a positive relation between perceived past trend in financial position and the expected future trend. Mean expectations of unemployment affect expectations of financial position negatively, but interest rate expectations do not. Again, both qualitative and quantitative measures of inflation expectations are significant. The coefficients are similar across models, and suggest that inflation is treated as a more serious threat to individual consumers than to the economy as a whole. A 1 per cent increase in unemployment expectations has the same impact on expected household financial position as a 2–3 per cent increase in inflation.

As with the model of expected business conditions, there is a positive relation between the dispersion of consumer unemployment expectations and the mean expected financial position of households. Similarly, the standard deviation of interest rate expectations does not correlate with financial expectations. The results for the dispersion of inflation expectations depend on how expectations are measured. The standard deviation of responses to the quantitative questions in the SRC survey is (insignificantly) negatively associated with household financial expectations. However, the Carlson–Parkin standard deviation measure is positive and marginally significant, and the time varying threshold model suggests a significant positive relation.

5 Conclusions

For many countries no quantitative inflation expectations data are available, and consumer sentiment about inflation and other variables is collected and reported in qualitative form. The results from this chapter have some good news and some bad news for users of such data.

One piece of good news is that estimators of mean expectations derived from qualitative data seem robust. There is plenty of room for disagreement about exactly how best to characterize the distribution of individual expectations, and how best to model consumer responses to survey questions. However, for practical purposes these problems do not seem to matter. The resulting series for mean inflation expectations have similar general properties, and to directly estimated expectations. And they seem to yield similar inferences when used in econometric modelling.

A second incidental piece of good news is that our extensions of the quantification technique to other variables have yielded some insights into consumer expectations formation. For example, consumers extrapolate trends in their own situation, but expect that trends in the general economy will mean-revert. Since the aggregate of individual household performance should match general business conditions, this suggests some irrationality or behavioural bias in individual perceptions of economic activity.

The bad news relates to the information content of the dispersion of expectations of inflation and other variables. The dispersion of unemployment has counterintuitive coefficients in both business conditions and household financial position models, with high dispersion associated with expectations of an improving economy. The standard deviations of inflation from qualitative data and from quantitative data have very different properties. The quantitative data may well be unduly influenced by outliers, and hence too noisy. However, this does not account for the large downward bias in the qualitative measures, or for the absence of any consistent pattern over time in the Carlson–Parkin type measures. Moreover, the qualitative inflation dispersion measures perform differently from the quantitative measures when used in models of consumer expectations, so the differences are operationally significant, and inferences from measures of "uncertainty" derived from these qualitative survey data cannot be regarded as reliable.

References

Balcombe, K. (1996), The Carlson–Parkin method applied to NZ price expectations using QSBO data, *Economics Letters*, 51: 51–57.

Batchelor, R.A. (1981), Aggregate expectations under the stable laws, *Journal of Econometrics*, 16: 199–210.

Batchelor, R.A. (1982), Expectations, output and inflation: the European experience, *European Economic Review*, 17: 1–25.

Batchelor, R.A. (1986a), Inflation uncertainty: theory and measurement for the European economy, in K. Oppenlander and G. Poser (eds), *Business Cycle Surveys in the Assessment of Economic Activity*, Proceedings of the seventeenth CIRET conference, Aldershot: Gower Press.

Batchelor, R.A. (1986b), The psychophysics of inflation, *Journal of Economic Psychology*, 7: 269–290.

Batchelor, R.A. (1986c), Quantitative v. qualitative measures of inflation expectations, *Oxford Bulletin of Economics and Statistics*, 48: 99–120.

Batchelor, R.A. and P. Dua (1992), Survey expectations in the time series consumption function, *Review of Economics and Statistics*, 74: 598–606.

Batchelor, R.A. and P. Dua (1996), Empirical measures of inflation uncertainty: a cautionary note, *Applied Economics*, 28: 333–341.

Batchelor, R.A. and A.B. Orr (1988), Inflation expectations revisited, *Economica*, 55: 317–331.

Batchelor, R.A. and A.B. Orr (1991), Inflation uncertainty, inflationary shocks and the credibility of counterinflation policy, *European Economic Review*, 35: 1385–1397.

Batchelor, R.A. and F. Zarkesh (2000), Variance rationality: a direct test, in F. Gardes and G. Prat (eds), *Expectations in Goods and Financial Markets*, London and New York: Edward Elgar, pp. 156–171.

Berk, J. (1999), Measuring inflation expectations: a survey data approach, *Applied Economics*, 31: 1467–1480.

Carlson, J.A (1975), Are price expectations normally distributed?, *Journal of the American Statistical Association*, 70: 794–754.

Carlson, J.A. and M. Parkin (1975), Inflation expectations, *Economica*, 42 (166): 123–138.

Curtin, R.E. (1996), Procedure to estimate price expectations, *Working Paper, University of Michigan Survey Research Center*.

DeGroot, M.H. (1970), *Optimal Statistical Decisions*, McGraw Hill: New York.

Fishe, R. and T.L. Idson (1990), Information induced heteroskedasticity in price expectations data, *Review of Economics and Statistics*, 72: 304–312.

Giordani, P. and P. Soderlind (2003), Inflation forecast uncertainty, *European Economic Review*, 47 (6): 1037–1059.

Henzel, S. and T. Wollmershauser (2005), Quantifying inflation expectations with the Carlson–Parkin method – a survey-based determination of the just-noticeable-difference, *Discussion Paper*, IFO Institut Munich.

Lahiri, K. and C. Teigland (1987), On the normality of probability distributions of inflation and GNP forecasts, *International Journal of Forecasting*, 3: 269–279.

Muth, J.R. (1961), Rational expectations and the theory of price movements, *Econometrica*, 29: 315–335.

Nielsen, H. (2003, Inflation expectations in the EU – results from survey data, *Discussion Paper*, Berlin: Free University and Humboldt University.

Pfanzagl, J. (1952), Zur Methodik des Kunjunkturtest-Verfahrens, *Statistische Vierteiljahresschrift*, 5: 161–173.

Rich, R.W., J.E. Raymond and J.S. Butler (1992), The relationship between forecast dispersion and forecast uncertainty: evidence from a Survey-ARCH model, *Journal of Applied Econometrics*, 7: 131–148.

Seitz, H. (1988), The estimation of inflation forecasts from business survey data, *Applied Economics*, 20: 427–438.

Theil, H. (1958, On the time shape of economic micro-variables and the Munich business test, *Review of the International Statistical Institute*, 20: 105–120.

Titterington, D.M., A.F. Smith, and U.E. Makov (1985), *Statistical Analysis of Finite Mixture Distributions*, Chichester: John Wiley.

3 Inflation expectations and empirical tests

Theoretical models and empirical tests

Richard Curtin

Realism and relevance

John Muth began his classic article on rational expectations by noting that survey data on expectations were as accurate as the elaborate models of economists, and he noted that there were considerable differences of opinion in the cross-sectional survey data (Muth, 1961). His basic insight was that economic agents form their expectations so that they are essentially the same as the predictions of the relevant economic theory. The assumption that expectations were formed rationally was, for Muth, the natural extension of economic theory, which already held that firms rationally maximize profits and consumers rationally maximize utility. Nonetheless, Muth noted that rationality was an assumption that could be tested by systematic comparison with alternative theories in explaining observed expectations.

Muth's hypothesis has indeed sparked an enormous amount of research, as well as wide divisions between disciplines, in how rationality should be conceptualized and how the hypothesis should be tested. Economics views rationality in terms of the choices it produces (substantive or full rationality), whereas other social sciences view rationality in terms of the process that is used to make choices (procedural or bounded rationality). It was Friedman's (1953) celebrated essay on methodology that declared the validity of economic theories as independent of their psychological assumptions. Economists have accordingly focused on whether the postulate of unbounded or bounded rationality was the more productive theoretical construct in terms of its predictive accuracy.

Compared with tests of utility maximization, expectations have the unique advantage that they can be measured and subjected to empirical tests.[1] The rigor of the tests of the rational expectations hypothesis ranges from tests of bias and predictive accuracy to how efficiently every possible piece of relevant information is used in forming the expectations. There is a virtual absence of empirical tests of the assumptions surrounding utility maximization, including tests on whether agents gather and process the relevant economic information and use it efficiently to maximize utility, and whether consumers know all the relevant facts at any given time or if there is informational heterogeneity.

There are some economists that take seriously the implicit assumptions that there are negligible costs associated with collecting and processing all the relevant information, and that all agents know the correct dynamic model. When asked about the stringent assumptions surrounding utility maximization, economists quickly allow that what those simplifying assumptions lack in realism they make up for in predictive performance. The lack of recognition of Friedman's basic methodological points in the discussion of rational expectations is quite amazing.

It should not be surprising that the debate about the rational expectations hypothesis has continued unabated in the nearly 50 years since Muth first published his theory. Perhaps it is as Lovell (1986) lamented two decades ago in his review of empirical tests of the rational expectations hypothesis: "Why should data spoil such a good story?" Indeed, the clear advantage of the rational expectations hypothesis is its theoretical strength. The hypothesis has proved to be enormously productive in transforming macroeconomic theory, given that the rationality assumption enables the powerful tools of optimization to systematically expand the depth and breadth of economic theories.

While the empirical tests have generally not fully supported the hypothesis, the criteria for acceptance are rigorous, and the lack of evidence is comparable to that found in tests of the full rationality postulate in many other aspects of economic theory. In contrast, while bounded rationality has frequently been confirmed in empirical studies, research on bounded rationality has not led to an integrated theoretical structure that could spark further theoretical advances. Indeed, the findings attributable to bounded rationality have been generally classified as "anomalies" rather than being incorporated into mainstream theory. The list of such anomalies includes the impact of framing, asymmetry of gains and losses, relative reference points, anchoring, and confirmatory bias, among other findings (Tversky and Kahneman, 1982; Earl, 1990; Thaler, 1991, 1992; Rabin, 1998; Rabin and Schrag, 1999). Only recently has there been a concerted effort to incorporate a more realistic account of expectations into mainstream economic theory, rather than relegating them to anomaly status.

Costs and benefits of rational expectations

Like most economic phenomena, inflation expectations can be integrated into mainstream theory by the systematic recognition of the costs and benefits associated with rational expectations. Rational expectations are costly to form and their benefits are derived from their use in economic decisions. As long as there is any positive cost involved in collecting and processing information using the relevant dynamic model, some agents will sometimes choose to hold less accurate expectations. The terms "sticky information" or "rational inattention" have been used to describe the impact of costs on the formation process (Mankiw and Reis, 2002; Sims, 2003; Bacchetta and Wincoop, 2005). These theories postulate that rational consumers may find the costs associated with updating their expectations to exceed the benefits. At any given time some people will find it worthwhile to incur the costs, especially if that information is critical to a pending decision. Most of the time, however, rational inattention is the optimal course. Alternatively, agents may base their expectations on imperfect information, which can be conceptualized as less costly than perfect information. Whatever the cause, the process creates staggered changes in expectations, whereby at any given time expectations reflect a combination of current and past information across different people.

Disagreement across people in their expectations at any given time is taken as an indication of such a process (Mankiw *et al.*, 2004). Some have modeled the disagreements as the result of factors other than costs, such as an epidemiological process in which "expert opinion" spreads slowly through a population, like the spread of a disease (Carroll, 2003). Costs can also be assumed to vary across demographic subgroups, as some encounter lower costs for acquiring and using information, and other, more economically active, subgroups derive greater benefits from updating their expectations more frequently. This interpretation of disagreements or inaccuracies in expectations stands in contrast to the older and still more common interpretation that the very existence of differences across demographic subgroups indicates non-rational expectations (Bryan and Venkatu, 2001; Souleles, 2004).

Staggered changes could be created by a wide range of processes that either encourage or discourage agents from updating their expectations. A common hypothesis for staggered updating holds that it is due to asymmetric responses to economic information, with agents updating their expectations much more quickly in response to bad news about inflation. Akerlof *et al.* (2001) suggest that bad economic news is perceived by consumers to contain more potentially relevant information about their financial situation. The volume of news also matters, especially the volume of bad news, as well as news that represents a sharp and negative break from the past (Carroll, 2003). Sims (2003) shows that, based on information theory, the tone and volume of economic reporting affects expectations beyond the information contained in the reports. This added impact of news, however, may be short-lived, usually lasting less than a few months (Doms and Morin, 2004).

It is not clear when the news media creates expectations and when their reporting simply responds to ongoing changes in expectations. Like any other business, the news media cater to consumers' preferences (Hamilton, 2004). For example, large shifts in expectations for future changes in the unemployment rate were found to change in advance of shifts in media reports about unemployment (Curtin, 2003).

The same staggered information flows have been hypothesized to result from uncertainty about the correct structural model of the economy. Since model uncertainty is costly to resolve, it results in less frequent updating of expectations (Branch, 2005). Although the data that indicates disagreement in expectations is similar to what could be expected to result from model uncertainty, these two concepts are distinct. More importantly, the prevalence of disagreement may be much more variable over time than uncertainty.

The models developed to capture the impact of staggered information are similar to consumption models that incorporate the division between "rule of thumb" and rational consumers. In this context, the switching models capture the difference between those that update their expectations regularly and those that base their expectations on pre-existing information. Mankiw and Reis (2003), Carroll (2003), and Khan and Zhu (2002) estimated that rather than continuously updating their expectations, most people update their expectations only a few times a year.

Sticky information theories result in differences in inflation expectations across agents. There are, however, other reasons to expect heterogeneity which represent more fundamental issues. Conventional economic theory assumes that the same information is available to all agents and the same models are used to generate expectations about the future. The result is that there is only one rational expectation at any given time for a given information set. Thus, while staggered information and model uncertainty may result in heterogeneity of expectations, there is no theoretical basis for expecting heterogeneity among those that have recently updated their expectations. The allowance of private information, in addition to public and official information, to influence the formation of expectations would provide a theoretical reason for heterogeneity in expectations. For example, the impact of private information has been found to be pivotal in the formation of unemployment expectations (Curtin, 2003).

Monetary policy implications of staggered information flows

Whatever the cause, the presence of sticky information is hypothesized to be the key to understanding dynamics of the macro economy. Sticky information has a long history in research on forward-looking Phillips curves (Woodford, 2003). The sticky information has ranged from staggered wage contracts, to staggered pricing models, to staggered information flows. Whatever the source, the existence of sticky information indicates the non-neutrality of monetary policy.

While there is now a widespread belief that monetary policy can influence output and employment, there is no consensus on the mechanisms that produce the impact. To be sure, if inflation expectations were fully rational, prices were perfectly flexible and the central bank was fully committed to price stability, there would be no impact on output and employment. Non-neutrality may derive from non-rationality in expectations, or from a lack of commitment to price stability on the part of the central bank.

The optimal situation is when the central bank enjoys widespread credibility and expectations are fully rational, allowing the central bank to reduce inflation without any loss in output or employment. Although central banks differ widely in the credibility they enjoy, economic losses cannot be completely avoided even among those that have the highest credibility.

When these optimal conditions are not present, expected inflation can become self-fulfilling due to what has been termed the "expectations trap" (Chari *et al.*, 1998; Albanesi *et al.*, 2002; Leduc *et al.*, 2003). The enticement into the trap is the higher cost in terms of output and employment that would result following the choices already made by households and firms in anticipation of higher inflation: consumers typically favor debt (whose repayment will be eroded by higher inflation), and firms typically raise prices in advance to protect the real value of their profits. These actions would imply relatively larger future losses in output and employment if the central bank adopted a policy aimed at price stability. Since the actions already taken by both consumers and firms act to lower the costs of inflation, the central bank is "trapped" into an accommodative policy that confirms the higher inflation expectations.

While full rationality and a fully committed central bank may seem too much to expect, Woodford (2005) advanced the notion that the main conclusions for optimal monetary policy also pertain to the assumption of near-rational expectations. While there is no accepted standard to judge whether expectations are "near-rational," the analysis of inflation expectations can help to sort out the various properties of expectations.

This chapter investigates a broad range of these issues, including whether inflation expectations are backward or forward looking, whether there is any support for the staggered information hypothesis, the interpretation of disagreement data, and some other methodological issues. Prior to the analytic sections, the rational expectations model and the adaptation models are defined. The analysis then turns to household inflation expectations collected by the University of Michigan, variously based on cross-section data, panel data, and times-series data. Finally, the analytic results are discussed along with their implication for monetary policies.

Theoretical models of expectations

Expectations are beliefs about the future. This definition was cited by Plato more than 2,000 years ago, and it remains to this day the generally accepted meaning of the term.[2] The formation of expectations depends on two factors: informational inputs (I) and the model or process of transforming information into expectations (f). Let the expectation of the inflation rate (P^e) formed by the i_{th} individual be defined as:

$$P_t^{e-1} = f(I_{t-1})$$

where the subscript t on P indicates the period for which the expectation applies, and the expectation formed based on the information that was available in a prior period denoted by e_{t-1}. The two dominant specifications of this equation are the rational expectations hypothesis and the extrapolative, adaptive, and error-learning models, which I will refer to collectively as "adaptive" expectations.

The format of the appropriate empirical tests of these two models is just as distinctive as their assumptions about rationality. The adaptive expectations models define what information is used and how it is used in the formation of expectations, including the availability and cost of information as well as the capacity of individuals to effectively utilize the information. The empirical tests were designed to determine whether variations in expectations are related to these hypothesized factors. In contrast, tests of the rational expectations hypothesis focus on whether the observed expectations are unbiased future forecasts and whether all of the information was used efficiently and optimally. In the former case, expectations are analyzed as the dependent variable, while in the latter case expectations are viewed as an independent variable in the analysis.

This difference makes the comparison of the relative merits of the two models difficult. For the adaptive expectations models, confirmation essentially entails finding a significant empirical relationship between expectations and some informational inputs. Confirmation of the rational expectations hypothesis, in contrast, requires finding unbiased and efficient future predictions. In tests of adaptive expectations, any statistically significant finding is taken as confirmation even if it accounts for a trivial proportion of the variance, whereas anything short of full rationality requires the rejection of the rational expectations hypothesis. This asymmetry in the evaluation of empirical evidence has stunted theoretical developments.

This situation is nowhere more important than in the assessment of the forward-looking content of expectations. Adaptive expectations models are inherently bound to the past. Aside from the special case where future outcomes are extrapolations of the past, no method is usually hypothesized to test the forward-looking content of expectations. Indeed, by their very construction, adaptive expectations models portray the formation process as a relatively transparent function of past outcomes where individuals never fully learn from their past errors. Rational expectations models, in contrast, place their entire emphasis on assessing the forward-looking information, but do not posit any specific process for the formation of expectations. When empirically rejected, the rational expectations framework provides no insight into which limitations on rationality prove most important.

Adaptive expectations

The various adaptive, extrapolative, and error-learning models can be summarized by the following autoregressive distributive lag representation:

$$P_t^e = \alpha + \sum_j \beta_j \, P_{t-j}^e + \sum_j \gamma_j \, P_{t-j} + \varepsilon_t$$

where P^e is inflation expectations, P is the actual inflation rate, j is the lag length, and ε_t is the error term, with the i subscript dropped for convenience. Variables other than the inflation rate that are part of the relevant information could also be included in the equation. Defining the unique characteristics of the various models involves the specification of coefficients α, β, γ, and ε.

Perhaps the most basic hypothesis is that expectations essentially represent random responses to the survey questions, unrelated to either the past realizations of the variable or even past expectations. In this case, the β, and γ coefficients would be hypothesized to be equal to 0, so that variations in expectations about its mean (α) are simply equal to the error term.

The pure extrapolative model is obtained by setting the coefficient β equal to zero, so that expectations solely depend on the lagged inflation rate. The most restricted version of this model can be characterized as "static expectations," where expectations simply depend on the most recent realization. The more general version holds that expectations represent a weighted average of past realizations. Under the extrapolative hypothesis, the γ coefficients are hypothesized to be any positive fraction between 0 and 1.

The adaptive or error-learning hypothesis posits that consumers revise their expectations for the following period based on the error in their expectations in the current period (Fisher, 1930; Cagan, 1956; Friedman, 1957; Nerlove 1958). In terms of the above equation, this implies that only one lag of the actual and expectation variables are used, with the coefficient on the difference between the expected and actual outcomes (the speed of the learning adjustment) hypothesized as being positive with an upper bound of 1.0. By use of the Koyck (1954) transformation, however, the adaptive expectations model can be shown to be equivalent to a weighted average of past realizations.

Another approach has been to utilize error correction models (ECM), which postulate equality in long-run equilibrium between inflation expectations and the inflation rate. The basic ECM can be expressed by using one lag of the expectations variable and two lags of the actual inflation rate, and fixing these coefficients at 1.0 to express the notion that the equilibrium rate of inflation is equal to its expectation. The ECM equation thus relates the change in expectations to past changes in the actual inflation rate, as well as the error in the prior period's expectation.

The reliance on information about past changes in inflation is the source of the most important disadvantage of all adaptive expectations models because systematic prediction errors result since expectations tend to underestimate (overestimate) the true change whenever the underlying variable is following an upward (downward) trend. In response to this deficiency, augmented models have been proposed which incorporate information on other variables that are assumed to influence the formation of expectations. The use of this additional information can help to offset the tendency toward systematic prediction errors.

Rational expectations

The strong appeal of the rational expectations hypothesis is that it avoids the bias toward systematic prediction errors by shifting its focus from the variable's history to its future realizations. The rational expectations hypothesis equates the expectation with the expected value of the actual subsequent realization, conditional on all available information (Muth, 1961). Unbiased expectations under the rational expectations hypothesis require that the coefficients α and β are 0 and 1, respectively, in the equation:

$$P_t = \alpha + \beta\, P_t^{e-j} + \varepsilon_t$$

The strong test of rationality also requires that all of the available information has been efficiently and optimally used in forming the expectation. This involves tests on the statistical properties of the prediction errors to determine if they are consistent with those stipulated by the hypothesis (orthogonality, efficiency, consistency, and unbiasedness). Tests of this assumption take the form:

$$\zeta_t = \alpha + \sum \beta_j P_{t-j} + \sum \gamma_j Z_{t-j} + \varepsilon_t$$

where ζ is the prediction error, the coefficients β and γ are expected to be zero, and the prediction errors are serially uncorrelated. This expresses the notion that if any of the available information was systematically related to the prediction errors, the information was not efficiently and optimally incorporated into the formation of the original expectation.

Reification of economic data in tests of expectations

Some economists seem to believe the only source of information about the actual inflation rate is the official announcements by the government's statistical agency. The assumption that consumers only utilize official sources of economic information reflects the widespread tendency to reify economic data—that is, treating conceptual measures as if they had a concrete existence. All economic data represent estimates of the underlying concepts, and some price indexes are measured with more error than others. There is no evidence that consumers revise their inflation expectations each time the government issues new monthly estimates, revises old figures or revises its measurement methodology. More importantly, aside for those who have their incomes or pensions indexed to official indices, theory suggests that consumers will use whatever measure best reflects their own expenditures. It would make no sense for consumers to take into account future prices that they will not face when making decisions.

The recent debate about whether tests on inflation expectations should be based on real-time data or revised data reflects this tendency toward data reification (Mehra, 2002; Croushore and Stark, 1999; Kean and Runcle, 1989; Zarnowitz, 1985). The information set at any given time is usually assumed to only include past data on the official inflation rate, usually outdated by at least one month (the official release of US data on the Consumer Price Index (CPI) for any given month is by the middle of the following month). While economists may condition their forecasts only on official data, consumers can be expected to actively use all the information available to them to gauge ongoing changes in price trends. Rather than relying on official information, consumers more often report and depend on private information.

If anything, consumers suffer from an overload of private information about prices. In comparison to the official information that has been released once a month in nearly the same format for decades, private information has increased substantially. The media have been repeatedly reinvented to provide expanded information, from newspapers, to television, to 24/7 operations of cable news, the internet, and the self-proclaimed experts that now inhabit all media. More importantly, people gain information on prices in every daily transaction in the marketplace. This personal collection of information is typically reported by consumers to be the most critical to the formation of their expectations.

One way of exploring the impact of private versus official information is to compare changes in expectations with the official release dates. The key analytic issue is how to devise a proxy measure of the unobserved inflation rate prior to the official announcement. This issue is easy to solve: the best estimate of the current month's inflation is the official inflation rate. And the hypothesis could be easily tested: the current month's price index should be dominated by last month's inflation index for the official information hypothesis to hold, and the current month's price index should dominate last month's official release if private information dominates. Such a test provides little support for the notion that consumers base their expectations on the official announcement.

The last issue is which inflation rate is the most appropriate to use to model consumer expectations. The inflation index most often favored by economists is a core rate that excludes energy and food prices, and is either based on the CPI or the personal consumption deflator. Consumers generally identify inflation with the overall CPI or personal consumption deflator as they best capture the prices of the goods and services that they actually purchase. The analyses included in this chapter focus on changes in the overall Consumer Price Index (CPI-u).

Data on inflation expectations

The University of Michigan has collected data on the inflation expectations of consumers for more than 50 years. Two questions are now asked of all consumers about expected price changes: the expected *direction* of change in prices and the expected *extent* of change. The question on the expected direction of change has been asked in a comparable format since 1946, while the question on the extent of change has been modified several times. In the 1940s and 1950s, the question simply asked whether prices would go up a little or go up a lot; from the 1960s to the mid-1970s, the question included a series of fixed percentage intervals from which the respondent was asked to choose; and from the mid-1970s to the present, the question simply asked the percentage rate of inflation that the consumer expected. This chapter focuses only on the monthly data collected since 1978 for the open-ended question on inflation expectations.

There is much cross-section and time-series variation in consumers' responses. The variation in responses is due to a number of factors, including differences in information and computational capacities, uncertainty about the correct dynamic model, and measurement errors.

These differences are discussed from several perspectives based on cross-section, time-series, and panel data.

Cross-section variation in responses

The unweighted distribution of responses across the surveys conducted between 1978 and 2005, covering about 200,000 cases, is shown in Figure 3.1. The response codes from 1 percent to 5 percent contain 54 percent of all the responses; including up to response code 10 percent adds another 16 percent; and including up to response code 15 percent adds another 4 percent for a total of 74 percent of all responses. As a result, three-quarters of all responses fell within the same range recorded by the CPI over the same time period—the year-over-year change in the CPI ranged from a low of 1.0 percent in 2002 to a high of 14.6 percent in 1980.

The upper tail of the distribution is quite long, although just 5 percent of all response codes were above 15 percent, and only 0.5 percent of all responses indicated an expected inflation rate of 50 percent or more. The lower tail of the distribution, in contrast, was sharply truncated, with just 3 percent of all responses expecting an overall decline in prices. The most distinctive, and perhaps the most difficult to explain, phenomena was the comparatively large number who expected a 0 percent inflation rate. Across the past 25 years, overall prices were anticipated to remain unchanged by 18 percent of all respondents. Yet, just 3 percent expected declines in prices.

One might have reasonably anticipated that the distribution of responses would not change so abruptly at zero. The lumping of inflation expectations at zero seems to suggest that a negative inflation rate incorporates some psychological aspects that consumers actively avoid, or perhaps that consumers consider the underlying probability distribution discontinuous at zero. The psychological hypothesis was more common in the decades following the depression of the 1930s, when consumers associated price declines with income declines, but in more recent years most consumers have eagerly embraced whatever product price declines they encountered in the marketplace. The single, and important, exception is house prices. Rather than a kink in the underlying probability distribution, the lumping at zero may simply reflect rounding, with consumers actually expecting a very low rate of inflation and not price declines.

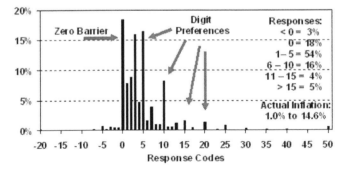

Figure 3.1 Year-ahead inflation expectations: distributions of responses, 1978–2005.

The truncation does not reflect the averaging of a few surveys where expectations of declines were common, with many more surveys where they were uncommon. Figure 3.2 shows the response distribution for 1980, when inflation expectations were at their highest levels; Figure 3.3 shows the response distribution for 2001, when inflation expectations were at their lowest levels. The same truncation in responses is evident in both cases. The major difference is that the 1980 distribution is shifted to the right and has a greater dispersion of responses.[3]

Whatever the cause, the data clearly indicate a truncated lower tail rather than a normal distribution. Importantly, the extent of the truncation provides information for those utilizing distribution assumptions to calculate a numerical estimate from qualitative response scales on inflation expectations, as is commonly done among EU countries.[4]

Digit preference

A close examination of the response distribution indicates the prevalence of certain digits, namely 0, 5, 10, 15, 20, and so on up to 50. This tendency to favor certain digits has been termed "digit preference." Digit preference is a wide-

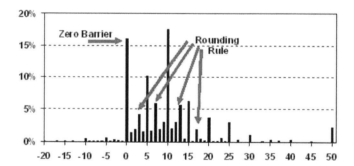

Figure 3.2 Year-ahead inflation expectations: distributions of responses, 1980.

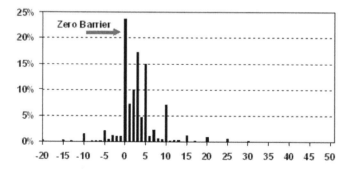

Figure 3.3 Year-ahead inflation expectations: distributions of responses, 2001.

spread phenomenon, exhibited in nearly all responses to open-ended numeric questions (Baker, 1992; Edouard and Senthilselvan, 1997). The questions could ask about dollar amounts of income, assets, debts, product prices, or probabilities of the occurrence of certain events, from the weather to a variety of economic or political outcomes, and even in response to attributes of the person, such as weight. The typical explanation of digit preference is that it represents "rounded" answers based on considerations of the cost of providing more exact responses. Economists may favor a "near rationality" interpretation whereby the rounding represents the level of precision that is associated with differences that matter to the respondent.

An even closer inspection will reveal the prevalence of 3, 7, 13, 17, and so on. This reflects coding rules implemented by the survey organization to provide a consistent means to code range responses. All responses are recorded as integers, and the very few decimal responses are rounded and coded as integers without any fractional values. The key part of the rule states that coders should round 0.5 to the nearest odd number, e.g. 3.5 would be rounded to 3 and 4.5 would be rounded to 5. This rule, in combination with the prevalence of range responses, produces the high prevalence of the coded values 3, 7, 13 and so forth. For example, a response of 5–10 percent would be coded as 7 percent; a response of 10–15 percent would be coded as 13 percent. Overall, range responses are quite rare. Whenever a respondent would give a range response, it was always probed for a more exact point estimate in the Michigan surveys, but some respondents insisted that they could not narrow the range to a single best integer estimate.

Digit preference and the frequency of range responses are usually considered survey measurement errors, given that they result in less precise measures. Experiments have been conducted with the data before rounding (from one decimal) and the characteristics of the response distribution have been nearly identical to the rounded figures, as one would expect. Range responses are likely to reflect uncertainty about the future course of inflation, or the lack of information that a more precise answer would require (presumably due to its high cost).

Some have misinterpreted digit preferences as "focal points" in the distribution, and suggest that this indicates that inflation expectations are more qualitative than quantitative in nature (Bryan and Palmqvist, 2005). The near-universal presence of digit preferences would mean that the same conclusion would also be valid for measurements of income, assets, prices, and so forth, meaning that surveys could measure only qualitative variables. The stability of the same integers as "focal points" in the distribution over time has been misinterpreted as indicating that the distribution of responses was not responsive to changes in the inflation or policies pursued by the central bank

Time-series variation

Rather than focusing on cross-section data, most economists are more interested in how the distribution changes from month-to-month. Given the pronounced skew in the distribution of inflation expectations, it is no surprise that the mean of the distribution always exceeds the median. Moreover, given that the long upper tail of the distribution is likely to represent measurement errors, the median rather than the mean of the distribution may provide the better measure of central tendency.[5] Indeed, the difference between the mean and median was substantial, with the mean being about 25 percent higher than the median, or 1.0 percentage points higher (see Figure 3.4). Over the period from January 1978–August 2005, the mean of the monthly distributions was 4.8 percent, while the median was 3.8 percent. Despite the difference in the levels, the time-series correlation between the mean and median was 0.98, indicating that either measure provided nearly identical time-series information. The median inflation expectation is typically the measure of choice, and I will restrict my focus to the median in this chapter.

The interquartile difference, defined as the difference between the twenty-fifth and seventy-fifth percentiles, can be used as an estimate of the variance in the monthly data.[6] Over the 1978–2005 period, the interquartile range averaged 4.7 percentage points, with the twenty-fifth percentile averaging 1.5 percentage points and the seventy-fifth percentile averaging 6.2 percentage points, meaning that half of all respondents held expectations within that range. The time-series correlations were quite high, as the correlation between the twenty-fifth percentile and the median was 0.91 and the correlation between the seventy-fifth percentile and the median was 0.97 (see Figure 3.5).

The interquartile range provides some interesting information about trends in inflation expectations. Increases in the variance occur abruptly, but decreases take place over an extended time period. Perhaps the clearest example is the sudden increase in variance at the time of the first war with Iraq in 1991. Following that increase, the variance of inflation expectation decreased gradually over the next decade (see Figure 3.6). Central banks have interpreted this to indicate that their credibility can be lost suddenly, and can then take a considerable period of time to re-establish.

What do the cross-section and time-series variations in inflation expectations indicate? There have been some that have used these variations as a strong

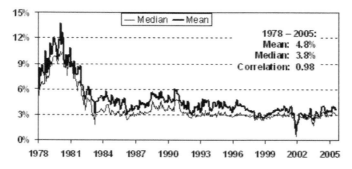

Figure 3.4 Median and mean inflation expectations (monthly data, 1978–2005).

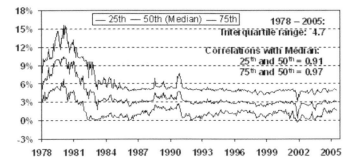

Figure 3.5 Inflation expectations: twenty-fifth, fiftieth, and seventy-fifth percentiles.

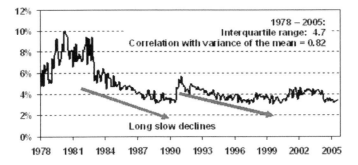

Figure 3.6 Inflation expectations: interquartile range.

indicator of vast measurement error, making the data worthless. Others, as I have already noted, interpret the variations as a reflection of the costs of collecting and processing information, which results in a staggered updating across respondents. While the more extreme responses may well reflect measurement errors, most of the disagreement or heterogeneity reflects the balancing of costs and benefits of updating expectations. To explore these issues in more detail, repeated measures on the same individuals are needed.

Panel data on expectations

The sample design of the monthly surveys of consumers includes a rotating panel. In the rotating panel design, each monthly sample is composed of a new representative subsample, as well as a re-interview subsample of all respondents who were first interviewed six months earlier. The design was chosen to enhance the study of change in expectations and behavior. In the present context, the sample design means that, for each respondent, two measures of inflation expectations were collected six months apart. In each interview, respondents were asked about the expected inflation rate during the following 12 months. As a result, the two instances of the question do not ask about identical time periods but do contain overlapping periods of six months.

This design enables a partial test of the hypothesis of staggered information flows. The staggered information hypothesis suggests that in any given monthly survey only some of the respondents would have updated their expectations. For this analysis, the sample was restricted to the range January 1993–August 2005, when the inflation rate was more stable, averaging 2.5 percent. More importantly, the average change in the actual inflation rate over all six-month intervals within this time period was nearly zero, or more exactly 0.0005 percentage points. In comparison, the average change in inflation expectations among identical individuals was −0.247, or a decrease of one-quarter of a percentage point. The negative change in inflation expectations probably reflects the persistent declines in the inflation rate over the 1993–2005 period. Overall, given that the consumer data on inflation expectations are collected as rounded integers, the two sources were remarkably close.

The average absolute differences, however, clearly indicate much greater change in the inflation expectations data among panel members. The average absolute differences were 0.48 percentage points for the change in the actual inflation rate and 2.8 percentage points for the change in inflation expectations. This amounted to absolute changes in expectations that were more than five times the change in the actual inflation rate.

A simple regression indicated that for each percentage point change in the actual annualized rate of inflation during the prior six months, consumers changed their inflation expectations by about 0.5 percentage points. This response indicates that consumers did not fully update their inflation expectations, as would be suggested by the staggered information hypothesis. Indeed, across all respondents from 1993 to 2005, 27 percent reported the same inflation expectation in the two surveys. Among the 73 percent that updated their expectations, 35 percent reported a higher inflation expectation in the second interview and 38 percent reported a lower inflation expectation.

Costs of updating expectations

Any observed change in inflation expectations over the six-month period cannot be taken as proof that inflation expectations were updated. The observed change may simply indicate measurement error rather than true change. A noted advantage of panel surveys is that stable sources of measurement error can be eliminated by taking the difference between the two interview measures. Since it is usually assumed that measurement error reflects specific questions and specific subgroups, by asking the same person the same question on two occasions, the measurement error would be eliminated by taking the difference of the two responses.

This by no means eliminates all measurement error, but it does eliminate errors that are likely to be associated with systematic bias. Random error in measurement remains, which increases the variance of the measurements. For example, if expectations were not updated, measurement errors could create a difference where none had existed. Such random variation increases the proportion of unexplained variance, but does not created biased estimates.

Based on the six-month differences, comparisons were made across selected demographic subgroups that could be reasonably expected to differ in the costs of updating inflation expectations. Education was selected given that the formation of inflation expectations is assumed to critically depend on the ability of the respondents to gather and interpret information; gender was selected since information gathered from personal shopping experience may provide advantage to women;[7] age and income were selected since the economic situation and experiences are likely to differ over the life cycle.

Given that the purpose of the analysis is to identify groups with relatively high or low heterogeneity, the overall sample mean was subtracted, with the analysis focused on the deviations from the mean. Recall that the observed change in inflation expectations was one-quarter of a percentage point, compared with the change in the actual CPI across all six-month intervals of zero in the 1993–2005 period.

A second measure of relative heterogeneity is the ratio of individual differences to the sample difference. Thus, when the ratio was above 1.0 for a particular subgroup, it would exhibit more heterogeneity than the rest of the panel during that six-month interval. The sample consisted of 26,611 cases that had complete data on both measures, with the interviews conducted from 1993 to 2005.

Consider the results for gender as shown in Table 3.1. Men raised their inflation expectations by +0.080 percentage points over the six-month interval on average, nearly the exact opposite of the −0.075 decline recorded by women. Recall that the overall sample mean was −0.247, so the positive deviation of +0.080 for men was closer to the average actual change in the CPI of 0.0. The absolute differences were also offsetting, although the average absolute differences were much larger: men recorded a smaller than average absolute error of −0.452 and women a larger error of +0.424. The ratio data indicated that the error among men was 67.6 percent of the average and for women it was 130.4 percent of the sample average. The difference was somewhat narrower with the ratio of the absolute errors.

The differences by education level conform to the hypothesis that the costs of collecting and processing relevant data decline as education increases. In the lowest education subgroup, the average change in inflation expectations was 2.9 times as large as the average, while among the highest education subgroup the change was just about half the average. The effect across education subgroups was nearly linear and significant, with higher education groups exhibiting less heterogeneity.

The results indicated that both the youngest and oldest age groups exhibited greater heterogeneity in expectations. The results, however, were not as large nor as consistent as those recorded by education. Indeed, none of the average deviations were significant, and only some of the absolute deviations proved to

Table 3.1 Change in inflation expectations over the six-month interval within selected demographic subgroups, panel data 1993–2005

Population subgroup	Deviations from sample means		Ratio to sample means	
	ΔP^e (standard error)	$|\Delta P|^e$ (standard error)	ΔP^e (standard error)	$|\Delta P|^e$ (standard error)
All households	0.000 (0.032)	0.000 (0.026)	1.000 (0.128)	1.000 (0.009)
Gender				
Male	0.080 (0.038)[a]	−0.452 (0.031)[a]	0.676 (0.152)[b]	0.843 (0.011)[b]
Female	−0.075 (0.050)	0.424 (0.042)[a]	1.304 (0.204)	1.147 (0.015)[b]
Education				
Less than high school	−0.476 (0.209)[a]	1.504 (0.179)[a]	2.925 (0.847)[b]	1.522 (0.062)[b]
High school	−0.176 (0.067)[a]	0.368 (0.055)[a]	1.713 (0.269)[b]	1.128 (0.019)[b]
Some college	0.078 (0.065)	0.086 (0.053)	0.683 (0.263)	1.030 (0.018)
College degree	0.157 (0.050)[a]	−0.425 (0.041)[a]	0.365 (0.203)[b]	0.852 (0.014)[b]
Graduate studies	0.122 (0.059)[a]	−0.631 (0.048)[a]	0.508 (0.240)[b]	0.781 (0.017)[b]
Age				
18–34	−0.097 (0.069)	0.326 (0.058)[a]	1.392 (0.280)	1.113 (0.020)[b]
35–44	−0.037 (0.061)	−0.084 (0.051)	1.151 (0.247)	0.971 (0.018)
45–54	0.075 (0.063)	−0.255 (0.052)[a]	0.696 (0.256)	0.911 (0.018)[b]
55–64	0.119 (0.081)	−0.203 (0.067)[a]	0.519 (0.325)	0.929 (0.023)[b]
65 or older	0.009 (0.086)	0.106 (0.072)	0.964 (0.346)	1.037 (0.025)
Household income				
Bottom fifth	−0.177 (0.130)	1.005 (0.109)[a]	1.714 (0.528)	1.349 (0.038)[b]
Second fifth	−0.122 (0.093)	0.453 (0.078)[a]	1.494 (0.378)	1.157 (0.027)[b]
Middle fifth	−0.172 (0.071)[a]	0.098 (0.059)	1.696 (0.289)[b]	1.034 (0.020)
Fourth fifth	0.111 (0.059)	−0.248 (0.048)[a]	0.552 (0.237)	0.914 (0.017)[b]
Top fifth	0.194 (0.048)[a]	−0.579 (0.039)[a]	0.216 (0.194)[b]	0.799 (0.014)[b]

Note
The average actual change in the CPI-u inflation rate was 0.0 across all six-month intervals.
a Significantly different from 0.0 at 95 percent confidence level.
b Significantly different from 1.0 at 95 percent confidence level.

be significant. The results by income groups indicate that the least heterogeneity was among the top 40 percent of the income distribution, and the largest heterogeneity was among those in the lowest fifth of the income distribution.

Overall, the data provide some support for the hypothesis that the costs involved in collecting and processing information play a role in the decision to update inflation expectations. Among groups that faced higher costs, the level of heterogeneity was greater, indicating less frequent updating, most notably among the least educated. Correspondingly, groups that faced lower costs and higher benefits exhibited more frequent updating and less heterogeneity, most strongly shown by upper income subgroups.

Staggered information flows

Although the two-wave panel data cannot rigorously test theories of staggered information flows, it can provide some guidance. The theory is typically expressed in terms of the delayed response in updating expectations. Since the panel includes a measure of only one change in expectations, an analysis of the timing of the updating of expectations over time is not possible. Instead, the process can be conceptualized in reverse: rather than postulating that a given change in the actual inflation rate has a staggered impact on a series of future changes in expectations, it is postulated that a given change in inflation expectations resulted from the staggered impact of a series of past changes in the actual inflation rate.

Past changes in the actual inflation rate were used as predictors in a regression analysis of the change in inflation expectations. For this analysis, the past change in the inflation rate was defined as the difference between the monthly change in the CPI (at annual rates) at time t and t_{-1}. Since the measured change in inflation expectations occurred over a six-month interval, changes in the actual inflation rate within that six-month interval would not unambiguously support the hypothesis of staggered information flows. Changes in the actual inflation rate that occurred more than six months ago could more reasonably be anticipated to support the hypothesis. Twelve lagged changes in the monthly inflation rate were entered into the regression. Dummy variables for the demographic characteristics discussed above were also included.

The results of the regression are shown in Table 3.2. While the first six lags of the actual change in the inflation rate were significant contributors to the change in inflation expectations, this could simply reflect normal updating, not the staggered information hypothesis. The coefficients increase from the first lag to the fourth lag and reach a peak at the sixth lag. The significance of the seventh to the tenth lags offers greater support for the hypothesis that staggered information flows have a significant impact on expectations. It is of some importance to note that all of these variables combined explained just 1 percent of the total variation in inflation expectations. So, even if the data support the staggered information hypothesis, the support is quite meager.

Table 3.2 Impact of lagged changes in actual inflation rate on change in inflation expectations, 1993 to 2005

	Coefficient	*Standard error*
Intercept	−0.188	0.113
Monthly change in CPI		
Lag 1	0.107*	0.016
Lag 2	0.167*	0.019
Lag 3	0.238*	0.024
Lag 4	0.301*	0.027
Lag 5	0.331*	0.029
Lag 6	0.339*	0.030
Lag 7	0.252*	0.029
Lag 8	0.177*	0.029
Lag 9	0.128*	0.027
Lag 10	0.087*	0.025
Lag 11	0.024	0.020
Lag 12	0.007	0.017
Sex		
Male (excluded)		
Female	−0.130*	0.064
Education		
Less than high school	−0.560*	0.151
High school	−0.241*	0.089
Some college (excluded)		
College degree	0.032	0.091
Graduate studies	−0.038	0.105
Age		
18–34	−0.138	0.094
35–44	−0.103	0.094
45–54 (excluded)		
55–64	0.078	0.112
65 or older	0.090	0.110
Income		
Bottom fifth	0.072	0.119
Second fifth	0.062	0.103
Middle (excluded)		
Fourth fifth	0.248*	0.092
Top fifth	0.276*	0.093
R^2 adjusted	0.010	
Cases	26,611	

Note
*Significantly different from 0.0 at 95 percent confidence level .

Asymmetric impact of information

The hypothesis that unfavorable information about inflation prompts widespread and prompt responses in inflation expectations can be tested by a comparison of positive and negative changes in the actual inflation rate with subsequent changes in expectations. For each six-month interval in the panel, the change in inflation expectations was compared with the change in the actual inflation rate during the prior six months, with negative and positive changes entered separately. The regressions included 26,611 cases from 1993 to 2005.

The estimated results were consistent with the hypothesis that increases in the inflation rate had a much larger impact than declines on inflation expectations. The coefficient for an increase in inflation was 0.117 (standard error of 0.020), nearly twice the size of the coefficient for declines in inflation of 0.068 (standard error of 0.020). The estimate that negative news about inflation was twice as powerful as positive news is consistent with prospect theory (Kahneman and Tversky, 1979).

The asymmetrical response of inflation expectations may mean that there is also an asymmetrical response to changes in the perceived credibility of central banks. Increases in inflation will more promptly diminish the credibility of central banks, but declines in inflation will only slowly rebuild lost credibility.

Backward- or forward-looking expectations?

Tests of whether the formation of inflation expectations represents a backward- or forward-looking process have typically been examined in separate equations, with the analyst having the responsibility of judging the comparative evidence. There is a way to nest both hypotheses in the same reduced-form equation by regressing current inflation expectations on both past and *future* changes in the actual inflation rate. Strong support for the adaptive hypothesis would be demonstrated if past, but not future, changes in the actual inflation rate were significant predictors, while support for forward-looking expectations would be shown if future, but not past, changes in the actual inflation rate were significant predictors. The resulting equation is simply another method to test for "Granger causality" (Geweke *et al.*, 1983). The estimated equation used from 1978 to 2005 was:

$$P_t^e = 0.895 + 0.291 \sum_{j=1}^{4} P_{t+j} + 0.318\, P_t - 0.089 \sum_{j=1}^{4}$$
$$\quad\ (0.276)\ (0.106) \qquad\qquad (0.148)\ \ (0.151)$$

$$P_{t-j} + 0.172 \sum_{j=1}^{4} P^e_{t-j}\, R^2 = 0.954$$
$$\quad\ (0.252)$$

The data indicate that higher *future* changes in the inflation rate were positively associated with increases in *current* expectations. The coefficients for the four-quarter lead (indicated by *t* ranging from +1 to +4) in the rate of inflation were both positive and significant, at more than twice its standard error. A separate chi-square test on the exclusion of the four-quarter lead was easily rejected ($p=0.006$). In contrast, the coefficients for the four-quarter lag (indicated by *t* ranging from −1 to −4) were clearly insignificant, thereby rejecting the adaptive hypothesis. Moreover, the coefficients were negative, exactly the opposite of what the adaptive hypothesis would predict.

Expectations also incorporate contemporaneous information on the inflation rate, even though the survey has always been completed well in advance of the announcement of the official inflation rate. Unlike past changes in inflation, contemporaneous changes in inflation had the anticipated positive impact on expectations. The significance of the contemporaneous inflation rate indicates that consumers obtain information about current inflationary trends from sources other than the official announcements.

Rational expectations hypothesis

Tests on whether the Michigan data on inflation expectations meet the rigorous criteria imposed by the rational expectations hypothesis have been repeatedly conducted during the past 25 years.[8] The data have never given unequivocal support to the rational expectations hypothesis, with the principle failing due to the lack of efficient use of all available information.[9,10] Thomas (1999: 141–142) summarized his findings by noting that "consensus household inflation forecasts do surprisingly well relative to those of the presumably better-informed professional economists." Indeed, the median consumer forecasts of year-ahead inflation rates "outperformed all other forecasts in the 1981–1997 period on simple tests of accuracy as well as on tests for unbiasedness." Mehra (2002: 35) also finds that Michigan's median inflation expectations outperforms the expectations of professional economists and forecasters: "They are more accurate, unbiased, have predictive content for future inflation, and are efficient with respect to economic variables generally considered pertinent to the behavior of inflation." As noted at the start of this chapter, it was findings such as these that originally motivated Muth to advance the rational expectations hypothesis.

Let us focus on the puzzle that consumers' performance at forecasting the inflation rate is comparable to forecasts by economists. This finding is more troublesome for those who favor some form of the adaptation hypothesis, but it is also quite difficult to argue that the costs of collecting and processing information are not significantly lower for economists than for consumers. Only under the hypothesis that the costs are trivial would no significant differences between economists and consumers be anticipated.

Another hypothesis is that the errors in consumer expectations are offsetting, and as a consequence the tests were misleading. Thus, the errors could be quite large – say, a significant underestimate among men is offset by a significant overestimate among women, or similar offsetting shifts among education or age subgroups. To examine this issue, a number of regressions were performed for a selection of demographic subgroups. Given that survey data usually involve some aggregation errors, the regression was calculated using nonlinear least squares to estimate a moving-average error term, using a consistent estimate of the covariance matrix that allows for serial correlation and heteroscedasticity. The overlapping forecast intervals generated by the survey questions could produce serially correlated errors even among perfectly rational agents (Croush-ore, 1998). In fact, a significant first order moving average error term was found in all equations. The residuals are also tested for the inefficient use of informa-tion on inflation, but no tests were attempted for the inefficient use of other rele-vant information (what is called strong efficiency).

Regressions were estimated for men and women, as well as for different edu-cation and age subgroups. The results are reported in Table 3.3. The regressions are based on quarterly observations from 1978 to 2005. Given the rather small monthly sample sizes, to ensure that estimates for each subgroup were based on a sufficient number of cases, the independent monthly samples were pooled into quarterly observations to calculate the median inflation expectations for each subgroup.[11]

The results of the analysis indicated that rather than offsetting errors, the year-ahead inflation expectations of each of the demographic groups were an unbiased estimate of the actual inflation rate. The null hypothesis that inflation expectations were a biased estimate was rejected for every demographic sub-group at the 95 percent confidence level: every constant term was insignificantly different from 0, and every estimated coefficient on inflation expectations was insignificantly different from 1. Every equation had a significant estimate of the moving average error term, but only among the least educated and the older respondents was there any evidence of the inefficient use of information about the inflation rate that was available at the time their expectations were formed.

These results have always been met with disbelief. Could it be that the costs of forming unbiased inflation expectations are more manageable based on stag-gered updating? Does the presumably lower cost and greater importance of private information play a more pivotal role in the formation of expectations than suggested by current theories? Or is the accuracy of expectations a property of groups and consensus forecasts? Could it be that the rational expectations hypothesis is true at the macro but not at the micro level?

Concluding comments

There are at least as many unresolved issues now as when the rational expecta-tions hypothesis was first advanced nearly a half century ago. Indeed, the find-ings from this analysis can be summarized in much the same way as Muth did in his classic article: consumers' inflation expectations are forward looking, they are generally as accurate as the forecasts of economic models, and they more closely correspond to the hypothesis of rational expectations than to the backward-looking hypothesis of adaptation.

There is no doubt that people sometimes engage in adaptive behavior, correct past errors, or simply rely on extrapolation to form expectations. These shortcuts are used to help reduce the costs involved in collecting and processing data. These costs result in staggered changes in expectations. In turn, staggered or sticky expectations are the likely cause of the findings that consumers do not take into account all available information when forming their expectations. It is

Table 3.3 Tests of rational expectations hypothesis based on University of Michigan's inflation expectations data, quarterly data 1978-2005

Population Subgroup	Unbiased → $\alpha = 0$ and $\beta = 1$ $P_t = \alpha + \beta P_t^{E,t-4}$				χ^2 for H_o	Efficiency → $\delta = 0$ and $\varphi = 0$ $e_t = \delta + \varphi P_{t-5}$		
	α	β	Θ	R^2		δ	φ	R^2
All households	-0.414 (0.533)	1.184 (0.181)	0.655* (0.108)	0.884	1.538 [0.464]	0.030 (0.158)	-0.035 (0.039)	0.005
Gender								
Male	-0.135 (0.524)	1.158 (0.177)	0.726* (0.081)	0.893	3.861 [0.145]	-0.004 (0.153)	-0.024 (0.037)	0.000
Female	-0.605 (0.594)	1.181 (0.186)	0.588* (0.145)	0.862	1.037 [0.594]	-0.011 (0.170)	-0.031 (0.042)	0.000
Education								
Less than high school	-0.323 (0.692)	1.148 (0.221)	0.574* (0.091)	0.800	0.722 [0.697]	-0.551* (0.195)	0.091* (0.033)	0.051
High school	-0.482 (0.610)	1.208 (0.189)	0.611* (0.076)	0.866	1.895 [0.388]	-0.121 (0.167)	0.001 (0.037)	0.000
Some college	0.082 (0.635)	1.064 (0.208)	0.607* (0.118)	0.850	1.946 [0.378]	-0.105 (0.204)	-0.009 (0.056)	0.000
College degree	0.113 (0.514)	1.049 (0.175)	0.568* (0.172)	0.853	1.960 [0.375]	-0.048 (0.187)	-0.021 (0.049)	0.000
Graduate studies	0.061 (0.588)	0.998 (0.189)	0.712* (0.081)	0.876	0.107 [0.948]	-0.027 (0.195)	-0.022 (0.058)	0.000
Age								
18–34	-0.139 (0.589)	1.068 (0.190)	0.556* (0.128)	0.849	0.243 [0.886]	-0.032 (0.199)	-0.026 (0.057)	0.000
35–44	-0.150 (0.585)	1.064 (0.184)	0.624* (0.129)	0.869	0.181 [0.914]	0.004 (0.194)	-0.029 (0.054)	0.000
45–54	-0.229 (0.582)	1.143 (0.187)	0.590* (0.095)	0.866	1.739 [0.419]	-0.052 (0.176)	-0.017 (0.041)	0.000

55–64	−0.153	1.233	0.647*	0.864	8.089*	−0.318*	0.048	0.012
	(0.569)	(0.188)	(0.071)		[0.018]	(0.158)	(0.029)	
65 or older	1.356	0.834	0.766*	0.789	8.538*	−0.929*	0.179*	0.218
	(0.774)	(0.271)	(0.074)		[0.014]	(0.175)	(0.042)	

Notes
Standard errors in parentheses; probability level of χ^2 in brackets. All standard errors and covariances calculated using the Newy–West procedure. All estimated equations included a moving average error term.
An asterisk indicates significance at the 0.05 percent level; significance tests on all coefficients except β were for differences from 0.0 and tests on β were for differences from 1.0. R^2 adjusted for degrees of freedom.

simply too costly given the expected benefit. These findings, however, do not contradict the rational expectations hypothesis, but act to incorporate the hypothesis more fully into the standard economic framework.

Moreover, the finding that consumers are not fully rational in forming their inflation expectations is as surprising as the finding that consumers do not fully maximize their utility. The profession needs to accept what amounts to a simplifying assumption that is roughly consistent with the evidence at the macro level. The acceptance should be based on its predictive performance, not on the realism of the theory's assumptions. To be sure, full rationality is not likely to be observed in everyday life among consumers, nor even among economists. Analysis at the micro level still needs to more fully incorporate aspects of bounded rationality and other innovations of behavioral theory.

Most of the theoretical implication of rationality for monetary policy, however, may be closely approximated by "nearly rational" expectations. Without a more exact and universal definition of what "near rationality" means, that glass will be seen as half empty by some and half full by others. It is that unresolved ambiguity that continues to makes monetary policy an interesting and challenging task.

Notes

1 Many economists have reinterpreted Muth's original hypothesis to apply at the micro rather than an the aggregate level (Begg, 1982). They reason that given that utility maximization is assumed to be true for each individual, the rational expectations hypothesis should be tested at the micro level. Some analysts have even claimed that the only appropriate test of the rational expectations hypothesis would be based on panel data. Some have also argued that the aggregation involved in time-series tests result in inconsistent estimates and masks offsetting individual differences (Figlewski and Wachtel, 1983; Kean and Runkle, 1990).

2 Plato wrote that "each man possesses opinions about the future, which go by the general name of expectations." (Plato, *Laws 644c*, 360 BC).

3 The larger variance that has often been associated with higher expected inflation rates in the literature may be partially due to the truncation of the distribution at zero.

4 Transforming qualitative expectations into quantitative estimates has been done for inflation expectations with mixed success. Different methods have been used to "quantify" qualitative measures of expectations, with the Carlson–Parkin (1975) technique the most widely known. These techniques involve an assumption about the underlying and unobserved distribution of expectations (typically assumed normal, but other distributional assumptions have been used) combined with an assumption that across the entire time-series, expectations are unbiased and equal to realizations (although other identifying assumptions are possible). See Batchelor (1986) and Pesaran (1987) for a review of these techniques.

5 There is a long-standing debate about whether large estimates (say, five or more times the median or mean) should be deleted and thus treated as missing data, or whether some information can be retained, namely that the respondent expected a large increase, and the data should simply be truncated.

6 The correlation between the interquartile range and the variance of the mean was 0.82.

7 Persistent differences in inflation expectations between men and women have been documented in the past (Bryan and Venkatu, 2001).

8 See Lott and Miller (1982), Gramlich (1983), Grant and Thomas (1999), Thomas

(1999), Mehra (2002), Roberts (1997), Badhestani (1992), Bryan and Gavin (1986), Noble and Fields (1982), and Batchelor and Dua (1989).

9 Cukierman (1986) has suggested that this is not a clear violation of the rational expectations hypothesis, since households may not always correctly distinguish between temporary and permanent shocks and thus their forecasts could exhibit serially correlated errors.

10 Similar comparisons were done for year-ahead forecasts of the national unemployment rate. Curtin (1999, 2003) found that consumers' forecasts of the year-ahead unemployment rate outperformed those of professional forecasters as well as forecasts from two prominent macroeconomic models.

11 Insufficient data in the first half of the period made it impossible to code real household income in a consistent fashion and so this variable was excluded from this analysis.

References

Akerlof, G.A., W. Dickens and G. Perry, "Near-Rational Wage and Price Setting and the Optimal Rates of Inflation and Unemployment," *Brookings Papers on Economic Activity* I, 1–60, 2000.

Albanesi, Stefania, V.V. Chari, and Lawrence Christiano, "Expectations Traps and Monetary Policy," NBER working paper 8912, 2002.

Bacchetta, Philippe and Eric van Wincoop, "Rational Inattention: A Solution to the Forward Discount Puzzle," Working paper 11633, National Bureau of Economic Research, September 2005.

Baghestani, H., "Survey Evidence on the Muthian Rationality of the Inflation Forecasts of U.S. Consumers," *Oxford Bulletin of Economics and Statistics*, vol. 54, pp. 173–186, 1992.

Baker, Michael, "Digit Preferences in CPS Unemployment Data," *Economic Letters*, vol. 39, no. 1, pp. 117–121, 1992.

Batchelor, R., "Quantitative versus Qualitative Measures of Inflation Expectations," *Oxford Bulletin of Economics and Statistics*, vol. 48, no. 2, pp. 99–120, 1986.

Batchelor, R. and Pami Dua, "Household versus Economists' Forecasts of Inflation: A Reassessment," *Journal of Money, Credit, and Banking*, vol. 21, pp. 252–257, 1989.

Begg, David K.H., *The Rational Expectations Revolution in Macroeconomics*, John Hopkins University Press, 1982.

Branch, William A., "Sticky Information and Model Uncertainty in Survey Data on Inflation Expectations," mimeo, July 2005.

Bryan, M.F. and W.T. Gavin, "Models of Inflation Expectations Formation: A Comparison of Household and Economist Forecasts," *Journal of Money, Credit, and Banking*, vol. 18, no. 4, pp. 539–544, 1986.

Bryan, Michael and Stefan Palmqvist, "Testing Near-Rationality using Detailed Survey Data," Economic Paper 228, European Commission, Economic and Financial Affairs, July 2005.

Bryan, Michael and Guhan Venkatu, "The Curiously Different Inflation Perspectives of Men and Women," Federal Reserve Bank of Cleveland, Economic Commentary Series, 2001.

Cagan, Phillip, "The Monetary Dynamics of Hyperinflation," in Milton Friedman ed.), *Studies in the Quantity Theory of Money*, pp. 25–117, University of Chicago Press, 1956.

Carlson, J. and M. Parkin, "Inflation Expectations," *Economica*, vol. 42, pp. 123–138, 1975.

Carroll, Christopher, "Macroeconomic Expectations of Households and Professional Forecasters," *Quarterly Journal of Economics*, vol. 118, no. 1, pp. 269–298, 2003.

Chari, V.V., Lawrence Christiano, and Martin Eichenbaum, "Expectation Traps and Discretion," *Journal of Economic Theory*, vol. 2, pp. 462–492, 1998.

Croushore, Dean, "Evaluating Inflation Expectations," Working Paper No. 98-14, Federal Reserve Bank of Philadelphia, 1998.

Croushore, Dean and Tom Stark, "Real Time Data Sets for Macroeconomists: Does the Data Vintage Matter?" Working paper 21, Federal Reserve Bank of Richmond, 1999.

Cukierman, Alex, "Measuring Inflationary Expectations," *Journal of Monetary Economics*, vol. 17, pp. 315–324, 1986.

Curtin, Richard, "The Outlook for Consumption in 2000," *The Economic Outlook for 2000*, University of Michigan, 1999.

Curtin, Richard, "Unemployment Expectations: The Impact of Private Information on Income Uncertainty," *Review of Income and Wealth*, vol. 49, no. 4, 2003.

Curtin, Richard, "What Recession? What Recovery? The Arrival of the 21st Century Consumer," *Business Economics*, vol. 39, no. 2, pp. 25–32, 2003.

Doms, Mark and Norman Morin, "Consumer Sentiment, the Economy, and the News Media," Working paper 2004-51, Federal Reserve Board, 2004.

Earl, Peter, "Economics and Psychology: A Survey," *Economic Journal*, vol. 100, pp. 718–755, 1990.

Edouard, L. and A. Senthilselvan, "Observer Error and Birthweight: Digit Preference in Recording," *Public Health*, vol. 111, no. 2, pp. 77–79, 1997.

Evans, George W. and Seppo Honkapohja, *Learning and Expectations in Macroeconomics*, Princeton University Press, 2001.

Figlewski, Stephen and Paul Wachtel, "Rational Expectations, Informational Efficiency, and Tests Using Survey Data: A Reply," *Review of Economics and Statistics*, vol. 65, pp. 529–531, 1983.

Fisher, Irving, *The Theory of Interest*, Macmillan, 1930.

Friedman, Milton, *Essays in Positive Economics*, University of Chicago Press, 1953.

Friedman, Milton, *The Theory of the Consumption Function*, Princeton University Press, 1957.

Geweke, J.-R., R. Meese and W. Dent, "Comparing Alternative Tests of Causality in Temporal Systems," *Journal of Econometrics*, vol. 21, pp. 161–194, 1983.

Gramlich, Edward M., "Models of Inflation Expectations Formation," *Journal of Money, Credit, and Banking*, vol. 15, pp. 155–173, 1983.

Grant, Alan P. and Lloyd B. Thomas, "Inflationary Expectations and Rationality Revisited," *Economic Letters*, vol. 62, pp. 331–338, 1999.

Hamilton, James, *All the News That's Fit to Sell*, Princeton University Press, 2004.

Kahneman, Daniel and Amos Tversky, "Prospect Theory: An Analysis of Decision Under Risk," *Econometrica*, vol. 47, no. 2, pp. 263–292, 1979.

Kean, Michael P. and David E. Runkle, "Are Economic Forecasts Rational?" *Federal Reserve Bank of Minneapolis Quarterly Review*, pp. 26–33, Spring 1989.

Kean, Michael and David Runkle, "Testing the Rationality of Price Forecasts: New Evidence from Panel Data," *American Economic Review*, vol. 80, pp. 714–735, 1990.

Khan, Hashmat and Zhenhua Zhu, "Estimates of Sticky Information Phillips Curve for the United States, Canada, and the United Kingdom," Working paper 2002-19, Bank of Canada, 2002.

Koyck, Leendert Marinus, *Distributed Lags and Investment Analysis*, North Holland, 1954.

Leduc, Sylvain, Keith Sill, and Tom Stark, "Self-Fulfilling Expectations and the Inflation of the 1970s: Evidence from the Livingston Survey," Working paper 02-13R, Federal Reserve Bank of Philadelphia, May 2003.

Lott, W. and S. Miller (1982), "Are Workers More Accurate Forecasters of Inflation than Capitalists?" *Eastern Economic Journal*, vol. 14, pp. 437–446.

Lovell, Michael C., "Tests of the Rational Expectations Hypothesis," *American Economic Review*, vol. 76, no. 1, pp. 110–124, 1986.

Mankiw, N. Gregory and Ricardo Reis, "Sticky Information Versus Sticky Prices: A Proposal to Replace the New Keynesian Phillips Curve," *Quarterly Journal of Economics*, vol. 117, no. 4, pp. 1295–1328, 2002.

Mankiw, N. Gregory and Ricardo Reis, "Sticky Information: A Model of Monetary Nonneutrality and Structural Slumps," in P. Aghion, R. Frydman, J. Stiglitz and M. Woodford (eds.), *Knowledge, Information and Expectations in Modern Macroeconomics: In Honor of Edmund S. Phelps*, Princeton University Press, 2003.

Mankiw, N. Gregory, Ricardo Reis, and Justin Wolfers, "Disagreement about Inflation Expectations," in Mark Gertler and Kenneth (eds.) *Macroeconomics Annual 2003*, NBER: 2004.

Mehra, Yash P., "Survey Measures of Expected Inflation: Revisiting the Issues of Predictive Content and Rationality," *Federal Reserve Bank of Richmond Economic Quarterly*, vol. 88, no. 3, pp. 17–36, 2002.

Muth, John F., "Rational Expectations and the Theory of Price Movements," *Econometrica*, vol. 29, no. 3, pp. 315–335, 1961.

Nerlove, Marc, "Adaptive Expectations and Cobweb Phenomena," *Quarterly Journal of Economics*, vol. 72, no. 2, pp. 227–240, 1958.

Noble, Nicholas R. and T. Windsor Fields, "Testing the Rationality of Inflation Expectations Derived from Survey Data: A Structure-Based Approach," *Southern Economic Journal*, vol. 49, no. 2, pp. 361–373, 1982.

Pesaran, M.H., *The Limits of Rational Expectations*, Basil-Backwell, 1987.

Rabin, M., "Psychology and Economics," *Journal of Economic Literature*, vol. XXXVI, pp. 11–46, 1998.

Rabin, M. and Schrag, J.L., "First Impressions Matter: A Model of Confirmatory Bias," *Quarterly Journal of Economics*, vol. 114, no. 1, pp. 37–82, 1999.

Roberts, John M., "Is Inflation Sticky?" *Journal of Monetary Economics*, vol. 39, pp. 173–196, 1997.

Sims, Christopher, "Implications of Rational Inattention," *Journal of Monetary Economics*, vol. 50, no. 3, pp. 665–690, 2003

Souleles, Nicholas S., "Expectations, Heterogeneous Forecast Errors, and Consumption: Micro Evidence from the Michigan Consumer Sentiment Surveys," *Journal of Money, Credit, and Banking*, vol. 36, no. 1, pp. 39–72, 2004.

Thaler, R.H., *Quasi-Rational Economics*, Russell Sage Foundation, 1991.

Thaler, R.H., *The Winner's Curse*, Princeton University Press, 1992.

Thomas Jr., Lloyd B., "Survey Measures of Expected U.S. Inflation," *Journal of Economic Perspectives*, vol. 13, no. 4, pp. 125–144, 1999.

Tversky, A. and Kahneman, D., "Causal Schemas in Judgements under Uncertainty," in D. Kahneman, P. Slovic, and A. Tversky (eds.), *Judgment under Uncertainty: Heuristics and Biases*, pp. 117–128, Cambridge University Press, 1982.

Woodford, Michael, *Interest and Prices: Foundations of a Theory of Monetary Policy*, Princeton University Press, 2003.

Woodford, Michael, "Robustly Optimal Monetary Policy with Near Rational Expectations," NBER Working paper 11896, 2005.

Zarnowitz, Victor, "Rational Expectations and Macroeconomic Forecasts," *Journal of Business and Economic Statistics*, vol. 3, pp. 293–311, 1985.

4 Heterogeneous expectations, adaptive learning, and forward-looking monetary policy

Martin Fukač[1]

1 Introduction

An empirical literature (Gurkaynak *et al.* 2006, Gurkaynak *et al.* 2007, Mishkin and Schmidt-Hebbel 2006) provides evidence that, in inflation targeting regimes, long-term inflation expectations are anchored to the target. This anchoring effect is usually explained by monetary policy being credible. On the other hand, short-term inflation expectations (1- to 2-year-horizon expectations, which is the time horizon of effective monetary policy) are typically more volatile, and there is a high degree of expectations heterogeneity (e.g. Mankiw and Wolfers 2003). Central bankers face problems in anchoring short-run expectations. This raises the issue of, what are the effects of expectations heterogeneity. This chapter contributes to this discussion.

I study the implications of inflation expectations heterogeneity in a standard closed economy New Keynesian business cycle model. Using numerical simulations, I find that if private agents (households and firms), and the monetary authority disagree about the expected inflation rate, then in an inflation targeting regime, a central bank should not respond aggressively to deviations from an inflation target that it itself anticipates. Weaker responses improve economic stability in the short run. They lead to falls in inflation volatility, in output volatility, and in the central bank's expected loss.

Heterogeneous expectations cause a mismatch in subjective real interest rates. The mismatch leads to higher volatility of both inflation and output than would occur when expectations are homogeneous across the economy. One of the worst scenarios is when private agents predict less inflation than the central bank. That leads the central bank to raise the policy interest rate. For private agents, who expect lower inflation, the *ex ante* real interest rate is higher due to that increase. Higher real rates cause private agents to substitute from present consumption so that aggregate demand drops. But consumption drops more than it would have if the private agents expected the same inflation rate as the central bank, because their subjective real rate is higher now. So the effect of monetary policy is stronger than the central bank itself intends. A similar situation, but with opposite implications, arises when the central bank expects low future inflation, and private agents expect high inflation. Implied, subjective real interest rates are low for private agents, which results in the economy growing too fast, at the cost of unnecessarily high inflation.

The role of monetary policy is complex in a heterogeneous expectations environment. Central bank's aversion to price inflation implies strong policy responses to deviations of expected inflation from the desired target. But if the central bank is too responsive, it multiplies the effect of the mismatch in the real rates even more. In the short run the mismatch matters most for monetary policy. In the mid- to long-run this phenomenon naturally disappears, and optimal monetary policy is standard, as in a homogeneous expectations environment.

The following text describes a simple numerical analysis of a New Keynesian model to assess its dynamics under incomplete and heterogeneous knowledge on the part of economic agents. A particular focus is on the implications that heterogeneous expectations have for the optimal behaviour of central bank. The next section sets up the experiment laboratory: a workhorse model, adaptive learning mechanism, and the source of expectations heterogeneity. In the third section, dynamics of the model environment are studied, and basic observations are summarized. The fourth section provides economic intuition for the results. The last part concludes with a general discussion about the results, and what lesson can be taken for monetary policy.

2 The model

The New Keynesian business cycle model is used as an approximation of the economy. As an extension to the standard model, the assumption that monetary policy is perfectly credible is relaxed. As a result private firms and households – as one economic group – form different expectations from the central bank. All agents use an adaptive (econometric) learning mechanism to learn about the actual structure of the economy, and they are allowed to disagree in their views. In the long run, the economy converges to standard, rational expectations equilibrium dynamics. But in the short run, the economic dynamics are driven by naïvely subjective expectations. The only source of expectations heterogeneity in my set-up is that the private agents and the central bank give different weights to past forecasting errors. They evaluate new pieces of information differently. They differ in the opinion about how much of the innovation is due to the fundamental error in their forecasting model – in other words, about how much they should update the model structure – and how much of it is due to an unanticipated shock that hits the economy.

The basic model is standard (e.g. see Walsh 2003, ch. 5.4; or Honkapohja and Mitra 2005). The aggregate dynamics are given by the IS curve (1), which is the households' Euler equation, linearized around a flexible price equilibrium; and the Phillips curve (2), which is the linearization of the firms' pricing rules. In a perfect-knowledge environment, the model is

$$x_t = E_t x_{t+1} - \sigma(i_t - E_t \pi_{t+1}) + g_t \qquad (1)$$

$$\pi_t = \beta E_t \pi_{t+1} + \lambda x_t + u_t \tag{2}$$

x_t is the output gap, defined as the deviation of actual output from the output arising in a flexible price environment; π_t is the inflation rate, and i_t is the interest rate set by the central bank. g_t and u_t are demand and cost-push shocks, respectively, assumed to follow AR(1) processes. β, σ, and λ, are the households' time preference parameter, risk aversion parameter, and inflation to output gap elasticity parameter, respectively.

The nominal side of the economy is anchored – at a zero inflation target rate – by a discretionary, expectations-based policy rule:

$$i_t = q_\pi E_t \pi_{t+1} + q_x E_t x_{t+1} \tag{3}$$

i_t is the nominal interest rate set by the central bank. q_π and q_x are the policy weights on inflation and the output gap, respectively. Here, the central bank *cannot* observe the shocks $\{g_t, u_t\}$ when making policy decisions.[2]

All expectations operators $E_t(.) = E_t(.|\Omega_t)$ stand for perfect knowledge, rational expectations. Ω_t is the perfect-knowledge information set, $\Omega_t = \{\beta, \lambda, \sigma, q_\pi, q_x, g_t, u_t, g_{t-1}, u_{t-1}, \ldots\}$.

Definition 1: Economic agents have *perfect knowledge* if an information set Ω_t is available at time t, where

$$\Omega_t^i = \{Q, g_t, u_t, g_{t-1}, u_{t-1}, \ldots\}.$$

The information set contains the true values of the structural parameters $Q = (\beta, \lambda, \sigma, q_\pi, q_x)$, and the current and past exogenous shocks u and g.

The key assumption of the workhorse model is that the perfect information set Ω_t is not available to agents. Agents have imperfect and heterogeneous knowledge, which leads to a heterogeneous expectations formation. The workhorse model takes the form

$$x_t = \hat{E}_t^P x_{t+1} - \sigma(i_t - \hat{E}_t^P \pi_{t+1}) + g_t \tag{4}$$

$$\pi_t = \beta \hat{E}_t^P \pi_{t+1} + \lambda x_t + u_t. \tag{5}$$

$$i_t = q_\pi \hat{E}_t^{CB} \pi_{t+1} + q_x \hat{E}_t^{CB} x_{t+1}. \tag{6}$$

where $\hat{E}_t^P(.) = E_t(.|\hat{\Omega}_t^P)$ are the subjective, imperfect-knowledge expectations of private agents, and $E_t^{CB}(.) = E_t(.|\Omega_t^{CB})$ are the subjective, imperfect knowledge expectations of central bank. The individual imperfect information sets $\hat{\Omega}_t^P$ and $\hat{\Omega}_t^{CB}$ are subsets of the perfect knowledge set, $\{\hat{\Omega}_t^P, \hat{\Omega}_t^{CB}\} \subset \Omega_t$.

Definition 2: Economic agents have *imperfect, homogeneous knowledge* if all agents share the same, incomplete information set $\hat{\Omega}_t$ at time t, where

$$\hat{\Omega}_t = \{\hat{\Theta}_t, \kappa_t, g_t, u_t, g_{t-1}, u_{t-1}, \ldots\}.$$

$\hat{\Theta}_t$ is the imperfect, time-varying belief about the true structural parameters $\{\beta, \lambda, \sigma, q_\pi, q_x\}$, and κ_t represents the information gain (willingness to learn, or the sensitivity to new information).

Definition 3: There are two groups of agents: (P) private agents, and (CB) the central bank. The private agents and central bank have *imperfect, heterogeneous knowledge* if the information they have differs, and is not perfect, $\hat{\Omega}_t^P \neq \hat{\Omega}_t^{CB}$.

I am interested in biasing this economy to an absurd extreme. To deviate from the homogeneous expectations case (the pooling-information assumption), and at the same time to avoid the problems of infinite-order expectations due to "forecasting others' forecasts", as raised by Towsend (1983), I suppose that agents believe that everyone shares their own expectations. And they do not learn from experience other than their own. Agents in this set-up are very naïve. Even though it might not seem to be a very realistic assumption, it is useful. It sets bounds for the results that one might expect for the convex combinations of two extreme assumptions – this one, and the imperfect homogeneous knowledge assumption.

Expectations heterogeneity is driven by an adaptive learning technology. The learning mechanism described below, resembles the assumption about the agents' knowledge. Honkapohja and Mitra (2005) show that the move from the perfect knowledge model to the imperfect and heterogeneous knowledge model is possible under Euler-equation learning. If all agents are learning (using recursive least squares, and the E-stability conditions hold), the originally heterogeneous knowledge $\hat{\Omega}_t^P$ and $\hat{\Omega}_t^{CB}$ is enriched over time so that it converges to the complete knowledge set Ω_t. It happens even despite the very restrictive assumption that agents believe that everyone shares their expectations, and they only trust their own experience.

The adaptive learning methodology relies on agents' learning about a reduced form model. The minimum-state representation to the structural model (4)–(6) is

$$\mathbf{Y}_t = \mathbf{a} + \mathbf{b}\mathbf{s}_t$$

$\mathbf{Y}_t$ is the vector of endogenous variables, $\mathbf{s}_t$ is the vector of exogenous shocks, and $\mathbf{a}, \mathbf{b}$ are the matrices collecting structural parameters.

The (P) private agents' and (CB) central bank's perceived law of motion (PLM) for the economy (4)–(6) is assumed to be

$$\hat{\mathbf{Y}}_t = \hat{\mathbf{a}}_t^i + \hat{\mathbf{b}}_t^i \mathbf{s}_t,$$

where $\{\hat{\mathbf{a}}_t^i, \hat{\mathbf{b}}_t^i\}$ is in $\hat{\Omega}_t^i$, and i = {P, CB} are the time-varying matrices of the model primitives, representing beliefs about the true structure $\{\mathbf{a}, \mathbf{b}\}$. Implicitly, in this framework agents have perfect knowledge about the structure of the economy, but they have imperfect knowledge about the true values of some structural parameters. Consequently, private agents and the central bank both learn about the structural matrices $\{\mathbf{a}, \mathbf{b}\}$ over time. The learning behaviour takes the form of econometric learning (recursive least squares). In the adaptive learning literature, it is believed that such a mechanism resembles actual behaviour of agents very closely (for all see Evans and Honkapohja 2003b, ch. 2.3). The algorithm is

$$\boldsymbol{\xi}_t^i = \boldsymbol{\xi}_{t-1}^i + \kappa_t^i (\mathbf{R}_t^i)^{-1} \mathbf{X}_t (\mathbf{Y}_t - \mathbf{X}_t' \boldsymbol{\xi}_{t-1}^i), \tag{7}$$

$$\mathbf{R}_t^i = \mathbf{R}_{t-1}^i + \kappa_t^i (\mathbf{X}_t \mathbf{X}_t' - \mathbf{R}_{t-1}^i), \tag{8}$$

i = {P,CB}, $\boldsymbol{\xi}_t^i = [\mathbf{vec}(\hat{\mathbf{a}}^i)' \; \mathbf{vec}(\hat{\mathbf{b}}^i)']'$ is the vector of the perceived-law-of-motion parameters. $\mathbf{X}_t$ is the matrix of appropriately stacked exogenous shocks s_t, and κ_t^i is the information gain. I also call this gain as the willingness to learn, or the sensitivity to new information. The information gain is the only source of heterogeneity. $\mathbf{R}_t^i$ is the information matrix available at time *t* to a group *i*.

3 Model dynamics

This section analyses the dynamics of the workhorse model. The goal is to assess the implications that expectations heterogeneity has in a forward-looking monetary policy regime for short-run economic fluctuations. I focus on two questions. The first question is: What is the contribution of expectations heterogeneity to inflation and output volatility? The benchmark is the standard, rational expectations model with optimized monetary policy. The second question is: How can a central bank's behaviour minimize the fluctuations in heterogeneous expectations environments?

To address both questions, the plan is to perform an intervention analysis. I expose the model economy to a one-period, unitary, cost-push shock, to a one-period, unitary, demand shock, and to a combination of the two. The REE serves as benchmark dynamics. There are no monetary policy shocks. To summarize the results, the central bank's expected loss is the prism. I report (*a*) the half life of the shock to central bank's expected loss (denoted as HL; it is the time it takes from the initial effect of the shock to the value of one half of the response amplitude), and (*b*) the amplitude of the response deviation from the rational-expectations dynamics (denoted as max). It is the maximum deviation of imperfect knowledge dynamics from REE dynamics. If it is positive, the adaptive learning (AL) economy is more responsive to the shock than under the rational expectations (RE); if negative, less.

Turning to model calibration, note that the paper by Clarida *et al.* (2000) calibrates the workhorse model. The calibrated values are: $\sigma = 1$, $\beta = 0.99$, and

$\lambda = 0.3$. Optimal weights are derived for the policy rule (3). Assuming that a central bank puts one-third weight on output stabilization, and two-thirds weight on inflation stabilization: $(q_\pi^*, q_x^*) = (1.5, 1)$. For comparison purposes, I also use two sets of non-optimal policy weights: $(q_\pi, q_x) = (1.3, 1)$, $(q_\pi, q_x) = (2.5, 1)$.

In all the simulations, I assume an econometric learning algorithm, which means that whenever a new piece of information (observation) arrives, the agents re-estimate their forecasting models. The recursive econometric learning is represented by (7) and (8) with $\kappa_t^i = c_i(t + 16)^{-1}$, where t denotes time, and $i = \{CB, P\}$; c_i is a positive constant and stands for a bias in the information gain. If $c_i = 1$, κ_t^i represents the recursive least squares technique. If $c_i > 1$, there is a greater willingness to update than under standard econometric learning. $\kappa_t^i \to 0$ as $t \to \infty$, thus the effect of $c_i \neq 1$ matters only initially. Next, I calibrate the autocorrelation in demand and cost-push shocks to 0.2. The reason for such a small number is that high persistence in the output gap and inflation is delivered by adaptive learning (see for instance Milani 2007). The value is set to replicate the empirical volatility of inflation and output. All the simulations are initialized from steady state values: $\boldsymbol{\xi}_0^i = [\text{vec(a)}' \ \text{vec(b)}']'$, for $i = \{P,CB\}$. $\mathbf{R}_0^i$ is an identity matrix.[3]

How is the experiment described? First, the reference results start with the case where knowledge is imperfect but homogeneous. Both the private agents and the central bank have the same sensitivity to new information/innovations, $\kappa_t^P = \kappa_t^{CB} = \kappa_t$. Then, the same technology is used to study the heterogenous expectations case. To see how expectations heterogeneity affects inflation and output volatility, the two groups of agents are assumed to have different sensitivity to new information, $\kappa_t^P \neq \kappa_t^{CB}$. The focus is on the instances in which (*a*) the private agents are more sensitive than the central bank, and (*b*) private agents are less sensitive then the central bank. To see how a central bank can minimize fluctuations, under the setup (*a*) and (*b*), I compare the effects of monetary policy which is (*i*) optimal in the rational expectations (RE) environment, (*ii*) more, and (*iii*) less responsive to inflation than under the optimal (RE) setting. All experiments begin from the economy's steady state – in the initial period, all agents know the structural parameters.

3.1 CB's expected loss in the homogenous case

Table 4.1 gives a representative set of results.[4] The left panel summarizes the impulse responses for the complete knowledge case (RE dynamics). The diagonals of the middle and right panel show the results for homogeneous knowledge case. The results for heterogeneous knowledge lie off the diagonal, and are discussed in the next subsection.

Adaptive learning contributes to volatility. Looking at the on-diagonal results, we can clearly see that the adaptive learning increases overall economic volatility. In all considered cases, $c_P = c_{CB} = \{0.8, 1, 1.2\}$, the amplitude (max), and the half life (HL) is a positive number, which means that the impulse response of

Table 4.1 Dynamics under rational expectations, and the contrast between adaptive learning and rational expectations

Shocks		c_p	RE dynamics				Absolute difference between adaptive learning and RE										
			$q_\pi = 1.3$		$q_\pi = 2.5$		$q_\pi = 1.3, c_{CB}$						$q_\pi = 2.5, c_{CB}$					
							0.8		1		1.2		0.8		1		1.2	
g_0	u_0		max	HL	max	HL	max	HL	max	HL	max	HL	max	HL	max	HL	max	HL
0	1	0.8	0.98	7	1.29	7	0.42	1,000+	0.44	1,000+	0.44	39	0.29	1,000+	0.27	54	0.26	64
1	0	0.8	0.72	7	0.43	7	0.09	1,000+	0.08	1,000+	0.07	170	0.04	1,000+	0.04	350	0.04	433
1	1	0.8	1.49	7	1.58	7	0.38	1,000+	0.36	1,000+	0.35	22	0.46	1,000+	0.40	29	0.40	32
0	1	1	0.98	7	1.29	7	0.53	883	0.56	463	0.58	19	0.43	253	0.38	23	0.35	28
1	0	1	0.72	7	0.43	7	0.20	83	0.10	1,000+	0.09	9	0.13	1,000+	0.06	58	0.05	158
1	1	1	1.49	7	1.58	7	1.02	8	0.51	1,000+	0.58	11	0.83	1,000+	0.67	13	0.58	16
0	1	1.2	0.98	7	1.29	7	0.79	50	0.73	51	0.76	11	0.69	37	0.60	12	0.52	14
1	0	1.2	0.72	7	0.43	7	0.48	6	0.30	6	0.12	5	0.29	1,000+	0.18	5	0.08	22
1	1	1.2	1.49	7	1.58	7	2.46	4	1.67	5	0.92	6	1.54	22	1.27	6	1.03	7

expected CB's loss is bigger than under the RE dynamics for all t. For example, if a demand shock hits the economy, $u_0 = 1$, $c_P = c_{CB} = 0.8$, and $q_\pi = 1.3$, the expected central bank's loss is higher by 0.42 basis points. The total loss amplitude is then 1.4, the sum of the RE response, 0.98, and the contribution of adaptive learning, 0.42. The HL of the shock exceeds the RE case by more than 1,000 periods (1,000+). If $q_\pi = 2.5$, then the contribution to the response amplitude is 0.29, and the total amplitude is 1.27. The HL is only 39 periods longer than in the RE case, where it takes the economy only seven periods to converge to its steady state.

We can also see that with higher sensitivity to new information, $c_i > 0.8$, the HL shortens. Examining the right panel of Table 4.1 for the demand shock again, we see that the HL drops from 39 periods, through 23, to only 14 periods, as $c_P = c_{CB}$ increases from 0.8 to 1.2. The same results hold for a cost-push shock, and for cost-push and demand shocks occurring jointly, $g_t = u_t = 1$.

What is the effect of monetary policy? The key result for the homogeneous case is that monetary policy can effectively influence both economic variability and the speed of learning (the convergence to the REE). The numbers in Table 4.1 demonstrate that increasing the inflation responsiveness from $q_\pi = 1.3$ to 2.5, the deviation from RE dynamics lowers. The shock response amplitude decreases in all three cases – by more than one-quarter. Also the speed of learning significantly improves. Its relation to the policy reactiveness is highly nonlinear. All these results confirm the findings made by Orphanides and Williams (2003), and Ferrero (2007). "Policy should respond more aggressively to inflation under imperfect knowledge than under perfect knowledge ... in order to anchor inflation expectations and foster macroeconomic stability" (Orphanides and Williams 2003: 26).

The results for the imperfect, homogeneous knowledge case can be summarized in two points:

• overall volatility increases with higher sensitivity to new information, but the increase in volatility is offset by faster learning;
• if the policy reacts aggressively to inflation, the central bank's expected loss decreases; the speed of learning increases.

3.2 CB's expected loss in the heterogeneous case

The results under heterogeneous expectations differ dramatically from the benchmark case. The summary of impulse response characteristics is again in Table 4.1. The representative results for the heterogeneous knowledge case lie off diagonal, in the middle and right panel. Volatility and speed of learning characteristics are represented by the impulse amplitude (max), and its half life (HL). There are two dimensions to the results: the effect of different sensitivity to new information ($\{c_P, c_{CB}\} \in \{0.8, 1, 1.2\}$: $c_P \neq c_{CB}$), and the policy inflation reactiveness ($q_\pi = \{1.3, 2.5\}$). We can read the following story from the Table 4.1:

The effect of expectations heterogeneity

- As the private sector becomes more sensitive to new information, economic variability increases. Fixing c_{CB}, the impulse amplitude of CB's expected loss increases with c_P.
- As the central bank becomes more sensitive to new information, economic variability decreases. Fixing c_P and shifting c_{CB}, amplitude falls.
- As both central bank and private sector become more of sensitive to new information (c_i increases), and at the same time monetary policy is less inflation responsive ($q_\pi = 1.3$), volatility falls.
- As the private sector becomes more sensitive to new information, the speed of convergence increases.
- As the central bank becomes more sensitive to new information, and at the same time the policy is too responsive, the speed of convergence decreases. If policy is not sufficiently responsive, the speed of convergence increases with the central bank's sensitivity.

The effect of monetary policy

- As policy becomes more inflation responsive, economic volatility decreases.
- A relative reduction in volatility depends on the degree of expectations heterogeneity (the ratio of c_P to c_{CB}).
- As policy becomes more inflation responsive, speed of convergence significantly increases.

The full results show that the short run implications for monetary policy are the opposite of those in the long run. In Figure 4.1, I plot the impulse response function of the central bank's expected loss for a different policy reactiveness to inflation. The impulse responses are presented in a static form. They are cut for horizons $t = \{4, 8, 16, 40\}$, and plotted for a different information gain bias, $\{c_P, c_{CB}\}$. Periods four to eight are here to represent the short run. The mid run, and long run is represented by 16, and 40 periods, respectively.

Figure 4.1 reveals that in the short run, monetary policy, which is less responsive to inflation ($q_\pi < 1.5$), delivers the lowest expected loss for almost all combinations of $\{c_P, c_{CB}\}$ – the dashed line lies at the bottom at $t = 8$. On the other hand, this is not a long-lasting phenomenon. There is a rising stabilizing effect of an inflation responsive policy ($q_\pi > 1.5$) in the mid run. At $t = 16$, it depends on the degree of information gain bias, but the dotted line shows that the responsive policy performs the best in the most cases. In the long run, for $t \geq 40$, the inflation responsive policy is a dominant one and is always connected with the lowest expected losses.

Remarkably, optimal (RE) monetary policy does not perform very well under heterogeneous expectations. In Figure 4.1, the continuous line, where $q_\pi(\alpha = 1/3)^* = 1.5$, is not connected with the lowest expected loss. Even though

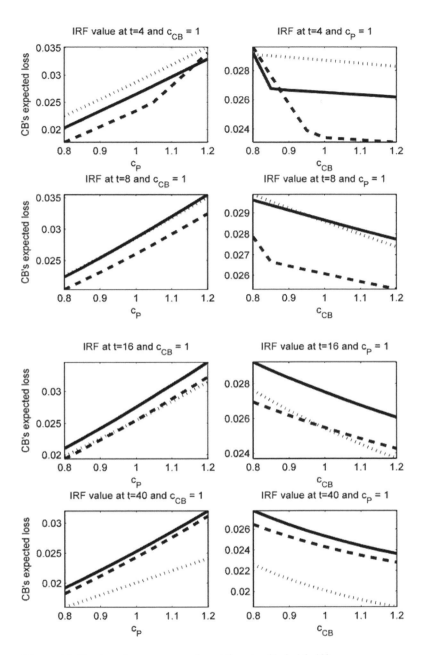

Figure 4.1 The impulse response value at time $t = \{4, 8, 16, 40\}$.

Note

The *dash line* is the response when $q_\pi = 1.3$, *continuous line* when $q_\pi^* = 1.5$, and *dotted line* when $q_\pi = 2.5$. The economy is subject to a unitary cost-push and demand shock ($u_0 = g_0 = 1$), and the impulse response function is evaluated in 3 dimensions: time, and information gain bias c_P and c_{CB}. The graphs above show the impulse response value at time $t = \{4, 8, 16, 40\}$.

it can be the second best option in some cases, it is always dominated by a policy that responds more or less than the optimal RE policy.

I turn now to consider robustness. The robustness of results is checked by changing the relative sizes of the shocks. The basic results remain mostly unchanged. As the variance of the demand shock g_t gets bigger in relative terms, there is a polarization of the policy effect at the short and long horizon. At $t = 16$, an inflation-reactive policy clearly dominates. On the other hand, as the variance of cost-push shock u_t gets bigger, in relative terms – approximately twice bigger – the picture slightly changes. At the short horizon, there is already a region of expectations heterogeneity in which inflation responsive policy is preferred, and over time it dominates.

4 Some intuition behind the results

One of the characteristics of adaptive learning is that, eventually, the boundedly rational equilibrium path converges to the REE (Evans and Honkapohja 2003b). Even though the two groups of agents are assumed not to communicate with one another, they can reach homogeneous and perfect knowledge. Over time, both groups, as a result of their own forecasting errors, end up with the same forecasting model and the same expectations. This is why we observe in Figure 4.1 that an inflation-responsive policy starts to dominate after 16 quarters. It is because expectations become homogeneous, and the economic environment evolves towards the REE. An important difference is that this does not hold early on, and an excessively responsive policy can actually considerably destabilize the economy. This observation leads to the conclusion that when expectations are heterogeneous, monetary policy should not be too active in order to improve stability in the short-term.

As for the numerical simulations, let us assume that the economy is initially in its rational expectations steady state.

A demand shock first hits the output gap, and then affects inflation for a while. Beginning in REE, agents were expecting equilibrium values of inflation and the output gap. In the RE and persistence-less environment, the shock would have just a one period impact. Under adaptive learning it influences expectations for subsequent periods. Being surprised, agents update their forecasting models. The policy rate is set so that it neutralizes the shock. A positive demand shock will cause an upward correction in the PLM's parameters, which will yield higher predictions of inflation and the output gap for the future periods. The policy rate reacts to those values. Because increasing c_{CB} causes higher expected values for inflation and output gap, monetary policy is suddenly more restrictive – policy rate increases. This is why the expected CB's loss declines as c_{CB} increases.

Using the same logic, we can interpret the effect of increasing private sector sensitivity to new information, c_P. A demand shock transmits to the future via expectations. Private agents update their model like the central bank. Their expectations influence the economic dynamics directly. A positive shock motivates model updates, yielding higher inflation and output gap forecasts in the future. Higher output gap expectations imply a higher current output gap, and consequently higher inflation. Higher inflation expectations have a direct effect on inflation, which increases, and an indirect effect on the output gap via a decrease in the real interest rate, which influences the output gap positively.

With a cost-push shock, after the first period, assuming no persistence, inflation would normally return to the REE. But because the private agents and the central bank update their model (bias their expectations upwards), the inflation rate and the output gap increase above the RE values. The mechanism of monetary policy works as in the previous shock case. An inflation averse policy pushes inflation down, and since the policy is now more aggressive than under the RE, the output gap decreases more.

The central bank's sensitivity to new information decreases the inflation rate responsiveness to a cost-push shock, but increases the responsiveness of the output gap. Again, monetary policy becomes more restrictive than under the RE, since the central bank predicts higher inflation due to the model updates. It tightens the interest rate, which closes the output gap, and the inflation rate returns to the RE dynamics. Thus by changing c_{CB}, we can explain why inflation becomes less responsive, and the output gap more so.

The private sector's sensitivity to new information helps the cost shock to trigger to inflation. As private agents become more to innovations sensitive, they anticipate higher inflation than under full knowledge. Actual inflation increases. With increasing c_P, agents update their models more, and produce higher forecasts of inflation. This immediately increases inflation due to higher expected inflation in the future. Agents also update their forecasts of the output gap. They will anticipate the reaction of the central bank, which they assume has the same expectations as themselves, which will lead to a policy rate adjustment. Since c_P will bias a policy reaction upwards, private agents will assume a lower output gap than under the RE. This explains why the output gap becomes more reactive if the private sector is more sensitive to new information. This is especially evident when the central bank responds to inflation too much.

5 Concluding discussion

A major challenge for future research is an analytical solution to the problem addressed in this chapter. Even having a simple model, heterogeneous expectations and adaptive learning lead to an uneasily tractable problem. Model transition functions are highly non-linear, which complicates and limits a comparative static analysis. An analytical evaluation of the speed of learning, as in Ferrero (2007), also seems complex. This chapter makes some headway in obtaining an intuition for analytical results. At present, a numerical analysis is the most viable approach.

The world is simpler if knowledge and beliefs are homogeneous. If knowledge is homogeneous, a central bank's aversion to price inflation helps to decrease inflation variability and speeds up learning. The speed of learning affects the persistence of inflation and its variability. If a central bank wishes to minimize its expected loss, it is desirable that agents learn the economy's actual law of motion as fast as possible. If knowledge and beliefs are heterogeneous, the central bank should not be too anti-inflationary, because if the bank is less inflation responsive, short-run economic stability improves. Thus, in a heterogeneous expectations world, the first goal of the central bank should aim to make expectations homogeneous across the economy, in order to minimize inflation target and output volatility. Once expectations have become homogeneous, the standard policy recommendations apply.

How can a central bank make expectations homogeneous in the short run? The expectations homogeneity is closely related to enhancing policy effectiveness. In this simple model, there are two ways this may work. First, either the central bank learns and adopts private agents' expectations. Or second, private agents get to know and acquire the central bank's expectations – and of course the two processes could be combined, with both sets of expectations converging on each other. In practice, neither is simple. The first will require reliable measures of private sector expectations. Central banks usually have surveys of private sector expectations on future economic developments. But the information that such surveys yield might be unreliable. The data collected may not truly represent market expectations, which drive agents' market behaviour – they could be subject to systematic measurement errors (due to inaccurate or collusive, game-playing responses, perhaps). In fact, the central bank can never be sure if the data being collected are useful for immediate policy decisions. Those considerations suggest it might be better for private agents to borrow central bank expectations, than the reverse. But how can this be done? And can it be relied upon? Central bank communications, through publications, speeches, and press conferences, clearly provide a crucial educative function. But when credibility is absent, the logic of this chapter is that the central bank really must furnish evidence of its commitment and capability to turn its expectations into reality.

Notes

1 Reserve Bank of New Zealand; e-mail: martin.fukac@rbnz.govt.nz. The views expressed in this chapter are those of the author(s) and do not necessarily reflect the views of the Reserve Bank of New Zealand. I would like to thank Michal Kejak, Kristoffer Nimark, Peter Sinclair, Sergey Slobodyan, participants at CERGE-EI seminars, Czech National Bank seminars, CFS Summer School 2005, a Bank of Poland conference on "Inflation expectations and monetary policy", and ESEM 2006, for their helpful comments. I am also indebted to Peter Sinclair for an outstanding editing support. All errors are my own.
2 Evans and Honkapohja (2003a) derive an expectations-based rule where a central bank observes shocks in current period.
3 The Matlab codes to replicate the simulation results may be obtained from the author upon request.
4 A full grid search was performed for all possible combinations of policy parameters ($q_\pi = (1, 5)$ and $\theta_x = 1$, and the information gain parameters $\{c_P, c_{CB}\} = (0.8, 1.2)$. Due to their complexity, I decided to present only a representative set. The full set of results can be obtained up on request.

References

Clarida, R., M. Gertler and J. Galí (2000), Monetary policy rules and macroeconomic stability: evidence and some theory, *Quarterly Journal of Economics*, 110: 127–159.

Evans, G.W. and S. Honkapohja (2003a), Expectations and the stability problem for optimal monetary policies, *Review of Economic Studies*, 70: 807–824.

Evans, G.W. and S. Honkapohja (2003b), Learning and expectations in macroeconomics, Princeton, NJ: Princeton University Press.

Evans, G.W. and S. Honkapohja (2004), Adaptive learning and monetary policy design, *Journal of Money, Credit and Banking*, 35 (supplement): 1045–1072.

Ferrero, G. (2007), Monetary policy, learning, and the speed of convergence, *Journal of Economic Dynamics and Control*, 31: 3006–3041.

Gurkaynak, R., A. Levin, and E. Swanson (2006), Does inflation targeting anchor long-run inflation expectations? Evidence from long-term bond yields in the U.S., U.K., and Sweden, *Federal Reserve Bank of San Francisco Working Paper*, 2006-09.

Gurkaynak, R., A. Levin, A. Marder, and E. Swanson (2007), Inflation targeting and the anchoring of inflation expectations in the western hemisphere, in F. Mishkin and K. Schmidt-Hebbel (eds) *Monetary Policy under Inflation Targeting*, Santiago: Central Bank of Chile, 415–465.

Honkapohja, S. and Mitra K. (2005), Performance of monetary policy with internal central bank forecasting, *Journal of Economic Dynamics and Control*, 29: 627–658.

Mankiw, N.G. and J. Wolfers (2003), Disagreement about inflation expectations, *NBER Macroeconomics Annual*, 18.

Milani, F. (2007), Expectations, learning and macroeconomic persistence, *Journal of Monetary Economics*, 54: 2065–2082.

Mishkin, F. and Schmidt-Hebbel (2006), Does inflation targeting make a difference?, *CNB Working Paper* 13/2006.

Orphanides, A. and J.C. Williams (2003), Imperfect knowledge, inflation expectations, and monetary policy, *NBER Working Paper* 9884.

Townsend, R.M. (1983), Forecasting the forecasts of others, *Journal of Political Economy*, 93: 546–588.

Walsh, C.E. (2003), *Monetary theory and policy*, second edition, Cambridge, MA: MIT Press.

5 Consumer inflation expectations

Usefulness of survey-based measures – a cross-country study

Ryszard Kokoszczyński,[1] *Tomasz Łyziak*[2] *and Ewa Stanisławska*[3]

Introduction

This chapter aims to analyse the role of consumer inflation expectations as a force driving inflation. Instead of assuming that inflation expectations are rational – which is a feature of the New Keynesian Phillips Curve (NKPC) – we refer to direct measures of consumer expectations quantified on the basis of qualitative surveys and use them in estimating the hybrid-type Phillips curve. Our attempts to perform such analysis for all CEE4 countries were not fully successful due to a constrained reliability of quantified measures of expectations in the case of Hungary and Slovakia. Hence, empirical tests verifying the degree of consumer inflation expectations' unbiasedness and their influence on price dynamics are done only for the Czech Republic and Poland.

The chapter is organized in the following way. The first section introduces the workhorse setup dominating inflation dynamics modelling in the last decade, the New Keynesian Phillips Curve. The second section outlines quantification methods used to quantify consumer inflation expectations on the basis of European Commission Consumer Surveys and evaluates their results for the Czech Republic, Hungary, Poland and Slovakia. The third section tests the role of inflation expectations of Czech and Polish consumers in affecting price dynamics and discusses the degree, to which the unbiasedness requirement of the rational expectations hypothesis is met. The last section concludes.

1 Theoretical aspects

In the late 1990s the New Keynesian Phillips Curve has become the standard macroeconomic model of inflation. It was introduced as a micro-founded model with clear theoretical foundations[4] that were to permit straightforward structural interpretation. The usual way of introducing the NKPC is based on the Calvo model of price setting.[5] This assumes that in each period of time a fraction $1 - \alpha$ of firms can reset their prices, while all other producers have to keep their prices unchanged. The (log) price level p_t is thus given by:

$$p_t = (1 - \alpha)p_t' + \alpha p_{t-1}, \tag{1}$$

where p'_t is the optimal price chosen by the producers who can change their prices in t. Producers would set their prices (in an imperfect competition framework) as a fixed markup over marginal cost, and the optimal price is given by:

$$\sum_{k=t}^{\infty} (\alpha\beta)^{k-t} E_t(p'_t - p_k - \lambda(fv)) = 0, \tag{2}$$

where β is a discount factor, and fv is a variable representing inflation pressure from economic activity. This is usually either an output gap or real marginal cost gap.[6] Solving (2) and combining with (1) we obtain the NKPC in the form:

$$\pi_t = \beta E_t \pi_{t+1} + \kappa(fv_t), \tag{3}$$

where $\kappa = \dfrac{(1-\alpha)(1-\alpha\beta)}{\alpha} \lambda > 0.$

Thus, the New Keynesian Phillips Curve links current inflation, π_t, to expected future inflation and the current excess demand indicator. Hence, this model is entirely forward-looking and there is no place for inflation persistence.

When confronted with data this basic formulation of the NKPC failed and the model has evolved into more empirically viable hybrid form with an added lagged inflation term.[7] Initial motivation for this change was mostly empirical (Galí and Gertler 1999). However, in the subsequent literature lagged inflation term found some behavioural explanation. If economic agents form their expectations in a backward-looking manner, past inflation becomes an important factor in explaining their price-setting behaviour. Within this framework a hybrid form of equation (3) given by:

$$\pi_t = \beta E_t \pi_{t+1} + \gamma \pi_{t-1} + \kappa(fv_t) \tag{4}$$

maintains its structural interpretation, with lagged inflation being simply a proxy for $E_{t-1}\pi_t$. An alternative interpretation is based directly on the rational expectations concept. Lagged inflation appears in equation (4) because it is correlated with the rational expectations of inflation in the next period. However, that changes the nature of the model – it is now only a reduced-form relationship.

Further developments include other theoretical explanations of the hybrid model. One of them suggests a different form of price adjustment – some fraction of price-setters reoptimize their prices, while others apply a simple price indexation formula, with indexation tied to the past inflation rate (Christiano *et al.* 2005). A similar explanation is the original proposal formulated by Galí and Gertler (1999), where standard Calvo model applies only to a subset of firms changing prices in the given period, while a remaining group adjusts their prices according to a rule of thumb depending on the lagged inflation.

The Relative Wage Model, introduced by Fuhrer and Moore (1995), results also in a hybrid such as equation (4), with β and γ equal to 0.5, but this model is based not on price-setting behaviour of firms, but on assumptions concerning the real wage contracting mechanism.

The quest for a microfounded theoretical and simple model of inflation dynamics has recently gone far beyond the sticky-price setup. Mankiw and Reis (2002) suggest that – because of costs of acquiring information and/or of price reoptimization – pricing decisions are not always based on current information. Hence current inflation depends on output (as a measure of demand conditions) and past expectations of current inflation and output growth. They call the resulting equation the sticky-information Phillips curve.

This sticky-information approach goes beyond the scope of this chapter, as it includes not only inflation expectations, but also output growth expectations. However, there is one important input here, developed further by Reis (2005) and Sims (2005), suggesting that the process of acquiring and processing information that is an important part of forming inflation expectations by economic agents should be in itself treated as an outcome of rational (optimizing) behaviour. This has serious implications for the traditional understanding of rationality of survey-based inflation expectations and the traditional way of testing for this rationality.[8] They may be summarized here as giving strong support to the idea of using agents' inflation expectations directly when modelling inflation dynamics within the Phillips curve framework (Section 3 describes this in greater detail).

2 Survey measures of inflation expectations

There are two major problems to be solved before applying direct measures of inflation expectations in inflation modelling. The first is the choice of type of agents who are surveyed. Most studies use either surveys of professional forecasters or household (consumer) surveys.[9] Data availability and comparability across countries under consideration meant that we had to limit ourselves to qualitative surveys conducted among households. The second issue is how to quantify qualitative responses in the households' survey. This section presents a detailed description of this process.

2.1 Survey data on consumers' inflation expectations

In our analysis we employ data from the European Commission's monthly Consumer Surveys, conducted in all European Union countries, including the new member states, which joined the EU in May 2004. In the chapter we focus on four Central European economies (CEE4): the Czech Republic, Hungary, Poland and Slovakia. Monthly data for the countries under consideration are available only for a relatively short period, beginning in January 2001 for the Czech Republic, February 1993 for Hungary, May 2001 for Poland and April 2000 for Slovakia. Although the survey data for Hungary start in 1993, we decided to use a shorter sample period 1999–2005. In this way in all CEE4 economies the periods we take into account display one-digit inflation dynamics, which makes our analysis more comparable across countries. In Section 3, we also use a comparable survey carried out by the Ipsos firm for Poland, covering a much longer period (since 1992).

The question concerning inflation expectations in the EC and Ipsos survey is designed in a qualitative way: the respondents do not give precise quantitative responses regarding future inflation, but declare the expected direction and magnitude of change in prices, comparing their predictions to the price movements currently observed. The question is:

> By comparison with the past 12 months, how do you expect that consumer prices will develop in the next 12 months? They will … (1) increase more rapidly, (2) increase at the same rate, (3) increase at a slower rate, (4) stay about the same, (5) fall, (6) don't know.

There is an additional question concerning the perception of current price movements in the EC survey, which can be useful in assessing the perceived rate of inflation. Responding to this question, consumers compare the present level of prices with the price level 12 months ago:

> How do you think that consumer prices have developed over the last 12 months? They have … (1) risen a lot; (2) risen moderately; (3) risen slightly; (4) stayed about the same; (5) fallen; (6) don't know.

In the common sample period, 2001–2005, survey responses on changes in prices perceived and expected by consumers point to some differences across countries analysed (Table 5.1, Table 5.2). In all of them a majority of respondents tend to notice increase in prices in the course of previous 12 months – however, the average fraction of these respondents is smaller in the Czech Republic (59.9 per cent) than Poland (77.3 per cent), Hungary (83.8 per cent) and Slovakia (91.0 per cent). In all economies, more respondents expect prices to increase over the next year than for prices to remain stable or fall. Consumers expecting an increase in the price level account for some 75 per cent in the Czech Republic and Poland, and even more in the two other countries (89.1 per cent in Slovakia and 93.8 per cent in Hungary). The comparison of fractions of respondents choosing the

Table 5.1 Survey data on perceived price changes[1]

Response:	Czech Rep. (%)	Hungary (%)	Poland (%)	Slovakia (%)
(1): "prices have risen a lot"	5.6	16.6	9.8	24.1
(2): "prices have risen moderately"	19.7	33.1	36.4	31.8
(3): "prices have risen slightly"	34.6	34.1	31.1	35.1
(4): "prices have stayed about the same"	28.9	11.6	18.2	6.4
(5): "prices have fallen"	6.5	3.4	1.2	0.7
(6): "I do not know"	4.7	1.3	3.2	1.9

Source: EC Consumer Survey, own calculations.

Note
1 Average fraction of respondents choosing respective responses, common sample: May 2001–July 2005.

Table 5.2 Survey data on expected price changes[1]

Response:	Czech Rep. (%)	Hungary (%)	Poland (%)	Slovakia (%)
(1): "prices will increase more rapidly"	23.2	27.6	15.6	29.1
(2): "prices will increase at the same rate"	43.5	53.0	48.0	47.1
(3): "prices will increase at slower rate"	7.4	13.2	13.1	12.9
(4): "prices will stay about the same"	13.5	1.1	13.9	6.7
(5): "prices will fall"	2.4	0.5	0.7	0.8
(6): "I do not know"	9.9	4.6	8.5	3.3

Source: EC Consumer Survey, own calculations.

Note
1 Average fraction of respondents choosing respective responses, common sample: May 2001–July 2005.

non-decisive response shows that uncertainty in assessing past and future price developments is higher in the Czech Republic (respectively 4.7 per cent, and 9.9 per cent of consumers do not know how prices evolved and how they will change) and Poland (3.2 per cent and 8.5 per cent) than in the remaining economies (1.3 per cent and 4.6 per cent in the case of Hungary, 1.9 per cent and 3.3 per cent in the case of Slovakia).

2.2 *Quantification methods*

The choice of quantification algorithm, with which expected inflation is extracted from the survey data, influences the outcome. Therefore, in order to check the robustness of the results, we use various versions of the two most popular quantification approaches: probability and regression methods.[10]

The original probability method first employed by Theil (1952), and later implementations by Knöbl (1974), Carlson and Parkin (1975) and Taylor (1988), refer to surveys in which respondents are questioned whether prices are expected to "go up", "stay the same" or "go down". The EC Consumer Survey contains more response categories. So the quantification procedure has to be adjusted. The adjusted probability method makes use of the fact that, in replying to the survey question regarding inflation expectations, respondents compare their predictions with the rate of price change as perceived at the time when the survey is carried out. Indeed, two replies – that prices will "rise at the same rate" or "stay at their present level" – are in fact quantitative in nature. The broader scope of information limits the number of assumptions made to only two – on the type of distribution of the expected rate of inflation, and a measure of perceived inflation. The probability approach used in this chapter refers to the canonical Carlson and Parkin (1975) method and assumes that, if the number of respondents is sufficiently large, the expected rate of price change is normally distributed in the population. The quantification outcome is a product of survey responses embodied in the balance statistics Φ consistent with the normal distribution assumption[11] and the perceived rate of inflation, which plays the role of a scaling factor. A frequently used proxy for the perceived rate of price change is the current rate of inflation (Berk 1997; Łyziak 2005), the most recent inflation rate available to respondents when answering the survey question regarding future prices. In this case, quantified measures of inflation expectations are described as "objectified", since they assume that the respondents perceive the current price dynamics correctly. Alternatively, the perceived rate of inflation may be derived on the basis of a survey question pertaining to the recently observed price developments (Berk 2000; Forsells and Kenny 2004). Indicators of inflation expectations quantified with a survey measure of recent price changes' perception are called "subjectified".[12]

The regression method of expectations quantification was introduced in application to business surveys by Pesaran (1984, 1987). He reinterpreted and developed Anderson's (1952) concept. In general, this method is based on estimation of the relationship between current inflation (measured by official statistics) and its perception by firms (survey respondents). The existence of such a relationship is justified by the fact that the inflation rate in the economy might be presented as a weighted average change of prices of goods sold by firms. It is assumed that the same relationship holds between inflation expectations (expressed quantitatively) and qualitative opinions of firms (respondents) about future inflation. As Pesaran (1987) stresses, this relationship should not be treated as causal, but rather as a simple tool to approximate unknown values. Simmons and Weiserbs (1992) interpreted the inflation rate in the economy as an average of inflation rates specific to each consumer which allowed them to employ this method for quantification of consumer surveys on expectations. Construction of the regression method restricts its application to surveys including questions on both expected and past inflation with appropriately long history. Moreover, questions on inflation perception and expectation should be symmetric.[13]

Table 5.3 Estimates of parameters of the regression model[1]

	Czech Republic	*Hungary*	*Poland*	*Slovakia*
α_0	0.023 (0.003)	–	0.006 (0.001)	0.009 (0.003)
α_1	0.823 (0.086)	0.977 (0.019)	0.934 (0.024)	0.956 (0.032)
α_2	−0.151 (0.070)	0.077 (0.015)	0.044 (0.006)	−0.019 (0.001)
β_0	–	0.151 (0.029)	−0.055 (0.028)	–
β_1	–	–	2.216 (0.738)	–
β_2	−2.040 (1.00)	–	–	–
Sample	2001:01–2005:07	1999:02–2005:07	2001:05–2005:05[2]	2000:04–2005:07
adj. R^2	0.83	0.70	0.94	0.51

Source: EC Consumer Survey, International Financial Statistics, own calculations.

Notes
1 NLS estimators; Newey–West standard errors in parentheses.
2 Due to disturbances in the recent survey responses (resulting probably from high oil prices), which caused some estimation problems, the sample was cut in May 2005.

There are several models which can be employed to approximate the relationship between inflation and the survey data.[14] In our chapter we use a version of the dynamic nonlinear regression model suggested by Smith and McAleer (1995). In this model the perceived price changes (both positive and negative) depend on the current and past inflation rates. These assumptions lead to the following specification:

$$\pi_t = \frac{\alpha_0 R_t - \beta_0 F_t + \alpha_2 R_t \pi_{t-12} + \beta_2 F_t \pi_{t-12}}{1 - \alpha_1 R_t - \beta_1 F_t} + \varepsilon_t, \ \alpha_1 R_t - \beta_1 F_t \neq 1 \tag{5}$$

where π_t indicates the yearly inflation rate, R_t and F_t are the proportions of respondents declaring that prices have risen and fallen during last 12 months, and ε_t is an error term.[15] Table 5.3 provides estimates of the parameters of the quantification equation.

2.3 Quantification results

By applying various quantification procedures we obtained three measures of inflation expectations for each country: the objectified and subjectified probability measures as well as the regression one (presented in the Appendix 5.1). As shown in Table 5.4, they exhibit a significant degree of convergence in Poland and Slovakia, while in the case of the Czech Republic and Hungary they are characterized by considerable dispersion. There are two factors in the quantification algorithms applied, which may affect the dispersion of analysed measures of inflation expectations. First is the volatility of the current rate of inflation, which enters all quantification methods, although in different ways. Second is the structure of responses to survey questions concerning inflation perception and expectations.[16] Table 5.4 suggests that differences in relative dispersion of inflation expectations in the economies analysed may be attributed to differences in survey data rather than in inflation volatility.

Due to limitations of the quantification procedures and specific features of survey data, some of the inflation expectations measures we obtained may be less reliable than others. Therefore, before moving to analysis of inflation

Table 5.4 Dispersion of inflation expectations' measures versus inflation volatility

	Czech Rep.	Hungary	Poland	Slovakia
(1) relative dispersion of inflation expectations' measures (in %)	59.6	43.1	28.4	23.0
(2) inflation volatility (standard deviation relative to the mean, in %)	81.1	33.4	64.9	38.8
Relative dispersion of quantified measures of inflation expectations expressed in units of inflation volatility (i.e. (1)/(2))	0.73	1.30	0.44	0.59

Source: EC Consumer Survey, International Financial Statistics, GUS, own calculations.

process, we assess the usefulness of measures of inflation expectations generated from different quantification algorithms according to a set of criteria. Objectified probability measures of inflation expectations are treated as trustworthy if the survey data on inflation perception are highly correlated with official indicators of price dynamics. In the context of our study, this condition is satisfied in Poland and the Czech Republic, but questionable in Hungary and Slovakia. The reliability of subjectified measures of inflation expectations is evaluated on two criteria. The first concerns the loss of information resulting from the aggregation of fractions of respondents declaring that in the previous 12 months they noticed: a sizeable; moderate; and a slight increase in the price level. The second compares balance statistics describing the patterns of responses to the survey question on inflation perception consistent with the normal-distribution-based quantification method with a more intuitive balance statistics calculated as a difference between the fractions of respondents reporting perceptions of an increase or decrease in prices. Significant differences between both balance statistics would suggest that changes in the perceived inflation quantified may not match the scale of changes in patterns of responses to the survey question. Verification of both these conditions shows that subjectified measures of inflation expectations are insufficiently reliable in Slovakia and Hungary, while they are useful in the Czech Republic. In the case of Poland, the results are mixed.

Since the regression method is based on the equation relating current inflation to survey data on inflation perceptions, as in the case of objectified probability measures, the closer the relation between survey fractions and the current price movements measured by official statistics, the better. Among CEE4 countries, respondents in Slovakia (probably due to rapid and considerable changes in regulated prices) and Hungary[17] had the greatest problems assessing current inflation. The second issue affecting the reliability of regression measures of inflation expectations concerns the aggregation of respondents claiming that prices are: much higher; quite a bit higher; and a little higher, into one group. Information on the intensity of price changes is more important than information on the direction of price changes in countries experiencing high inflation rates, like Hungary.

Table 5.5 summarizes the usefulness of inflation expectations measures in economies under consideration. Detailed assessment criteria are given in Appendix 5.2. According to the criteria adopted, the only reliable measures of inflation expectations are those from the Czech Republic and Poland. For Hungary and Slovakia, none of the quantified measures is trustworthy; so we do not use them in testing the relationship between inflation expectations and price dynamics.

3 Inflation expectations in the Phillips curve

3.1 Unbiasedness of inflation expectations

A necessary requirement of the rational expectations hypothesis tested in this section is that expectations constitute an unbiased predictor of future inflation.

Table 5.5 Usefulness of different measures of expectations in economies considered

	Probability measure		Regression measure
	Objectified	*Subjectified*	
Czech Republic	*Useful* Survey data on inflation perception highly correlated with CPI inflation *Limited usefulness*	*Useful* Aggregation of respondents' fractions does not constrain information content of the survey, volatility of perceived inflation intuitive *Limited usefulness*	*Useful* Aggregation of respondents' fractions does not constrain information content of the survey, survey data on inflation perception highly correlated with CPI inflation *Limited usefulness*
Hungary	Survey data on inflation perception relatively less correlated with CPI inflation *Useful*	Aggregation of respondents' fractions leads to considerable loss of information, quantification procedure generates unintuitive volatility in perceived inflation *Useful/limited usefulness*	Aggregation of respondents' fractions leads to considerable loss of information, survey data on inflation perception relatively less correlated with CPI inflation *Useful*
Poland	Survey data on inflation perception highly correlated with CPI inflation *Limited usefulness*	Aggregation of respondents' fractions does not constrain information content of the survey, quantification procedure generates unintuitive volatility in perceived inflation *Limited usefulness*	Aggregation of respondents' fractions does not constrain information content of the survey, survey data on inflation perception highly correlated with CPI inflation *Limited usefulness*
Slovakia	Survey data on inflation perception relatively less correlated with CPI inflation	Aggregation of respondents' fractions leads to considerable loss of information, quantification procedure generates unintuitive volatility in perceived inflation	Aggregation of respondents' fractions leads to considerable loss of information, survey data on inflation perception relatively less correlated with CPI inflation

Source: own assessment, see Appendix 5.2 for details.

The unbiasedness assumption means that economic agents fully exploit all available information and do not commit systematic forecast errors, thus the actual inflation is equal to expected inflation on average, and to expected inflation plus a random forecast error period by period. In line with the hypothesis of unbiasedness, the coefficients α and β in the equation (6) should be equal to zero and one, respectively:[18]

$$\pi^e_{t/t-n} = \alpha + \beta\pi_t + \varepsilon_t, \tag{6}$$

where π_t denotes the actual inflation in period t, $\pi^e_{t/t-n}$ is the expectation of inflation at time t formed at time $t - n$, while ε_t is white-noise error.

The results of unbiasedness tests of consumer inflation expectations in the Czech Republic and Poland (Table 5.6, Table 5.7) show that this assumption is violated. In the period 2001–2004, the relationship between actual inflation ex-post and expected inflation in both economies was insignificant. This may reflect the extremely small number of observations, which imposes constraints on verifying unbiasedness, a long-run phenomenon.[19] The period under consideration was also characterized by different types of shocks. Both economies experienced rapid disinflation, and largely unexpected falls in inflation to their historically lowest levels in 2003. Moreover, starting from mid-2003 the perspective of accession to the European Union (May 2004) made consumers afraid of a rapid price increase. This effect was noted in both countries, although in the Czech Republic it was weaker than in Poland.[20] Peculiarities of the period limit the economic interpretation of the unbiasedness test results. Using alternative survey data on Polish consumers' inflation expectations covering a much longer period (1992–2004), there is a cointegration between both variables, but the unbiasedness hypothesis is still rejected.[21]

As mentioned above, biasedness of inflation expectations may (to some extent) result from the short samples available to verify this long-run phenomenon. Even in the Polish case, with survey data on inflation expectations available from 1992, expectation formation might have been substantially disrupted by high and volatile inflation, which reached one-digit levels only at the end of 1998. So it is

Table 5.6 Unbiasedness test – Czech Republic[1]

	Probability measure		Regression measure
	Objectified	*Subjectified*	
Sample period	2001:01–2004:07	2001:01–2004:07	2001:01–2004:07
α	0.03 (0.01)	0.03 (0.01)	0.04 (0.01)
β	−0.53 (0.43)	−0.43 (0.32)	0.30 (0.24)
F [H$_0$: (α, β) = (0, 1)]	8.07 (0.00)	18.51 (0.00)	26.24 (0.00)

Source: EC Consumer Survey, International Financial Statistics, own calculations.

Note
1 OLS estimators; Newey–West standard errors in parentheses.

Table 5.7 Unbiasedness test – Poland[1]

	Probability measure		Regression measure
	Objectified	Subjectified	
Sample period	2001:05–2004:09 [1992:01–2004:09][2]	2001:05–2004:09	2001:05–2004:09
α	0.04 (0.01) [0.01 (0.01)]	0.04 (0.01)	0.05 (0.01)
β	−0.62 (0.19) [1.32 (0.09)]	−0.45 (0.16)	−0.83 (0.22)
F [H$_0$: $(\alpha, \beta) = (0, 1)$]	74.81 (0.00) [19.83 (0.00)]	47.27 (0.00)	48.20 (0.00)

Source: EC Consumer Survey, Ipsos, GUS, own calculations.

Notes
1 OLS estimators; Newey–West standard errors in parentheses.
2 Tests performed with the use of alternative indicators of inflation expectations quantified on the basis of Ipsos survey data.

important to check whether inflation expectations converge towards rational expectations in the long-run. Estimating the following equation:

$$\pi^e_{t/t-n} = \alpha_1 \pi^e_{t-1/t-n-1} + \alpha_2 \pi_t + \varepsilon_t, \tag{7}$$

a long-run convergence of inflation expectations towards the actual inflation takes place if the coefficients α_1 and α_2 add to one. Moreover, lower α_1 speeds up the convergence process (Figure 5.1).

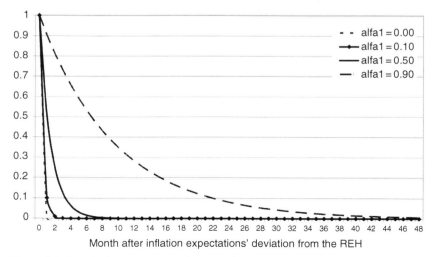

Figure 5.1 Speed of convergence of expectations towards actual inflation (source: own calculations).

Consumer inflation expectations in the Czech Republic and Poland seem to converge to the actual inflation in the long run,[22] although the speed of convergence is very low. According to estimation results presented in Table 5.8 and Table 5.9, the coefficient α_1 amounts to 0.9–0.95 for the measures of inflation expectations considered. It is a bit lower (0.81), when Polish consumer inflation expectations are analysed over the longer time span, 1992–2004.

Table 5.8 Long-run convergence of expectations towards actual inflation – Czech Republic[1]

	Probability measure		Regression measure
	Objectified	*Subjectified*	
Sample period	2001:02–2004:07	2001:02–2004:07	2001:02–2004:07
α_1	0.95 (0.04)	0.93 (0.02)	0.91 (0.04)
α_2	0.05 (0.03)	0.04 (0.03)	0.20 (0.07)
F [H_0: $\alpha_1 + \alpha_2 = 1$]	0.00 (0.95)	0.39 (0.54)	4.10 (0.05*)
Speed of convergence (half life of expectations' deviation from REH)	14 months	10 months	–

Source: EC Consumer Survey, International Financial Statistics, own calculations.

Note
1 OLS estimators; Newey–West standard errors in parentheses.

Table 5.9 Long-run convergence of expectations towards actual inflation – Poland[1]

	Probability measure		Regression measure
	Objectified	*Subjectified*	
Sample period	2001:06–2004:09 *[1992:02–2004:09][2]*	2001:06–2004:09	2001:06–2004:09
α_1	0.93 (0.03) *[0.81 (0.05)]*	0.91 (0.02)	0.90 (0.03)
α_2	0.05 (0.02) *[0.24 (0.07)]*	0.08 (0.03)	0.07 (0.04)
F [H_0: $\alpha_1 + \alpha_2 = 1$]	0.48 (0.49) *[2.56 (0.11)]*	0.01 (0.91)	0.54 (0.47)
Speed of convergence (half life of expectations' deviation from REH)	10 months *[4 months]*	8 months	7 months

Source: EC Consumer Survey, Ipsos, GUS, own calculations.

Notes
1 OLS estimators; Newey–West standard errors in parentheses.
2 Estimated with the use of alternative indicators of inflation expectations quantified on the basis of Ipsos survey data.

3.2 Estimates of the Phillips curve

Should direct measures of inflation expectations quantified on the basis of qualitative surveys play any role in macroeconometric models, or should they constitute a fully independent source of information, clearly separated from others? On
the one hand, the information content of quantified measures of inflation expectations may be limited due to the fact that respondents may not base their actual
decisions on the survey responses (Berk 2000). On the other hand, survey data
may be useful in identifying how inflation expectations are formed, which is
crucial for modelling price behaviour. Estimating the New Keynesian Phillips
curves presumes that inflation expectations are rational. This assumption is questionable theoretically (Section 1), and most empirical researchers examining
survey expectations find they are not perfectly rational.[23] Therefore, the most
general use of survey measures of inflation expectations in macroeconometric
models would aim at replacing the assumption of perfectly rational expectations
with survey indicators. Direct measures of inflation expectations may also be
used to estimate weights on backward- and forward-looking behaviour in the
hybrid-type Phillips curves.

   There are attempts to make use of direct measures of inflation expectations in
macroeconometric modelling. When estimating the Phillips curve, Driver *et al.*
(1999) employ the measure of expected inflation constructed from Gallup and
GfK consumer confidence surveys, while Paloviita (2002) refers to OECD forecasts as empirical proxies of economic agents' inflation expectations. Adam and
Padula (2003) allow for non-rationality of inflation expectations in the forward-
looking New Keynesian Phillips curve for the United States by employing
Survey of Professional Forecasters data. In a similar analysis conducted for
France, Germany and Italy, Gorter (2005) uses direct measures of inflation
expectations constructed from Consensus Economic surveys. Estimating hybrid
Phillips curves, Forsells and Kenny (2004) show that consumer expectations do
affect inflation dynamics in the euro area. Similarly, direct measures of Polish
consumers' inflation expectations are used in the small structural model of monetary transmission mechanism in Poland (Łyziak 2002) and one of the forecasting models of the National Bank of Poland, the NSA model (Kłos *et al.* 2005).

   The hybrid Phillips curve, which we use to show the role of consumer inflation
expectations in the price formation, has the following form:

$$\pi_t = \alpha_0 + \alpha_1 \pi_{t+4/t}^e + \alpha_2 \pi_{t-4} + \alpha_3 x_{t-i} + \alpha_4 e_{t-j}^r + \varepsilon_t, \tag{8}$$

As in the version of the aggregate supply curve used by Forsells and Kenny
(2004) in analysing price dynamics in the euro area, the annual inflation (π) is
driven by its past values, inflation expectations (π^e) and a measure of excess
demand in the economy (x). The real exchange rate (e^r) is added, reflecting the
greater openness of the Czech and Polish economies. Instead of estimating the
Phillips curve via headline inflation, we use core inflation measures, excluding
regulated prices in the case of the Czech Republic and foodstuffs and fuels in the

case of Poland. Excess demand in the economy is measured by the output gap, defined as a percentage deviation of actual output from its HP-filter-value. Since the dynamic homogeneity restriction (that the coefficients α_1 and α_2 add to one) is rejected for almost all specifications estimated for both countries,[24] we present unrestricted estimates only (Table 5.10, Table 5.11). The exception is the Phillips curve estimated with the regression measure of Czech consumers' inflation expectations, for which both unrestricted and restricted estimates are shown.

The estimation results show that direct measures of inflation expectations help to explain price dynamics in both economies – in all equations estimates of the parameter α_1 are positive and differ statistically from zero at 10 per cent significance levels at most. In the case of OLS estimation, they vary from 0.23 to 0.53 for Poland, while for the Czech Republic they are a bit higher and range from 0.51 to 0.62. All other variables enter the estimated equations significantly and their signs are consistent with theoretical requirements. The only exception is a negative sign of the coefficients on the past inflation in the case of the Phillips curves with probability measures of inflation expectations estimated for the Czech Republic.

To address the problem of the low number of observations available for our analysis, we estimated the Phillips curve (8) on pooled data from both countries (Appendix 5.3). The results do not differ much and confirm our conclusions on the significance of direct inflation expectations measures in inflation modelling.

4 Concluding remarks

Probability and regression methods offer a useful way of measuring inflation expectations on the basis of qualitative survey data. However, the reliability of measures of this kind should be assessed rigorously before using them in macroeconomic modelling. Raw survey data may not make economic sense; and distortions may be induced by quantification algorithms. So before making use of different measures of consumers' inflation expectations in the CEE4 countries, we evaluated their trustworthiness by analysing the dispersion of inflation expectation measures, the correlation of survey data on inflation perception with CPI inflation figures, the loss of information resulting from the need to aggregate some fractions of respondents and the consistency between changes in quantified indicators of inflation perceptions and intuition based on simple balance statistics. According to the criteria adopted, the only reliable measures of consumer inflation expectations are those for the Czech Republic and Poland. In the case of Hungary and Slovakia none of the quantified measures is trustworthy; so we do not use them to test the relationship between inflation expectations and price dynamics.

Czech and Polish consumers' inflation expectations seem to converge, in the long run, to the actual inflation. But convergence is very slow. They do not fulfil the unbiasedness requirement of the rational expectations hypothesis: so we relax this assumption when estimating the hybrid-type Phillips curve. Estimation results indicate that direct measures of inflation expectations are useful in explaining price dynamics in both economies.

Table 5.10 Estimates of the hybrid Phillips curve – Poland[1]

	a_1	a_2	a_3	a_4	R^2_{adj}	n
Objectified probability measure (i = 3, j = 1), OLS	0.53 (0.06) [0.28 (0.10)]²	0.38 (0.03) [0.57 (0.07)]	0.15 (0.08) [0.42 (0.17)]	−0.03 (0.01) [−0.04 (0.02)]	0.98 (0.98)	18 (34)
Objectified probability measure (i = 4, j = 1), TSLS	0.56 (0.06) [0.31 (0.13)]²	0.36 (0.02) [0.55 (0.08)]	0.15 (0.09) [0.37 (0.16)]	−0.03 (0.01) [−0.04 (0.02)]	0.97 (0.98)	17 (34)
Subjectified probability measure (i = 3, j = 2), OLS	0.38 (0.10)	0.45 (0.05)	0.38 (0.06)	−0.06 (0.02)	0.98	18
Subjectified probability measure (i = 3, j = 2), TSLS	0.45 (0.10)	0.44 (0.05)	0.35 (0.06)	−0.06 (0.02)	0.97	17
Regression measure (i = 3, j = 2), OLS	0.23 (0.07)	0.44 (0.05)	0.41 (0.07)	−0.07 (0.02)	0.98	18
Regression measure (i = 3, j = 2), TSLS	0.36 (0.13)	0.39 (0.08)	0.34 (0.08)	−0.07 (0.02)	0.96	17

Source: own calculations.

Notes

1 OLS/TSLS estimators; Newey–West standard errors in parentheses. In the case of TSLS the list of instruments comprises explanatory variables with inflation expectations replaced with their lag.

2 The Phillips curve estimated with the use of alternative indicators of inflation expectations quantified on the basis of Ipsos survey data, i = 2, j = 1.

Table 5.11 Estimates of the hybrid Phillips curve – Czech Republic[1]

	α_1	α_2	α_3	α_4	R^2_{adj}	n
Objectified probability measure ($i = 1, j = 1$), OLS	0.54 (0.08)	−0.23 (0.04)	0.30 (0.11)	−0.06 (0.02)	0.93	18
Objectified probability measure ($i = 1, j = 1$), TSLS	0.49 (0.15)	−0.22 (0.04)	0.39 (0.21)	−0.09 (0.04)	0.93	17
Subjectified probability measure ($i = 2, j = 1$), OLS	0.62 (0.27)	−0.49 (0.13)	0.84 (0.19)	−0.04 (0.06)	0.86	18
Subjectified probability measure ($i = 2, j = 1$), TSLS	1.12 (0.38)	−0.58 (0.18)	0.70 (0.11)	0.05 (0.10)	0.89	17
Regression measure ($i = 1, j = 0$):						
• unrestricted estimates, OLS	0.51 (0.10)	0.27 (0.10)	1.15 (0.10)	−0.07 (0.03)	0.88	18
• unrestricted estimates, TSLS	0.90 (0.13)	0.50 (0.11)	1.03 (0.19)	−0.01 (0.00)	0.80	17
• restricted estimates, OLS	0.63 (0.03)	0.37	1.13 (0.09)	−0.05 (0.02)	0.88	18

Source: own calculations on the basis of IFS data.

Note

1 OLS/TSLS estimators; Newey–West standard errors in parentheses. In the case of TSLS the list of instruments comprises explanatory variables with inflation expectations replaced with their lag.

Appendix 5.1

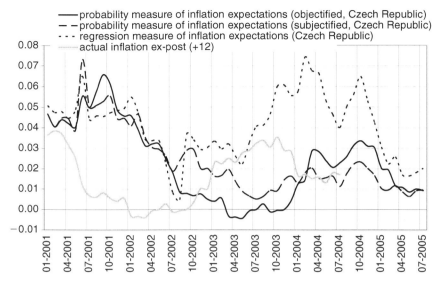

Figure 5.2 Measures of consumer inflation expectations in the Czech Republic (source: EC Consumer Survey, International Financial Statistics, own calculations).

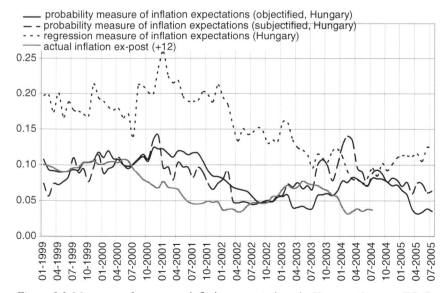

Figure 5.3 Measures of consumer inflation expectations in Hungary (source: EC Consumer Survey, International Financial Statistics, own calculations).

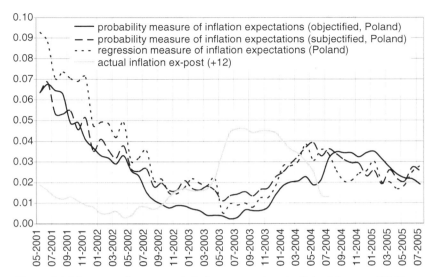

Figure 5.4 Measures of consumer inflation expectations in Poland (source: EC Consumer Survey, International Financial Statistics, own calculations).

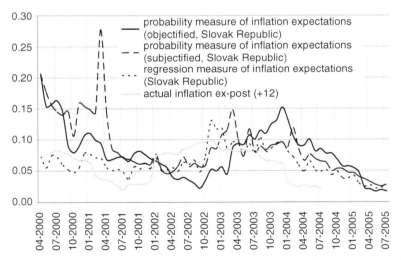

Figure 5.5 Measures of consumer inflation expectations in Slovakia (source: EC Consumer Survey, International Financial Statistics, own calculations).

Appendix 5.2

Table 5.12 Overall degree of uncertainty

	Czech Republic	Hungary	Poland	Slovakia
Relative dispersion of quantified measures of inflation expectations expressed in units of inflation volatility (see: Table 5.4)	0.73	1.30	0.44	0.59
Correlation:				
objectified probability measure and subjectified probability measure	0.85	0.59	0.90	0.66
objectified probability measure and regression measure	0.39	0.71	0.88	0.42
subjectified probability measure and regression measure	0.31	0.19	0.95	0.43

Source: own calculations.

Table 5.13 Usefulness of objectified probability measures of inflation expectations

	Czech Republic	Hungary	Poland	Slovakia
Correlation:				
CP balance statistics[1] and CPI inflation	0.80	0.68	0.86	0.54
AC balance statistics[2] and CPI inflation	0.75	0.09	0.83	0.68

Source: own calculations.

Notes
1 CP balance statistics show the impact of patterns of responses to the survey question on inflation perception on the quantification outcome in the standard Carlson and Parkin (1975) quantification method (normal distribution of the perceived rate of inflation).
2 AC balance statistics are defined as the difference between fractions of respondents claiming that there was an increase and decrease in the price level.

Table 5.14 Usefulness of subjectified probability measures of inflation expectations

	Czech Republic	Hungary	Poland	Slovakia
Correlation (CP[1] and AC balance statistics[2])	0.96	−0.04	0.91	0.66
Relative volatility of CP balance statistics expressed in units of relative volatility of AC balance statistics	0.41	5.00	1.29	6.08
The loss of information resulting from the aggregation of respondents declaring that they noticed a sizeable, moderate and slight increase in the price level[3]	1.21	3.12	1.57	2.47

Source: own calculations.

Notes
1 CP balance statistics show the impact of patterns of responses to the survey question on inflation perception on the quantification outcome in the standard Carlson and Parkin (1975) quantification method (normal distribution of the perceived rate of inflation).
2 AC balance statistics are defined as the difference between fractions of respondents claiming that there was an increase and decrease in the price level; it is the simplest and the most intuitive quantitative description of patterns of responses to the survey question.
3 Relative volatility of the balance statistics considering all 5 fractions of respondents (weights: 3 for respondents noticing a sizeable increase in prices, 2 – a moderate increase, 1 – a slight increase, 0 – for respondents declaring no change in the price level, −1 – for those perceiving a fall in the price level) expressed in units of relative volatility of the AC balance statistics.

Table 5.15 Usefulness of regression measures of inflation expectations

	Czech Republic	Hungary	Poland	Slovakia
Correlation:				
Current inflation and fraction of respondents declaring perceived rise in prices	0.80	0.54	0.82	0.66
Current inflation and fraction of respondents declaring perceived fall in prices	−0.67	0.29	−0.49	−0.46
The loss of information resulting from the aggregation of fractions of respondents declaring that they noticed a sizeable, moderate and slight increase in the price level[1]	1.21	3.12	1.57	2.47
The loss of information resulting from the aggregation of fractions of respondents declaring that they expect that prices will rise at a faster rate, the same rate and a slower rate[2]	1.34	6.57	1.56	2.40

Source: own calculations.

Notes
1 Relative volatility of the balance statistics considering all 5 fractions of respondents (weights: 3 for respondents noticing a sizeable increase in prices, 2 – a moderate increase, 1 – a slight increase, 0 – for respondents declaring no change in the price level, −1 – for those perceiving a fall in the price level) expressed in units of relative volatility of the AC balance statistics.
2 Relative volatility of the balance statistics considering all 5 fractions of respondents (weights: 3 for respondents expecting that prices will rise at faster rate, 2 – at the same rate, 1 – at slower rate, 0 – for respondents expecting no change in the price level, −1 – for those predicting a fall in the price level) expressed in units of relative volatility of the AC balance statistics.

Appendix 5. 3

We estimated the Phillips curve, as specified in equation (8), on pooled data for Poland and the Czech Republic, using both pooled and fixed effect estimators.[25] As group specific effects turned out insignificant in models with probability measures of inflation expectations, these results are not presented (Table 5.16). Estimates of all parameters – except the output gap coefficient in the specification with the probability measure of inflation expectations – have correct signs and are highly significant. The dynamic homogeneity restriction, as in the Phillips curves estimated for both countries separately, is mostly unfulfilled.

Notes

1 National Bank of Poland, Economic Institute, Ryszard.Kokoszczynski@nbp.pl, and Department of Economics, University of Warsaw, rkokoszczynski@wne.uw.edu.pl.
2 National Bank of Poland, Economic Institute; Tomasz.Lyziak@nbp.pl.
3 National Bank of Poland, Economic Institute; Ewa.Stanislawska@nbp.pl. Opinions expressed in this chapter are those of the authors and do not necessarily represent the views of the institutions they work for. The authors wish to thank Martin Fukač, Christina Gerberding, Maritta Paloviita and Peter Sinclair for their insightful remarks and the participants in the workshop "The role of inflation expectations in modelling and monetary policy making" at the National Bank of Poland (9 – 10 February 2006, Warsaw), the "Chief Economists Workshop" at the Bank of England (8 – 10 May 2006, London), 28th CIRET Conference "Cyclical Indicators and Economic Policy Decisions" (20–23 September 2006, Rome) and the "Conference on Price Measurement for Monetary Policy" (24–25 May, 2007, Federal Reserve Bank of Dallas, US) for their comments and discussions. All remaining errors are those of the authors.
4 See Woodford (2003), ch. 3, or Paloviita (2005), Annex 2, for a detailed derivation.
5 Roberts (1995) shows that both Taylor model of staggered price setting and Rotemberg model of quadratic price adjustment costs may have the same closed-form solutions, relating current inflation to future inflation and the current state of (excess) demand.
6 Gap means a deviation of the variable from its value for a frictionless state of the economy. There is a number of approaches used in empirical models for representing both output gap and real marginal cost, though it seems that there is still no consensus on the best way of doing that (cf. Rudd and Whelan 2005; Neiss and Nelson 2005).
7 This failure also triggered a lengthy discussion about issues beyond the model specification – such as estimation methods, and the exact nature of regressors representing the current state of demand. Those issues, beyond the scope of this chapter, are nicely summarized in Rudd and Whelan (2005) and a special 2005 issue of the *Journal of Monetary Economics* on the econometrics of the New Keynesian price equation.
8 See also Andolfatto *et al.* (2005) and Branch (2004).
9 See Roberts (1995) and other papers quoted in Section 3.2 of this chapter.
10 The detailed description of the versions of probability and regression method used in this chapter can be found in Łyziak (2005) and Łyziak and Stanisławska (2006).
11 Balance statistics Φ is calculated in the following way:

$$\Phi = \frac{F^{-1}(1-a-b-c) + F^{-1}(e)}{F^{-1}(1-a-b-c) + F^{-1}(e) - F^{-1}(1-a) - F^{-1}(1-a-b)},$$

where F^{-1} denotes the inverse of the cumulative standardized normal distribution function and a, b, c are fractions of respondents declaring that prices will, respectively,

Table 5.16 Estimates of the hybrid Phillips curve – pooled Poland and Czech Republic data[1]

	α_1	α_2	α_3	α_4	R^2_{adj}	$H_0: \alpha_1 + \alpha_2 = 1$
Objectified probability measure ($i = 2, j = 1$)	0.77 (0.10)	0.24 (0.10)	−0.17 (0.17)	−0.001 (0.000)	0.92	0.28[3]
Subjectified probability measure ($i = 2, j = 1$)	0.56 (0.10)	0.34 (0.10)	0.30 (0.09)	−0.001 (0.000)	0.89	0.00[3]
Regression measure($i = 2, j = 1$)	0.42 (0.09)	0.31 (0.05)	0.38 (0.01)	−0.002 (0.000)	0.91	0.00[3]
Regression measure[2] ($i = 3, j = 1$)	0.44 (0.09)	0.31 (0.04)	0.40 (0.01)	−0.057 (0.019)	0.90	0.00[3]

Source: own calculations on the basis of IFS data.

Notes
1 GLS estimators with cross-section weights; White period standard errors in parentheses; sample: 2001Q1–2005Q3; unbalanced panel; n = 36;
2 Fixed effects model (constant);
3 P-value for Wald coefficient restriction test.

rise faster, at the same rate and more slowly, while *e* is a percentage of respondents expecting prices to go down.

12 The probability method of quantifying perceived inflation used in this chapter is consistent with the approach followed by Forsells and Kenny (2004) while deriving numerical measures of the perceived inflation in the euro area.

13 Therefore we aggregate some categories of responses in the EC survey in such a way as to obtain information only about direction of price movements.

14 As pointed out by Smith and McAleer (1995), in the probability method the quantified measures are a function of a specific probability distribution, whereas in the regression method a function of a specific regression model.

15 We use 12-month lagged inflation rate in order to avoid overlapping periods.

16 Both these factors are closely related to each other. In particular, the reaction of quantification outcomes to changes in the current rate of inflation depends on the patterns of responses to survey questions.

17 In the case of Hungary, the share of respondents declaring a fall in prices in the perception question is positively correlated with the current rate of inflation.

18 See: H. Bakhshi and A. Yates (1998), p. 9.

19 Cf. Andolfatto *et al.* (2005), pp. 5 and 6.

20 As shown in Łyziak (2005), there were significant shifts in the patterns of responses to the survey question on inflation expectations in a majority of the acceding countries before the EU enlargement. It seems that the perspective of EU accession was the major cause of those shifts with some country-specific factors (changes in indirect taxes, price deregulations, increase of the current domestic inflation) and external factors (the increase of the oil price in international markets) playing a minor role. A substantial increase of inflation expectations relative to the current rate of inflation was recorded in the majority of EU acceding countries with Cyprus and Slovenia the only exceptions.

21 Also another aspect of the rational expectations hypothesis, macroeconomic efficiency, is rejected in the case of Polish consumer inflation expectations (Łyziak 2005).

22 The only exception is the regression measure of inflation expectations of Czech consumers.

23 For instance, Bakhshi and Yates (1998), analysing inflation expectations of UK employees, conclude that respondents are making systematic errors in forecasting inflation; they appear – like consumers in Poland – to be over-predicting. Pesaran (1987) demonstrates that neither do inflation expectations of UK manufacturing sector's firms support rational expectations hypothesis. Svendsen (1996) finds that Norwegian firms' price expectations (or plans) are not rational. Roberts (1997) estimates the degree of nonrationality in two US survey-based measures of inflation expectations (the "Livingston" survey of economists' inflation forecasts and the University of Michigan survey for households). He concludes that they reveal an intermediate degree of rationality, being neither perfectly rational nor as unsophisticated as simple autoregressive models would suggest. Forsells and Kenny (2004) show that consumer inflation expectations in the euro area satisfy an intermediate form of rationality: they provide an unbiased predictor of inflation one year ahead, but they are not fully rational with respect to all available information.

24 F statistics for H_0: $\alpha_1 + \alpha_2 = 1$: 6.93 (75.0) for the Phillips curve estimated with OLS, in which the objectified probability measure of inflation expectations of Polish (Czech) consumers is used, 8.59 (16.39) for the specification with subjectified probability measure and 159.77 (1.41) for the specification with the regression measure. In the price equation using alternative indicators of Polish consumers' inflation expectations quantified on Ipsos survey data, the F statistic equals 20.21.

25 Due to a low number of cross-section units relative to the number of coefficients to be estimated, we were not able to estimate a random effects model, which from a theoretical point of view would be the most appropriate.

References

Adam, Klaus and Mario Padula (2003), Inflation dynamics and subjective expectations in the United States, *ECB Working Paper*, 222, European Central Bank.

Anderson, Oskar, Jr. (1952), The business test of the IFO-Institute for economic research, Munich, and its theoretical model, *Revue de l'Institut International de Statistique*, 20: 1–17.

Andolfatto, David, Scott Hendry and Kevin Moran (2005), Are inflation expectations rational?, *Macroeconomics*, 0501002, EconWPA.

Bakhshi, Hasan and Anthony Yates (1998), Are UK inflation expectations rational? *Bank of England Working Paper* series, 81.

Berk, Jan M. (1997), Measuring inflation expectations: a survey data approach. *DNB-Staff Reports*, De Nederlandsche Bank.

Berk, Jan M. (2000), Consumer inflation expectations and monetary policy in Europe, *DNB-Staff Reports*, De Nederlandsche Bank.

Branch, William A. (2004), The theory of rationally heterogenous expectations: evidence from survey data on inflation expectations, *Economic Journal*, 114: 592–621.

Carlson, John A. and Parkin, Michael (1975), Inflation expectations, *Economica*, 42: 123–138.

Christiano, Lawrence, Martin Eichenbaum and Charles Evans (2005), Nominal rigidities and the dynamic effects of a shock to monetary policy, *Journal of Political Economy*, 113: 1–45.

Driver, Rebecca L., Paul G. Fisher, Lavan Mahadeva and John D. Whitley (1999), Inflation and the output gap, typescript, Bank of England.

Forsells, Magnus and Geoff Kenny (2004), Survey expectations, rationality and the dynamics of euro area inflation, *Journal of Business Cycle Measurement and Analysis*, 1: 13–42.

Fuhrer, Jeffrey and George Moore (1995), Inflation persistence, *Quarterly Journal of Economics*, 110: 127–159.

Galí, Jordi and Mark Gertler (1999), Inflation dynamics: a structural econometric analysis, *Journal of Monetary Economics*, 44: 195–222.

Gorter, Janko (2005), Subjective expectations and New Keynesian Phillips curves in Europe, *DNB Working Paper* 049/2005, De Nederlandsche Bank.

Kłos, Bohdan, Ryszard Kokoszczyński, Tomasz Łyziak, Jan Przystupa and Ewa Wróbel (2005), Structural econometric models in forecasting inflation at the National Bank of Poland, *NBP Paper*, 31, National Bank of Poland.

Knöbl, Adalbert (1974), Price expectations and actual price behavior in Germany, *International Monetary Fund Staff Papers*, 21: 83–100.

Łyziak, Tomasz (2002), Monetary transmission mechanism in Poland: the strength and delays, *NBP Paper,* 26, National Bank of Poland.

Łyziak, Tomasz (2005), Inflation targeting and consumer inflation expectations in Poland: a success story? *Journal of Business Cycle Measurement and Analysis*, 2 (2): 185–212.

Łyziak, Tomasz and Ewa Stanisławska (2006), Consumer inflation expectations: survey questions and quantification methods – the case of Poland, *NBP Papers*, 37, National Bank of Poland.

Mankiw, N. Gregory and Ricardo Reis (2002), Sticky information versus sticky prices: a proposal to replace the New Keynesian Phillips Curve, *Quarterly Journal of Economics*, 117: 1295–1328.

Neiss, Katharine S. and Edward Nelson (2005), Inflation dynamics, marginal cost, and the output gap: evidence from three countries, *Journal of Money, Credit, and Banking*, 37 (6): 1019–1045.

Noble, Nicholas R. and T. Windsor Fields (1982), Testing the rationality of inflation expectations derived from survey data: a structure-based approach, *Southern Economic Journal*, 49: 361–373.

Paloviita, Maritta (2002), Inflation dynamics in the euro area and the role of expectations, *Discussion Paper* 20/2002, Bank of Finland.

Paloviita, Maritta (2005), The role of expectations in euro area inflation dynamics, *Bank of Finland Studies E:32.*

Pesaran, Hashem M. (1984), Expectations formations and macroeconometric modelling, in Pierre Malgrange and Pierre-Alain Muet (eds), *Contemporary Macroeconomic Modelling*, Oxford: Basil Blackwell.

Pesaran, Hashem M. (1987), *The Limits To Rational Expectations*. Oxford: Basil Blackwell

Reis, Ricardo (2005), Inattentive producers, *NBER Working Paper*, 11820.

Roberts, John M. (1995), New Keynesian Economics and the Phillips Curve, *Journal of Money, Credit, and Banking*, 27 (4): 975–984.

Roberts, John M. (1998), Inflation expectations and the transmission of monetary policy, *Finance and Economics Discussion Series*, 1998-43, Federal Reserve Board.

Rudd, Jeremy and Karl Whelan (2005), Modelling inflation dynamics: a critical review of recent research, *Finance and Economics Discussion Series*, 2005-66, Federal Reserve Board.

Simmons, Peter and Daniel Weiserbs (1992), Consumer price perceptions and expectations, *Oxford Economic Papers*, 44: 35–50.

Sims, Christopher A. (2005), Rational inattention: a research agenda, *Discussion Paper*, 34/2005, Deutsche Bundesbank.

Smith, Jeremy and Michael McAleer (1995), Alternative procedures for converting qualitative response data to quantitative expectations: an application to Australian manufacturing, *Journal of Applied Econometrics*, 10: 165–185.

Svendsen Ingvild (1996), Empirical evidence on expectations, *Økonomiske Doktoravhandlinger 28*, Universitetet I Oslo.

Taylor, Mark P. (1988), What do investment managers know?: an empirical study of practitioners' predictions, *Economica*, 55: 185–202.

Theil, Henri (1952), On the time shape of economic microvariables and the Munich business test, *Revue de l'Institut International de Statistique*, 20: 105–120.

Woodford, Michael (2003), *Interest and Prices. Foundations of a Theory of Monetary Policy*, Princeton, NJ: Princeton University Press.

6 Further evidence on the properties of consumers' inflation expectations in the euro area

Magnus Forsells and Geoff Kenny[1]

1 Introduction

Recent empirical evidence has emphasized the importance of inflation expectations in the inflationary process.[2] This chapter uses the European Commission's qualitative survey data to analyse and assess the empirical properties of consumers' inflation expectations in the euro area and explore their role in explaining the observed dynamics of inflation. The chapter builds on and updates previous research (Forsells and Kenny 2004), to take account of new empirical evidence since the start of stage three of EMU. This previous research only covered the period up to the end of 2001 and, in particular, did not cover the period since the introduction of euro notes and coins in January 2002. This chapter also enhances the understanding of the properties and role of consumers' inflation expectations as a determinant of inflation by taking a cross country perspective of euro area patterns. The analysis is based on a quantification of the qualitative replies provided by the European Commission's regular monthly survey conducted throughout the EU.

Our analysis tends to confirm previous findings on the important information content of surveyed consumer expectations. Yet it suggests that consumers' expectations are unlikely to satisfy the very strong restrictions implied by the Rational Expectations Hypothesis (REH). The predictive performance of the surveyed expectations at the area-wide level seems to reflect counterbalancing errors at the country level, a finding which cautions against drawing strong conclusions about rationality on the basis of area-wide indicators alone. Last, estimates of a hybrid Phillips curve – which nests both backward and forward-looking inflation dynamics – suggests that consumer expectations play an important role in determining the actual dynamics of inflation over the period 1985–2004. This finding is also robust across the five largest euro area countries.

The layout of the remainder of the chapter is as follows. Section 2 considers the predictive performance of a quantitative indicator of consumers' inflation expectations in the euro area and the five largest euro area countries. Section 3 presents more formal tests for bias in expectations, while Section 4 considers the dynamic properties and the adjustment of expectations relative to actual inflation. Section 5 reports the evidence on the macroeconomic efficiency of inflation expectations, while Section 6 presents evidence on the role of surveyed expectations as a determinant of actual inflation. Section 7 concludes.

2 The predictive performance of consumers' inflation expectations

This section considers the predictive performance of a quantitative indicator of consumers' inflation expectations in the euro area, and across the euro area countries. We present a number of forecast performance summary statistics. The available survey data on consumers' inflation expectations in the euro area provide only qualitative information on the likely direction of change in consumers' inflation expectations. As a result, an assessment of the predictive performance of consumers must be based on quantitative estimates derived from such qualitative surveys. In what follows, the quantification procedure suggested by Berk (1999) is applied to derive estimates of inflation expectations for the euro area and the five largest constituent countries.[3]

Figure 6.1 plots the derived measure of inflation expectations in the euro area together with the actual year-on-year rate of increase in the Harmonised Index of Consumer Prices (HICP) over the period January 1986 to September 2005.[4] Figure 6.1 also reports the estimates of perceived inflation upon which consumers are assumed to condition their expectations. According to these estimates consumers have consistently overestimated the actual inflation rate since the mid-1990s, with a further widening of the gap between perceived and actual inflation following the introduction of euro notes and coins in January 2002. This jump in measures of perceived inflation is also a relatively common feature across the five euro area countries considered, although in some countries the divergence with actual inflation has proved more transitory than in others.[5]

Despite these consistent misperceptions about past inflation, the evidence in Figure 6.1 suggests a strong relationship between actual and expected inflation. In particular, although there is some evidence to suggest that consumers underpredicted inflation towards the end of the 1980s, they appear to have broadly anticipated the trend decline in inflation over the course of the 1990s. Indeed, over the period from the beginning of the 1990s to the start of Economic and Monetary Union in January 1999, the euro area evidence supports a significant degree of forward-looking information in the derived expectations series. In particular, at the area-wide level, consumers appear to have performed much better than if they had attached a very high weight to past inflationary trends when forming their expectations.

To provide a more quantitative evaluation of the expectations series, Table 6.1a and Table 6.1b present two standard forecast performance statistics: the Mean error and the Root Mean Squared Error (RMSE). For comparison, the performance measures have also been calculated for two alternative measures of expectations:

a   a naïve expectation which simply extrapolates the current year-on-year rate as the expectation for the next 12 months ($\pi_t^e = \pi_{t-12}$) and

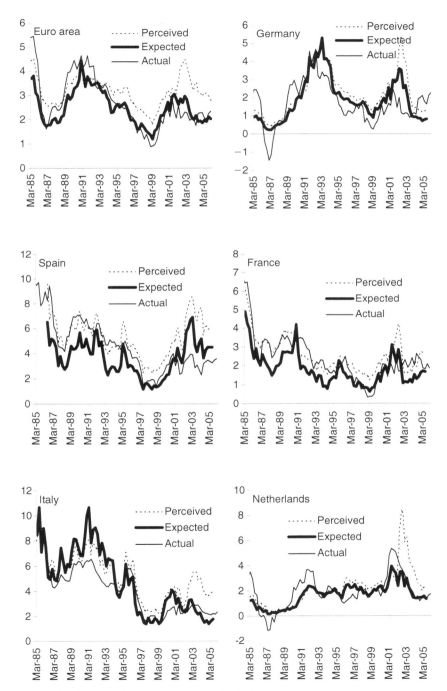

Figure 6.1 Perceived, actual and expected inflation.

b   a forecast based on an AutoRegressive (AR) equation

$$\left(\pi_t^e = \alpha + \sum_{i=12}^{23} \beta_i \pi_{t-i}\right).$$

The performance statistics are then calculated for the whole sample (January 1986–October 2005) as well as three sub-samples: 1985 – 1989, 1990 – 1999 and 2000–2005. This breakdown of the sample is somewhat arbitrary. Nonetheless, given the observed decline in inflation during the 1990s as well as subsequent changes in the monetary policy regime, not least associated with the introduction of the single currency in January 1999, it is interesting to examine the stability over time in the behaviour and forecasting performance of consumers' inflation expectations.

At the area-wide level, the performance statistics in Table 6.1a and Table 6.1b indicate quite strongly the change in the performance of the derived expectation series in the 1990s and the 2000s compared with the late 1980s. The tables suggest that most of the bias in expectations relates largely to the late 1980s, with the mean error falling from 0.34 in the 1980s (indicating a substantial underprediction of inflation on average) to only around −0.1 in the 1990s and the 2000s (indicating a significantly smaller over prediction on average). Similarly, there is also an improvement in terms of the root mean squared error (RMSE), which falls from 1.20 to 0.63 between the 1980s and the 2000s. A striking feature of the surveyed expectations for the euro area is their relative precision as a predictor of one-year-ahead inflation compared with the two other benchmarks. Over the whole sample period both the mean error and the RMSE are

Table 6.1a Mean error: alternative measures of expected inflation

	Euro area	Germany	France	Italy	Spain	Netherlands
Mean error (full sample)						
Expectations	−0.01	−0.27	0.33	−0.97	0.49	0.20
Naive	−0.14	−0.01	−0.19	−0.35	−0.28	−0.05
AR	−0.24	0.37	−0.44	−0.74	−0.36	−0.76
Mean error (1980s)						
Expectations	0.34	0.14	0.41	−1.20	1.61	−0.40
Naive	−0.27	0.11	−0.59	−0.78	−0.51	−0.43
AR	–	–	–	–	–	–
Mean error (1990s)						
Expectations	−0.09	−0.40	0.24	−1.33	0.87	0.32
Naive	−0.27	−0.20	−0.29	−0.44	−0.46	0.13
AR	−0.28	0.58	−0.79	−0.93	−0.63	0.80
Mean error (2000s)						
Expectations	−0.11	−0.34	0.43	−0.18	−0.65	0.38
Naive	0.18	0.22	0.24	0.09	0.19	−0.10
AR	−0.17	0.03	0.16	−0.42	0.10	0.70

Table 6.1b Root mean squared error: alternative measures of expected inflation

	Euro area	*Germany*	*France*	*Italy*	*Spain*	*Netherlands*
RMSE (full sample)						
Expectations	0.81	1.36	0.95	1.98	1.85	1.21
Naive	0.89	1.16	1.04	1.31	1.35	1.31
AR	0.85	1.36	0.91	1.37	1.37	1.37
RMSE (1980s)						
Expectations	1.20	1.42	1.32	2.17	2.59	0.92
Naive	1.61	1.94	1.84	2.11	2.34	1.54
AR	–	–	–	–	–	–
RMSE (1990s)						
Expectations	0.71	1.36	0.72	2.34	1.49	1.13
Naive	0.56	0.88	0.70	1.20	0.92	1.02
AR	1.02	1.65	1.10	1.65	1.60	1.33
RMSE (2000s)						
Expectations	0.63	1.32	0.94	0.88	2.02	1.49
Naive	0.59	0.80	0.74	0.60	1.00	1.56
AR	0.43	0.64	0.45	0.68	0.85	1.42

lower for the expectation series than for the two benchmarks. In terms of overall accuracy, however, this outperformance of the area-wide indicator is not maintained in the most recent sub-period (2000s).

The performance is generally worse at the country level than for the euro area aggregate. Regarding the mean error, it turns out that a naïve method produces a better forecast for all five countries compared with the estimated survey indicators (when considering the whole sample period). The RMSE analysis broadly suggests a similar conclusion with the exception of the Netherlands where the expectation series turns out to be most accurate in predicting future inflation. Indeed, the out-of sample errors at the country level are generally considerably larger than for the area as a whole. This finding suggests that parts of the accuracy of the expectation series at the area-wide level is due to counterbalancing behaviours at the country level. It also suggests a need for caution about inferences about rationality of expectations based on the area-wide indicator alone.

3 Testing for bias in inflation expectations

When considering the full sample, the summary statistics reported in Table 6.1a and Table 6.1b suggest relatively little evidence of bias in the area wide indicator of expectations but more considerable and potentially significant evidence of bias at the country level. So we should consider a more formal test of bias by applying, for example, the equation:

$$\pi_t = \alpha + \beta \pi_t^e + u_t, \tag{1}$$

where π_t is the observed inflation rate in month t and π_t^e represents expectations for inflation in month t and formed in month $t - 12$. If the joint null hypothesis H_0: $(\alpha, \beta) = (0, 1)$ cannot be rejected, the expectations are unbiased in a statistical sense. In line with the previous evidence of an improved performance of the euro area expectations indicator in the 1990s and the 2000s compared with the 1980s, the hypothesis of unbiased inflation expectations is conducted for the full sample period and the three sub-samples defined earlier. The results are presented in Table 6.2 in the form of p-values. Over the whole sample, the results suggest that consumers' inflation expectations have been a somewhat biased predictor of inflation 12 months ahead. This conclusion is relatively robust across countries and different time periods. However, in line with the results in Table 6.1a and Table 6.1b, at the area wide level we are unable to reject the hypothesis of unbiased expectations in the 1990s sub period.

A closer look at the country dimension reveals no major differences in terms of bias compared with the results for the euro area when considering the full sample and the three sub-samples. However, when looking at the 1990s subsample it turns out that the expectation series are biased for all countries despite being unbiased at the area-wide level. This behaviour is consistent with the idea that part of the accuracy of the expectation series at the area-wide level is due to counterbalancing errors at the country level. Again, it highlights the perils of drawing inferences about the rationality of euro area consumers' inflation expectations based on area-wide indicators alone.

4 Dynamic properties: the adjustment of consumers' expectations

Tests of bias shed no light on the dynamics of the expectations' formation process over time. As to how much consumers revise their expectations to reflect the flow of new information, including knowledge of the errors in their own previous forecasts assuming they know them at the point when they form their expectations, those past errors should not be correlated with future errors. To analyse this, Figure 6.2 reports the autocorrelation function for these errors. While they decay gradually over time, there does appear to be some positive autocorrelation for lags greater than 12.[6] Interestingly, the correlation fades away somewhat faster for the five countries than for the euro area as a whole.

Table 6.2 Test for unbiasedness, sub-periods, $(\pi_t = \alpha + \beta\pi_t^e + u_t)$ (*p-values*)

	1980s	*1990s*	*2000s*	*1985–2005*
Euro area	0.00	0.26	0.00	0.02
Germany	0.06	0.00	0.00	0.00
France	0.00	0.05	0.00	0.00
Italy	0.00	0.00	0.00	0.00
Spain	0.00	0.00	0.00	0.00
Netherlands	0.00	0.00	0.05	0.11

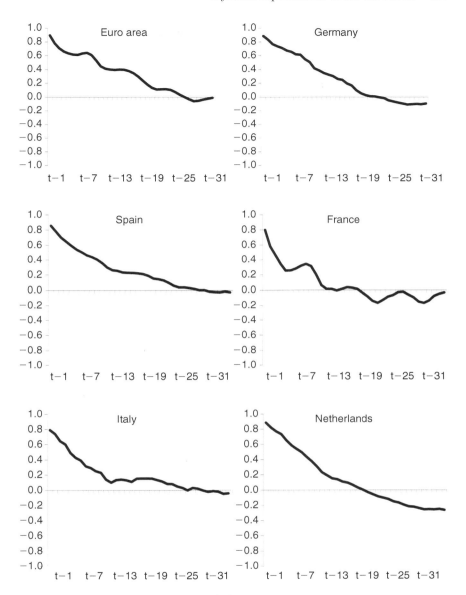

Figure 6.2 Expectation errors: autocorrelations.

However, even if uncertainty about the nature of the shocks affecting the inflationary process may give rise to such persistence in expectational errors, they should not persistent indefinitely. In particular, as argued in McCallum (1980), because errors are costly (e.g. they can lead to poor decisions) "purposeful agents" have an incentive to acquire sufficient information to weed out systematic expectational error (see also Carlson 1987).

Forsells and Kenny (2004) suggested the estimation of the two equation error correction model in order to assess the speed with which consumers revise their expectations to take account of the flow of new information and weed out any systematic error. If actual and expected inflation are cointegrated with cointegrating vector $[1, -1]$, it is possible to estimate an error correction model whereby the adjustment of expected inflation toward its fully rational value can be examined.[7] The bi-variate model is given by (2) and (3) below:

$$\Delta \pi_t^e = \alpha_o^e + \sum_{i=1}^{p} \varphi_i^e \Delta \pi_{t-i}^e + \sum_{i=1}^{p} \psi_i^e \Delta \pi_{t-i} + \alpha^e [\pi_{t-1}^e - \pi_{t-1}] + \varepsilon_t^e \tag{2}$$

$$\Delta \pi_t = \alpha_o + \sum_{i=1}^{p} \varphi_i \Delta \pi_{t-i}^e + \sum_{i=1}^{p} \psi_i \Delta \pi_{t-i} + \alpha [\pi_{t-1}^e - \pi_{t-1}] + \varepsilon_t \tag{3}$$

Under the hypothesis of cointegration, either α or α^e is non-zero.[8] As the preliminary step in testing for the existence of such an error correction representation, Table 6.3 reports standard unit root tests for both actual and expected inflation over the period 1985–2005. In general, the tests suggest that both actual and expected inflation have unit roots but that they are stationary when differenced once. Yet, one can reject the null hypothesis of a unit root in the expectation error. So actual and expected inflation cointegrate with known cointegrating vector $[1, -1]$.

In estimating the bi-variate error correction model ((2) and (3)), consistent with the monthly frequency of the data, the lag length p is set equal to 12.[9] The equilibrium correction coefficients (α^e, α) and p-values based on F-tests for Granger-causality associated with the parameters φ_i^e, ψ_i^e, φ_i and v_i are reported in Table 6.4 for both the euro area and the individual countries. In the regression for the change in expectations, the adjustment parameter on the expectational error is significant in all instances and suggests that consumers revise their

Table 6.3 Unit root tests

	Infl.	d(infl.)	Exp.	d(exp.)	error
Euro area	−1.59	−3.72***	−2.24	−16.21***	−3.52***
Germany	−1.90	−14.96***	−1.75	−24.72***	−2.62*
France	−1.62	−6.17***	−3.57***	−12.62***	−4.98***
Italy	−2.60*	−12.84***	−1.92	−23.82***	−3.42**
Spain	−2.67*	−13.52***	−3.25**	−21.25***	−4.05***
Netherlands	−2.05	−15.50***	−2.12	−6.50***	−3.20**

Notes
ADF presents the augmented Dickey-Fuller test-statistic for the null hypothesis of a unit root in the indicated series against the alternative hypothesis of stationarity.
d() denotes the first difference of each series.
*, ** and *** indicate that it is possible to reject the null of a unit root at the 10 per cent, 5 per cent and 1 per cent levels of significance, respectively.

Table 6.4 Error correction coefficients (*coefficients and p-values*)

	Expectations regression			Inflation regression		
		F^1	F^2		F^3	F^4
	α^e	$\phi_i^e \equiv 0$	$\psi_i^e \equiv 0$	α	$\phi \equiv 0$	$\psi_i \equiv 0$
Euro area	−0.10***	0.10	0.00	0.00	0.10	0.00
Germany	−0.11***	0.00	0.00	−0.02	0.79	0.00
France	−0.13***	0.11	0.05	0.03	0.02	0.00
Italy	−0.12**	0.00	0.03	0.00	0.84	0.00
Spain	−0.07*	0.00	0.00	0.01	0.32	0.00
Netherlands	−0.13***	0.00	0.012	0.07**	0.84	0.00

Notes
*, ** and *** indicate that the coefficients (α^e and α) are significant at the 10 per cent, 5 per cent and 1 per cent level, respectively.
For the F-statistics, F^i (i = 1, 2, 3, 4), the p-values are reported.

expectations and adjust them to be in line with the actual outcome. In terms of the speed of this adjustment, given the monthly frequency of the data, the estimated coefficient (−0.10) implies quite low persistence in deviations of actual from expected inflation. The other adjustment coefficient (α), however, is not significant, thereby suggesting that the adjustment of actual inflation plays no significant role in maintaining the cointegrating relation. All these findings are robust across individual countries.

To shed further light on the dynamic interaction between actual and expected inflation, Table 6.4 also reports the p-values for the tests that the other short-run coefficients φ_i^e, ψ_i^e, φ_i and v_i can be excluded from the bi-variate model. In line with the previous results of Forsells and Kenny (2004) there is, at the area-wide level, a significant role for actual inflation as a determinant of changes in expectations in a Granger-causal sense (F^2). But the feedback from expectations to actual changes in inflation is quite weak and insignificant at standard levels (F^3). These conclusions are also reasonably robust across the five euro area countries considered.

5 Test of macroeconomic efficiency

Another optimality condition implied by the rational expectations hypothesis is that the expectational errors should be orthogonal to the information set that was known to consumers at the time they formed their expectations: the *ex post* error should not be explained by past economic developments. The *efficiency* of consumers' inflation expectations may be tested by estimating the equation:

$$\pi_t - \pi_t^e = \delta + \varphi\Omega_{t-12} + u_t, \tag{4}$$

where Ω_{t-12} represents the set of information variables that are relevant for predicting inflation. In the empirical analysis below, this set of information includes past inflation as well as a wide range of other macroeconomic indicators capturing demand and cost pressures as well as monetary and financial conditions. A statistically significant φ suggests that the effect on inflation from past developments in the information variable (Ω_{t-12}) has been incorrectly estimated.

The results from the macro efficiency tests at area-wide data are given in Table 6.5a for the whole sample period and the sub-periods. Earlier findings based on forecasting performance and tests of unbiasedness indicate that expectations have become more rational over the sample period. They also seem to have become more efficient. Over the full sample-period, past price developments do not explain consumers' prediction errors (suggesting some evidence of weak form efficiency). As for the other variables, neither the cost indicators nor the two euro exchange rate measures explain any of the prediction error. However, consumers' inflation expectations do not appear to be fully efficient with respect to the information in the demand variables, the monetary aggregates, or some of the other interest rate variables.[10] The three sub-samples give clear evidence of improving efficiency. In the first sub-sample ten variables significantly explain the errors, while in the third sub-sample six variables enter with a statistically significant coefficient. On the role of M3 in explaining the expectational error the results are particularly interesting given the ECB's monetary policy strategy. Over the whole sample and for most sub-samples, φ is positive, suggesting that consumers have underestimated its impact on inflation. In

Table 6.5a Test for efficiency, euro area sub-periods, $(\pi_t - \pi_t^e = \delta + \varphi\Omega_{t-12} + u_t)$ (*estimates of φ*)

	Full sample	*1980s*	*1990s*	*2000s*
Demand variables				
GDP	0.30***	0.89***	0.23**	0.16
Industrial production	0.08***	0.20***	0.06**	0.09***
Unemployment	−0.45***	−3.18***	−0.40**	−0.44***
Monetary and financial variables				
M1	0.07***	−0.34	0.06	0.10***
M3	0.18***	0.67***	0.18***	−0.10
3-month interest rate	0.17***	0.09	0.22***	0.05
Long-term interest rate	0.21***	0.21	0.26***	0.18
12-m. real interest rate	0.11***	−0.66**	0.17***	0.03
US$/euro	0.00	−0.06***	0.01	−0.01
Nominal eff. exchange rate	0.00	−0.08***	0.02	−0.02
Price and cost variables				
Inflation	0.09	−0.13	0.29***	−0.78***
Compensation p. employee	0.08	−0.74	0.08	−0.67***
Producer prices	0.03	0.19***	0.20**	0.01
Commodity prices	0.00	0.02***	0.01	0.01
• Energy	0.00	0.01	0.01	0.00**
• Non-energy	0.01	0.03***	0.00	0.01

Notes
** and *** indicate that the coefficient is significant at the 5 per cent and 1 per cent level, respectively.

Table 6.5b Test for efficiency, euro area countries ($\pi_t - \pi_t^e = \delta + \varphi \Omega_{t-12} + u_t$) (estimates of φ)

	Euro area	Germany	France	Italy	Spain	Netherland
Demand variables						
GDP	0.30***	0.42***	0.09***	0.18***	0.13***	0.26***
Industrial production	0.08***	0.18***	0.00	0.08	0.03	0.08***
Unemployment	−0.45***	−0.07***	0.00	0.00	−0.01	−0.02***
Monetary and financial variables						
M1	0.07***	0.05	−0.01	0.08**	0.10**	−0.02
M3	0.18***	−0.05	0.02	−0.21***	0.12**	0.09**
3-month interest rate	0.17***	0.53***	0.02	−0.20	−0.10	0.54***
Long-term interest rate	0.21***	0.62***	0.03	−0.05	0.09	0.57***
12-m. real interest rate	0.11***	0.14	0.06	−0.25***	0.26***	0.11**
US$/euro	0.00	−0.02	−0.02**	−0.02	0.04**	0.03**
Nominal eff. exchange rate	0.00	−0.01	0.00	0.05***	−0.05	−0.10**
Price and cost variables						
Inflation	0.09	−0.17	0.09	−0.58***	0.16	0.03
Compensation p. employee	0.08	−0.04	0.17	−0.22***	0.15	−0.01
Producer prices	0.03	0.10	0.04	−0.21***	0.09	0.12***
Commodity prices	0.00	0.01	0.00	0.00	0.00	0.02***
• Energy	0.00	0.01**	0.00	0.00	0.00	0.02***
• Non-energy	0.01	0.00	0.01	0.03**	0.02	0.01

Notes
** and *** indicate that the coefficient is significant at the 5 per cent and 1 per cent level, respectively.

particular, this result tends to support the independent and incremental information role assigned to M3 in the strategy.

Table 6.5b reports the degree of significance of φ for the euro area as well as the countries for the whole sample period. The role of the various variables in explaining the expectational error differs quite a lot across the countries. There is little evidence against overall efficiency in France and much stronger evidence in countries such as the Netherlands, Italy and Spain.

6 Expectations and euro area inflation dynamics

As discussed in the introduction, a key insight of the REH is that rational expectations of inflation have a strong influence on actual inflation.[11] As discussed in Forsells and Kenny (2004), this view has been re-articulated in recent new Keynesian models of price dynamics. If D_t is an excess demand measure and Z_t a cost shock variable, the role of expectations as a driving variable for actual inflation can be tested using the hybrid Phillips curve in equation (5):

$$\pi_t = \alpha + \gamma_f \pi^e_{t+4} + \gamma_b \pi^e_{t-4} + \beta D_t + \delta Z_t + u_t \tag{5}$$

In applying (5) to the data, to ensure robustness of the results with respect to the chosen measure of excess demand, two alternative proxies for D_t are used. First, a standard output gap is defined as the log of actual GDP in the euro area minus the log of potential GDP (estimated using a HP filter). Second, we also consider the primitive version of the New Keynesian Phillips Curve (NKPC) suggested by Galí *et al.* (2001) where the deviations in real marginal costs from their steady state value replace traditional output gap measures. The deviation of real unit labour costs from their sample mean is used as a proxy for marginal costs. The real price of oil is used to capture the impact of transitory cost shocks (Z_t). The equations are estimated over the period 1985Q1–2004Q4 (80 observations).

Table 6.6a reports the coefficients from the estimated hybrid Phillips curves. The two equations appear to capture quite adequately the dynamics of inflation over the sample period. A striking feature at the area-wide level is that for both specifications, the surveyed measure of inflation expectations enters with a highly significant positive coefficient, which is close to unity. The results at the country level are fully consistent with this, although they indicate slightly lower coefficients (except in the Netherlands). This testifies to a forward-looking dimension to the inflationary process in line with the previous findings in Forsells and Kenny (2004).[12] However, the backward-looking component is also mostly significant but quantitatively less important. Surprisingly, the real price of oil only enters significantly for the euro area, France and the Netherlands.

Table 6.6b reports the results of similar regressions but under the restrictions that the weights on the backward and forward looking components sum to unity. This restriction is accepted only (at the 5 per cent level of significance) in the equations using the output gap for France, Spain and the Netherlands. However, in all equations using the deviation from real unit labour costs, including the

Table 6.6a Estimates of hybrid Phillips curve ($\pi_t = \alpha + \gamma_f \pi_{t+4}^e + \gamma_b \pi_{t-4} + \beta_1 D_t + \delta Z_t + u_t$)

Output gap

	α	γ_f	γ_b	β_1	δ	R^2	n
euro area	−0.54**	0.87***	0.35***	0.05	0.00*	0.83	80
Germany	0.27	0.53***	0.22	0.14	0.01	0.57	80
France	0.26	0.55***	0.41***	−0.05	0.01**	0.75	80
Italy	0.41*	0.41***	0.39***	0.15	0.00	0.88	80
Spain	0.15	0.40***	0.59***	0.07	0.00	0.67	75
Netherlands	−0.01	1.06***	0.09	0.45***	−0.01	0.73	80

Real unit labour cost gap

	α	γ_f	γ_b	β_1	δ	R^2	n
euro area	−0.40	0.94***	0.24**	0.06*	0.00**	0.84	80
Germany	0.14	0.57***	0.25*	−0.01	0.01	0.56	80
France	0.70**	0.49***	0.31***	0.07*	0.01**	0.76	80
Italy	−0.57*	0.58***	0.41***	−0.11***	0.00	0.90	80
Spain	0.13	0.44***	0.57***	0.05	0.00	0.68	75
Netherlands	0.01	1.07***	0.07	−0.07	−0.01**	0.65	66

Notes
*, ** and *** indicate that the coefficient is significant at the 10 per cent, 5 per cent and 1 per cent levels, respectively, n denotes the number of observations.

Table 6.6b Restricted estimates of hybrid Phillips curve ($\pi_t = \alpha + \gamma_f \pi_{t+4}^e + (1 - \gamma_f)$
$\pi_{t-4} + \beta_2 D_t + \delta Z_t + u_t$)

Output gap

	α	γ_f	$1 - \gamma_f$	β_2	δ	R^2	n
euro area	0.00	0.61***	0.39***	0.15**	0.00	0.81	80
Germany	−0.18	0.63***	0.37***	0.04	0.01*	0.54	80
France	0.19*	0.60***	0.40***	−0.06	0.01**	0.75	80
Italy	−0.52***	0.47***	0.53***	0.15	0.00	0.83	80
Spain	0.11	0.41***	0.59***	0.07	0.00	0.68	75
Netherlands	0.24**	0.91***	0.09	0.47***	−0.01	0.73	80

Realunit labour cost gap

	α	γ_f	$1 - \gamma_f$	β_2	δ	R^2	n
euro area	0.07	0.77***	0.23*	0.07**	0.00*	0.83	80
Germany	−0.19	0.65***	0.35**	−0.03	0.01*	0.54	80
France	0.27*	0.66***	0.34***	0.03	0.01**	0.75	80
Italy	−0.60***	0.58***	0.42***	−0.11***	0.00	0.90	80
Spain	0.14	0.43***	0.57***	0.05	0.00	0.68	75
Netherlands	0.26	0.90***	0.10	−0.11	−0.01**	0.65	66

Notes
*, ** and *** indicate that the coefficient is significant at the 10 per cent, 5 per cent and 1 per cent levels, respectively, n denotes the number of observations.

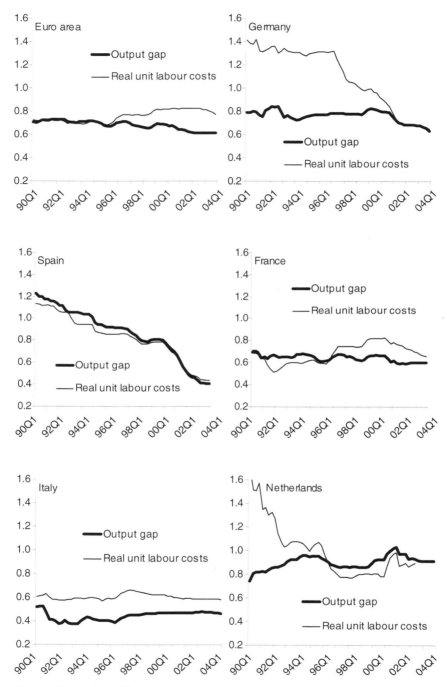

Figure 6.3 Hybrid Phillips curve – recursive parameter estimates (γ_f).

euro area, this restriction is accepted. For both specifications the role for expectations in determining actual inflation dynamics is strongly maintained. However, the weight on past inflation and, hence the backward-looking component in the inflation process, is significant in most euro area countries and generally quantitatively larger than estimated for the euro area as a whole. These finding are therefore more in favour of the hybrid rather than a pure forward-looking version of the Phillips curve.

Last, in order to check for stability, Figure 6.3 plots recursive estimates of the restricted parameter on consumers' expectations in each of the two models for the euro area. While there is some evidence that the weight attached to the forward looking component has risen in the real unit labour costs specifications but fallen for the output gap equation, the estimated parameters range between 0.61 and 0.77. Across countries, there is some hint of instability in the parameter estimates. In particular, for Germany and Spain, the recursive estimates suggest a decline in the size of the forward looking parameter.

7 Conclusions

This chapter has revisited the important topic of household inflation expectations and their possible link with price formation in the euro area. Previous research (Forsells and Kenny 2004) has been updated to take account of new empirical evidence since the start of stage three of EMU. It also enhances our understanding of the properties and role of consumers' inflation expectations as determinants of inflation, by taking a richer cross country perspective.

Overall, the results provide further insights into the empirical features and usefulness of quantified survey indicators for economic analysis and the modelling of inflation. In particular, the extended country analysis confirms previous results that consumers' expectations are unlikely to satisfy the very strong restrictions implied by the Rational Expectations Hypothesis but still contain potentially relevant information about future prices. Importantly, the good predictive performance of the quantified indicator of surveyed expectations at the area-wide level seems to reflect counterbalancing errors at the country level. This finding cautions against drawing strong conclusions about rationality on the basis of area-wide indicators alone. Lastly, estimates of a hybrid Phillips curve suggest that consumer expectations play an important role in driving the actual dynamics of inflation over the period 1985–2004. This finding is also robust across the five largest euro area countries.

Notes

1 European Central Bank; Frankfurt am Main; Germany. The views expressed in this chapter are those of the authors and do not necessarily reflect those of the European Central Bank. We would like to thank Fabien Curto Millet, Tomasz Łyziak, Peter Sinclair and other participants at the conference on inflation expectations organized by the National Bank of Poland (9 – 10 February 2006) for helpful comments and suggestions.

2 See, for example, Roberts (1995), Roberts (1998), Sbordone (2000a) and (2000b), Galí and Gertler (1999), Galí, Gertler and Sólido Lopez (2001).
3 This methodology is based on the so called probabilistic approach. Recent literature (e.g. Berk 1999; and Berk 2000), building on the earlier contributions of Carlson and Parkin (1975), Batchelor (1981, 1982 and 1986) and Batchelor and Orr (1988) and others, has further developed this approach. An important feature of these recent advances in methodology is that, unlike earlier approaches, long-term unbiasedness is not imposed in deriving a measure of expected inflation. See Forsells and Kenny (2004) for the underlying methodology and the dataset used in evaluating the estimated expectations series.
4 The expectations reported for month t in Figure 6.1 were formed in month $t-12$. Hence, the difference between the two lines in Figure 6.1 represents the expectational error.
5 Several factors underlie the sharp increase in perceptions around the time of the cash changeover. First, consumers appear to have attached a very high weight to price developments in goods and services they buy more frequently and/or individually. A number of such items were affected by various price shocks around and before 2002. Second, consumers became more aware of price movements and/or changes in their purchasing power due to the large media reporting following the introduction of euro coins and bills, which was a one-off event of an unprecedented nature. Third, the higher awareness of consumers in combination with uncertainties regarding the conversion rates to the euro could have led consumers to answer the survey question differently than before. Instead of comparing the current price level with the one prevailing one year ago, it may be the case that the base of comparison became the price level prevailing before the cash changeover in the legacy currency. Box 4 in the 2002 Annual Report of the ECB provides a more detailed analysis of the effects of the introduction of the euro banknotes and coins on consumer prices.
6 Given that the expectation horizons are overlapping due to the monthly frequency of the data, some correlation up to order $12-1$ could be expected. Cuckierman (1986) argued that even perfectly rational agents may not be able to distinguish permanent from transitory shocks. If this is the case and if permanent shocks are mistakenly perceived to be transitory, agents may make repeated one-sided errors in forming their expectations.
7 Other papers applying cointegration techniques to shed light on the rationality of expectations include Grant and Thomas (1998), Dutt and Ghosh (2000), Berk (1999) and (2000). See also Paquet (1992).
8 Granger (1988) pointed out that, if two series are cointegrated, then there must be Granger causality in at least one direction.
9 This was the lowest number of lags that was consistent with serially uncorrelated residuals in the bi-variate system.
10 The consistent lack of efficiency with respect to monetary variables that is found for the euro area is at odds with the evidence reported in Ball and Croushore (1998) for US inflation expectations.
11 The finding in Section 4 that expectations adjust towards actual inflation, rather than the other way around, suggests that the process generating inflation is not strongly influenced by expectations, which in turn contrasts with New Keynesian theories of price dynamics. Such a hypothesis, however, warrants further investigation in a multivariate context (e.g. using the Phillips curve framework adopted in this section).
12 Curtin (2005) and Kokoszczyński *et al.* (2005) reach similar conclusions using data for the United States, and Poland and the Czech Republic, respectively.

References

Ball, L. and D. Croushore (1998), Expectations and the effects of monetary policy, *Federal Reserve Bank of Philadelphia*, WP 98-13.

Batchelor, R.A. (1981), Aggregate expectations under the stable laws, *Journal of Econometrics*, 16: 199–210.

Batchelor, R.A (1982), Expectations, output and inflation: the European experience, *European Economic Review*, 17: 1–25.

Batchelor, R.A. (1986), Quantitative versus qualitative measures of inflation expectations, *Oxford Bulletin of Economics and Statistics*, 48: 99–120.

Batchelor, R.A. and A.B. Orr (1988), Inflation expectations revisited, *Economica*, 55: 317–331.

Berk, J.M. (1999), Measuring inflation expectations: a survey data approach, *Applied Economics*, 3: 1467–1480.

Berk, J.M. (2000), Consumers' inflation expectations and monetary policy in Europe, *Research Memorandum, Vrije Universiteit, Amsterdam*, 2000-20.

Carlson, J.A. and M. Parkin (1975), Inflation expectations, *Economica*, 42: 123–138.

Carlson J.B. (1987), Learning, rationality, the stability of equilibrium and macroeconomics, *Federal Reserve Bank of Cleveland, Economic Review, Fourth Quarter*: 1–12.

Cukierman, A. (1986), Measuring inflation expectations, *Journal of Monetary Economics*, 17: 315–324.

Curtin, R. (2005), Inflation expectations: theoretical models and empirical tests, *Presented at a conference at the National Bank of Poland (Warsaw)*, 9–10 February 2006.

Dutt, S.D. and D. Ghosh (2000), Inflation expectations: are they rational?: an empirical examination, *Applied Economics Letters*, 7: 103–106.

European Central Bank (2002), Effects of the introduction of the euro banknotes and coins on consumer prices, *Annual Report*: 40–42.

Forsells, M. and G. Kenny (2004), Survey expectations, rationality and the dynamics of euro area inflation, *Journal of Business Cycle Measurement and Analysis*, 1: 13–41.

Galí, J. and M. Gertler (1999), Inflation dynamics: a structural econometric analysis, *Journal of Monetary Economics*, 44: 195–222.

Galí, J., M. Gertler and D. López-Salido (2001), European inflation dynamics, *NBER Working Paper*, w8218.

Granger, C. (1988), Recent development in the concept of causality, *Journal of Econometrics*, 39: 199–211.

Grant, A.P. and L.B. Thomas (1998), Inflationary expectations and rationality revisited, *Economics Letters*, 62: 331–338.

Kokoszczyński, R., T. Łyziak and E. Stanisławska (2005), Consumer inflation expectations: usefulness of survey-based measures – a cross-country study, *Presented at a conference at the National Bank of Poland (Warsaw)*, 9–10 February 2006.

McCallum, B.T. (1980), Rational expectations and macroeconomic stabilization policy: an overview, *Journal of Money, Credit and Banking*, XII: 697–746.

Paquet, A. (1992), Inflationary expectations and rationality, *Economic Letters*, 40: 303–308.

Roberts, J.M. (1995), New Keynesian economics and the Phillips Curve, *Journal of Money, Credit and Banking*, 27 (4): 939–1506.

Roberts, J.M. (1998), Inflation expectations and the transmission of monetary policy, *Finance and Economics Discussion Series*, 1998-43, Federal Reserve Board, Washington, DC.

Sbordone, A.M. (2000a), Prices and unit labour costs: a new test of price stickiness, unpublished manuscript, Rutgers University.

Sbordone, A.M. (2000b), An optimizing model of US Wage and Price Dynamics, unpublished manuscript, Rutgers University.

7 Household versus expert forecasts of inflation

New evidence from the European survey data

Christina Gerberding[1]

1 Introduction

There is a broad consensus that inflation expectations play a key role in the transmission of monetary policy to aggregate output and prices. Hence, the question of how economic agents form expectations is of interest to model builders and monetary policy makers alike. However, empirical studies of the process of expectations formation face the problem that expectations are inherently unobservable. One approach to solving this problem is to derive market players' inflation expectations from financial asset prices.[2] Alternatively, one can ask market participants directly what their expectations are over a certain time horizon through a survey. The main advantage of surveys is that they yield direct observations of inflation expectations which do not depend on certain a priori assumptions, for instance regarding the level and the structure of *ex ante* real interest rates.[3]

In the United States, the use of survey data on price expectations obtained as part of the Michigan, Livingston and ASA-NBER surveys has a long tradition.[4] By contrast, measures of inflation expectations derived from surveys conducted in the member states of the European Union have received little attention until recently. This chapter analyses survey measures of expected inflation for four major EU member countries, Germany, France, Italy and the United Kingdom. The data are taken from the European Commission's Consumer Survey and from the Survey of Professional Experts conducted by the London-based institute Consensus Economics. Drawing on these two sources enables us to compare the relative performance of household versus expert forecasts of inflation.

The survey data, and the method used for quantifying the qualitative data from the Consumer Survey, are described in Section 2. Section 3 compares the predictive power of the two sets of survey expectations and submits them to standard tests of unbiasedness and informational efficiency. While most of them pass the test of unbiasedness, the orthogonality tests indicate the surveyed households and experts did not make efficient use of all the information available at the time they formed their expectations. As a next step, we analyse the dynamic interactions of the survey expectations and the subsequently realized inflation rates in an error correction framework. Finally, to shed more light on expectations formation, and the inflation process, we estimate simple trivariate VARs of inflation, one-year-ahead inflation expectations and output. Section 5 summarizes the findings and discusses their monetary policy implications.

2 The data

2.1 The European Commission Consumer Survey of expected price developments

In the European Union member states, a harmonized consumer survey, which also includes an assessment of past and future price developments, is conducted monthly. The surveys are carried out by national institutions, such as the Gesellschaft für Konsumforschung (GfK) in Germany. Each country's sample comprises at least 1,500 persons selected by a special procedure. For the larger countries – France, Italy, Spain and the United Kingdom – the sample size is 2,000, for Germany 2,500. From January 1997, the GfK included 500 respondents from East Germany in the survey (that is, until December 1996, the data are for West Germany only). Results from these surveys are available from 1985 onwards.

In the EC survey, respondents may choose from among several categories of responses. Table 7.1 shows the exact wording of the questions and the categories of responses available. The terms A', B', etc. denote the percentages of the respondents in each response category. Owing to the large sample size and the selection criteria applied by the polling institutes, the basket of goods relevant for the surveyed households should more or less correspond to the basket of goods of the average household used by statistical offices to measure consumer price movements. The survey data may thus be interpreted as an assessment of the direction of change of the respective national consumer price index.[5]

An argument in favour of gathering qualitative rather than quantitative data is that the surveyed households are more likely to have an opinion on the expected direction of future price changes than they are to give precise forecasts for a

Table 7.1 Questions and response categories of the EU Consumer Survey on price developments (Question 5 and 6)

Q5: How do you think that consumer prices have developed over the last 12 months? They have . . .	*Q6: By comparison with the past 12 months, how do you expect that consumer prices will develop in the next 12 months? They will . . .*
Fallen (A')	Fall (A)
Stayed about the same (B')	Stay about the same (B)
Risen slightly (C')	Increase at a slower rate (C)
Risen moderately (D')	Increase at the same rate (D)
Risen a lot (E')	Increase more rapidly (E)
Don't know (F')	Don't know (F)

certain time horizon.[6] This advantage is offset somewhat, however, by the fact that empirical applications often require a quantification of the survey results which, in turn, is only possible under certain assumptions, some of which may not be testable.[7]

To obtain quantitative data, I follow the probability method developed by Carlson and Parkin (1975) which was extended to the five-category case by Batchelor and Orr (1988).[8] Due to the wording of Question 6 (see Table 7.1), the procedure requires the specification of a variable that captures respondents' perceptions of the rate of inflation over the past 12 months. In terms of the conversion method, the mean expected inflation rate, $E_t\pi_{t+12}$, is the product of the (mean) assessment of price developments over the past 12 months, π'_{t-1}, and a factor x_t (calculated using the cumulative density function) which reflects the change in the assessment of future relative to past price developments:[9]

$$\pi^e_{t+12} = \pi'_{t-1}x_t \tag{1}$$

In principle, this problem can be solved by using the assessment of past price trends from Question 5 (see Table 7.1) to construct a measure of π'_{t-1}. Unfortunately, quantification of the responses to this question is further complicated by the fact that the response categories C', D' and E' refer to the assessment of past price trends in relation to a benchmark considered "moderate". So equation (1) may be expressed as:

$$\pi'_{t-1} = \pi^m_{t-1}x'_{t-1} \tag{2}$$

where x'_t reflects the assessment of past price trends relative to the rate of price rise considered to be moderate by the average respondent. To evaluate the responses to this part of the question, one needs to learn what respondents consider a moderate rate of inflation. Such information is not available; other conceivable methods of defining the "moderate" rate of inflation require additional critical assumptions; so this approach will not be pursued further here.[10]

Instead, we use two methods to measure the perceived rate of inflation proposed in the literature. The first one is to assume that the respondents' assessment of past price developments matches the actual rate of change of the respective national consumer price index over the past 12 months. Under this assumption, the most recent inflation figures available to consumers are used as a scaling parameter (i.e. $\pi'_{t-1} = \pi_{t-1}$).[11] However, more recently, the marked discrepancy between perceived inflation and inflation as measured by the consumer price index which occurred after the euro changeover at the beginning of 2002 in some member countries of the euro area has thrown some doubt on the validity of this assumption.[12] Hence, we also consider a second, survey-based measure of perceived inflation. To obtain this measure, the last three categories of Question 5 are aggregated into one category "prices have risen", thereby transforming the responses into the traditional three-category case for which the Carlson–Parkin-method was originally developed.[13] In this case, the indifference interval around zero (the response threshold) takes the role of a scaling parameter. This parameter can be obtained by equating the mean of the perceived past inflation rate with the mean of the actual past inflation rate (Carlson and Parkin 1975).[14] This assumption is obviously much weaker than the assumption that perceived inflation always equals inflation as measured by the CPI, but some information is lost by merging three response categories into one.

In Figure 7.1, the survey-based measures of perceived inflation (method 2) are contrasted with the inflation rates as measured by the CPI (method 1). Interestingly, the rate of inflation perceived by the surveyed households at times differs considerably from the official figures. For Germany, the difference is especially marked after the currency changeover at the beginning of 2002. As a consequence, the survey-based measures of expected inflation differ, depending on the choice of the scaling parameter.

In Figure 7.2, the quantified survey expectations for period *t*, scaled with either actual or perceived inflation, are contrasted with actual inflation at time *t* (quarterly averages). Missing observations reflect the fact that the quantification method breaks down when the share of respondents in one of the categories is equal to zero.[15] As the expectations series is dated back one year (four quarters), the vertical differences between the two series measure the forecast error. At first glance, the survey expectations seem to follow actual price developments quite closely. However, there are also periods when the future trend in the inflation

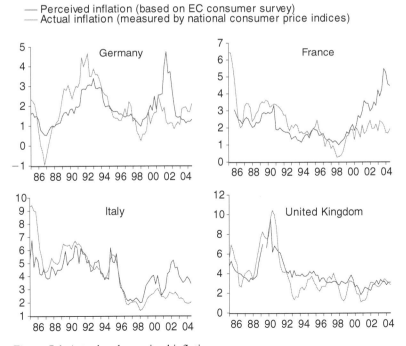

Figure 7.1 Actual and perceived inflation.

rate is anticipated correctly. Table 7.2 compares the two scaling methods in terms of the root mean squared errors (RMSE) of the resulting expectations series. The RMSEs of the two expectations measures are fairly similar for Germany and France. But for Italy and the United Kingdom, the expectations series scaled with perceived past inflation perform much better than those based on actual past inflation.

Despite the fact that the EC consumer survey is supposed to be harmonized across all participating countries, the wording of the questions and the response categories in some countries – notably France – displays some peculiarities which have to be kept in mind when further analysing the data. The French households are asked for their assessment of expected price developments "in the coming months" without this time period being specified more precisely.[16] Since the first part of the question refers to the assessment of price trends in the past six months (again different from the Commission's blueprint), some respondents could likewise relate the question on future price developments to that time horizon. The danger that the price expectations calculated from the EU survey are subject to measurement errors is greater for France than for the other countries.

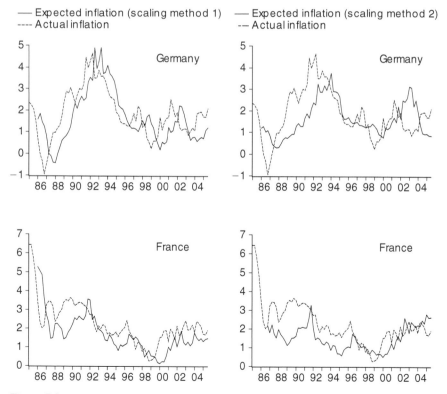

Figure 7.2 Expected inflation according to EC Consumer Survey.

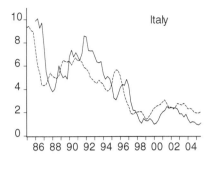 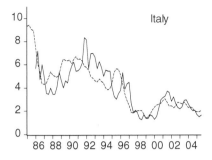

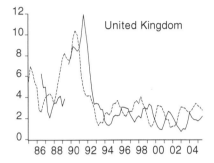 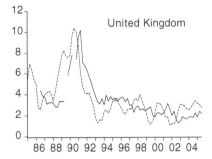

Figure 7.2 continued.

Table 7.2 Comparison of RMSEs of alternative scaling procedures estimation period: 1986Q1–2005Q3 (79 obs)

Price expectations according to	*Root mean square forecast error*			
	Germany	*France*	*Italy*	*United Kingdom*
EC Consumer Survey (1)	1.01	0.98	1.53	1.97
EC Consumer Survey (2)	1.09	0.96	1.17	1.55

2.2 Consensus forecasts for consumer prices

A potential weakness of consumer and business surveys is that the respondents have little incentive to state their expectations correctly. Some critics therefore recommend to restrict attention to surveys of professional forecasters who also sell their forecasts on the market.[17] However, professional forecasters may have strategic incentives to report forecasts that deviate from their "true" expectations.[18]

Since the autumn of 1989, the London-based firm Consensus Economics has been conducting a survey at the beginning of each month in which renowned experts are asked to give their forecasts for the development of a range of important macroeconomic variables in over 20 countries. For each of the seven largest industrial countries (United States, Japan, Germany, France, United Kingdom, Italy and Canada), a separate panel of professional forecasters is recruited from the major banks, investment firms, economic research institutes and other business services in that country.[19] For our purposes, the usefulness of the regular monthly Consensus Forecasts is limited by the fact that they are

Table 7.3 Structure of quarterly consensus forecasts for consumer prices[20]

Germany: quarterly consensus forecasts

Percentage change (year-on-year) from survey of 12 September 2005

	2005				2006				2007	
	Q1	*Q2*	*Q3*	*Q4*	*Q1*	*Q2*	*Q3*	*Q4*	*Q1*	*Q2*
Consumer prices[†]	1.7	1.7	*2.0*	*2.1*	*2.3*	*1.9*	*1.5*	*1.4*	*1.4*	*1.4*

Note
† Consensus forecasts shown in italics

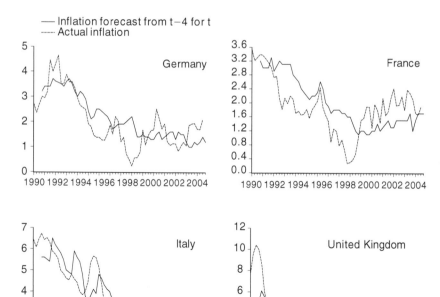

Figure 7.3 Consensus forecasts of inflation.

"fixed event" forecasts with changing forecast horizons. However, once every quarter, Consensus Economics asks the country panellists to provide additional forecasts of key macro variables, including consumer prices, for each of the following one to six quarters. The arithmetic means of these quarterly forecasts are then published in separate tables (individual forecasts are not available). Table 7.3 illustrates the structure of these data.

To match the 12-month horizon of the price expectations from the EC consumer survey, we focus on the year-ahead forecasts of the country panellists. Consensus Forecasts with this horizon are available for the G7-countries from November 1989. Figure 7.3 shows the resulting time series of inflation forecasts for Germany, France, Italy and the United Kingdom (reported in $t–4$) along with actual price developments. As forecasts for West German consumer prices became forecasts for all-German consumer prices in December 1996, we use all-German CPI data from the fourth quarter of 1997. The UK Consensus Forecasts from 1997Q2 refer to the underlying rate of inflation (RPIX) which explains the smoothness of both series from 1998Q2 to the end of the sample.[21]

One striking feature is that the professional experts polled by Consensus Economics failed to anticipate either the deceleration of inflation in the first half of the 1990s or the further sharp slowing of inflation rates in the run-up to European monetary union. The tendency to overestimate actual inflation was particularly marked in France but visible in the German forecasts too, especially at the turn of 1998 to 1999. Nor were the price increases after the beginning of EMU predicted correctly.

3 Empirical results

3.1 Comparison of predictive power

In Table 7.4, the accuracy of the household expectations from the EC survey and the expert forecasts polled by Consensus Economics is compared in terms of their mean absolute forecast errors (MAE), their root mean square errors (RMSE) and of Theil's inequality coefficient which gives the forecast error relative to the "naïve" extrapolative forecast ("no change in the inflation rate"). For Germany, Italy and the United Kingdom, the expert forecasts are substantially more precise than the household expectations. The difference is less marked for France, where the MAE of the household expectations scaled with actual past inflation is even smaller than the MAE of the expert forecasts. In fact, with respect to French consumer prices, all of the survey expectations considered here performed worse than the naïve extrapolative forecast during the sample period. The lack of predictive power of the French households' expectations may reflect the ambiguity of the forecast horizon. But this does not explain the disappointing performance of the Consensus Forecasts for France. By contrast, the Consensus Forecasts for Germany, Italy and the United Kingdom managed to outperform the naïve extrapolative forecast by considerable margins. The same is true for the inflation expectations of the UK households when perceived past inflation is used as the scaling variable.

Table 7.4 Comparison of predictive power. Estimation period: 1990Q4 to 2005Q3 (60 obs)

Price expectations according to	Germany	France	Italy	United Kingdom
	Mean absolute forecast error			
EC consumer survey (1)	0.74	0.58	1.01	1.42
EC Consumer Survey (2)	0.78	0.61	0.84	1.14
Consensus forecasts	0.57	0.59	0.74	0.65
	Root mean square forecast error			
EC consumer survey (1)	0.85	0.70	1.25	1.92
EC consumer survey (2)	1.01	0.73	1.11	1.34
Consensus forecasts	0.69	0.68	0.86	1.07
	Theil's inequality coefficient[1]			
EC consumer survey (1)	0.94	1.11	1.16	0.98
EC consumer survey (2)	1.11	1.15	1.03	0.68
Consensus forecasts	0.76	1.07	0.79	0.61

Note
1 Forecast error of the survey data relative to the naive extrapolative forecast ($E_t\pi_{t+4} = \pi_{t-1}$). Values smaller than unity imply that the forecasts of the surveyed households and experts outperform the naive extrapolative forecast.

3.2 Tests of unbiasedness and efficiency

This section asks whether the survey measures of expectations are "rational" in the sense of Muth (1961). Since the monetary policy implications of rational expectations are very different from those of other, more backward-looking models of expectations formation, the issue is of considerable interest to monetary policy makers. In his definition of rational expectations, Muth assumes that the subjective expectations of economic agents match the predictions of the relevant economic theory.[22] The evidence presented so far suggests that the surveyed households and expert often did not anticipate future price developments. Rational expectations do not imply that economic agents' forecasts are always correct, but that they exhibit no systematic mistakes.

The popularity of the rational expectations hypothesis in macroeconomic modelling has motivated numerous authors to test it on survey data.[23] The tests build on certain properties of the forecast errors which must be met in a rational expectations scenario. Most importantly, under the hypothesis of RE, the expectations errors must have a mean value of zero (criterion of unbiasedness):

$$E(\eta_t) = 0 \qquad (3a)$$

and they must not be correlated with variables which were included in the agents' information set Ω_{t-j} at the time the expectations were formed (criterion of orthogonality):

$$E(\eta_t|\Omega_{t-j}) = 0 \qquad (3b)$$

The most common test of unbiasedness consists of regressing actual inflation on the inflation forecast and a constant and testing the null hypothesis $c_0 = 0$ and $\beta = 1$:

$$\pi_t = c_0 + \beta E_{t-4}\pi_t + \varepsilon_t \tag{4}$$

However, Holden and Peel (1990) have shown that while the condition $c_0 = 0$ and $\beta = 1$ is sufficient for unbiasedness, it is not necessary (that is, unbiasedness is still possible even if $c_0 = 0$ and $\beta = 1$ is rejected by the data). They regress the forecast error on a constant instead and test whether the constant can be restricted to zero:[24]

$$\pi_t - E_{t-4}\pi_t = c_0 + \varepsilon_t \tag{4b}$$

As demonstrated by Holden and Peel, the condition $c_0 = 0$ is both necessary and sufficient for unbiasedness. Table 7.5 summarizes the results of this test for the household and expert inflation forecasts considered here. Accordingly, most of the survey expectations pass the test of unbiasedness. In fact, only the mean forecast error of the surveyed French households is significantly different from zero (independently of the scaling method).

The informational efficiency of the survey data may be tested by regressing the forecast error on a range of variables which may have been of help in forecasting inflation and were commonly available at the time the forecasts were made:

$$\pi_t - E_{t-4}\pi_t = \beta\Omega_{t-5} + \varepsilon_t \tag{5}$$

If β is significantly different from zero, informational efficiency is rejected. However, the vector Ω must contain only variables which were actually available

Table 7.5 Are the forecasts unbiased?

H_0: $c_0 = 0$ (p-values)	Germany	France	Italy	United Kingdom
EC consumer survey (1)	0.38 ($c_0 = 0.17$)	0.01 ($c_0 = 0.43***$)	0.50 ($c_0 = -0.20$)	0.62 ($c_0 = 0.19$)
EC consumer survey (2)	0.33 ($c_0 = 0.21$)	0.00 ($c_0 = 0.57***$)	0.85 ($c_0 = 0.04$)	0.80 ($c_0 = 0.08$)
Consensus forecasts	0.28 ($c_0 = -0.17$)	0.30 ($c_0 = -0.17$)	0.59 ($c_0 = 0.11$)	0.19 ($c_0 = -0.28$)

Notes
Estimated equation: $\pi_t - E_{t-4}^s\pi_t = c_0 + \varepsilon_t$
Estimation method: OLS, Newey–West correction of standard errors
Sample periods: EC Survey 1986Q1–2005Q3; Consensus Forecasts 1990Q4–2005Q3.
***(**/*) denotes significance at the 1 per cent (5 per cent/10 per cent) level.

to the survey respondents when answering the survey ("real-time data"). So time series subject to major revisions after initial publication, such as industrial output or gross domestic product, are inadmissible (unless real-time data are still available). To circumvent this problem, I use three-month national money market rates (which are never revised), rates of change in the national consumer price indices (which are subject only to minor revisions) and past forecast errors as elements of the vector Ω. First, I regress the forecast errors on each of these variables in turn. Then a multivariate test includes the most up-to-date values of all information variables (dated $t-5$) as well as their respective previous year's values (dated $t-9$) in the information set. Table 7.6 summarizes the results.

Most of our survey measures of inflation expectations are found to be efficient with respect to the information contained in past forecast errors (thereby providing evidence of weak-form efficiency). However, none of the forecast errors is completely orthogonal to all of the information variables considered here, the one possible exception being the expectations of Italian consumers (when scaled with perceived past inflation). These results agree with previous empirical studies, nearly all of which find that survey expectations are not fully efficient in the sense of Muth.[25]

3.3 Inflation expectations dynamics

Yet might the concept of "strong rationality" be too strict a criterion? The notion that economic agents know all the relevant structural relationships is extreme,

Table 7.6 Are the forecast errors orthogonal to selected information variables?

H_0: $\beta = 0$; p-values	Germany	France	Italy	United Kingdom
EC consumer survey (1)				
$\Omega_{t-5} = \eta_{t-5}$	0.91	0.36	0.75	0.85
$\Omega_{t-5} = \pi_{t-5}$	0.00***	0.01**	0.00***	0.00***
$\Omega_{t-5} = i_{t-5}$	0.04**	0.24	0.00***	0.01***
$\Omega_{t-5} = (\eta_{t-5}, \eta_{t-9}, \pi_{t-5}, \pi_{t-9}, i_{t-5}, i_{t-9})$	0.00***	0.42	0.00***	0.00***
EC consumer survey (2)				
$\Omega_{t-5} = \eta_{t-5}$	0.05*	0.00***	0.96	0.13
$\Omega_{t-5} = \pi_{t-5}$	0.78	0.12	0.26	0.05*
$\Omega_{t-5} = i_{t-5}$	0.24	0.00***	0.58	0.14
$\Omega_{t-5} = (\eta_{t-5}, \eta_{t-9}, \pi_{t-5}, \pi_{t-9}, i_{t-5}, i_{t-9})$	0.00***	0.00***	0.07*	0.00***
Consensus Forecasts				
$\Omega_{t-5} = \eta_{t-5}$	0.95	0.01***	0.80	0.44
$\Omega_{t-5} = \pi_{t-5}$	0.59	0.55	0.08*	0.69
$\Omega_{t-5} = i_{t-5}$	0.61	0.06*	0.01**	0.90
$\Omega_{t-5} = (\eta_{t-5}, \eta_{t-9}, \pi_{t-5}, \pi_{t-9}, i_{t-5}, i_{t-9})$	0.00***	0.00***	0.00***	0.00***

Notes
Estimation equation: $\eta = c_0 + \beta\Omega_{t-5} + \varepsilon_t$ with $\eta_t = \pi_t - E^s_{t-4}\pi_t$
Estimation method: OLS, Newey–West correction of standard errors
Sample periods: EC Survey 1986Q1–2005Q3; Consensus Forecasts 1990Q4–2005Q3.
***(**/*) denotes significance at the 1 per cent (5 per cent/10 per cent) level.

and can hardly be maintained outside the tranquillity of a prolonged steady state.[26] Many critics have pointed to the importance of information problems and have stressed the need to take into account the costs of making optimal forecasts and also to explicitly model learning processes.[27] For instance, with incomplete information about the nature of the shocks hitting the economy, forecasters may rationally adjust their forecasts only gradually in response to new information. However, even if data and model uncertainty give rise to such persistence in expectational errors, they should not persist indefinitely. The adjustment process may take considerable time; but rationality implies that the long-run movements in actual and expected inflation should be linked.

Such links may be explored through pairwise Granger-causality tests for inflation expectations $(E_{t-4}\pi_t)$ and subsequently realized inflation rates (π_t), or in a vector error correction framework. Many recent empirical studies on the inter-action between inflation expectations and inflation are conducted with bi-variate error correction models of the form:[28]

$$\Delta E_{t-4}\pi_t = \delta_{\pi e}(\pi_{t-1} - E_{t-5}\pi_{t-1}) + \Sigma a_{11}(i)\Delta E_{t-4-i}\pi_{t-i} + \Sigma a_{12}(i)\Delta \pi_{t-i} + a_{10} + \varepsilon_{t\pi e} \text{ (6a)}$$

$$\Delta \pi_t = \delta_{\pi}(\pi_{t-1} - E_{t-5}\pi_{t-1}) + \Sigma a_{22}(i)\Delta \pi_{t-i} + \Sigma a_{21}(i)\Delta E_{t-4-i}\pi_{t-i} + a_{20} + \varepsilon_{te} \quad \text{(6b)}$$

Provided that actual and expected inflation are cointegrated with cointegrating vector $[1, -1]$, the error correction model given by equations (6a) and (6b) can be used to evaluate the issue of forecast rationality and the behaviour of prices and inflation expectations in general. First, the adjustment coefficient $\delta_{\pi e}$ provides information useful in assessing the rationality of forecasters' behaviour. A significantly positive value of $\delta_{\pi e}$ implies that the change in expectations (between period $t-5$ and $t-4$) is such that the level of inflation expected for period t will be closer to the rational outcome (which is unknown at the time expectations are formed).[29] Second, the VEC system highlights the potential two-way feedback between inflation and inflation expectations. If both $\delta_{\pi e}$ and δ_{π} are significant (with $\delta_{\pi e} > 0$ and $\delta_{\pi} < 0$), then not only do expectations adjust to the fully rational outcome, but actual inflation also adjusts to the level expected by consumers and/or professional forecasters (as implied by the Friedman-Phelps models of inflation). Third, the coefficients α_{12} and α_{21} capture additional short-run effects of changes in actual inflation on changes in expectations and vice versa.

Whether the VEC model given by the equations (6a) and (6b) is the best framework to analyse the issue of expectations adjustment, depends on the order of integration of the variables concerned. We therefore start off our analysis by estimating simple bi-variate VAR models of inflation expectations and inflation and determining the number of cointegration vectors via the Johansen method. The lag length of the VARs is chosen according to standard lag length criteria and the requirement of serially uncorrelated errors. The results of the trace tests on the number of cointegrating equations (CEs) are reported in Table 7.7.[30] The hypothesis of no cointegration between inflation expectations and inflation is rejected at high confidence for all measures of expectations but one, the second measure of the French consumers' expectations (where perceived inflation has drifted far from actual inflation; see Figure 7.1). In most cases, as the null of at most one CE is also rejected at the 5 per cent-level of significance, the variables in question do seem stationary. The trace test favours the null of at most one CE only in the second measure of Italian consumers' expectations. These results are somewhat at odds with Doepke *et al.* (2005) who subject the same set of variables

Table 7.7 Survey forecasts und subsequently realized inflation rates ($E_{t-4}\pi_t$, π_t)

	EC survey, method 1	EC survey, method 2	Consensus forecasts
Germany			
VAR analysis:			
• lag length	4 lags	5 lags	4 lags
• no of CE(s):[1] H_0: none	p = 0.00 (***)	p = 0.007 (***)	p = 0.008 (***)
H_0: *at most 1*	p = 0.010 (**)	p = 0.009 (***)	p = 0.045 (**)
• Granger causality (p-values):			
$E_{t-4}\pi_t$ does not Granger-cause π_t	0.55	0.80	0.61
π_t does not Granger-cause $E_{t-4}\pi_t$	0.00	0.00	0.056
VEC analysis:			
• lag length	3 lags	4 lags	3 lags
• adjustment coefficients			
δ_π	−0.12	−0.11	−0.24***
$\delta_{\pi e}$	0.61***	0.15**	0.11**
• Granger causality (p-values):			
$a_{21} = 0$	0.89	0.65	0.59
$a_{12} = 0$	0.00	0.10	0.38
France			
VAR analysis:			
• lag length	5 lags	4 lags	4 lags
• no of CE(s):[1] H_0: none	p = 0.000 (***)	p = 0.33	p = 0.009 (***)
H_0: at most 1	p = 0.014 (**)	p = 0.57	p = 0.035 (**)
• Granger causality (p-values):			
$E_{t-4}\pi_t$ does not Granger-cause π_t	0.014	(0.06)	0.46
π_t does not Granger-cause $E_{t-4}\pi_t$	0.000	(0.13)	0.04
VEC analysis:			
• lag length	4 lags	(3 lags)	3 lags
• adjustment coefficients			
δ_π	0.03	−0.15*	−0.07
$\delta_{\pi e}$	0.65***	(0.05)	0.12***
• Granger causality (p-values):			
$a_{21} = 0$	0.009	(0.046)	0.34
$a_{12} = 0$	0.00	(0.17)	0.42

Notes
Unrestricted Cointegration Rank Test (Trace).
Results of the restricted model in parentheses. When the restriction is not rejected, we only report results of the restricted model.
Sample period: 1990Q4–2005Q3.

Table 7.7 continued Italy and United Kingdom

	EC survey, method 1	EC survey, method 2	Consensus forecasts
Italy			
VAR analysis:			
• lag length	8 lags	4 lags	7 lags
• no of CE(s):[1] H_0: none	p = 0.00 (***)	p = 0.01 (**)	p = 0.000 (***)
H_0: at most 1	p = 0.02 (**)	p = 0.12	p = 0.012 (**)
• Granger causality (p-values):	0.00	0.03	
$E_{t-4}\pi_t$ does not Granger-cause π_t	0.00	0.00	0.00
π_t does not Granger-cause $E_{t-4}\pi_t$			0.00
VEC analysis:			
• lag length	7 lags	3 lags	6 lags
• adjustment coefficients			
δ_π	0.00	−0.10*	−0.19**
$\delta_{\pi e}$	0.10*	0.25**	0.44***
• Granger causality (p-values):			
$a_{21} = 0$	0.22	0.55	0.00
$a_{12} = 0$	0.00	0.0995	0.31
United Kingdom			
VAR analysis:			
• lag length	5 lags	2 lags	6 lags
• no of CE(s):[1] H_0: none	p = 0.00 (***)	p = 0.00 (***)	p = 0.002 (***)
H_0: at most 1	p = 0.00 (***)	p = 0.00 (***)	p = 0.012 (**)
• Granger causality (p-values):			
$E_{t-4}\pi_t$ does not Granger-cause π_t	0.61	0.95	0.28
π_t does not Granger-cause $E_{t-4}\pi_t$	0.00	0.14	0.00
VEC analysis:			
• lag length	4 lags	1 lag	5 lags
• adjustment coefficients			
δ_π	−0.03	−0.10	−0.17**
$\delta_{\pi e}$	0.59***	0.17***	0.07
• Granger Causality (p-values):			
$a_{21} = 0$	0.09	0.84	0.24
$a_{12} = 0$	0.00	0.51	0.00

Notes
Unrestricted Cointegration Rank Test (Trace).
Results of the restricted model in parentheses. When the restriction is not rejected, we only report results of the restricted model.
Trend assumption: no deterministic trend.
Sample period 1990Q4–2005Q3.

to standard univariate unit root tests and find that for most of them, it is hard to reject the null of nonstationarity.[31]

Taking the results of the trace tests seriously, simple bi-variate VARs for the levels of expected and actual inflation constitute the appropriate framework for our analysis. Testing for Granger causality in this framework, the null hypothesis that actual inflation does not Granger-cause inflation expectations has to be rejected for all but three of our measures of expectations. So in most cases, there is significant adjustment towards the fully rational level. The three exceptions are the survey expectations of the French and British households (when scaled with perceived past inflation) and the Consensus Forecasts for Germany (where the p-value of the null is still close to 0.05). On how inflation expectations affect inflation, the results are less clear-cut. In some cases, for instance Germany and the United Kingdom, we find that inflation expectations do not Granger-cause subsequently realized inflation rates. In other cases, we find evidence of two-way rather than one-way causation between the two variables, particularly in the Italian data.

For the sake of comparability with other studies, we also report the results of the corresponding VEC analysis for all our measures of expectations (even though the null of at most one CE is rejected in most cases). With one CE imposed, the estimated values of the adjustment coefficient $\delta_{\pi e}$ are generally significant, with the expected positive sign. However, in three out of 12 cases, the estimates are too close to zero or too imprecise to be significant. For the Italian consumers' expectations (when scaled with actual past inflation) and the UK Consensus Forecasts, the VEC results are somewhat at odds with the VAR results. There is little evidence that our measures of consumer expectations exert any significant influence on actual inflation. However, as far as the Consensus Forecasts are concerned, the estimates of δ_{π} are significant with the expected negative sign in three out of four cases, suggesting that there may be some adjustment of inflation towards inflation expectations and not just the other way around.

Overall, we find that with only two exceptions, our measures of inflation expectations are Granger-caused by actual inflation (but less frequently the other way around), suggesting that the expectations of the surveyed households and experts are forward-looking (rational) in the sense that they ultimately revert to their long-run "rational" values. With one or two exceptions, the results of the Granger-causality tests in the stationary VAR framework are confirmed by the results of the bivariate VEC models.

3.4 Inflation, expectations and output dynamics

For three of the four countries, results agree with previous empirical studies in finding that the process generating inflation is not strongly influenced by inflation expectations (the one possible exception is Italy).[32] However, this finding need not conflict with New Keynesian theories of price dynamics as is sometimes claimed. For one thing, the adjustment coefficient δ_{π} tests the influence of past expectations on current inflation, whereas, in the New Keynesian model of aggregate supply, inflation depends on current expectations of future inflation (as well as on a measure of the output gap). This proposition is different from the one examined so far, but again, survey measures of inflation expectations may be used to test it directly.

Our first step follows Paloviita and Virén (2005) and estimates a simple VAR model of inflation, π_t, one-year-ahead inflation expectations, $E_t \pi_{t+4}$, and the output gap, y_t for each of the four countries. Measures of the output gaps are obtained by detrending the (log) GDP series with an HP-filter. While Paloviita and Virén focus on the inflation equation of the model, we are also interested in the expectations equation as a model of the expectations formation process. Paloviita and Virén note a potential problem – the apparent non-stationarity of some of the time series. However, the analysis in the last section, showed most of our time series of inflation expectations and inflation to be stationary in the period 1990Q4–2005Q3. Since our measure of economic activity is by construction stationary, too, the analysis may be safely conducted with the levels of the three

Table 7.8 Inflation, inflation expectations and output

	EC survey, method 1	EC survey, method 2	Consensus forecasts
Germany			
VAR $\{\pi_t, E_t\pi_{t+4}, y_t\}$			
• lag length	3 lags	lag 1–3, 8–9	3 lags
• Granger causality (p-values)			
Dependent variable: π_t	0.39	0.49	0.59
• excluded: $E_t\pi_{t+4}$	0.00	0.00	0.00
• excluded: y_t	0.00	0.00	0.00
• excluded: all			
Dependent variable: $E_t\pi_{t+4}$			
• excluded: π_t	0.007	0.04	0.02
• excluded: y_t	0.00	0.03	0.20
• excluded: all	0.00	0.00	0.03
Dependent variable: y_t			
• excluded: π_t	0.19	0.00	0.00
• excluded: $E_t\pi_{t+4}$	0.19	0.34	0.33
• excluded: all	0.00	0.007	0.00
France			
VAR $\{\pi_t, E_t\pi_{t+4}, y_t\}$			
• lag length	5 lags	5 lags	5 lags
• Granger causality (p-values)			
Dependent variable: π_t	0.23	0.00	0.20
• excluded: $E_t\pi_{t+4}$	0.63	0.32	0.41
• excluded: y_t	0.38	0.01	0.36
• excluded: all			
Dependent variable: $E_t\pi_{t+4}$			
• excluded: π_t	0.06	0.27	0.13
• excluded: y_t	0.07	0.33	0.17
• excluded: all	0.05	0.18	0.099
Dependent variable: y_t			
• excluded: π_t	0.52	0.82	0.87
• excluded: $E_t\pi_{t+4}$	0.53	0.76	0.74
• excluded: both	0.82	0.93	0.93

Note
Sample period: 1990Q4 to 2005Q3.

Table 7.8, continued Italy and United Kingdom

	EC survey, method 1	EC survey, method 2	Consensus forecasts
Italy			
VAR $\{\pi_t, E_t\pi_{t+4}, y_t\}$			
• lag length	Lags 1–2, 8–9	Lags 1–2, 8	2 lags
• Granger causality (p-values)			
Dependent variable: π_t	0.03	0.02	0.00
• excluded: $E_t\pi_{t+4}$	0.02	0.00	0.00
• excluded: y_t	0.00	0.00	0.00
• excluded: all			
Dependent variable: $E_t\pi_{t+4}$			
• excluded: π_t	0.19	0.01	0.45
• excluded: y_t	0.95	0.42	0.90
• excluded: all	0.38	0.046	0.60
Dependent variable: y_t			
• excluded: π_t	0.72	0.85	0.24
• excluded: y_t	0.54	0.58	0.33
• excluded: all	0.44	0.60	0.33
United Kingdom			
VAR $\{\pi_t, E_t\pi_{t+4}, y_t\}$			
• lag length	4 lags	2 lags	5 lags
• Granger causality (p-values)			
Dependent variable: π_t	0.16	0.11	0.18
• excluded: π_t	0.40	0.48	0.002
• excluded: y_t	0.20	0.29	0.006
• excluded: all			
Dependent variable: $E_t\pi_{t+4}$			
• excluded: π_t	0.00	0.27	0.22
• excluded: y_t	0.10	0.04	0.22
• excluded: all	0.00	0.06	0.24
Dependent variable: y_t			
• excluded: π_t	0.23	0.005	0.44
• excluded: y_t	0.53	0.36	0.89
• excluded: all	0.22	0.008	0.48

Note
Sample period: 1990q4 to 2005q3.

variables which enter the New Keynesian Phillips curve. Again, we restrict our attention to the results of simple Granger-causality tests. A full-fledged analysis of the dynamic interactions of the three variables, including the impulse responses and the variance decompositions, is left to future research.

As a starting point, we estimate trivariate VARs with lag length four (consistent with the quarterly frequency of the data). We then check the residuals and, where necessary, include more lags to remove any remaining serial correlation. In some cases, we can reduce the lag length to three or even two lags (applying standard lag length criteria); in others, we have to increase it to five lags or to add lags eight and nine (see Table 7.8). In Table 7.8, we report the results of Granger Causality (Block Exogeneity Wald) Tests for each of the three endogenous variables across the three measures of expectations and the four countries considered here.[33] According to these tests, the output gap (HP-filter) is exogenous to both inflation and inflation expectations in most cases, notably in France, Italy and the United Kingdom (except for the VAR with the second measure of British consumers' expectations). For Germany, however, the joint hypothesis that inflation and inflation expectations do not Granger-cause the output gap is rejected on all measures of expectations.

What of the process governing expectations formation? The Granger causality test results are mixed: four of our eight measures of consumers' expectations display a significant response to lagged values of the output gap or of inflation or to both of them, while the other four don't. In contrast, exogeneity of the Consensus Forecasts can only be rejected in one case (Germany). Again, this may be interpreted as evidence against simple backward-looking models of expectations formation. But we still need to check the robustness of these results, for instance to different measures of the output gap.

Finally, as to the inflation process itself, our results suggest that our measure of the output gap Granger-causes inflation in Germany and Italy but not in France, or, if expectations are measured by the EC survey data, the United Kingdom. As to how inflation expectations affect inflation, the evidence is again mixed. In Italy, each of our measures of inflation expectations exerts a significant influence on inflation. By contrast, inflation in Germany and the United Kingdom does not seem to depend on any of our measures of inflation expectations. This points against the New Keynesian model of inflation. However, our VARs do not fully capture the forward-looking nature of the New Keynesian Phillips curve as they make inflation depend on the lags of the expectations variable, not its contemporaneous value. Furthermore, the overlapping nature of the inflation variable (which measures inflation over the past *four* quarters) inevitably leads to highly significant coefficients of the first three lags of inflation which may well soak up some of influence of inflation expectations and the output gap. Re-estimation at annual frequency might shed more light on this issue.

4 Conclusions

In this chapter, we compare the properties of two sets of survey expectations which are drawn from the European Commission's consumer survey and from the expert surveys conducted by Consensus Economics. Our analysis yields the following results:

- The quantification of the qualitative data from the consumer survey requires the choice of a scaling variable to capture respondents' perceptions of past inflation. This chapter uses actual past inflation, as well as a measure of perceived past inflation calculated from the answers to Question 5 of the survey, as scaling variables. Comparing the resulting expectations series, we find that the errors[34] of the alternative expectations measures differ little in Germany and France, while the expectations series scaled with perceived past inflation perform much better than those based on actual past inflation for Italy and the United Kingdom.

• Comparing the predictive power of the two sets of survey expectations, we find that for three of the four countries (Germany, Italy and the United Kingdom), experts' forecasts are much more precise than household expectations. The Consensus Forecasts for Germany, Italy and the United Kingdom manage to outperform the naïve extrapolative forecast by considerable margins.

• On rationality, most of our survey measures of inflation expectations prove unbiased. Most are efficient vis-à-vis the information in past forecast errors (evidence of weak-form efficiency). However, only one of the forecast errors is orthogonal to all of the information variables considered.

• As to the interaction of expected and actual inflation in a VAR framework, most measures of expectations are Granger-caused by subsequently realized inflation rates (but less often the other way around). The surveyed households and experts appear forward-looking in that their expectations ultimately revert towards fully "rational" values.

• Finally, to shed more light on both expectations formation and on the inflation process, we estimate simple trivariate VARs of inflation, one-year-ahead inflation expectations and output. While some of our measures of inflation expectations depend on lagged values of the output gap and/or of inflation, others do not. For three out of four countries, the expert expectations collected by Consensus Economics are exogenous to both lagged output and inflation. This may be taken as evidence against simple backward-looking models of expectations formation.

Overall, our results suggest that expectations are neither fully rational (in the sense of Muth) nor completely backward-looking. Both dimensions of expectations formation have important monetary policy implications. On the one hand, backward-looking elements in the formation of expectations introduce additional lags into the transmission mechanism which reinforce the need for monetary policy makers to adopt a forward-looking approach. On the other, if expectations are at least partly forward-looking, the efficacy of monetary policy depends on the ability of the central bank to stabilize private sector expectations. A clear definition of the ultimate objective and the announcement of a comprehensible and transparent monetary policy strategy play key roles in this context.

Notes

1 Wilhelm-Epstein-Strasse 14, 60431 Frankfurt/Main, Germany, e-mail: christina.gerberding@bundesbank.de. Please note that the chapter represents the author's personal opinions and does not necessarily reflect the views of the Deutsche Bundesbank.
2 For more see ECB, *Monthly Bulletin*, May 2000, pp. 37–55, or also Mylonas and Schich (1999).

3 Pesaran (1989, p. 210) therefore calls these types of calculations "theory-loaded implicit methods" and notes: "such 'implicit' methods of the measurement of inflation expectations are, however, only as good as the theory and the auxiliary assumptions that underlie them".

4 An overview of this literature is given in Thomas (1999).

5 Cf. Reckwerth (1997), p. 13f.

6 For more on this see Pesaran (1989), p. 210.

7 At the microeconomic level it is also possible to work directly with ordinal responses. Nerlove (1983) may be regarded as a pioneer in this field. However, the use of ordinal measures of expectations in conventional, aggregated time series models is extremely time-consuming, if not impossible altogether; therefore, qualitative data generally need to be quantified for studies of this type.

8 For a detailed description, see Reckwerth (1997) or Nielsen (2003). By contrast, the regression approach proposed by Pesaran is better suited to the enterprise survey data he uses. Cf. Pesaran (1989), p. 221ff. and Batchelor and Orr (1988), p. 322.

9 The precise method of deriving this term is described in Reckwerth (1997), p. 56ff.

10 Batchelor and Orr (1988) use a complicated method to determine the moderate rate of inflation; this method requires, *inter alia*, quantifying the "natural" rate of inflation. For more see Batchelor and Orr (1988), p. 322f.

11 Simmons and Weiserbs (1992) and Berk (1999, 2002) use this approach.

12 See Deutsche Bundesbank (2002, 2004).

13 See Berk (1999, 2002).

14 Another method, which does not rely on the assumption of unbiasedness, is to estimate the threshold parameter by regressing the official inflation rate on the unscaled mean of the perceived inflation rate (Bennett 1984). As both methods lead to very similar results, we pursue only the first one here.

15 See Berk (1999), p. 9.

16 See Gerberding (2001), p. 36.

17 Cf. Keane and Runkle (1990), p. 715.

18 See Laster *et al.* (1999).

19 In Germany, 26 institutions are surveyed at present (in France: 17, in Italy: 13, in Spain: 10, in the Netherlands: 9): DG Bank, BHF Bank, Deutsche Bank Research, DGZ Deka Bank, JP Morgan, MM Warburg, WGZ Bank, Bank Julius Baer, BfG Bank, Commerzbank, Dresdner Bank, Invesco Bank, RWI Essen, Sal Oppenheim, Bayerische Landesbank, FAZ Institut, HypoVereinsbank, Bankgesellschaft Berlin, Helaba Frankfurt, IW Cologne, DIW Berlin, HSBC Trinkaus, IFO Munich, IfW Kiel, Merrill Lynch, Westdeutsche LBank.

20 See: Consensus Economics, *Consensus Forecasts*, September 2005, p. 8.

21 In 1990 (1991) the country panellists were asked to provide additional forecasts for individual quarters as part of the February (March), July and November surveys. In 1992 and 1993, the quarter-by-quarter forecasts were part of the February, May, August and November surveys, and since the beginning of 1994, they have been included in the March, June, September and December surveys. In Figure 7.2, the two missing observations for the second quarter of 1990 and 1991 were approximated by interpolating the preceding and succeeding "observation".

22 In Muth's own words: "Expectations, since they are informed predictions of future events, are essentially the same as the predictions of the relevant economic theory" Muth (1961), p. 316.

23 Many of these studies make use of the Michigan and Livingston surveys of inflation expectations. See Roberts (1997), Croushore (1998), Grant Thomas (1999) and the older studies quoted there.

24 For more see Holden and Peel (1990), p. 124.

25 Examples include Baghestani (1992), Batchelor and Dua (1989) and Roberts (1997).

26 Cf. Pesaran (1989), p. 2.

27 Among these critics are Akerlof and Yellen (1985a/b, 1987), Pesaran (1989), Ball (1991) and Evans and Honkapohja (2000).
28 See, for instance, Grant and Lloyd (1998), Berk (1999, 2000) or Forsells and Kenny (2002).
29 See Forsells and Kenny (2002), p. 20.
30 Based on visual inspection of the data, we decided to allow for deterministic trends in the data (but not in the CE). However, the results are reasonably robust to changes in the trend assumptions.
31 See Doepke *et al.* (2005), p. 7f.
32 See, for instance, Forsells and Kenny (2002), p. 21, and Mehra (2002).
33 The full set of estimation results is available from the author on request.
34 As revealed by RMSE (root mean squared errors).

References

Akerlof, G.A. and J.L. Yellen (1985a), A near-rational model of the business cycle, with wage and price inertia, *Quarterly Journal of Economics*, 100 (supplement): 823–838.

Akerlof, G.A. and J.L. Yellen (1985b), Can small deviations from rationality make significant differences to economic equilibria?, *American Economic Review*, 75 (4): 709–720.

Akerlof, G.A. and J.L. Yellen (1987), Rational models of irrational behavior, *AEA Papers and Proceedings*, May 1987: 137–142.

Baghestani, H. (1992), Survey evidence on the Muthian rationality of the inflation forecasts of U.S. consumers, *Oxford Bulletin of Economics and Statistics*, 54: 173–186.

Batchelor, R.A. and P. Dua (1989), Household versus economist forecasts of inflation: a reassessment, *Journal of Money, Credit, and Banking*, 21: 252–257.

Batchelor, R.A. and A.B. Orr (1988), Inflation expectations revisited, *Economica*, 55: 317–331.

Batini, N. and A. Haldane (1999), Forward-looking rules for monetary policy, *Bank of England Working Paper*, 91.

Berk, J.M. (1999), Measuring inflation expectations: a survey data approach, *Applied Economics*, 3: 1467–1480.

Berk, J.M. (2002), Consumers' inflation expectations and monetary policy in Europe, *Contemporary Economic Policy*, 20 (2): 122–132.

Carlson, J.A. and M. Parkin (1975), Inflation expectations, *Economica*, 42: 123–137.

Consensus Economics (no date), *Consensus Forecasts – A Digest of International Economic Forecasts*, London: Consensus Economics, various editions.

Croushore, D. (1998), Evaluating inflation forecasts, *Working Paper*. 98-14, Federal Reserve Bank of Philadelphia.

Deutsche Bundesbank (1998), Financial market prices as monetary policy indicators, *Monthly Report*, July 1998: 49–67.

Deutsche Bundesbank (2001), The information content of survey data on expected price developments for monetary policy, *Monthly Report*, January 2001: 35–49.

Deutsche Bundesbank (2002), Consumer prices and the changeover from Deutsche Mark to euro, *Monthly Report*, July: 15–24.

Deutsche Bundesbank (2004), The euro and prices two years on, *Monthly Report*, January: 15–28.

Doepke, J., J. Dovern, U. Fritsche and J. Slacalek (2005), European inflation expectations dynamics, *Deutsche Bundesbank Discussion Paper*, 1, 37/2005.

European Central Bank (2000), Monetary policy transmission in the euro area, *Monthly Bulletin*: July 2000, 43–58.

Forsells, M. and G. Kenny (2002), The rationality of consumers's inflation expectations: survey-based evidence for the euro area, *ECB Working Paper*, 163, August.

Gerberding, C. (2001), The information content of survey data on expected price developments for monetary policy, *Deutsche Bundesbank Discussion Paper*, 9/01.

Grant, A.P. and L.B. Thomas (1999), Inflationary expectations and rationality revisited, *Economic Letters*, 62, (3) March: 331–338.

Hansen, L.P. and R.J. Hodrick (1980), Forward exchange rates as optimal predictors of future spot rates: an econometric analysis, *Journal of Political Economy*, 88: 829–853.

Holden, K. and D.A. Peel (1990), On testing for unbiasedness and efficiency of forecasts, *Manchester School*, 58 (2) June: 120–127.

Keane, M.P. and D.E. Runkle (1990), Testing the rationality of price forecasts: new evidence from panel data, *American Economic Review*, 80, 4: 714–735.

Laster, D., P. Bennet and I.S. Geoum (1999), Rational bias in macroeconomic forecasts, *Quarterly Journal of Economics*, 114: 293–318.

Łyziak, T. (2003), Consumer inflation expectations in Poland, *ECB Working Paper*, 287, November 2003.

McCallum, B.T. (1976), Rational expectations and the estimation of econometric models: an alternative procedure, *International Economic Review*, 17: 484–490.

Mehra, Y. (2002), Survey measures of expected inflation: revisiting the issues of predictive content and rationality, *Federal Reserve Bank of Richmond Economic Quarterly*, 88/3: 17–36.

Muth, J.F. (1961), Rational expectations and the theory of price movements, *Econometrica*, 29: 315–335.

Naish, H.F. (1993), The near optimality of adaptive expectations, *Journal of Economic Behavior and Organization*, 20: 3–22.

Nerlove, M. (1983), Expectations, plans and realizations in theory and practice, *Econometrica*, 51: 1251–1279.

Nielsen, H. (2003), Essays on expectations, Aachen 2003.

Paloviita, M. and M. Virén (2005), The role of expectations in the inflation process in the euro area, *Bank of Finland Discussion Paper*, 6/2005.

Pesaran, M.H. (1989), *The Limits to Rational Expectations*, Oxford and New York: Basil Blackwell.

Reckwerth, J. (1997), Inflation and output in Germany: the role of inflation expectations, *Deutsche Bundesbank Discussion Paper*, 5/97.

Roberts, J.M. (1998), Inflation expectations and the transmission of monetary policy, *Board of Governors of the Federal Reserve System Working Paper*, Washington, DC, October 1998.

Sargent, T.J. (1973), Rational expectations, the real rate of interest and the natural rate of unemployment, *Brookings Papers on Economic Activity*, 2: 429–472.

Theil, H. (1954), *Linear Aggregation of Economic Relations*, Amsterdam: North-Holland.

Thomas Jr., L.B. (1999), Survey measures of expected US inflation, *Journal of Economics Perspectives*, 12 (4): 125–144.

8 The role of expectations in the inflation process in the euro area

Maritta Paloviita and Matti Virén[1]

1 Introduction

Controlling inflation is the primary objective of central banks. For this purpose, central banks need to know both the determinants of inflation and the basic features of its transmission mechanism. Given that both theoretical considerations and empirical evidence suggest that inflation expectations are a crucial element in these matters, the nature of inflation expectations must be carefully examined.

Somewhat surprisingly, inflation expectations have been analysed relatively little. This is mainly because we have only a limited amount of data on "realized" inflation expectations. In most cases, inflation expectations have been derived not from observed survey or published forecast data but by using the orthogonality conditions connected with the Rational Expectations Hypothesis (REH) and employing the GMM estimator. This enables estimation and testing of key behavioural equations, but it does not really allow for an analysis of the determinants of inflation expectations. Thus the estimation results for Phillips curves are not very informative in terms of the inflation propagation mechanism and inflation expectations. Nor are they very informative for policy decisions. Take the simple question of how to reduce inflation. Conventional Phillips curve results just show the impact of the cyclical situation (e.g. output gap) on current inflation, while the role of inflation expectations stays in a "black box", even though inflation expectations is clearly the most important variable.[2] Phillips curves suffer from other problems as well. They usually fit the data poorly, and reasonable results can be obtained only by adding some auxiliary variables to the estimating equations (such as lags, in the case of the "hybrid" New Keynesian Phillips curve). Against this background, we clearly need a more general – and more data-consistent – representation of the model.

The situation is quite different if we use data on "realized" inflation expectations. Then we can at least observe the independent role of inflation expectations. We can also see how inflation expectations react to other variables or policies or policy regimes.

The main sources for expectations data are the regularly published macroeconomic forecasts of governments (finance ministries), research institutes and international organizations such as OECD. All these publish at least some form of inflation forecast. The problem with most of the data is that they cannot be compared across countries, and it is difficult to construct a consistent aggregate euro area data from these series. Thus we are often limited to OECD data. Fortunately, the Consensus Forecast also provides survey-based inflation forecasts in the same format for all European countries. The problem is that the data only cover the period 1989–2003 which is very short for all analytical purposes.[3]

Recently, we have seen a growing interest in the nature and role of inflation expectations. Thus, for instance, Levin *et al.* (2004) provide an analysis of the volatility of inflation expectations and the sensitivity of expectations to realized inflation.[4] A special emphasis in the chapter is on the distinction between inflation targeting (and non-targeting) countries. We continue these analyses by specifying a small VAR model which not only includes inflation and inflation expectations but also the real economy driving variable, output, or more precisely the output gap. This model can be seen as an empirical generalization of the Phillips curve and an umbrella that nests Phillips curve variants. And it enables us to analyse the determinants of inflation expectations.

In what follows, we briefly introduce the analytical framework. Then in Section 3, we report and discuss the results. Section 4 presents some concluding remarks.

2 Analysis

Our empirical analysis deals with the euro area and so the data are from the euro area countries only. The analysis is based on a simple VAR model, which in its basic form consists of three variables: inflation (Δp), inflation expectations (Δp^e), and the output gap. In some instances the model is completed with world (US) inflation, which gives us a type of VARX representation. Moreover the output gap is replaced by the labour share (LS), GDP growth (ΔGDP), or by a simple time trend deviation of GDP.[5] The choice between these measures is known to be a difficult conceptual and measurement issue, but in this study the choice does not play a crucial role as it turns out from subsequent estimation results. It may well be that the issue is more compelling when estimating a conventional one-equation Phillips curve.

The key variable is inflation expectations. The series come from the OECD, although Consensus Forecast data are also used. In the basic set-up, Δp^e is the inflation forecast for the following year, which is published by the OECD in June of the current year. Thus it is assumed that the decisions on pricing and volume of output, as well as the formation of inflation expectations, occur at the same moment.[6] We cannot pin down the exact timing of decisions with annual data, so we do the analysis with the forecast for the following year, which is published in December of the current year, and with the forecast for the current year, which is published in December of the previous year.[7] The quality of OECD forecasts from the point of view of Rational Expectations has been analysed on several occasions (see e.g. OECD 1993 and Virén 2005). The analyses have shown that there are some problems with unbiasedness, especially in the early days, but that the quality of the data is reasonable also in this respect. Basically, the same result is also reached in this study (see Appendix 8.1 for details).[8]

In identifying the shocks we use the simple Cholesky decomposition. This is mainly motivated by the fact that our VAR model encompasses several theoretical models and at this stage we do not want to tie it to any of them. Moreover, if one considers the structural VAR identification schemes, none of them would appear to be an obvious candidate in this case. The Blanchard-Quah (1989) identification scheme, which is widely applied, is not easily applicable to our three-variable case, considering especially the difference in perceived roles of actual and expected inflation. As for more general schemes (Amisano and Giannini 1997), we found that adopting one of them might bring too much specification uncertainty into the analysis.

Moreover, the variable ordering with the Cholesky decomposition needs only a small amount of experimenting. The recursive system we have in mind comes down to the following variable ordering: output gap, inflation expectations (for the next period) and actual inflation. The first two variables could be reversed in order, to give the following alternatives for application and comparison: $var1 = \{y, \Delta p^e, \Delta p\}$ and $var2 = \{\Delta p^e, y, \Delta p\}$. These orderings can be viewed from a purely technical perspective although they reflect deeper differences in economic modelling strategies. First, one may consider the determination of output in an RBC framework and see output shocks as deriving mainly from non-monetary factors (e.g. technology) and hence only weakly responding to inflation shocks. Alternatively, one could see the output gap as determined by the future path of the real interest rate and hence exogenous to current inflation and inflation expectations.

These considerations would put the output gap first (ordering $var1$). But one could also see inflation expectations as having a more profound role in the model. One may think that inflation expectations are related to expectations of future monetary policy. Thus inflation-expectation shocks are related to such things as changes in the credibility of monetary policy, perceived changes in the effectiveness of monetary policy, and policy prerequisites (e.g. from the institutional point of view). Not all of these need be conditional on output developments, so that the $var2$ ordering could be plausible as well.

What is clear, however, is that actual inflation cannot be first in the ordering because actual inflation reflects both output and expected inflation shocks. In addition, it reflects all kinds of short-term shocks which are related e.g. to imperfect control over monetary policy and to price shocks induced by market imperfections. If we had a recursive system in which both actual inflation and output would precede expected inflation we could interpret that system as a representation of the New Keynesian Phillips curve from the point of view of rational expectations. Then, however, there would be very little room for an independent role for inflation expectations. They would merely reflect changes in actual inflation and output – in the same way as in the "instrumental equations" for expected inflation in the single-equation model. The idea of estimating the VAR was, however, to get more of a general assessment of the role of inflation expectations and not a priori to restrict its role to something of little importance.

In what follows, we use the two above-mentioned orderings, and the results turn out qualitatively similar. They differ somewhat because the residuals are contemporaneously correlated. This is due to the annual frequency, which is dictated by the OECD forecasting system.

The analyses make use of the euro area data which cover (after two lags) the period 1979–2003 (25 observations). The sample is very small, and artificial in that the euro area did not exist before 1999. Partly because of this, we also use individual country data, and pooled cross-country data with different pooling and estimation restrictions. With the pooled data, the total number of observations is 292.

The main problem in our analysis is the apparent non-stationarity of some of the time series (within our sample period). If we use the output gap as the real economy driving variable, it is, at least in its Hodrick–Prescott variant, stationary.[9] But with the sample period of 1977–2003 both inflation and inflation expectations are non-stationary by standard tests. If we want to preserve the set of variables as in the Phillips curve, we must resort to first differences of the three variables (i.e. second differences of price level and output and first differences of inflation expectations). If we used labour share as the driving variable, we would end up with all three variables (inflation, inflation expectations and labour share) being non-stationary. Finally, we could use GDP (Gross Domestic Product in constant prices) directly. The growth rate of GDP is roughly stationary in the same way as the deviation of GDP from linear time trend.[10] Both are used in the analysis – mainly to evaluate the robustness of the results.

Using the Vector Error Correction Model would solve some of the problems and we carry out the analysis within that framework also. More precisely, we impose an error-correction term on the inflation and inflation expectations terms, assuming that inflation and inflation expectations cannot diverge in the long-run. Unfortunately, the whole sample is characterized by declining inflation, so that inflation expectations are always below current inflation. Hence the cointegrating restriction, $\Delta p^e = \Delta p$, is not consistent in the long run with the data in this sample.[11] But it makes little difference whether a more data-consistent error-correction term is used (see Appendix 8.2). In fact, the Vector Error Correction model's results are so close to the simple VAR results that they are not considered in detail here.[12]

The VAR model suffers as well from some other well-known shortcomings. All analyses are related to shocks in different variables. Thus we cannot consider the effects of expected changes in different variables. Shocks to inflation expectations may seem a bit difficult to interpret, but since inflation expectations essentially reflect the general public's expectations of policy credibility and effectiveness, the corresponding shocks are just as plausible as actual inflation and/or output shocks. Measurement is then another issue. It may well be that our measures (data) of inflation expectations suffer more from measurement errors than do actual inflation and the output gap. Here we can do very little to clarify this point. Using different (survey) data might give some idea of the seriousness of this problem.

3 Reporting and interpreting the results

The main data are illustrated in the following figures: Figure 8.1 contains the aggregate data and Figure 8.2 the (pooled) individual country data, which are more volatile; Figure 8.3 illustrates difference between different forecasts and, finally, Figure 8.4, the nontrivial relationship between actual and forecast inflation with the aggregate data. As for the VAR analysis, we follow here the standard practice of reporting three sets of results: parameter estimates of the VAR model(s), variance decompositions and impulse responses. Because we have so many alternatives for specifying the output variable (price index, country set, and lag structure), we must be selective in presenting the results. In any case, we try to cover all relevant combinations.[13]

In estimating the VAR, we must fix the lag length. In our case, it was difficult to choose between one lag, VAR(1), and two lags, VAR(2), which are the only relevant alternatives for our data. The problem is due to the fact that the second lag is only marginally significant (Table 8.1 and Table 8.2). Generally, it is (only) the output gap which requires the second lag. Fortunately, the lag length does not essentially affect the qualitative nature of the results, but it does make some difference, as can be seen from Table 8.3. As for the Cholesky decomposition, we report the majority of results for the *var1* ordering. This is motivated by the fact that output is more persistent than inflation expectations and that the *var1* ordering is more conservative as regards inflation expectations. Thus, in terms of variance decompositions, it may give the lower bound for the relative importance of various shocks.

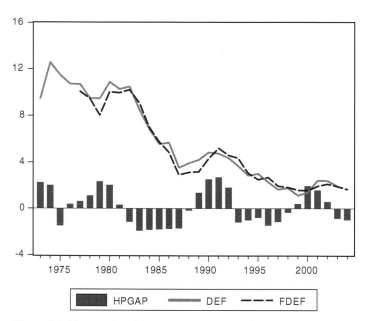

Figure 8.1 Time series with aggregate euro area data.

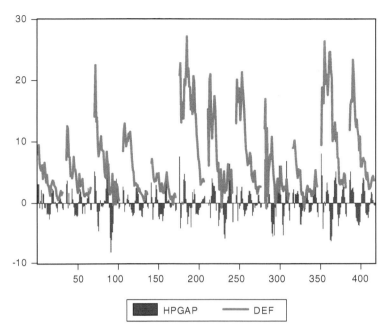

Figure 8.2 Time series with pooled euro area data.

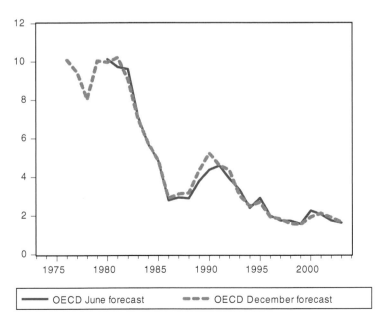

Figure 8.3 OECD inflation forecasts for the following year.

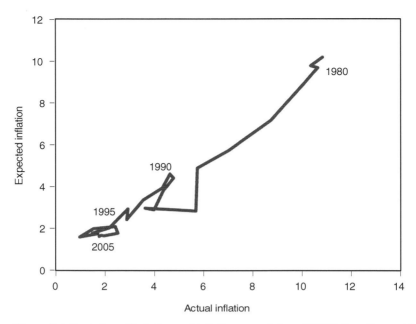

Figure 8.4 Evolution of inflation and inflation expectations (OECD June forecasts).

In addition to the choice of the lag length and variable ordering in the Cholesky decomposition, we face the choice of inflation variable. Thus we must choose between GDP deflator (DEF) and consumer prices (PC). Both alternatives can be defended, and partly for this reason, we estimated our models with both variables (concerning both actual data and expected/forecast values). In what follows, we report primarily the results for the GDP deflator because this choice seems more consistent with the choice of scale variable (GDP gap) and because we focus on economy-wide developments in prices and output.

Technically, the reporting runs as follows: estimation results are reported in Table 8.1 and Table 8.2, variance decompositions for different Cholesky decompositions and data sets in Tables 8.3–8.6, and impulse responses (with analytical confidence intervals) in Figures 8.5–8.6. Here we mainly consider aggregated data and pooled cross-country data.[14] In presenting the variance decompositions, we scrutinize only the very short-run results (for horizons of one and two years) and long-run results (in practice, a time horizon of 20 years). These three data points illustrate most of the interesting changes: all changes are more or less monotonic (as can be seen already from the reported impulse responses).

A brief summary of the main findings and discussion of their implications for monetary policy and further research follows.

1   In general, our VAR model performs reasonably well for both the aggregate data and pooled cross-country data.[15] Moreover, the results for different

Table 8.1 Estimation results with aggregate euro area and pooled (stacked) cross-country data

Dependent variable	gap	Δp^e	Δp	gap	Δp^e	Δp
Data	Aggregate euro area			Pooled cross-country		
gap, 1	1.047	0.370	0.300	1.094	0.137	0.223
	(4.33)	(1.79)	(1.81)	(19.42)	(2.46)	(3.71)
gap, 2	−0.509	−0.177	−0.172	−0.489	−0.050	−0.172
	(2.60)	(1.06)	(1.28)	(8.95)	(0.92)	(2.95)
Δp^e, 1	0.333	0.604	0.643	−0.105	0.797	.0735
	(0.94)	(2.00)	(2.64)	(1.37)	(10.51)	(9.01)
Δp^e, 2	−0.527	−0.139	−0.396	−0.150	−0.022	0.022
	(1.33)	(0.41)	(1.46)	(1.76)	(0.26)	(0.24)
Δp, 1	−0.127	0.174	0.317	0.155	0.044	0.171
	(0.33)	(0.53)	(1.21)	(2.19)	(0.63)	(2.27)
Δp, 2	0.243	0.172	0.383	0.025	0.008	0.055
	(0.73)	(0.61)	(1.68)	(0.40)	(0.14)	(0.83)
R2/SEE	0.795	0.912	0.959	0.703	0.890	0.915
	0.825	0.705	0.568	1.409	1.396	1.503
	Δgap	$\Delta^2 p^e$	$\Delta^2 p$	Δgap	$\Delta^2 p^e$	$\Delta^2 p$
Δgap, 1	0.449	0.553	0.275	0.365	0.153	0.156
	(1.63)	(2.57)	(1.65)	(5.58)	(2.60)	(2.38)
Δgap, 2	−0.101	−0.164	−0.079	−0.053	0.120	0.036
	(0.38)	(0.80)	(0.50)	(0.81)	(2.04)	(0.55)
$\Delta^2 p^e$, 1	0.330	−0.056	0.805	−0.101	−0.001	0.608
	(0.85)	(0.19)	(3.44)	(1.23)	(0.01)	(7.41)
$\Delta^2 p^e$, 2	−0.127	0.009	0.334	0.127	−0.031	0.293
	(0.26)	(0.02)	(1.15)	(1.49)	(0.39)	(3.46)
$\Delta^2 p$, 1	−0.576	0.244	−0.484	0.040	0.047	−0.463
	(1.23)	(0.67)	(1.70)	(0.55)	(0.71)	(6.32)
$\Delta^2 p$, 2	−0.180	0.396	−0.006	−0.005	0.060	−0.147
	(0.45)	(1.26)	(0.02)	(0.07)	(0.98)	(2.17)
R2/SEE	0.336	0.349	0.591	0.134	0.010	0.203
	1.029	0.801	0.622	1.690	1.518	1.683

Notes
The first six rows correspond to level-form model and subsequent six rows are from the first-difference specification. Pooled cross-country data are un-weighted; the corresponding variance decompositions are reported in Tables 8.5 and 8.6. All estimates are OLS estimates.

variable definitions and specifications of the VAR are very similar (see Table 8.4). To be sure, differencing makes some difference, and this is a bit alarming as it could reflect some weaknesses in the dynamic specification. Most likely the result reflects the changing nature of inflation which in turn reflects the change in inflation objectives. One way to solve this problem would be to introduce an explicit inflation target to the system in the manner e.g. Gerlach and Svensson (2003). We have not experimented with this option, but introducing world (US) inflation could be seen as one manner of solution to this problem. It does not, however, provide a solution to the open

Table 8.2 Estimation results with pooled cross-country data

Dependent variable	gap	Δp^e	Δp
gap, 1	1.119	0.158	0.257
	(21.79)	(4.05)	(4.87)
gap, 2	−0.529	−0.105	−0.188
	(10.89)	(2.82)	(3.76)
Δp^e, 1	−0.048	0.634	0.579
	(0.73)	(8.85)	(7.38)
Δp^e, 2	−0.158	0.081	0.064
	(2.20)	(1.17)	(0.79)
Δp,1	0.108	0.122	0.304
	(1.68)	(2.24)	(4.26)
Δp,2	0.028	−0.054	0.001
	(0.50)	(1.06)	(0.01)
R2/SEE	0.705/1.374	0.889/1.364	0.913/1.485
Wald	7.30	74.78	3.72
	Δgap	$\Delta^2 p^e$	$\Delta^2 p$
Δgap, 1	0.417	0.161	0.223
	(6.86)	(3.78)	(3.82)
Δgap, 2	−0.120	0.026	0.057
	(1.95)	(0.59)	(0.98)
$\Delta^2 p^e$, 1	−0.044	−0.069	0.502
	(0.60)	(0.98)	(6.53)
$\Delta^2 p^e$, 2	−0.115	−0.032	0.270
	(1.58)	(0.47)	(3.52)
$\Delta^2 p$,1	0.003	0.137	−0.349
	(0.45)	(2.54)	(4.94)
$\Delta^2 p$,2	−0.052	0.042	−0.166
	(0.83)	(0.82)	(2.51)
R2/SEE	0.135/1.646	0.027/1.492	0.187/1.663
Wald	11.48	109.22	68.96

Notes
As in Table 8.1, the first 6 rows correspond to the level form model and the subsequent 6 rows the first difference model. Wald test statistics test the hypothesis that lagged inflation terms in the gap sum up to zero and in the inflation and expected inflation equations to one. The 5 per cent critical value is 3.80. Estimates are (un-weighted) OLS estimates with a fixed effects LS estimator; in the difference form, the fixed effects are disregarded.

issue (Table 8.4). For us, what is more important is that introducing this variable does not essentially change the results.

2   Inflation expectations are very important in the determination of inflation. Innovations in expectations account for more than one-third of the (forecast) variance of inflation, irrespective of time horizon. Even in the long run, inflation expectations exert a significant and independent effect on actual inflation developments and their relative importance increases rather than decreases with the length of the time horizon. The percentage share can go up to 50 per cent. In other words, changes in output growth and (past) inflation cannot fully explain the future path of inflation.

Table 8.3 Variance decompositions for time horizons 1, 2 and 20

Ordering	var1, 2 lags			var2, 2 lags			var1, 1 lag			var1, 1 lag			var1, 1 lag		
Data	OECD 1979–2003			OECD 1979–2003			OECD 1979–2003			Consensus 1991–2003			OECD 1991–2003		
	gap	Δp^e	Δp	Δp^e	gap	Δp	gap	Δp^e	Δp	gap	Δpc^e	Δpc	gap	Δpc^e	Δpc
gap, 1	100.0	0.0	0.0	17.7	82.3	0.0	100	0.0	0.0	100.0	0.0	0.0	100.0	0.0	0.0
gap, 2	97.7	2.0	0.2	27.0	72.7	0.2	99.2	0.0	0.8	98.7	0.3	0.9	97.4	0.1	2.5
gap, 20	93.1	5.2	1.7	31.0	67.3	1.7	92.1	5.4	2.4	92.0	5.4	2.5	92.9	1.7	5.4
Δp^e, 1	17.7	82.3	0	100.0	0.0	0.0	25.5	74.5	0.0	4.3	95.7	0	6.5	93.5	0.0
Δp^e, 2	36.0	63.2	0.8	91.3	7.9	0.8	40.6	57.7	1.7	7.5	90.7	1.8	10.7	88.2	1.2
Δp^e, 20	47.7	40.7	11.6	71.7	16.7	11.6	64.7	33.9	1.4	26.1	71.8	2.1	25.0	73.7	1.2
Δp, 1	2.7	20.8	76.5	23.3	0.2	76.5	19.0	14.6	66.4	10.7	31.1	58.2	9.0	28.6	62.3
Δp, 2	28.1	38.3	33.5	60.6	5.9	33.5	30.9	30.9	38.2	24.6	35.3	40.1	19.5	41.0	39.5
Δp, 20	42.9	28.3	28.8	56.0	15.2	28.8	62.2	25.1	12.7	42.7	32.5	24.8	36.2	41.1	22.7
	Δgap	$\Delta^2 p^e$	$\Delta^2 p$	$\Delta^2 p^e$	Δgap	$\Delta^2 p$	Δgap	$\Delta^2 p^e$	$\Delta^2 p$	Δgap	$\Delta^2 pc^e$	$\Delta^2 pc$	Δgap	$\Delta^2 pc^e$	$\Delta^2 pc$
Δgap, 1	100	0.0	0.0	19.1	80.9	0.0	100	0.0	0.0	100.0	0.0	0.0	100.0	0.0	0.0
Δgap, 2	93.4	0.2	6.4	19.5	74.0	6.4	94.9	0.1	5.0	99.0	0.8	0.2	99.7	0.0	0.3
Δgap, 20	90.4	3.5	6.1	23.0	70.9	6.1	89.3	5.5	5.2	98.4	1.3	0.3	99.6	0.0	0.3
$\Delta^2 p^e$, 1	19.1	80.9	0.0	100.0	0.0	0.0	9.8	90.2	0.0	0.2	99.8	0	4.7	95.3	0.0
$\Delta^2 p^e$, 2	45.1	53.2	1.7	73.6	24.7	1.7	22.5	76.1	1.5	7.5	87.3	5.2	9.9	88.8	1.3
$\Delta^2 p^e$, 20	47.9	50.3	1.9	73.6	24.5	1.9	30.5	66.9	2.6	10.5	84.4	5.1	11.8	86.9	1.4
$\Delta^2 p$, 1	1.1	26.4	72.5	25.7	1.7	72.5	0.1	32.8	67.1	7.1	33.6	59.2	5.0	41.6	53.4
$\Delta^2 p$, 2	31.4	30.8	37.7	52.1	10.1	37.7	16.8	48.0	35.2	12.6	34.4	53.1	13.4	41.9	44.6
$\Delta^2 p$, 20	41.6	26.7	31.7	50.4	17.9	31.7	26.0	42.0	32.0	15.5	33.1	51.4	15.8	40.7	43.5

Notes

The first nine rows correspond to level-form model and the subsequent nine rows correspond to first-difference specification. Δ^2 denotes second (log) difference. The data are aggregate euro area data. Inflation expectations are derived from either OECD or Consensus Forecast.

Table 8.4 Comparison of variance decompositions using different specifications

Variable to be decomposed (below), horizon	gap	Δp^e	Δp
Level, HP gap	42.9	28.3	28.8
Level, HP gap, December forecast	67.5	15.1	17.4
Level, HP gap, December forecast for the current year	51.9	4.4	43.7
Level, LS, trend	28.2	51.4	20.4
Level, ΔGDP	29.7	41.8	28.6
Level, GDP trend	39.9	41.5	18.5
Level, HP gap, + US Def	29.6	7.1	63.4
Level, HP gap, consumer prices	36.6	53.5	10.0
Difference, HP gap	41.6	26.7	31.7
Difference, Δ²GDP	17.9	50.1	32.0
Difference, HP gap + US Def	25.6	18.1	56.2
Difference, HP gap, consumer prices	25.3	61.0	13.7
Difference, HP gap, December forecast	41.6	32.2	26.2
Difference, HP gap, December forecast for the current year	36.4	40.5	23.1

Notes
All numbers are long-run inflation variance decompositions, Δp, 20 in a VAR model with two lags and var1 variance decomposition. The data are aggregate euro area data.

Table 8.5 Variance decompositions with pooled cross-country data for the euro area

Variable to be decomposed (below), horizon	gap	Δp^e	Δp
gap, 1	100.0	0.0	0.0
gap, 2	99.2	0.0	0.8
gap, 20	95.1	2.3	2.6
Δp^e, 1	3.8	96.2	0.0
Δp^e, 2	7.3	92.6	0.1
Δp^e, 20	15.1	84.1	0.7
Δp, 1	2.0	35.6	62.4
Δp, 2	8.8	54.5	36.7
Δp, 20	13.5	69.2	17.3
	Δgap	$\Delta^2 p^e$	$\Delta^2 p$
Δgap, 1	100.0	0.0	0.0
Δgap, 2	99.5	0.4	0.1
Δgap, 20	97.8	2.1	0.1
$\Delta^2 p^e$, 1	2.6	97.4	0.0
$\Delta^2 p^e$, 2	5.4	94.4	0.2
$\Delta^2 p^e$, 20	9.5	90.2	0.4
$\Delta^2 p$, 1	0.3	29.3	70.4
$\Delta^2 p$, 2	3.9	29.4	66.6
$\Delta^2 p$, 20	5.6	29.1	65.3

Notes
Estimates are based on an artificial euro economy obtained by stacking the time series of gap, Δp^e and Δp from the 12 countries as a single (unweighted) time series. Var1 Cholesky decomposition with one lag is used in both models.

Table 8.6 Variance decompositions with individual country data

Variable to be decomposed (below), horizon	gap	Δp^e	Δp
Austria, Δp, 20	28.6	46.9	24.5
Belgium, Δp, 20	16.2	52.5	31.3
Finland, Δp, 20	37.8	44.6	17.6
France, Δp, 20	36.9	49.2	13.8
Germany, Δp, 20	30.7	42.1	27.2
Greece, Δp, 20	13.7	81.9	4.3
Ireland, Δp, 20	16.3	38.6	45.1
Italy, Δp, 20	51.9	20.4	27.7
Luxembourg, Δp, 20	1.0	29.9	69.1
Netherlands, Δp, 20	36.9	30.2	32.9
Portugal, Δp, 20	54.4	33.9	11.6
Spain, Δp, 20	16.2	47.4	36.3
	Δgap	$\Delta^2 p^e$	$\Delta^2 p$
Austria, Δp^e, 20	38.5	18.5	43.0
Belgium, Δp^e, 20	4.6	33.2	62.2
Finland, Δp^e, 20	13.6	28.2	58.3
France, Δp^e, 20	6.5	57.3	36.2
Germany, Δp^e, 20	34.4	7.0	58.6
Greece, Δp^e, 20	0.7	44.9	54.4
Ireland, Δp^e, 20	9.6	26.1	64.3
Italy, Δp^e, 20	26.0	47.4	26.6
Luxembourg, Δp^e, 20	1.7	12.7	85.6
Netherlands, Δp^e, 20	24.0	25.5	50.5
Portugal, Δp^e, 20	19.3	42.2	38.5
Spain, Δp^e, 20	3.9	30.8	65.3

Notes
With all countries, var1 variance decomposition is used.

3   Inflation and inflation expectations explain only a small fraction of output (forecast) variance. This suggests that the direct linkage between monetary/price shocks and output is quite weak. But the nature of this linkage still makes sense. Scrutinizing the impulse responses (Figures 8.5 and 8.6), we see that inflation expectations shocks have negative, statistically significant and quite persistent effects on the output gap while the effect of actual inflation on output is somewhat sensitive to the specification and data. In general, it has either a positive or a negative short-run effect, but in all cases a negative long-run effect. Interpretation of these results is not clear because we do not have interest (exchange) rates in the model, but it is tempting to interpret the negative output effect of inflation expectations as coming from adverse supply (cost) shocks and the positive effects of actual inflation as consequences of temporary demand disturbances.

4   There seems to be only a minor difference between the effects with OECD forecasts and Consensus (survey) Forecasts (Table 8.3). Thus the performance

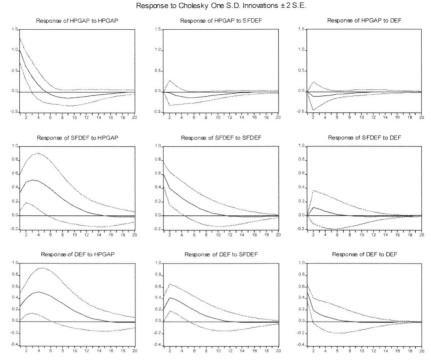

Figure 8.5 Impulse responses for aggregate euro area data (Impulse responses correspond to level data with one lag in the VAR).

of inflation expectations is not due to the specific OECD data but probably
reflects overall market sentiment about future inflation. Future experiments
with national data sets may allow more affirmative conclusions here.

5   Inflation expectations react in the same way to both output and inflation
shocks. It is hard to say which of these variables is "more important" in determining expectations because in this respect the variance decompositions
produce slightly conflicting results, depending on specification and data set.
But clearly there is some propagation mechanism between output and inflation
developments, on the one hand, and inflation expectations, on the other. Even
then, the most important element is the persistence of inflation expectations:
even after 20 years, almost half of the forecast variance of inflation expectations can be attributed to this variable alone. Thus, errors in inflation expectations do not die out over a typical business-cycle. It is interesting to compare
this result with the behaviour of actual inflation; there the shocks are much
more short-lived and less persistent. This is remarkable even if the effects of
own shocks to expectations diminish faster than to the output gap variables.

6   The impulse responses suggest that the effects of inflation and output shocks
last more than ten years. In the aggregate euro area data, the duration of

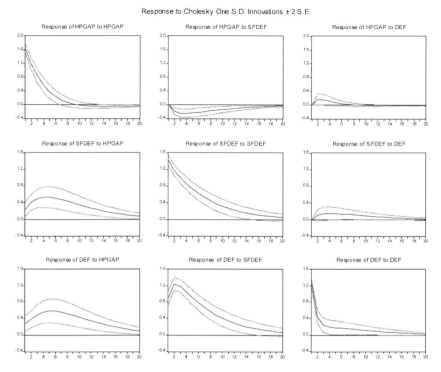

Figure 8.6 Impulse responses for pooled euro area data (Impulse responses correspond to level data with one lag in the VAR).

effects is typically shorter than the pooled cross-country data. In the latter, where country differences appear and high-inflation countries bear more weight, the inflation-duration effects linger much longer, especially expected inflation (see Tables 8.5 and 8.6). This also shows up in individual country estimates. The individual data reveal some sensitivity to differencing, but otherwise the results follow the same pattern. That may reflect some regime shifts that merit more detailed analysis in further analyses.

4 Concluding remarks

Inflation cannot be modelled or understood without analysing inflation expectations. This fact is again confirmed in our analysis, and in recent data. In the euro area, inflation expectations have come down quite dramatically since the 1970s. Actual inflation has followed the same pattern, reinforcing the falling trend in inflation expectations. Although we cannot say exactly what have been the contributions of various factors, including policy targets, to changes in inflation expectations, we can conclude that the (independent) role of expectations in the inflation process has been, and obviously still is, of crucial importance.

The central role of expectations in inflation dynamics has strong implications for the design of monetary policy. It means that if inflation expectations are anchored by credible monetary policy, inflation will be more stable. Moreover, if the persistence of inflation indeed comes from the persistence of expectations, as this study suggests, policies affecting expectations are crucial in all efforts at disinflation. Stable and low inflation would in turn minimize losses to the economy and provide the best environment for strong and balanced growth.

Against this background, the role and nature of inflation expectations clearly deserves even more attention and analysis. Much effort has gone into identifying and measuring inflation expectations, but very little is known empirically about the possible independent role of expectations in the inflation process and, equally important, about the determinants of expectations.[16] Knowing merely that inflation expectations are unbiased is not very informative from the policy point of view. In this respect, VAR analysis gives us at least a rough idea of the nature and magnitudes of the main interrelationships.

Because the data strongly favour the interpretation that inflation expectations do not immediately adjust to changes in actual inflation and output, we have ample reason to study their origins more thoroughly. The VARs which we have used here represent one way of tackling the issue. There may be other ways to do it. Perhaps event studies – say, in the form of analyses of major policy decisions – could provide further insight to the determination of expectations.[17] The dispersion of expectations in survey-based data could also throw light on the possible role of forecast uncertainty.

Appendix 8.1

Table 8.7 Wald tests for unbiasedness of inflation expectations

Euro area/country	June forecast		December forecast	
	F-statistic	*Probability*	*F-statistic*	*Probability*
Euro area, aggregated	0.757	0.482	1.938	0.165
Euro area, pooled	5.532	0.004	5.883	0.003
Austria	0.481	0.625	1.008	0.379
Belgium	1.952	0.167	9.994	0.001
Finland	0.488	0.621	1.346	0.279
France	4.234	0.029	0.516	0.603
Germany	0.550	0.585	0.268	0.767
Greece	4.716	0.020	3.928	0.033
Ireland	1.088	0.355	0.518	0.602
Italy	3.419	0.052	3.636	0.041
Luxembourg	0.433	0.655	1.436	0.261
Netherlands	1.374	0.275	2.710	0.086
Portugal	2.400	0.115	1.992	0.160
Spain	3.892	0.037	2.099	0.144

Notes
All Wald tests are computed for the parameter restrictions $a_0 = 0$ and $a_1 = 1$ in $\Delta p_t = a_0 + a_1 \Delta p_t^e + e_t$.

Appendix 8.2

Table 8.8 Pooled cross-country results with a VECM (2) model

Dependent variable	Δgap	$\Delta^2 p^e$	$\Delta^2 p$
EC-term	−0.176	−0.112	0.085
	(7.43)	(3.54)	(3.45)
Δgap, 1	0.334	0.141	0.179
	(5.52)	(2.66)	(2.84)
Δgap, 2	−0.022	0.166	0.051
	(0.37)	(3.11)	(0.80)
$\Delta^2 p^e$, 1	0.433	0.256	0.263
	(4.02)	(2.71)	(2.34)
$\Delta^2 p^e$, 2	0.183	0.110	0.084
	(2.01)	(1.38)	(0.88)
$\Delta^2 p$,1	−0.299	−0.196	−0.326
	(3.66)	(2.65)	(3.82)
$\Delta^2 p$,2	−0.125	−0.049	−0.125
	(1.91)	(0.86)	(1.85)
R2/SEE	0.306	0.226	0.300
	1.555	1.365	1.621

Variance decompositions	Gap	Δp^e	Δp
Δgap, 2	96.7	0.5	2.8
Δgap, 20	72.6	10.5	16.9
$\Delta^2 p^e$, 2	0.3	97.7	2.0
$\Delta^2 p^e$, 20	1.7	74.7	23.6
$\Delta^2 p$,2	6.9	55.5	37.5
$\Delta^2 p$,20	14.3	47.6	38.1

EC-term: HPGAP + $4.54\Delta p^e$ − $3.58\Delta p$
EC-term: $1.00\Delta p^e$ − $0.76\Delta p$, $\chi^2 (1) = 8.04$
EC-term: $1.00\Delta p^e$ − $1.00\Delta p$, $\chi^2(2) = 71.74$

Notes
Numbers inside parentheses are t-ratios. The χ^2-test statistics are related to the restrictions of the β-matrix. The first (unrestricted) EC is used in deriving the variance decompositions.

Notes

1 Economist, Bank of Finland, and professor of economics, University of Turku, and scientific advisor, Bank of Finland, respectively. E-mail addresses: maritta.paloviita@ bof.fi and matvir@utu.fi. Useful comments from Juha Tarkka and Jouko Vilmunen (Bank of Finland), an anonymous referee and the participants of the conference of the Eurosystem Inflation Persistence Network in Vienna, April 2005, and NBP conference on the Role of Inflation Expectations in Warsaw, February 2006, as well as financial support from The Yrjö Jahnsson Foundation are gratefully acknowledged. Finally, we want to express special thanks to Peter Sinclair for numerous conceptual and editorial comments.
2 Note that published expectations (forecasts) are not even used as instruments for expected inflation in the REH framework. See, however, Paloviita and Mayes (2005).
3 More precisely, Consensus Economics provides data for consumer prices. The data are monthly and so include a large number of observations, but when used with

annual (output) data the high-frequency properties cannot be utilized. In what follows, we use the data only in pooled cross-country analysis, where the degrees of freedom are reasonable.

4 In addition, a number of papers have recently been published using survey or forecast – based inflation expectations data in estimating the Phillips curve(s). See, for instance, Adam and Padula (2003) and Paloviita (2006, 2008). Alternative measures of euro area inflation expectations can be found in Gerlach (2004).

5 In this connection, we bypass discussion on the proper concept or measure of the output gap. Results with alternative proxies suggest that the choice is not a crucial issue here.

6 Because we use annual data, one might presume that mid-year values correspond to average annual values of production and the price level.

7 The latter concept, in fact, corresponds to the Expectations Augmented Phillips curve specification.

8 A similar result is reached in Forsells and Kenny (2002) for the EU Commission's Consumer Survey.

9 The generally used Hodrick-Prescott filter suffers from several problems which may affect the results in a crucial way (see e.g. Cogley and Nason 1995). Therefore, we also used the OECD output gap to check the robustness of the results. As these data do not cover the whole period, we used the HP filtered output gap series.

10 If the output gap is created by introducing a linear trend to the estimating equation, all the other variables are of course also (similarly) affected.

11 The cointegration properties of actual and forecast variables is analysed e.g. in Aggarwal *et al.* (1995).

12 Before turning to the results, we should point out that our VAR model is not very suitable to the open economy environment, which obtains for all countries for most of the sample period. A tempting alternative would be to extend the model with some open-economy variables, but that would unnecessarily complicate our analysis at this stage. Hence we only do the following: we add foreign (US) inflation as an exogenous variable in our VAR specification. The idea is again to see whether that makes any difference in results compared to the basic three-variable VAR model.

13 See Paloviita and Virén (2005) for more complete set of results. A full set of results is available by email upon request from the authors.

14 The analyses were also done for individual countries (see Paloviita and Virén 2005). No big differences were detected between different countries and subsets of countries (for instance, looking separately at countries which presumably have more closely followed the German inflation norm). The long-run percentage share of p^e in variance decompositions was almost identical for the big countries (France, Germany and Spain). Only in the case of Italy was the share somewhat smaller (see Table 8.6).

15 This shows up in estimation results reported in Table 8.1. If the VAR (inflation) equations are compared with Phillips curves estimated using the same sample and data, the VAR equations have slightly bigger standard errors. The problem is only that with e.g. the pooled cross-country data the coefficients of the New Keynesian Phillips curve are incorrect (the coefficient of output gap is negative and the coefficient of the expected inflation exceeds one). The Expectations Augmented Phillips curve performs better, especially in terms of coefficient estimates. However, it cannot be directly compared with the VAR equations because it has current period values on the right-hand side. With the supply curve, similar arguments apply. See Tillman (2005) for the most recent evaluation of the performance of the New Keynesian Phillips Curve.

16 Some interesting analyses do exist, however. See e.g. Bonato *et al.* (1999), who try to estimate the role of policy announcements on (monetary conditions) expectations.

17 A preliminary attempt to measuring the effects of different policy regimes is made in Virén (2005).

References

Adam, K. and Padula, M. (2003), Inflation dynamics and subjective expectations in the United States, *ECB Working Paper*, 222.

Aggarwal, R., Mohanty, S. and Song, F. (1995), Are survey forecasts of macroeconomic variables rational?, *Journal of Business*, 68: 99–119.

Amisano, G. and Giannini, C. (1997), *Topics in Structural VAR Econometrics*, Lecture Notes in Economics and Mathematical Systems, Springer-Verlag, Berlin.

Blanchard, O. and Quah, D. (1989), The dynamic effects of aggregate demand and supply disturbances, *American Economic Review*, 79: 655–673.

Bonato, L., St. Clair, R. and Winkelman, R. (1999), Survey expectations of monetary conditions in New Zealand: determinants for the transmission of policy, *Reserve Bank of New Zealand Working Paper* 6/99.

Cogley, T. and Nason, J. (1995), Effects of Hodrick Prescott Filter on trend and difference stationary time series: implications for business cycle research, *Journal of Economics Dynamics and Control*, 19: 253–278.

Forsells, M and Kenny, G. (2002), The rationality of consumers' inflation expectations: survey-based evidence for the euro area, *ECB Working Paper*, 163.

Gerlach, S. (2004), The two pillars of the ECB, *Economic Policy*, 19: 389–439.

Gerlach, S. and Svensson, L. (2003), Money and inflation in the euro area: a case for monetary indicators, *Journal of Monetary Economics*, 50: 1649–1672.

Levin, A., Natalucci, F. and Piger, J. (2004), Explicit inflation objectives and macroeconomic outcomes, *ECB Working Paper*, 383.

OECD (1993), How accurate are OECD projections?, *OECD Economic Outlook*, 53: 48–54.

Paloviita, M. (2006), Inflation dynamics in the euro area and the role of expectations, *Empirical Economics*, 31: 847–860.

Paloviita, M. (2008), Comparing alternative Phillips curve specifications: European results with survey-based expectations, *Applied Economics*, 14: 2259-2270.

Paloviita, M. and Mayes, D.G. (2005), The use of real time information in Phillips Curve relationships for the euro area, *North American Journal of Economics and Finance*, 16: 415–434.

Paloviita, M. and Virén, M. (2005), The role of expectations in the inflation process in the euro area, *Bank of Finland Discussion Paper*, 6/2005.

Tillman, P. (2005), The new Keynesian Phillips Curve in Europe: does it fit or does it fail?, *Discussion Paper*, Deutsche Bundesbank 2/2005.

Virén, M. (1998), OECD forecasts for the G7 countries in 1969–1997, *Government Institute for Economic Research (VATT) Discussion Papers*, 197.

Virén, M. (2005), Inflation expectations and regime shifts in the euro area, *Bank of Finland Discussion Papers*, 25.

9 The European consumer and monetary policy

Jan Marc Berk and Gerbert Hebbink[1]

1 Introduction

Expectations of economic agents are crucial for a central bank and its monetary policy design. This view is supported by much recent work on monetary theory, and the seminal expositions of Walsh (2003) and Woodford (2003). At the heart of this work lies the combination of dynamic stochastic general equilibrium models, and simple models of price stickiness. This combination has a fairly recent origin. But much earlier, central banks had grasped the importance of credibility for the conduct of their monetary policies. Indeed, the credibility of a central bank is probably the single most important factor determining whether an anti-inflation policy entails significant output and employment losses.[2] When a central bank lacks credibility, the public does not believe that the central bank is going to do what it says it is going to do. As a result, expected inflation in the private sector will exceed the central bank's objective for inflation. These expectations will feed into the wage and price decisions of households and firms, causing some businesses and workers to overcharge their goods and services. The resulting decline in employment and real activity complicates the environment for monetary policy, making the central bank's job more difficult.

The public's expectations of inflation therefore need to be taken into account by the central bank when determining the stance of monetary policy, in order to achieve its objective (Kydland and Prescott 1977; Barro and Gordon 1983). Moreover, central banks need to assess the credibility of their monetary policy on an ongoing basis. A key to this ongoing assessment is knowing how the inflation expectations of the general public compare with the price stability objective pursued by the central bank. However, measures of expected inflation are also of interest by themselves, as forecasting inflation is a major task of any central bank. Measures of expected inflation play an important role in any such exercise, given that the inflation expectations of firms and households over various horizons influence their wage and price decisions, thereby feeding into the measured inflation rate.

Broadly speaking, there are two approaches to gauging inflation expectations.[3] The first is to try to infer the expected inflation rate from the prices of financial instruments (Bank of Canada 1998; Mylonas and Schich 1999). The primary advantage of looking at the prices of financial instruments is that these prices reflect the expectations of agents upon which they have been willing to act. This forward-looking nature makes financial asset prices popular among central bankers (see Hördahl 2000, and Angeloni and Rovelli 1998, for recent examples). If, for example, both nominal and index-linked bonds with identical risk, liquidity and maturity characteristics are traded, it is in principle possible to obtain a very accurate measure of expected inflation (Barr and Campbell 1997; Schmidt 1999). However, in practice index-linked bonds are still scarce, and where they are issued, it is usually more than just the determination of their returns that varies from nominal bonds. Thus, it is often necessary to make strong auxiliary assumptions to infer expected inflation from the prices of these nominal assets, thereby clouding the information content of the expected inflation series that has been derived.[4] The alternative approach is to simply ask a sample of the general public what they expect inflation to be over some specified time horizon by means of a survey. This direct approach has the advantage of obtaining a measure of expected inflation which is undistorted by any auxiliary assumptions. The primary drawback is that participants may not base their actual decisions on their survey responses. Moreover, the results of sample surveys are overly sensitive to sampling errors and to the precise formulation of the questions posed (Chan-Lee 1980).

This chapter deals with the use of quantitative information on inflation expectations and perceptions of European consumers as derived from qualitative survey data for monetary policy purposes. More specifically, following the suggestion of Goodhart (1997), we investigate the information content of the expected inflation measures in the context of movements in actual inflation and short-term interest rates in Europe. We seek to explore whether the inflation expectations of European consumers react to these events, and whether the reaction of consumers in countries with more credible central banks differs from the reaction of consumers in countries with less credible central banks. While the main focus of the chapter is on expectations, we also use our method to quantify survey information on the price developments as perceived by consumers (as opposed to developments as expected by them). This will prove to be especially interesting in cases of monetary policy interventions that are likely to have immediate effects on actual and perceived prices. We apply this to a unique policy experiment that occurred in 2002, i.e. the introduction of a new currency, the euro. We are thus in a position to see how this new currency shaped price perceptions of European consumers.

Answers to these questions are of considerable importance to the European Central Bank (ECB), which as a relatively new central bank attaches a high priority to establishing credibility, and which will be confronted with introducing the euro currency in new member's states in the future. But the relevance of a study of the relationship between the actual inflation rate and that expected by a large class of economic agents (consumers) extends beyond Europe. This is illustrated by the definition of price stability used by the former chairman of the Board of Governors of the Federal Reserve, Greenspan. He argues that "price stability obtains when economic agents no longer take account of the prospective change in the general price level in their economic decision making" (Greenspan 1996: 1). Our results indicate that consumers' inflation expectations in most European countries form a long-term equilibrium relationship with actual future inflation. However, and counter intuitively, they do not seem to react in any systematic way to actual upturns in inflation and surprise movements in short-term interest rates.

The remainder of the chapter is structured as follows. The next section describes the methodology used to derive the measures of expected inflation, as well as some of the properties of the constructed inflation expectations. Section 3 then conducts some monetary policy experiments, including a post mortem exercise on the effects of euro introduction on price perceptions of consumers. Section 4 concludes.

2 Quantification of survey-based expected inflation

Following Simmons and Weiserbs (1992), Madsen (1996) and Papadia (1983), we make use of the survey conducted monthly under the aegis of the European Commission. In this survey, European consumers are asked the following questions regarding prices: "(i) Is the price level now compared to 12 months ago a) much higher, b) moderately higher, c) a little higher, d) the same, e) lower?" and "(ii) Do you expect prices over the next 12 months a) to rise faster, b) to show a similar rise, c) to rise less fast, d) to stay the same, e) to decline?"[5] The first question is backward looking and relates to the price level as perceived by the consumer. We can use this question to calculate the so-called perceived inflation rate, as opposed to the "official" inflation rate based on published CPI statistics. The second question is forward looking, and aims to capture expectations of consumers regarding future inflation. The method we use for extracting measures of perceived as well as expected inflation is an extension of the method made popular by Carlson and Parkin (1977), requiring less restrictive assumptions, such as a priori assuming rationality and normality of inflation expectations. In this respect we extend the analysis of Bakhshi and Yates (1998) to 13 European countries or regions.[6] The modifications to the Carlson–Parkin or CP-method are described in more (technical) detail in Berk (1999).

An informal description of our method is as follows. Within a cross-sectional sample of size N surveyed at time t, each agent i is presumed to answer questions about the future behaviour of prices at time $t + 12$ (in months) on the basis of a subjective conditional probability distribution. This distribution is conditional on the information set available to the consumer at t. Agents are then presumed to report that no change in the price level is expected if the expected future inflation rate falls within an interval centred around zero. Similarly, agents will report that no change in the rate of inflation is expected if their expectation falls within an interval centred on the price increase that they perceive to have occurred in the past 12 months. The boundaries of both intervals, denoted as the response thresholds, are to be determined by the data.

The survey results can be regarded as N drawings from the aggregate population and we are able to derive expressions of this expected inflation rate, the standard deviation and the response thresholds as functions of the survey responses.[7] These expressions are given in relation to the perceived inflation rate (i.e. the price rise that consumers perceive to have occurred in the past 12 months). In order to obtain actual values for these variables, the form of the aggregate density function and the perceived inflation rate over the last 12 months, which performs a scaling role with respect to the expected future inflation rate, must be known. Both issues are addressed in Berk (2000), who finds that the normal distribution outperforms non-normal alternatives, such as (symmetric and asymmetric) t-distributions. In addition, it is concluded that the most recent inflation rate available to consumers when answering the survey question regarding future prices (Simmons and Weiserbs 1992) is superior to the other available measure of the perceived inflation rate – i.e. the answers of consumers to the survey question pertaining to price developments in the past 12 months. We therefore proceed using the expected inflation rate based on the normal distribution as our preferred measure of inflation expectations. In our post-mortem of the effects of the euro introduction (see Section 3) we use the survey-based measure of the perceived inflation rate.

In most of our empirical work, we use monthly data, covering the period from January 1986 up to December 1999. Our choice of sample period is governed by the objective of studying to study the information content of the survey data for monetary policy purposes. We therefore decided against using more recent data, as those might be affected by (the anticipation of) a policy regime shift, namely the introduction of the euro. Indeed, we analyse the euro's introduction in more detail as a separate case study, see below.[8] The data pertain to the countries comprising the EU (excluding Luxembourg) and two regions: the euro area (i.e. the European countries which adopted the euro as their currency) and the EU. We prefer a country-by-country analysis over, for example, system or panel approaches as we are interested in exploring whether the relationship between the inflation rate expected by consumers and the actual future inflation rate differs between countries with more or less credible central banks. Upon prior investigation of the data, we eliminated Austria, Sweden and Finland from our sample because of insufficient observations. The survey responses are complemented by data on consumer price inflation, calculated as the increase of the CPI over the relevant 12 months.

The constructed expectation measures have a number of desirable properties.[9] As is shown elaborated in the working paper version of this chapter, expected and actual future inflation rates (i.e. the inflation rate prevailing in the coming 12 months) are cointegrated for all countries except France, Italy, Portugal and Denmark. The concept of cointegration, which stresses long-term relationships, is a suitable methodology given the orientation of monetary policymakers, who frequently stress the medium- to long-term horizons when striving for price stability (Bernanke and Mishkin 1997). Cointegration implies that, although both the actual 12-month-ahead and expected inflation rates show substantial persistence and show no mean-reverting behaviour, both series form an equilibrium relationship in the sense that deviations from this relationship are temporary. Moreover, the forecast error (that is, the difference between expected and actual future inflation) is stationary. This implies that the inflation forecasts show consistency, as defined by Cheung and Chinn (1997). The concept of consistency focuses on the long-run property of forecasts, and hence is weaker than the one conventionally used in evaluating forecast rationality. It does not impose any further restrictions on the forecast errors, beyond the requirement that they be weakly covariance stationary.

The economic rationale of this weak form test of rationality follows Cukierman and Meltzer (1982), who show that following a large permanent disturbance, the possibility of confusion about the persistence of the shock can account for the serial dependence in finite samples without implying violation of the rationality principle. The weak form test implies that this uncertainty on the permanence of shocks can lead to transitory deviations between actual and expected inflation. In the long run, however, expected inflation responds fully to changes in the actual rate of inflation, as agents cannot be systematically fooled. As our survey forecasts of expected inflation are very likely to be subject to measurement errors (Smyth 1992), this concept of forecast consistency is especially useful, since it allows for serially correlated forecast errors. Serially correlated forecast errors can happen, for example, when stationary measurement errors are present (see Lee 1994; Cheung and Chinn 1997, for details).[10] They result in a rejection of the standard, strong form, rationality test, which focuses on a combination of unbiasedness, efficiency and orthogonality. Indeed, earlier studies by and large reject the rationality of survey-based inflation expectations measures; see, for example, Batchelor and Dua (1987), Evans and Gulamani (1984), Holden and Peel (1977), Pesando (1975), De Menil and Bhalla (1975), De Leeuw and McKelvey (1981), Madsen (1996), Pearce (1979), Pesaran (1985), Thomas (1995) and Figlewski and Wachtel (1981). These results could be interpreted as meaning that the speed of adjustment of unemployment towards the NAIRU following a monetary shock is less than it would be in a world in which consumers hold fully rational expectations. This is because the sluggishness in expectations (as exemplified by the serially correlated forecast errors) inhibits the allocative role of the price mechanism.

3 Monetary policy analysis

The monetary policy strategy of the Eurosystem (i.e. the ECB and the national central banks of the countries which adopted the euro as their currency as of 1 January 1999) combines a privileged role for money in the monetary policy decision making process with a broad-based assessment of prospective inflationary pressures. The latter implies that Eurosystem monetary policy decisions will be based not only on money, but also on a host of other (non-money) indicators for future euro area inflation (see Berk *et al.* 2000, for details). So measures of inflation expectations derived from survey data could thus be useful as information variables.

It is important to stress the role played by non-monetary variables in the monetary policy strategy of the Eurosystem. This applies in particular to inflation expectations, as they are often confused with inflation expectations under a inflation targeting strategy such as that conducted by, for example, the Bank of England. A central element of an inflation targeting strategy is inflation forecast targeting (Svensson 1999), in which an internal conditional inflation forecast is used as an intermediate target. The inflation rate expected by consumers obviously is not the same as the internal inflation forecast of the central bank, which is usually based on a structural model of the economy (Berk 2001). So, even in inflation targeting, countries consumers' inflation expectations should not directly enter the monetary policy reaction function of the central bank. And the Eurosystem does not target a conditional inflation forecast. In contrast, the Eurosystem treats expectational variables as pure indicator variables (as defined in Svensson and Woodford 2000). That is, survey-based inflation expectations are interpreted as one of many indicators of future inflation.

In order for expected inflation to fulfil a role as an indicator variable, there needs to be a stable statistical relationship between expected and future actual inflation, see Shigehara (1996) and Groeneveld *et al.* (1996). Our findings that current inflation expectations and future realizations of inflation are cointegrated, and that the forecast error is stationary, seem to confirm the usefulness of the former as an information variable for monetary policy: expected inflation derived from consumer surveys shows identical long-run behaviour to the actual inflation 12 months ahead. Unfortunately, this interpretation is not that straightforward, as it is well known (Engle and Granger 1991) that cointegration per se provides no information on the direction of causality in the long-term relationship, while it is crucial for the policy maker to know whether currently observed consumer expectations provide "advance knowledge" of future inflation. Indeed, the formulation of the survey questions seems to imply causality running from current expected inflation to actual future inflation.

A statistical concept which is frequently used to gauge the direction of causality is the traditional Granger causality test, which consists of F-tests on exclusion restrictions in regressions of changes in the (expected) inflation rate. In addition to this test, we investigate the issue of causality by analysing vector error correction models (VECMs). These models are VARs which include error correction terms consisting of the lagged residual from the cointegrating relations. By Granger's Representation Theorem (Engle and Granger 1987), the error correction terms provide additional information on the direction of causality.[11] The intuition is this: that if expected and actual inflation rates have a common stochastic trend, the current change in the actual inflation rate is partly the result of its moving into alignment with the trend value of the expected inflation rate. Whereas the traditional Granger tests pertain to causality in the short-term dynamic adjustment, the ECM-based test relates to causality in the long-term relationship, see Kremers *et al.* (1992). Both dimensions of causality are relevant to policymakers. For practical purposes, however, the usefulness of long-term concepts is hampered by the uncertainty surrounding, and the sometimes low speed of, adjustment towards the long term.

Results of the causality tests are presented in Table 9.1. The first part of the table relates to the null hypothesis that the expected inflation rate does not cause the actual future inflation rate, and the second part pertains to the reverse hypothesis. Columns labelled "F-test" relate to the traditional Granger test, and columns labelled "t-test on ECM" pertain to the error correction-based tests. The models on which both tests are based do not include contemporaneous variables as regressors and uniformly include 12 lags of changes in the (expected) inflation rate, as suggested by the Akaike information criterion and tests for serial correlation.[12] It follows from Table 9.1 that the traditional Granger causality tests provide, at best, only scant evidence in favour of the hypothesis that the expected inflation rate causes the actual future inflation rate 12 months ahead.

The statistics on the significance of the error correction terms point to a somewhat different conclusion. For some large euro area countries which show cointegration between actual future and expected inflation, the hypothesis that causality runs from expected inflation to the actual future inflation rate could not be rejected. The evidence therefore seems to indicate that for Germany, Ireland, Spain, the Netherlands and the euro area as a whole, the expectations measures do have predictive power, in a long-run causal sense, for future inflation.[13]

Notwithstanding the outcomes of the Granger tests, the long-term causality result is of interest from the point of view of central bankers. It suggests the possibility for them to influence the future actual inflation rate by affecting the expectations of consumers, an issue to which we will return below. This indicates that our measure of expected inflation for the euro area could enter the monetary policy strategy of the Eurosystem.

Note that the preceding analysis concentrates on the *statistical* concept of causality, which focuses on forecasting future inflation. The survey-based meas-

Table 9.1 Testing for causality between expected and actual future inflation

	$\pi^e \neq \pi$		$\pi \neq \pi^e$	
	F-test	*t-test on ECM*	*F-test*	*t-test on ECM*
Belgium	1.15	8.07**	5.22**	1.41
Germany	1.90*	8.21**	3.49**	0.49
France	1.77	4.89**	2.46**	0.86
Ireland	0.59	8.13**	3.37**	2.48*
Italy	1.16	3.20**	2.17*	0.06
Netherlands	1.16	4.46**	1.52	0.90
Spain	0.62	7.16**	3.30**	0.29
Portugal	2.17*	7.49**	1.37	4.68**
Euro area°	2.45**	4.88**	3.49**	2.62*
Denmark°	3.10**	6.26**	2.25*	0.10
Greece°	2.63*	6.11**	1.98*	3.41**
United Kingdom	3.06**	8.27**	6.11**	0.09
EU	2.07*	6.44**	5.39**	2.11*

Notes
Investigated is causal relationship between actual future inflation rate (12 months ahead) and expected inflation rate. **(*) indicates significance at 1% (5%). Sample period 1986–2005.

ures of expected inflation cannot be seen as a causal determinant of (future) inflation in an *economic* sense. By this we mean that our measures are not by themselves measures of the underlying causes of inflation. The policymaker should concentrate on, and react to movements in, variables that are proximate causes of inflation, rather than to variables that reflect the expectations of economic agents. These expectations respond only to the underlying causes of inflation insofar as agents are aware of them and actually expect inflation to result.

Put differently, consumers need to be able to recognise inflationary pressures for the expectations measures to become useful. As illustrated by Fuhrer and Moore (1992), Woodford (1994) and Bernanke and Woodford (1997), the use of forecasts in setting monetary policy would change the relationship between the forecasters' information variables and the policy goal, and so would lead them to change the way in which they form their forecasts. But once they did, the relation between their forecasts and the underlying sources of inflationary pressure would change, so that the policy maker's optimal response to the forecast would change. And if the latter changes its response, this again changes the way in which forecasters ought to form their forecasts. The result of this game-theoretic problem may be that no equilibrium exists, or that a multiplicity of equilibria exist. Other arguments for not basing monetary policy on market expectations include the sometimes irrational character of decisions of economic agents (overreaction, for example) and the implicit shortening of the horizon of monetary policy when the central bank bases its monetary policy on private sector expectations. This is at odds with the main argument in favour of central bank independence, i.e. that monetary policy is not subject to the short-term horizon of politicians (Blinder 1998).

Besides being used as an indicator of future consumer price inflation, our expectations measures can, in principle, be used to gauge how consumers' perceptions of future price developments are influenced by certain events relevant to the monetary policy maker. More specifically, we investigate the effects on inflation expectations across European countries of a rise in past inflation (which is expected by definition) and an unanticipated rise in short-term interest rates. To highlight the monetary policy relevance of this exercise, note that our sample consists of countries such as Germany and the Netherlands, the central banks of which have built up a reputation for credibly holding future inflation to a low stable level, and also countries such as Greece and Spain, for which (during our sample period at least) no such conclusion could be drawn. Obviously, we have to restrict our sample to the period before the establishment of the European Central Bank.

Based on the literature on central bank credibility and independence (see, for example, Cukierman 1994), one might expect that in the more credible countries an upturn in inflation has less effect on expectations of future inflation, as the reputation of the central bank prevents the inflationary shock from becoming persistently embedded in the public's inflation expectations of economic agents such as consumers (Goodhart 1997).[14] Similarly, an unanticipated rise in short-term interest rates in countries with more credible central banks should reduce expectations of inflation by more than in countries with less credible central banks.

Having survey-based measures of expected inflation available for several countries and over a relatively long time period should allow us to empirically test these hypotheses.

We explore these hypotheses using a VECM-framework. This allows us to take the persistence of both actual and expected inflation into account and at the same time make maximum use of the information provided by the levels of these variables. We first investigate the effect on inflation expectations of European consumers of a change in the most recent actual inflation rate available to them when responding to the survey, that is $\Pi(t-1)$. Table 9.2 below documents both the long-run reaction of expected inflation (i.e. the coefficient of the error correction term in the VECM) and the short term reaction (i.e. the one-period effect on expected inflation).

As is well known (see Kremers *et al.* 1992, for details), statistical significance of the long run coefficient implies that the expected inflation and the one-period lagged inflation rates are cointegrated. Most coefficients are insignificant, often of the wrong sign, and do not allow us to discern a pattern between even the polar cases with respect to countries with very high credibility (Germany) or very low credibility (Greece). A possible explanation of this somewhat disappointing result is that the changes in inflation had been widely anticipated by consumers. As illustrated by Kuttner (2000), forward-looking expectations should respond, if at all, only to surprise elements, and not to anticipated movements, in key variables such as the inflation rate.

We explore this issue further in a second experiment, in which we analyse the effects of monetary policy surprises on our measures of expected inflation. As a prelude to this experiment, we construct time series of unanticipated short-term interest rates for the countries in our sample. To do this, we collect data (season-

Table 9.2 Effect on expected inflation of change in actual inflation

	Long-run (ECM)	*Short term (one period)*
Belgium	0.19* (2.07)	0.21 (0.14)
Germany	−0.02 (0.25)	−0.13 (0.74)
France	0.31** (3.25)	−0.36* (1.89)
Ireland	−0.45** (3.39)	−0.14 (0.81)
Italy	0.01 (0.14)	0.54 (1.92)
Netherlands	−0.13* (1.89)	0.19 (1.43)
Spain	−0.27* (2.59)	−0.10 (0.71)
Portugal	−0.21* (2.91)	0.05 (0.25)
Euro area	−0.08 (1.51)	−0.12 (0.75)
Denmark	−0.09 (1.27)	−0.03 (0.51)
Greece	−0.14* (2.16)	−0.03 (0.21)
United Kingdom	0.10 (0.75)	0.55* (2.43)
EU	−0.12 (1.82)	−0.15 (0.84)

Notes
The table shows the effects of a change in lagged inflation, estimated with an VECM/VAR with 12 lags. Absolute t-values in parentheses. **(*): significant at 1% (5%). Sample: 1986–1999.

ally unadjusted) on industrial production, a monetary aggregate (M1 because of maximum data availability), and a money market rate (i.e. one-month euro rates).[15] We could not reject the hypothesis that these data contain a single unit root. We then construct a five-variable VECM for each country, consisting, in most cases, of the home money market rate, a foreign equivalent, the consumer price inflation rate, industrial production and the money stock. For Germany, the US money market rate is included as the foreign interest rate. For most other European countries, the German short-term interest rate performs this role. Exceptions are the United Kingdom, for which both the US and the German rate are included, and Ireland, for which the UK money market rate is included. We then proxy the unexpected short-term interest rate by the residual of the interest rate equation in the VECM. The VECMs, who take into account both the unit roots and possible long-term relationships between the levels of the variables used to model our policy surprises, prove to be reasonably robust and plausibly signed. The results of this analysis, are not shown here in order to save space, but are available from the author upon request.

Our constructed series of unanticipated movements in the short-term interest rate are then included as exogenous variables in a VECM otherwise consisting of expected and actual inflation. We construct the experiment in such a way that only the most recent actual inflation rate and unanticipated interest rates available to consumers when responding to the survey enter the analysis. The results are presented in Table 9.3 below. They indicate that in all countries considered, unanticipated movements in the money market rate fail to elicit statistically significant reactions from our measures of expected inflation.[16] Moreover, the

Table 9.3 Effects on expected inflation rate of change in

	Actual inflation rate		Unexpected interest rate
	Long-run (ECM)	Short term (one period)	
Belgium	−0.02 (0.83)	−0.05 (−0.73)	0.02 (0.25)
Germany	−0.01 (0.61)	0.02 (0.15)	−0.13 (0.56)
France	−0.16* (3.68)	0.10 (0.82)	−0.09 (0.84)
Ireland	−0.01 (0.20)	−0.03 (0.33)	−0.01 (0.31)
Italy	−0.04 (1.93)	−0.15 (0.73)	−0.03 (0.28)
Netherlands	−0.00 (0.04)	−0.23 (1.78)	0.01 (0.24)
Spain	0.08* (2.20)	0.23** (2.21)	−0.14 (1.18)
Denmark	−0.04 (0.49)	−0.10 (1.52)	0.01 (0.84)
Greece	−0.01 (0.20)	0.03 (0.31)	−0.04 (0.77)
United Kingdom	0.01 (0.81)	−0.10 (0.75)	0.19 (0.70)

Notes
The table shows the effects of a change in lagged inflation and an unexpected change in short-term interest rates, estimated with an VECM/VAR with 12 lags, with unexpected interest rate change taken as exogenous. See main text for discussion on the construction of unexpected interest rate. Absolute t-values in parentheses. **(*): significant at 1% (5). Sample: 1986–1999.

results presented in Table 9.2 are re-confirmed. That is, effects on expected inflation of movements in actual inflation are limited.

To summarize, Tables 9.2 and 9.3 suggest that inflation expectations of consumers across European countries do not react to movements in inflation or
unanticipated changes in short-term interest rates in a way that is systematically
related to the credibility of central banks (as suggested by Goodhart 1997). To
the extent that these consumers' expectations enter wage negotiations, our results
imply that the adjustment of unemployment towards the NAIRU following a
monetary shock is rather relatively slow, and that demand shocks will influence
unemployment.

Nevertheless, our results are subject to several caveats. First, they are of
course contingent on our constructed measures of expected inflation and unanticipated movements in short-term interest rates. It is possible that these measures are too crude to pick up the effects anticipated by Goodhart (1997).[17] With
respect to our measures of expected inflation, a recent study by Van Lelyveld
(2000) argues that the dataset under consideration, and more specifically the
formulation of the survey questions, implies a shift towards bimodal distributions as the inflation rate falls. Moreover, the experiments are set up in quite a
relatively rudimentary way. For example, the modelling of the reaction of consumers' inflation expectations to jumps in inflation and surprise movements in
short-term interest rates is somewhat arbitrary. Investigating the robustness of
the results to changes in these assumptions and the modelling strategy are
important topics for future work.

Finally, as a third experiment, we investigate the effects on inflation perceptions
(i.e. the information contained in the backward looking survey question) of a
major event that is related to monetary policy. As will be elaborated upon below,
and in contrast to the analysis underlying Tables 9.2 and 9.3, we now include the
period after the establishment of the ECB. In 1999, 11 European countries
adopted the euro as a common currency. To the European consumers however,
the new currency became reality three years later, when the euro coins and banknotes were introduced. We investigate the effects of this policy shock on inflation as it is perceived by consumers, instead of expected inflation. This is the
most appropriate, since it is implausible that consumers anticipated an inflationary effect of the euro in the period before the cash-changeover and adjusted their
expectations about future inflation prior to the cash changeover. That would
require *ex ante* knowledge of the conversion rate and information on possible
economic effects, like additional costs encountered by retailers. Moreover, a
rapid conversion of all prices into a new currency has an immediate effect on
inflation – and hence on perceived inflation – compared to an interest rate adjustment, which will mainly affect future prices and expected inflation. For this
reason we assume that the initial effect of the cash changeover was its impact on
perceived inflation.

To the monetary policymaker, this effect is relevant, since a sudden adjustment of perceptions of current inflation might feed into expectations about future
inflation. Moreover, actual behavior is based on expectations about future prices,

as well as perceived current prices. Hence, a policy shock like this may have additional real economy effects.

Whether an effect of the euro conversion on perceived inflation has economic grounds has attracted a significant amount of research. Dziuda and Mastrobuoni (2009) focus on higher inflation for lower priced goods, which might have had a more than proportional effect on perceived inflation. The European Central Bank has also noted that prices of the most "visible", daily items have risen more than other prices (ECB 2003). Psychological factors might also have played a role. The well-known concept of money illusion is still valid here (Fisher 1928; Shafir *et al.* 1997). According to Traut-Mattausch *et al.* (2004), the conviction that prices would be raised seems to have boosted inflation perceptions. Some persistence in perceived inflation due to the euro could be explained by consumers' inability to adapt to the euro and to problems they may have with conversion calculations (Mastrobuoni 2004).

In order to assess the impact of the euro conversion on perceived inflation, we use survey data, quantified similarly to the data on expected inflation.[18] Our period of analysis focuses on the years before and after the cash-changeover, 1986–2005, using quarterly observations from 15 European countries.[19] Note that we include European countries that have not adopted the euro to provide us with a cross-check of the validity of our hypothesis that the euro-introduction affected perceived inflation rates.

Our econometric analysis is based on an autoregressive time series model of perceived inflation rates, for each country.[20] We assume that the euro introduction can be viewed as a policy intervention that results in aberrant observations with respect to the model of perceived inflation. The significance of these observations is tested through the significance of single-observation dummy variables, using standard *t*-tests at a 5 per cent-level (Franses 1998). Significant dummies in the period 2002–2003 are then included in the model. The resulting equation is tested for autocorrelation in the residuals, as well as non-normality of the residuals, where the latter might indicate any remaining outliers in the data.[21]

It appears that the largest euro-effect on perceived inflation is found for the Netherlands. The final column of Table 9.4 below reports the size of this effect, scaled by average inflation over the sample period. No effect to speak of, or a very small effect is found for the United Kingdom, Denmark and Sweden. These countries have not adopted the euro, which gives additional support for the hypothesis that the temporarily higher rate of perceived inflation was caused by the introduction of the euro.

One explanation that has been given for a significant effect of the euro on perceived inflation is a relative price increase of the most "visible" expenditure items in the period around the euro-introduction.[22] However, a comparatively high rate of inflation for these goods is not unusual in a historic sense (see for example ECB 2003). Figure 9.1 indicates that the relationship between "visible" and "perceived" inflation is limited, at best. Döhring and Mordonu (2007) find that a similar indicator of visible inflation ("out-of-the-pocket expenditure") does not explain inflation perceptions better than the HICP index. Indeed, the graph

Table 9.4 Effects on perceived inflation of euro introduction

	No. of observations (1)	No. of lagged endogenous variables (2)	R^2 (3)	Significant dummy variables (4)	Impulse response (8 quarters) (5)	Effect (by quarter) (6)	Effect (scaled by average inflation) (7)
Belgium	73	1	0.81	–	5.93	0.00	0.00
Greece	80	1	0.64	Q2	4.33	2.26	0.22
Spain	75	1	0.81	Q2	5.09	1.16	0.25
Finland	37	1	0.96	Q1	5.06	0.75	0.28
Portugal	73	1	0.75	Q3, Q5, Q8	4.60	1.70	0.25
Sweden	37	1	0.56	Q1, Q2	2.44	0.26	0.08
Austria	37	1	0.97	Q1, Q3	6.88	1.12	0.49
Germany	77	4	0.93	Q1, Q2, Q3	7.11	1.07	0.54
Denmark	73	1	0.92	–	6.55	0.00	0.00
Italy	79	1	0.77	–	5.02	0.00	0.00
Netherlands	77	4	0.96	Q1, Q2, Q3, Q4, Q5, Q6	5.17	2.51	1.23
United Kingdom	57	1	0.88	–	4.88	0.00	0.00

Notes
1 Estimation period 1986–2005. Later first observation for FI, SW, AU, UK.
2 Optimal lags based on Akaike and Hannan-Quinn criteria.
  Equations include a constant, and quarterly dummy variables for 2002 and 2003.
  Additional dummy variables: 91Q3 (GE), 95Q2 (IT), 01Q2 (NL).
3 All equations stable, no residual autocorrelation, and normally distributed residuals not rejected (p > 0.05).
4 Numbers refer to quarters in 2002 and 2003.
5 Calculated with 1 per cent residual shock.
6 Product of impulse response and sum of estimated dummy variables (significant at 5% level).
7 Average inflation calculated over entire estimation period.

Percentage points

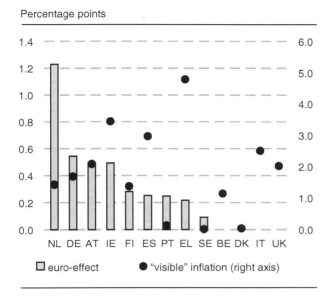

Figure 9.1 Euro-effect and indicator of "visible" inflation.

Notes
Explanation: euro-effect see Table 4, last column.
"Visible" inflation in divergence from HICP-inflation, 2001–2002.

illustrates that there is no cross-sectional relationship between the euro-effect on perceived inflation and "visible" inflation in 2001 and 2002.[23] A full analysis of the cross-sectional differences in the euro-effect on perceived inflation is beyond the scope of this chapter. We conclude that a major monetary policy intervention, like the euro introduction, may have a sizeable impact on perceived inflation rates.

4 Concluding remarks

In this chapter we developed and analysed measures of perceived past and expected future inflation extracted from consumer surveys in the European Union. We showed that currently observed inflation expectations of consumers and the unobserved 12-months-ahead inflation rate have identical long-run properties, a point which is of interest for policymakers. But as our expectations variables do not identify the underlying causes of inflation, caution is warranted in making use of this long-term relationship for monetary policy purposes.

We furthermore find that inflation expectations of European consumers are not affected by unexpected changes in interest rates. To the extent that these expectations play an important role in private sector decisions, our results imply that consumers only gradually adapt to monetary policy shocks. So for example, with respect to wage bargaining, this may imply that the labour market reacts sluggishly to monetary policy changes. However, we find evidence that perceived inflation – the inflation rate as it is observed seen by consumers – has been affected significantly by the advent of the euro in 2002. This implies that a major monetary policy intervention might have significant side effects, to the extent that private sector decisions, like spending and saving, are affected by perceived inflation rates.

Notes

1 Division Economics and Research, De Nederlandsche Bank, Amsterdam. Corresponding author: PO Box 98, 1000 AB Amsterdam, Netherlands. Email: j.m.berk@dnb.nl. Views expressed are those of the authors and do not necessarily reflect the position of De Nederlandsche Bank. The authors wish to thank, without implication, Bryan Chapple, Tomasz Łyziak, Job Swank and participants of the workshop on the role of inflation expectations in modelling and monetary policy making, organized by the National Bank of Poland in Warsaw in February 2006, for constructive comments. Henk van Kerkhoff provided excellent research assistance.
2 Moreover, as credibility increases, the stabilizing role of monetary policy becomes more effective, and output volatility is reduced. The finding of Alesina and Summers (1993) that the high degree of independence of the Deutsche Bundesbank is associated with low inflation with no attendant cost in terms of greater output volatility is generally seen as reflecting the high degree of credibility of that institution.
3 An alternative, third route is to construct an economic model that includes expectations as variables and certain assumptions about how these expectations are formed. Estimating and solving the model then generates projected values for, e.g. the inflation rate. In this case, empirical analysis of the expectations can be carried out only indirectly, and is conditional on the behavioural model. As a result, the conclusions concerning the expectations will not be invariant to the choice of the underlying behavioural model (Kuismanen and Spolander 1994).
4 Other problems include the unreliability of financial market indicators in general. Financial markets tend to over-react to shocks and are susceptible to herding and speculative phenomena, leading to time-varying risk premia that hinder the use of such measures for monetary policy purposes.
5 Both questions also include a "don't know" category. In what follows, we allocate the numbers of this category proportionally to the other response categories. See Visco (1984: 30, 32) for a discussion.
6 Moreover, Bakhshi and Yates (1998) base their analysis on quantitative survey responses whereas we must rely on a quantification of qualitative survey responses.
7 See Berk (1999) for details.
8 A discussant to this chapter by and large corroborated our findings presented below using an updated sample, see Łyziak (2006).
9 Notwithstanding these desirable properties, our method has certain pitfalls. For example, the method breaks down whenever a response category is equal to zero, as such a data point is inadmissible under continuous probability distributions. Second, the transformation of the original frequencies to a form which makes it possible to derive the moments of the assumed distribution is highly non-linear. Small sampling variations could therefore produce large changes in the estimates of these distributional parameters, see Löffler (1999). Third, we assume the process of formation of the expected future inflation rate to be independent of the formation of the perceived past inflation rate. See Berk (2001) for details.
10 The test that actual future inflation and expected inflation are cointegrated with zero

constant term and unit coefficient is effectively a test of the joint hypothesis of unbiasedness and negligible measurement errors (Engsted 1991).

11 Note that the traditional Granger causality tests should be formulated in terms of changes in (expected) inflation because of the non-stationarity of the variables, see Hayo (1999). As we know from the money-output literature, different assumptions about the time series properties can make a difference to the outcome of causality tests, see for example Hafer and Kutan (1997). The significance of the error correction terms in a VECM can be investigated using a conventional *t*-test, see Johansen (1995).

12 We acknowledge that the relatively large number of coefficients to be estimated could adversely affect the power of the tests.

13 As our measure of expected inflation is scaled using the past actual inflation rate, our bivariate causality results might be affected by the behaviour of this scaling variable. More specifically, the causality results may reflect inflation inertia, given the unit root in this inflation process. We checked this by recalculating Table 9.1 using the raw survey data, i.e. the balance statistic consistent with our quantification procedure, see Berk (1999). The results remained qualitatively the same to those in Table 9.1; results are available on request. We thank Tomasz Łyziak for this insight.

14 Hayo (1998) argues that the public attitude towards price stability also plays a role in this respect.

15 We dropped the euro area and the EU from our analysis, because of lack of relevance for this purpose. Portugal was omitted because of data problems.

16 We also examined the direct bivariate relationship, estimated with single-equation OLS, between changes in expected inflation and unexpected interest rate movements, with qualitatively similar results. In addition, we investigated the effects of unanticipated interest rate changes on inflation uncertainty, as derived from the survey responses. They proved to be insignificant.

17 It would be interesting, for example, to compare our measures with measures of monetary policy shocks directly derived from financial market information, as in Bagliano and Favero (1999). We plan to investigate this issue in subsequent research.

18 A scaling factor was chosen so as to equate the mean of the perceived past inflation rate with the mean of the actual past inflation rate.

19 Since our econometric methodology mainly consists of an analysis of aberrant observations, requiring dummy variables, we converted the data to quarterly observations. This keeps the number of independent variables tractable.

20 The null hypothesis of stationarity of the perceived inflation series cannot be rejected for all countries, except Denmark and Ireland, based on the KPSS-test. The ADF-test for a unit root is rejected for all countries, except Ireland and Austria (at 10% level; lag length based on AIC; trend term included where significant at 5% level).

21 We have also tested an alternative, more restrictive model, with one lag and two possible dummy variables (2002Q1 and 2002Q2). The results are similar to those presented here.

22 Our measure of visible inflation includes the following HICP categories: food and non-alcoholic beverages; alcoholic beverages, tobacco and narcotics; other major durables for recreation and culture; other recreational items and equipment, gardens and pets; recreational and cultural services; newspapers, books and stationery; restaurants and hotels; hairdressing salons and personal grooming establishments.

23 In a simple linear regression between the two variables, R^2 is 0.01.

References

Alesina, A. and Summers, L. (1993), Central bank independence and macroeconomic performance: some comparative evidence, *Journal of Money, Credit and Banking*, 25: 151–162.

Angeloni, I. and Rovelli, R. (1998), *Monetary Policy and Interest Rates*, London: Macmillan.

Bagliano, F.C. and Favero, C.A. (1999), Information from financial markets and VAR measures of monetary policy, *European Economic Review*, 43: 825–837.

Bakhshi, H. and Yates, A. (1998), Are UK inflation expectations rational?, *Bank of England Working Paper*, 81.

Bank of Canada (1998), *Information in Financial Asset Prices*, Ottawa: Bank of Canada.

Barr, D.G. and Campbell, J.Y. (1997), Inflation, real interest rates, and the bond market: a study of UK nominal and index-linked government bonds, *Journal of Monetary Economics*, 39: 361–383.

Barro, R.J. and Gordon, D.B. (1983), A positive theory of monetary policy in a natural rate model, *Journal of Political Economy*, 91: 589–610.

Batchelor, R.A. and Dua, P. (1987), The accuracy and rationality of UK inflation expectations: some quantitative evidence, *Applied Economics*, 19: 819–828.

Berk, J.M. (1999), Measuring inflation expectations: a survey data approach, *Applied Economics*, 31: 1467–1480.

Berk, J.M. (2000), Consumers' inflation expectations and monetary policy in Europe, *DNB Staff Reports*, 55/2000, De Nederlandsche Bank, Amsterdam.

Berk, J.M. (2001), *The Preparation of Monetary Policy: Essays on a Multi-model Approach*, Boston, MA: Kluwer Academic Publishers.

Berk, J.M., Kakes, J.I. and Houben, A.C.J.F. (2000), Monetary policy and strategy of the Eurosystem, in: Bergeijk, P.A.G. van, Berndsen, R.J. and Jansen, J. (eds), *Euro Area Economics*, Cheltenham: Edward Elgar.

Bernanke, B.S. and Mishkin, F.S. (1997), Inflation targeting: a new framework for monetary policy?, *Journal of Economic Perspectives*, 11: 97–116.

Bernanke, B.S. and Woodford, M. (1997), Inflation forecasts and monetary policy, *Journal of Money, Credit, and Banking*, 29: 653–686.

Blinder, A.S. (1998), *Central Banking in Theory and Practice*, Cambridge, MA: MIT Press.

Carlson, J.A. and Parkin, M. (1977), Inflation expectations, *Economica*, 42: 123–138.

Chan-Lee, J.H. (1980), A review of recent work in the area of inflationary expectations, *Weltwirtschaftliches Archiv*, 116: 45–86.

Cheung, Y.W. and Chinn, M.D. (1997), Integration, cointegration and the forecast consistency of structural exchange rate models, *NBER Working Paper*, *5943*, Cambridge, MA: NBER.

Cukierman, A. (1994), *Central Bank Strategy, Credibility, and Independence*, Cambridge, MA: MIT Press.

Cukierman, A. and Meltzer, A.H. (1982), What do tests of market efficiency show in the presence of the permanent-transitory confusion, *mimeo*, Carnegie-Mellon University, Pittsburgh.

Döhring, B. and Mordonu, A. (2007), What drives inflation perceptions? A dynamic panel data analysis, *European Economy*, 284, Economic and Financial Affairs, European Commission.

Dziuda, W. and Mastrobuoni, G. (2009), The euro changeover and its effects on price transparency and inflation, *Journal of Money, Credit and Banking*, 41 (1): 101–129.

ECB (2003), *Monthly Bulletin*, October.

Engle, R.F. and Granger, C.W.J. (1987), Co-integration and error correction: representation, estimation and testing, *Econometrica*, 55: 251–276.

Engle, R.F. and Granger, C.W.J. (1991), *Long-run Economic Relationships: Readings in Cointegration*, Oxford: Oxford University Press.

Engsted, T. (1991), A note on the rationality of survey inflation expectations in the United Kingdom, *Applied Economics*, 23: 1269–1275.

Evans, G. and Gulamani, R. (1984), Tests for rationality of the Carlson–Parkin inflation expectations data, *Oxford Bulletin of Economics and Statistics*, 46: 1–19.

Figlewski, S. and Wachtel, P. (1981), The formation of inflationary expectations, *Review of Economics and Statistics*, 63: 1–10.

Fisher, I. (1928), *The Money Illusion*, New York: Adelphi.

Franses, P.H. (1998), *Time Series Models for Business and Economic Forecasting*, Cambridge, UK: Cambridge University Press.

Franses, P.H. and McAleer, M. (1998), Cointegration analysis of seasonal time series, *Journal of Economic Surveys*, 12: 651–679.

Fuhrer, J. and Moore, G. (1992), Monetary policy rules and the indicator properties of asset prices, *Journal of Monetary Economics*, 29: 303–336.

Goodhart, C.A.E. (1997), Why do the monetary authorities smooth interest rates?, in Collignon (ed.), *European Monetary Policy*, London: Pinter, pp. 119–178.

Greenspan, A. (1996), Opening remarks to the 1996 Jackson Hole Symposium: Achieving Price Stability, *Federal Reserve Bank of Kansas City*: 1–5.

Groeneveld, J.M., Knot, K.H.W. and Wesseling, A.A.T. (1996), De Monetaire Beleidsstrategie van de ECB, *ESB*, 81: 618–621.

Hafer, R.W. and Kutan, A.M. (1997), More evidence on the money-output relationship, *Economic Inquiry*, 35: 48–58.

Hayo, B. (1998), Inflation culture, central bank independence and price stability, *European Journal of Political Economy*, 14: 241–263.

Hayo, B. (1999), Money-output Granger causality revisited: an emprirical analysis of EU countries, *Applied Economics*, 31: 1489–1501.

Holden, K. and Peel, D.A. (1977), An empirical investigation of inflationary expectations, *Oxford Bulletin of Economics and Statistics*, 39: 291–299.

Hördahl, P. (2000), Estimating the implied distribution of the future short-term interest rate using the Longstaff-Schwartz model, *ECB Working Paper*, 16.

Johansen, S. (1995), *Likelihood-based Inference in Cointegrated Vector Autoregressive Models*, Oxford: Oxford University Press.

Jong, E. de (1988), Expectation formation: criteria and assessment, *The Economist*, 136: 435–467.

Kremers, J.J.M, Ericsson, N.R. and Dolado, J.J. (1992), The power of cointegration test, *Oxford Bulletin of Economics and Statistics*, 54: 325–348.

Kuismanen, M. and Spolander, M. (1994), Measuring inflation expectations in Finland: a survey data approach, *Bank of Finland Discussion Papers*, *21/94*, Bank of Finland, Helsinki.

Kuttner, K.N. (2000), Monetary policy surprises and interest rates: evidence from the Fed Funds futures market, *Working Paper*, Federal Reserve Bank of New York.

Kydland, F.E. and Prescott, E.C. (1977), Rules rather than discretion: the inconsistency of optimal plans, *Journal of Political Economy*, 85: 473–491.

Lee, K.C. (1994), Formation of price and cost inflation expectations in British manufacturing industries, *Economic Journal*, 104: 372–385.

Leeuw, F. de and McKelvey, M.J. (1981), Price expectations of business firms, *Brookings Papers on Economic Activity*, 1: 299–313.

Lelyveldt, I.P.P. van (2000), *Inflation, Institutions, and Preferences*, unpublished PhD thesis.

Löffler, G. (1999), Refining the Carlson–Parkin method, *Economics Letters*, 64: 167–171.

Lucas, R.E. (1976), Econometric policy evaluation: a critique, in R.E. Lucas (ed.), *Studies in Business-Cycle Theory*, Cambridge, MA: MIT Press, pp. 104–130.

Łyziak, T. (2006), Consumers' inflation expectations and monetary policy in Europe: a discussion, *mimeo*, National Bank of Poland.

Madsen, J.B. (1996), Formation of inflation expectations: from the simple to the rational expectations hypothesis, *Applied Economics*, 28: 1331–1337.

Mastrobuoni, G. (2004), The effect of the euro-conversion on prices and price perceptions, *CEPS Working Paper*, 101.

Menil, G. de and Bhalla, S.S. (1975), Direct measurement of popular price expectations, *American Economic Review*, 65: 169–180.

Mylonas, P. and Schich, S.T. (1999), The use of financial market indicators by monetary authorities, *OECD Economics Department Working Paper*, 223.

Newey, W.K. and West, K.D. (1987), A simple, positive semi-definite, heteroskedasticity and autocorrelation consistent covariance matrix, *Econometrica*, 55: 703–708.

Papadia, F. (1983), Rationality of inflationary expectations in the European Economic Community Countries, *Empirical Economics*, 8: 187–202.

Pearce, D.K. (1979), Comparing survey and rational measures of expected inflation, *Journal of Money, Credit and Banking*, 11: 447–456.

Pesando, J.E. (1975), A note on the rationality of the Livingston price expectations, *Journal of Political Economy*, 83: 849–858.

Pesaran, M.H. (1985), Formation of inflation expectations in British manufacturing industries, *Economic Journal*, 95: 948–975.

Schmidt, F.A. (1999), Extracting inflation expectations from bond yields, *Monetary Trends*, April, Federal Reserve Bank of St Louis.

Shafir, E., Diamond, P. and Tversky, A. (1997), Money illusion, *Quarterly Journal of Economics*: 341–374.

Shigehara, K. (1996), The options regarding the concept of a monetary policy strategy, in Deutsche Bundesbank (ed.), *Monetary Policy Strategies in Europe*, München: Vahlen-Verlag, pp. 7–44.

Simmons, P. and Weiserbs, D. (1992), Consumer price perceptions and expectations, *Oxford Economic Papers*, 44: 35–50.

Smyth, D.J. (1992), Measurement errors in survey forecasts of expected inflation and the rationality of inflation expectations, *Journal of Macroeconomics*, 14: 439–448.

Svensson, L.E.O. (1999), Monetary policy issues for the Eurosystem, *NBER Working Paper*, *7177*, Cambridge, MA: NBER.

Svensson, L.E.O. and Woodford, M. (2000), Indicator variables for monetary policy, *ECB Working Paper*, *12*, Frankfurt: ECB.

Thomas, D.G. (1995), Output expectations within manufacturing industry, *Applied Economics*, 27: 403–408.

Traut-Mattausch, E., Schulz-Hardt, S., Greitemeyer, T. and Frey, D. (2004), Expectancy confirmation in spite of disconfirming evidence: the case of price increases due to the introduction of the euro, *European Journal of Social Psychology*, 34: 739–760.

Visco, I. (1984), *Price Expectations in Rising Inflation*, Amsterdam: North-Holland.

Walsh, C.E. (2003), *Monetary Theory and Policy*, 2nd edition, MIT Press.

Woodford, M. (1994), Nonstandard indicators for monetary policy: can their usefulness be judged from forecasting regressions?, in N.G. Mankiw (ed.), *Monetary Policy*, Studies in Business Cycles, 29, Cambridge, MA: NBER.

10 Testing near-rationality using survey data[1]

Michael F. Bryan[2] and Stefan Palmqvist[3]

1 Introduction

Since Phelps (1967) and Friedman (1968), economists have generally accepted the proposition that, in an environment in which expectations converge to fully rational, the natural rate of unemployment represents the threshold to which a central bank can permanently reduce unemployment without accelerating inflation. Akerlof *et al.* (2000), hereafter ADP, have proposed that some agents form "nearly-rational" inflation expectations, a behavioral assumption that agents either underweight inflation (only incorporate a fraction of it) when making decisions or, in the extreme, ignore it altogether. Further, as the economic incentive to anticipate inflation varies from agent to agent, the proportion of nearly-rational agents in the economy is an inverse function of inflation, producing a "kink" in the long-run Phillips curve below the natural rate of unemployment (see Figure 10.1, which reproduces the long-run Phillips curve derived by ADP

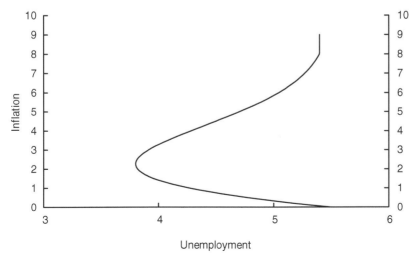

Figure 10.1 Long-run Phillips curve under near-rationality (source: Akerlof *et al.* (2000), figure 1).

from their theoretical model). The mechanism by which this kink is produced is as follows: At zero inflation, rational as well as nearly-rational individuals expect no inflation, which makes actual inflation equal to expected. As inflation rises above zero, the nearly-rational agents underestimate inflation, and thus overestimate their real wage increases, work more, and thereby drive down unemployment. However, as inflation rises, some of the agents that were nearly-rational at lower inflation rates find it worthwhile to start predicting inflation accurately and thus switch to forming rational inflation expectations. As a consequence, as inflation increases, a smaller proportion of households form nearly-rational expectations, which tends to push their unemployment in the opposite direction. The interaction of these two effects suggests that unemployment is minimized (employment is maximized) at a low, but strictly positive rate of inflation.

In the ADP model, the conventional natural rate of unemployment is merely a special case of the sustainable long-run unemployment rates, in which either the rate of inflation is zero or so high that all agents find it advantageous to make decisions using rational inflation expectations. The authors stop short of providing precise estimates of the inflation rate that minimizes unemployment and, indeed, they "resisted the temptation to call the unemployment-minimizing rate of inflation the optimal rate."[4] The welfare implications of the ADP model are not perfectly clear since, via the efficiency wage assumption, productivity also varies with the rate of inflation. Further, the wedge between actual and perceived real wages that causes an unwitting substitution between labor and leisure needs to be evaluated relative to the distortions created by wage and price frictions in the model. But subsequent discussion by ADP is less cautious, and they state that:

> Zero inflation is an inappropriate policy target [of the central bank] because it raises the sustainable rate of unemployment by a significant amount.... Moderate inflation, which includes the range of [US] experience of recent years, with the core CPI rising at a 2 to 2.5 percent annual rate, allows the economy to operate with low unemployment. Such an inflation rate yields maximum prosperity.[5]

Whether it provides a prescription for an optimal inflation rate or not, the ADP model gives a rationale for why a central bank might target inflation at a moderately positive level, which, in practice, virtually every central bank with an inflation target has chosen to do.[6] The existence of nearly-rational agents as described in ADP implies that a central bank must produce a modest inflation if the minimization of unemployment is among its long-run objectives.[7]

This chapter tests whether the assumption of near-rationality conforms to households' inflation expectations as measured by survey data. Section 2 argues that the evidence provided in ADP is consistent with any set of expectations that are less-than-fully rational. To test their particular form of expectations formation – near-rationality – one needs to bring the theory to actual data on agents' expectations. We do this in Section 3, which considers the case of near-rationality using survey data for households, first in the aggregate data, and then in micro-survey data. We find that these survey data fail to reveal the correspondence between nearly-rational agents and inflation that ADP suggest. Section 4 concludes.

2 Re-examining the evidence of near-rational inflation expectations

To test the near-rationality hypothesis, Akerlof *et al.* (2000) estimate Phillips curves of the following general form using US data,

$$\pi_t = c + \beta\pi_{t,\,t-n}^e + \gamma(L)U_t + \varepsilon_t, \tag{1}$$

where π is realized inflation, π^e is expected inflation formed at some earlier date (typically, one year ago), and U is the unemployment rate.[8] Equation (1) is estimated in two subperiods, high inflation, where the five-year inflation trend exceeds 4 percent, and low inflation, where the inflation trend is less than 3 percent, or, alternatively, less than 2.5 percent. For each subperiod, they specify equation (1) using different lag structures and alternative measures of inflation, inflation expectations, and the unemployment rate. Inflation is alternatively measured as the annual percentage change in the CPI, the GDP deflator, or the PCE (personal consumption expenditure) deflator, expected inflation is taken from the University of Michigan's Survey of Consumer Attitudes or the Livingston Survey of Professional Forecasters, and unemployment is measured as the rate for all civilian workers, the rate for 25- to 54-year-old males, or as Shimer's (1988) demographically adjusted series.[9] The alternative specifications of the high- and low-inflation samples and the different lag structures, combined with the different measures of inflation, inflation expectations, and the unemployment rate yield a total of 144 alternative estimated price equations for each sample (see Figure 10.2, which reproduces the high- and low-inflation βs estimated this way by ADP.) ADP find that while the constellation of the estimated βs is approximately unity in the high-inflation sample (mean = 1.00), it is significantly less than one in the low-inflation sample (mean = 0.25). This finding is consistent with their near-rationality hypothesis as it shows that only a fraction of aggregate expected inflation enters the estimated Phillips curve equations in the low-inflation sample, while in the high-inflation sample, aggregate expectations are fully incorporated into the estimated equations.

Having found evidence consistent with the near-rationality hypothesis, ADP turn to the long-run Phillips curve. Using a nonlinear representation, ADP approximate their model using a variety of alternative "right-hand side" variables. Regarding the inflation rate that minimizes long-run unemployment, ADP conclude that

> The densest cluster of estimates spans a range from 1.5 to 3 percent for the inflation rate that maximizes employment in the long run. The estimated

unemployment reduction from operating the economy at that inflation rate (rather than at zero or high inflation) falls mainly in the range from 0.5 to 3 percentage points.[10]

Lundborg and Sacklén (2006) follow the approach used by ADP to estimate a long-run, expectations-augmented Phillips curve for Sweden. When survey measures of inflation expectations are used, they find that the unemployment-minimizing rate of inflation is about 4 percent, compared to Sweden's current inflation target of 2 percent. If Sweden were to raise its inflation target to 4 percent, the authors claim, unemployment would be permanently reduced from 4–5 percent to about 2–3 percent. In Lundborg and Sacklén (2003), the authors show that under the conditions laid out by ADP, raising the inflation target reduces unemployment as well as workers' effort. But the increased employment more than offsets the lower effort levels, and hence, output rises. The authors therefore argue that raising the inflation target by 2 percentage points is welfare improving.

A decline in the estimated β in equation (1) below unity for a low-inflation regime is merely the observation that the covariance of actual and expected inflation (given the cyclical state of the economy) falls relative to the variance of inflation expectations. But this may be true for any number of less-than-fully-rational expectation assumptions. As an example, suppose that a fraction of the population expects an inflation rate that on average equals the central bank's

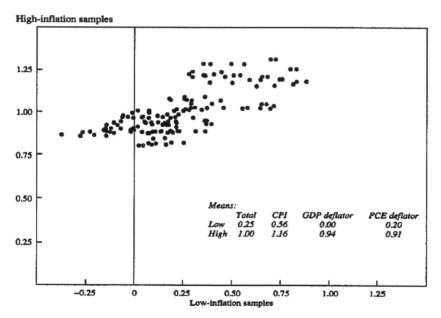

Figure 10.2 Coefficients on expected inflation for alternative Phillips curve specifications in high- and low-inflation samples (source: Akerlof *et al.* (2000), figure 6).

long-run inflation target and the remainder form rational expectations. Suppose further that if observed inflation remains close to the target, the central bank gains credibility and a rising proportion of agents expect the central bank to deliver the stated objective. Under those expectations, β would appear less than unity if one estimated equation (1) in the low-inflation sample, but unity in the high-inflation sample. Indeed any expectations scheme where a part of the population hold expectations centered on *any* constant is consistent with the findings in Figure 10.2.

The method and data used by ADP and Lundborg and Sacklén cannot distinguish between their specific form of near-rationality and other, less-than-fully-rational inflation expectations. So we follow the approach suggested by Nordhaus in the general discussion of ADP, and "test whether inflationary expectations in fact have responded to experienced inflation in the nonlinear way suggested by the paper."[11] To conduct such tests one needs direct measures of inflation expectations, and we therefore use survey measures of inflation expectations. This is a topic to which we now turn.

3 Evidence of near-rationality in survey data

Our data on inflation expectations consists of two surveys. For the United States we use individual responses from the Michigan Survey of Consumer Attitudes for the period 1978–1999. These data are collected monthly from a national survey of at least 500 respondents. For Sweden, we use the Households Purchasing Plans (HIP) survey for the period 1979–2001.[12] The HIP survey was conducted on a quarterly basis from 1979 until 1992 and on a monthly basis thereafter. The HIP originally consisted of about 10,000 households, but its size has been reduced over time to reach the current levels of about 1,500 respondents.

Both surveys ask similarly posed and structured questions. In the Michigan survey, respondents are first asked: "During the next 12 months, do you think that prices in general will go up, or go down, or stay where they are now?" Respondents are then asked to quantify their answer by the question: "By about what percent do you expect prices to go up (down) on average, during the next 12 months?" In Sweden, respondents are asked: "If you compare with the situation today, do you think prices in general over the next 12 months will: increase, be about the same, decrease somewhat?" which is followed with: "By how many percent do you think they will: increase/decrease?"[13, 14]

There are no dynamics in the model used by ADP to derive the long-run Phillips curve, making direct tests of near-rationality virtually impossible. As an example, suppose that the economy is hit by a transitory shock to the inflation rate, causing the inflation rate to rise temporarily. Should such a shock induce the nearly-rational agents to start forming rational inflation expectations, or does a change in behavior require that the shock have persistent effects on the inflation rate? As the ADP model provides no guidelines on what triggers a change in behavior, we proceed along two paths. We first identify different inflation "regimes" in the two countries. This approach only requires that a change in the expectations formation occurs when permanent changes in the inflation trend are observed. But, by using all available inflation information, we also consider the case where every change in inflation – temporary or not – has the potential to induce a change in expectations formation in accordance with near-rationality.

To identify the different inflation regimes in the two countries, we conducted Bai-Perron (1998) break-points tests on the US CPI and the core CPI in Sweden.[15,16] These break-points are shown in Figure 10.3 together with the average inflation rate between two break dates, henceforth referred to as the "inflation trend." The tests reveal that both nations experienced two inflation break-points, yielding three distinct inflation regimes. The regimes are remarkably similar for the two countries. In the United States, the first inflation break is estimated between July and August of 1982, when the inflation trend drops from 10.2 percent to 3.9 percent. The second break occurs between January and February of 1991, when the inflation trend falls to 2.7 percent. In Sweden, the first break in the inflation data is estimated between December of 1983 and January of 1984 as the inflation trend drops from 9.6 percent to 6.0 percent. The second break occurs between March and April of 1991, when the inflation trend is reduced to 2.5 percent. Sweden announced a formal inflation target in January 1993, but at the time of the introduction of inflation targeting the inflation rate had already fallen substantially. Thus, our test picks up a break prior to the announcement of inflation targeting. Note that since the early 1990s, the United States and Sweden have followed nearly identical low-inflation paths, regarding actual as well as trend inflation, after having formerly followed higher trends.

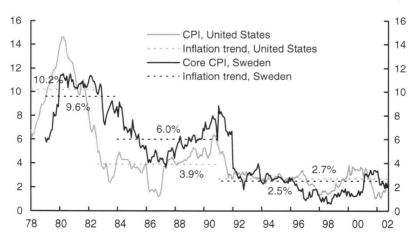

Figure 10.3 Inflation regimes in the United States and Sweden (sources: Bureau of Labor Statistics, Statistics Sweden, and own calculations).

Note
The inflation trends refer to the average inflation rate between two break dates, where the break dates are identified by the Bai-Perron (1998) break-point test.

Near-rationality implies that household inflation expectations errors should correspond to inflation in a nonlinear way: At zero inflation, there should be no difference between those who ignore inflation and those who are fully rational. Hence, the ADP model implies that in the aggregate (the average across households) expectations errors should be zero at price stability. In a low, but positive inflation environment, however, as some fraction of individuals ignore inflation while the rest form their expectations rationally, the ADP model predicts that aggregate inflation expectations will be less than realized inflation. As inflation continues to rise, a larger proportion of the population form their expectations in a fully rational way, so that the aggregate expectations error, eventually, shrinks as the added accuracy of the rational agents more than offsets the increasingly negative expectations errors of the nearly-rational. Eventually (at very high inflation), the ADP framework assumes everyone is fully rational and the aggregate expectations error tends to zero again.

3.1 Evidence of near-rationality in the aggregate survey data

Our first test of near-rationality computes the average aggregate expectations errors across the different regimes, and checks whether these expectations errors correspond to inflation in such a nonlinear way. In Table 10.1 we report the average aggregate inflation expectations errors for the United States and Sweden in the full sample period as well as in the different regimes.

In the United States, aggregate inflation expectations errors are, on average, small (about 8 percent of the realized inflation rate), and positive. This is problematic. Rational expectations imply that these average aggregate errors should be zero, and near-rationality would turn them negative. However, a large number of studies have found a positive "bias" in mean survey data for the United States when the benchmark for comparison is an aggregate consumer price index.[17] US survey data on household inflation expectations are typically higher than the

Table 10.1 Household inflation expectations errors and inflation in the United States and Sweden

Country	Period	Average aggregate expectations error	Average inflation
United States	1978:01–1999:12	0.39	4.8
United States	1978:01–1982:07	−1.28	10.2
United States	1982:08–1991:01	0.63	3.9
United States	1991:02–1999:12	1.01	2.7
Sweden	1979:I–2001:12	−0.09	5.2
Sweden	1979:I–1983:IV	−0.88	9.6
Sweden	1984:I–1991:I	0.73	6.0
Sweden	1991:II–2001:12	−0.16	2.5

Notes
The inflation measures refer to the CPI in the United States and the core CPI (CPIX) in Sweden. Expectations errors are calculated as the expected inflation minus 12-month forward inflation.

officially reported CPI-measures. These survey data do not record household predictions of any particular inflation statistic, but rather the growth rate of "prices in general," leaving ambiguous the benchmark against which respondent accuracy should be judged.[18] To compensate for any potential benchmark error, we focus on the differences in the expectations errors across the three regimes. In the United States, as inflation is reduced from about 10 percent to about 4 percent, households switch from under- to over-predicting inflation. As inflation is reduced further, from about 4 percent to about 3 percent, US households overestimate inflation even more. That average aggregate inflation expectations errors in the United States increase as inflation falls strongly contradicts the ADP near-rationality hypothesis.

In Sweden, households' inflation expectations roughly coincide on average with realized inflation. However, as inflation fell from about 10 percent to 6 percent, households, on average went from under- to overestimating inflation, and, as inflation was reduced further, from about 6 percent to 2.5 percent, households again, on average, underpredicted inflation. While the behavior of aggregate expectations errors across the last two regimes in Sweden is broadly consistent with ADP near-rationality, the "inverted U-shape" observed across all three regimes is hard to reconcile with near-rationality.

It is not clear from the ADP model whether a transitory increase in inflation should cause the nearly-rational households to start forming rational expectations or if the increase must be more persistent to induce a change in the process of inflation expectations formation. Table 10.1 looked at changes in the inflation trend, which can be thought of as representing permanent changes in the inflation rate. In what follows, we instead consider all fluctuations in inflation and regress aggregate household inflation expectations errors on the rate of inflation with the simple, nonlinear form,

$$\pi^e_{t,\,t-12} - \pi_t = \alpha + \beta_1 \pi_t + \beta_2 \pi_t^2 + \varepsilon_t, \tag{2}$$

where π^e is aggregate expected inflation from the survey 12 months ago, and π is the inflation rate. If ADP-type near-rationality holds, we expect to find $\alpha = 0$, $\beta_1 < 0, \beta_2 > 0$, and $|\beta_1| > \beta_2$. The results of this experiment are in Table 10.2.

The first two rows depict the results from the Michigan survey. Aggregate expectations errors are about 3 percent at zero inflation. A significant constant in the US data need not tell against near-rationality. Consistent with ADP-type near-rationality, we find that the coefficient on the inflation rate is correctly signed and significant, but the coefficient on squared inflation, while it has the expected sign, is insignificant. In the case of Sweden, as ADP-type near-rationality predicts, aggregate expectations errors are not significantly different from zero at price stability. However, the coefficients on inflation and squared inflation are insignificant and wrongly signed. That does not accord with ADP-type near-rationality.

Figure 10.4 shows the expectations errors for the US data, together with the fitted values from equation (2), as well as the U-shaped relation predicted by the

Table 10.2 Expectations errors as a nonlinear function of inflation in the United States and Sweden

Country	Period	α	β₁	β₂	R²
United States	1978:01–1999:12	2.97***	−0.68***	0.02	0.68
		(0.40)	(0.15)	(0.01)	
United States[a]	1978:01–1999:12	2.62***	−0.50**	0.01	0.52
		(0.51)	(0.21)	(0.01)	
Sweden	1979:I–2001:12	−0.24	0.20	−0.03	0.10
		(0.37)	(0.20)	(0.02)	

Notes
Standard errors using the Newey–West procedure are shown within parenthesis. ***, **, and * denote significance at the 1, 5, and 10 percent level. [a] Uses expectation values posted on University of Michigan's Survey of Consumer Attitudes website which imputes values for "up, don't know" and "down, don't know" based on the distribution of known responses.

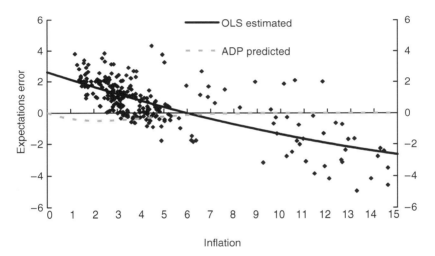

Figure 10.4 Aggregate expectations errors and inflation in the United States (sources: Bureau of Labor Statistics, University of Michigan's Survey of Consumer Attitudes, and own calculations).

Notes
The data refer to the period 1978–1999. The dashed line represents the predicted relation under near-rationality. The dots represent actual expectations errors, plotted against the 12-month forward inflation rate, and the solid line is the estimated relationship from equation (2).

ADP model. The dashed line is the expected relationship under near-rationality, where we have assumed that at zero inflation half of the agents are fully rational and at 5 percent inflation 95 percent of the agents are fully rational, which corresponds to the assumptions made by ADP in their theoretical work. The dots are the actual expectations errors from the Michigan survey plotted against the realized CPI-inflation. Figure 10.5 shows the corresponding findings from

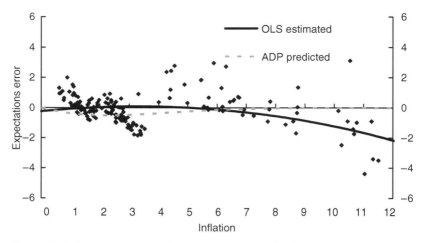

Figure 10.5 Aggregate expectations errors and inflation in Sweden (sources: Statistics
         Sweden and own calculations).

Notes
The data refer to the period 1979–2001. The dashed line represents the predicted relation under near-
rationality. The dots represent actual expectations errors, plotted against the 12-month forward inflation rate, and the solid line is the estimated relationship from equation (2).

Swedish data. These figures further illustrate the findings in Table 10.2: the
expectations errors do not vary with the rate of inflation as predicted by the ADP
near-rationality hypothesis. The figures also suggest that the evidence against
that hypothesis is robust to the simple, quadratic, functional form in equation
(2), since they indicate that there is no other natural specification that would pick
up a nonlinear relation supporting it.

Overall, we find evidence for ADP near-rationality lacking in the aggregate
household survey data. The relationship between errors in household inflation
expectations and inflation does not match the model's prediction. However, a
complete evaluation of the ADP model requires a more careful examination of
the behavior of the individual household inflation predictions, a topic to which
we now turn.

3.2 Evidence of near-rationality in the micro survey data

A key implication of the near-rationality hypothesis is that when inflation is
below some threshold, some individuals underpredict inflation, or, in the
extreme, they ignore it altogether. The lower the inflation rate the greater is the
proportion of households that underpredict or ignore inflation. A simple test of
near-rationality would therefore be to check whether the proportion of households that ignore or underpredict inflation is inversely related to inflation.
However, before doing that we need to address the evidence that households
hold very different expectations about inflation.[19]

In terms of the ADP-framework, allowing for heterogeneous responses from the proportion of households that form rational expectations implies that we no longer know whether a household that expects no inflation belongs to the nearly-rational or rational proportion of the population. Also, if we allow for heterogeneity among the rational individuals it seems plausible that the fraction of zero responses among the rational individuals increases when inflation falls. We would therefore expect the fraction of households expecting no inflation to vary inversely with inflation even in the case where all agents form rational expectations.

Near-rationality combined with heterogeneity of responses among rational individuals therefore implies that the test for near-rationality must be modified. As inflation falls, there will be more nearly-rational households expecting no (or underpredicting) inflation, and more rational households expecting no inflation. In the extreme case, where nearly-rational households ignore inflation, the fraction of households expecting no inflation should thus vary nonlinearly with inflation in order to be consistent with near-rationality. In the case where the nearly-rational individuals underpredict inflation, ADP near-rationality only requires that the fraction of households underpredicting inflation varies inversely (i.e. not necessarily nonlinearly) with inflation. In Table 10.3 we show the fraction of households expecting no inflation, and the fraction of households underpredicting inflation in the full sample and the three regimes.

In the United States, there are on average 18 percent of the respondents that expect no inflation over the next year, and 54 percent of the respondents underpredict inflation on average. As we go from one inflation regime to another, the proportion of households expecting no inflation is almost unaffected, whereas the proportion of households underpredicting inflation falls with the inflation trend. Thus, irrespective of which form of near-rationality we are considering (ignoring or underpredicting inflation), these findings are inconsistent with near-rationality. If anything, Table 10.3 suggests that more households underpredict inflation at high rates of inflation.

In Sweden, the proportion of households expecting no inflation increases as inflation is reduced from about 10 percent to about 6 percent, and it increases substantially as inflation is reduced further, which is consistent with the predictions of the extreme version of ADP where the nearly-rational individuals ignore inflation. The substantial increase in the proportion of households expecting no inflation is also associated with a rise in the proportion of households underpredicting inflation. The only evidence against ADP in the case of Sweden is that the proportion of households underpredicting inflation falls by almost 20 percentage points when Sweden goes from the first to the second inflation regime.

Looking at the full data set, we regress the fraction of households expecting no, or underpredicting, inflation on the rate of inflation with the simple, nonlinear form,

$$f = \gamma + \delta_1 \pi_t + \delta_2 \pi_t^2 + \varepsilon_t, \tag{3}$$

Table 10.3 Fraction of households expecting no inflation, fraction of households underpredicting inflation, and inflation in the United States and Sweden

Country	Period	Fraction of zeros	Fraction underpredicting	Average inflation
United States	1978:01–1999:12	0.18	0.54	4.8
United States	1978:01–1982:07	0.18	0.66	10.2
United States	1982:08–1991:01	0.17	0.56	3.9
United States	1991:02–1999:12	0.18	0.47	2.7
Sweden	1979:I–2001:12	0.41	0.62	5.2
Sweden	1979:I–1983:IV	0.07	0.65	9.6
Sweden	1984:I–1991:I	0.10	0.49	6.0
Sweden	1991:II–2001:12	0.54	0.65	2.5

Note
The inflation measures refer to the CPI in the US and the core CPI (CPIX) in Sweden.

Table 10.4 Proportion of households expecting no inflation and proportion of households underpredicting inflation as a nonlinear function of inflation in the United States and Sweden

Country	Period	γ	δ_1	δ_2	R^2
United States, no inflation	1978:1–1999:12	0.17^{***} (0.02)	0.01 (0.01)	0.00 (0.00)	0.12
United States, underpredicting	1978:1–1999:12	0.20^{***} (0.05)	0.11^{***} (0.02)	-0.01^{***} (0.001)	0.62
Sweden, no inflation	1979:I–2001:12	0.77^{***} (0.04)	-0.14^{***} (0.02)	0.01^{***} (0.00)	0.80
Sweden, underpredicting	1979:I–2001:12	0.72^{***} (0.04)	-0.06^{***} (0.02)	0.01^{***} (0.00)	0.12

Notes
Standard errors using the Newey–West procedure are shown within parenthesis. ***, **, and * denote significance at the 1, 5, and 10 percent level.

where f is the fraction of households expecting no, or underpredicting, inflation, and π is the inflation rate. We expect to find $\gamma = 0.5$, $\delta_1 < 0$, $\delta_2 > 0$, and $|\delta_1| > \delta_2$ if ADP near-rationality holds. The results of this experiment are in Table 10.4.

Table 10.4 shows that, in the United States, the proportion of households expecting no inflation is unrelated to the actual inflation rate. For the households that underpredicted inflation, we find that the coefficients on both inflation and squared inflation are wrongly signed and significant. For Sweden we find that the fractions of households expecting no inflation, and underpredicting inflation, conform to the predictions of near-rationality.

Figures 10.6 and 10.7 show the fraction of households expecting no inflation over the coming year as a function of the realized inflation rate in the United States and Sweden, respectively. We have also included the estimated relationship from Table 10.4 in the figures. In the US data, there is no relationship between the realized rate of inflation and the proportion of households predicting price stability. Thus, our findings for the United States in Table 10.4 are robust to the simple quadratic functional form we assume in equation (3). Yet the results are very different in the HIP data for Sweden. The proportion of Swedish households predicting no inflation jumps substantially when the realized rate of inflation falls below 3 percent, a finding broadly in line with the prediction of ADP.

Similarly, we can check the proportions of US and Swedish households who underpredict inflation as a function of realized inflation (Figures 10.8 and 10.9), and again, we observe a striking difference between the two nations. In the United States, the proportion of households underestimating inflation is negatively related to inflation, in conflict with the predictions of ADP near-rationality. However, in Sweden, the proportion of households under-predicting inflation rises appreciably as inflation falls under 3 percent, again, seemingly consistent with the predictions of the ADP framework. However, at rates of inflation above 5 percent, the under-prediction of inflation by Swedish households rises again, which is hard to reconcile with that model.

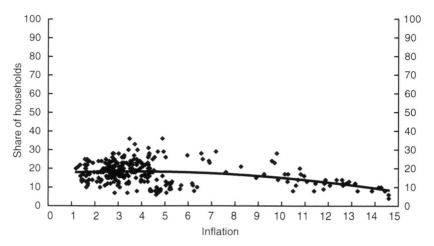

Figure 10.6 Share of US households expecting no inflation and inflation (sources: Bureau of Labor Statistics, University of Michigan's Survey of Consumer Attitudes, and own calculations).

Notes
The data refer to the period 1978–1999. The dots represent the proportion of households expecting no inflation, plotted against the 12-month forward inflation rate, and the solid line is the estimated relationship from equation (3).

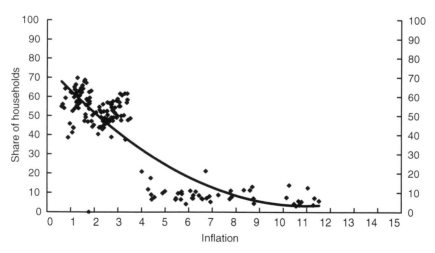

Figure 10.7 Share of Swedish households expecting no inflation and inflation (sources: Statistics Sweden and own calculations).

Notes
The data refer to the period 1979–2001. The dots represent the proportion of households expecting no inflation, plotted against the 12-month forward inflation rate, and the solid line is the estimated relationship from equation (3).

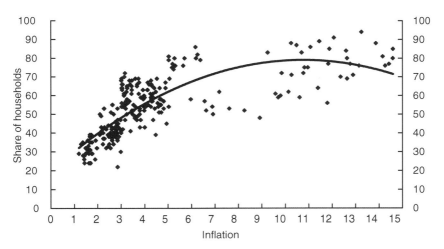

Figure 10.8 Share of US households underpredicting inflation and inflation (sources: Bureau of Labor Statistics, University of Michigan's Survey of Consumer Attitudes, and own calculations).

Notes
The data refer to the period 1978–1999. Each dot represents the proportion of households underpredicting inflation, plotted against the 12-month forward inflation rate, and the solid line is the estimated relationship from equation (3).

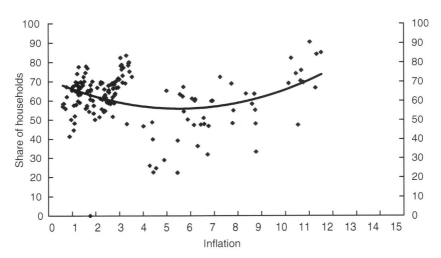

Figure 10.9 Share of Swedish households underpredicting inflation and inflation (sources: Statistics Sweden and own calculations).

Notes
The data refer to the period 1979–2001. Each dot represents the proportion of households underpredicting inflation, plotted against the 12-month forward inflation rate, and the solid line is the estimated relationship from equation (3).

In sum, the evidence in aggregate survey data is unsupportive of near-rationality, both in the United States and in Sweden. In the US micro survey data reveal further evidence against near-rationality, whereas the Swedish micro data seem more supportive of it.

4 Conclusion

This chapter has considered the evidence of "near-rationality" in household inflation expectations using detailed survey data. We reject the specific form of near-rational inflation expectations suggested by Akerlof *et al.* and are unable to demonstrate several of the key testable propositions of their theory, at least as it applies to households.

We have been able to show that households' inflation expectations are not near-rational in the particular form ADP suggest. But other types of less-than-fully-rational inflation expectations formation are not excluded. Indeed, our investigation of the household survey data for Sweden and the United States have revealed new insights into the expectations formation process. Households in both nations tend consistently to underestimate inflation during a high-inflation regime, but consistently over-estimate it when inflation is moderate. We have also uncovered intriguing differences between the two countries in the most recent, low-inflation period. Although both the United States and Sweden followed a nearly identical inflation trend, Swedish households, on average, formed more accurate inflation expectations. Further, an unusually large share of Swedish households reported an expectation of zero inflation compared to the United States during this low-inflation period. Whether the advent of inflation targeting in Sweden contributed to the break in similarity between the expectations of inflation for Swedish versus US households remains an intriguing open question.

Notes

1 We would like to thank Lars Jonung for comments as well as suggesting this line of research, George Akerlof, John Carlson, Christoph Knoppik, and John Roberts for comments, Guhan Venkatu, Linsey Molloy, and Pat Higgins for excellent research assistance, Richard Curtin at the Survey Research Center of the University of Michigan, the NIER, and Anita Olsson-Malmberg of Statistics Sweden for supplying the data. We have also benefited from presenting the chapter at the EEA-ESEM conference in Madrid, the European Commission, the Bank of Poland's conference on Inflation Expectations, the Federal Reserve System's Macroeconomic Research Group, the NIER, the Reserve Bank of Australia, Sveriges Riksbank, and Växjö University. The views expressed in this chapter are solely the responsibility of the authors and should not be interpreted as reflecting the views of the Federal Reserve Bank of Atlanta, the Federal Reserve System, or the Executive Board of Sveriges Riksbank.
2 Federal Reserve Bank of Atlanta, Research Department, 1000 Peachtree Street N.E., Atlanta, GA 30309-4470. E-mail: Mike.Bryan@atl.frb.org.
3 Sveriges Riksbank, Monetary Policy Department, SE-103 37 Stockholm, Sweden. E-mail: Stefan.Palmqvist@riksbank.se.
4 Akerlof *et al.* (2000), p. 19.

5 Akerlof *et al.* (2001), pp. 7–8.
6 See e.g. Kuttner (2004).
7 Giavazzi and Mishkin (2006) discuss the optimal inflation target for Sweden in the context of the ADP framework, although they dismiss the notion by claiming that, among other reasons, "the evidence for the Akerlof–Dickens–Perry mechanism is not at all clear cut."
8 They also estimate wage Phillips curves, with similar empirical results. We therefore only describe the results and method used to estimate the price Phillips curves.
9 As an alternative to using survey data on expectations, they also report results from adaptive expectations using a distributed lag of past inflation rates with similar results.
10 Akerlof *et al.* (2001), p. 7.
11 Brookings Paper on economic activity 2000–2001, p. 56.
12 There was a significant break in the mean survey response at the beginning of 2002, see Palmqvist and Strömberg (2004). We therefore choose to end the Swedish sample in 2001.
13 Both surveys probe the "stay the same" response with a follow-up question, albeit with somewhat different purposes. The Michigan survey follow-up question concerns whether the respondent intended to say that *prices* would remain the same, or whether *inflation* would remain the same. The follow-up question in the HIP tries to separate those who think that prices will be constant over the next 12 months from those who believe in a small, but non-zero, rate of inflation. In the case of the Michigan survey, extreme responses are asymmetrically truncated at the values of −10 percent and +50 percent. No truncation is used in the HIP.
14 From October 1995 and onwards there are five qualitative response options available, so this account refers to the surveys January 1979–September 1995. For a description of the current surveys, see Palmqvist and Strömberg (2004).
15 The Bai-Perron test uses a sequential procedure that jointly identifies the number of breaks implied by the data, and estimates the timing of those breaks.
16 The US CPI measures costs of owner occupied housing on a rental equivalence basis. The Swedish CPI includes mortgage rates as a cost of owner occupied housing. Thus, to get comparable inflation measures we use the Swedish core CPI (called CPIX, formally UND1X) as our inflation benchmark throughout the chapter, since it excludes mortgage rates (as well as the direct effects of changes in indirect taxes and subsidies). However, all of the results presented in the chapter are robust to the choice of inflation benchmark in Sweden.
17 One study of this "bias" is Mehra (2002).
18 Bryan and Venkatu (2001b) analyze, among other things, the responses in the *FRBC/ OSU Inflation Psychology Survey* and show that about 66 percent of the interviewed households had heard of the CPI. While those 66 percent gave very accurate estimates of what had happened to the CPI, their average response to the question about "prices in general" was more than twice as high as the increase recorded by the CPI. This finding suggests that whatever price measure households have in mind when they answer the question about "prices in general," it is probably not the CPI.
19 That households hold heterogeneous inflation expectations is documented in, e.g. Jonung (1981), Bryan and Venkatu (2001a), and (2001b), Carroll (2003), Mankiw *et al.* (2003), Souleles (2004), and Palmqvist and Strömberg (2004). From the early work on survey measures of expectations, it is clear that the causes of heterogeneity in inflation opinions are important to consider when testing the assumption of rational expectations formation. See, e.g. the discussion about rationality in survey measures between Figlewski and Wachtel (1981) and (1983) and Dietrich and Joines (1983). Keane and Runkle (1990) provide further insights on this note. The fact that households form heterogeneous inflation expectations is, however, something that must be considered when testing *any* hypothesis about expectations formation.

References

Akerlof, George A., William T. Dickens, and George L. Perry (2000), Near-rational wage and price setting and the long-run Phillips curve, *Brookings Papers on Economic Activity*, 2000-1: 1–60.

Akerlof, George A., William T. Dickens, and George L. Perry (2001), Options for stabilization policy: a new analysis of choices confronting the Fed, *Policy Brief*, 69, Brookings Institution.

Bai, J., and P. Perron (1998), Estimating and testing linear models with multiple structural changes, *Econometrica*, 66 (1): 47–78.

Bryan, Michael F. and Guhan Venkatu (2001a), The demographics of household inflation surveys, *Economic Commentary*, Federal Reserve Bank of Cleveland.

Bryan, Michael F. and Guhan Venkatu (2001b), The curiously different inflation perspectives of men and women, *Economic Commentary*, Federal Reserve Bank of Cleveland.

Carroll, Christopher D. (2005), The epidemiology of macroeconomic expectations, in Larry Blume and Steven Durlauf, (eds.), *The Economy as an Evolving Complex System III*, Oxford: Oxford University Press.

Dickens, William T. (2001), Comments on Charles Wyplosz's "Do we know how low inflation should be?," Brookings Institution.

Dietrich, J. Kimball, and Douglas H. Joines (1983), Rational expectations, informational efficiency, and tests using survey data: a comment, *Review of Economics and Statistics*, 65 (3): 525–529.

Figlewski, Stephen, and Paul Wachtel (1981), The formation of inflationary expectations, *Review of Economics and Statistics*, 63 (1): 1–10.

Figlewski, Stephen, and Paul Wachtel (1983), Rational expectations, informational efficiency, and tests using survey data: a reply, *Review of Economics and Statistics*, 65 (3): 529–531.

Friedman, Milton (1968), The role of monetary policy, *American Economic Review*, 58 (1): 1–17.

Giavazzi, Francesco, and Frederic S. Mishkin (2006), An evaluation of Swedish monetary policy between 1995 and 2005, *Riksdag Press Release*.

Jonung, Lars (1981), Perceived and expected rates of inflation in Sweden, *American Economic Review*, 71 (5): 961–968.

Keane, Michael P., and David E. Runkle (1990), Testing rationality of price forecasts: new evidence from panel data, *American Economic Review*, 80 (4): 714–735.

Kuttner, Kenneth N. (2004), A snapshot of inflation targeting in its adolescence, in Christopher Kent and Simon Guttmann (eds.), *The Future of Inflation Targeting*, Sydney, NSW: Reserve Bank of Australia Conference Volume.

Lundborg, Per, and Hans Sacklén (2003), Low-inflation targeting and unemployment persistence, *FIEF Working Paper*, 188.

Lundborg, Per, and Hans Sacklén (2006), Low-inflation targeting and long-run unemployment, *Scandinavian Journal of Economics*, 108 (3): 397–418.

Mankiw, N. Gregory, Ricardo Reis, and Justin Wolfers (2003), Disagreement about inflation expectations, in Mark Gertler and Kenneth Rogoff (eds.), *NBER Macroeconomics Annual*, Cambridge, MA: MIT Press, pp. 209–248.

Mehra, Yash P. (2002), Survey measures of expected inflation: revisiting the issues of predictive content and rationality, *Economic Quarterly*, 88 (3) Federal Reserve Bank of Richmond.

Palmqvist, Stefan, and Lena Strömberg (2004), Households' inflation opinions – a tale of two surveys, *Sveriges Riksbank Economic Review*, 4: 23–42.

Phelps, Edmund S. (1967), Phillips curves, expectations of inflation and optimal unemployment over time, *Economica*, new series, 34 (135): 254–281.

Shimer, Robert J. (1998), Why is the U.S. unemployment rate so much lower?, in Ben S. Bernanke and Julio Rotemberg (eds.), *NBER Macroeconomics Annual*, Cambridge, MA: MIT Press, pp. 11–73.

Souleles, Nicholas S. (2004), Expectations, heterogeneous forecast errors, and consumption: micro evidence from the Michigan Consumer Sentiment Surveys, *Journal of Money, Credit, and Banking*, 36 (1): 39–72.

11 400,000 observations on inflation perceptions and expectations in the EU

What do they tell us?

Staffan Lindén

1 Introduction

The ability to measure inflation expectations accurately is more than of academic interest; it is an integral part of central bank policy. According to the present approach to monetary policy making, founded on inflation targeting, central banks should be forward-looking, framing their policies today on the basis of forecasts of the future rate of inflation one to two years ahead. This approach calls for reliable, frequent and timely data on the public's inflation expectations. Furthermore, expectations about the future course of the price level are important to decision-makers in all markets: for goods, labour, money, financial assets and currencies. Decisions on these markets underlie the actual rate of inflation, nominal wage rates, interest rates, exchange rates as well as real variables such as the rate of unemployment. Expectations actually determine all types of economic behaviour, as human action is forward-looking. Such information, however, is difficult to compile for the simple reason that inflationary expectations are not directly measurable in a way similar to variables such as interest rates, monetary aggregates, rates of unemployment, consumer and producer prices etc. The expectations of the future behaviour of prices are held by individuals in their minds. To measure them in a representative way is a major challenge for economists and for policy-makers.

A straightforward way to measure the inflation expectations of the public is to ask people about their expectations, and in fact, a few surveys do exactly that. Examples of such surveys are the Swedish Household Survey, the University of Michigan survey of consumer attitudes, and the Inflation Psychology Survey conducted by the Federal Reserve Bank of Cleveland in association with the Ohio State University. Other countries, such as Australia and South Africa, have also included direct questions on inflation in their respective consumer surveys. In May 2003, two new questions were added to the harmonized consumer survey for the European Union, thus adding to the number of surveys that explicitly ask a selection of respondents (representing the public at large) about their inflation perceptions and expectations. The two new questions were introduced on a voluntary and experimental basis. They aimed at obtaining point estimates of the perception and expectation, using a quantitative formulation on past (perceived) and future (expected) inflation.

Some common features are usually obtained with such surveys of inflation expectations and perceptions. Based on the Swedish Household Survey, Jonung (1981) and Palmqvist and Strömberg (2004) report on the demographic properties of inflation perceptions and expectations. They find that low-income households say inflation is higher than respondents in higher income classes, both for perceptions and expectations. Education matters in the same way: the higher the education, the lower the inflation rate reported, and women report higher inflation than men. Furthermore, young and old people report inflation to be higher than the middle-aged (a U-shaped relationship). The same patterns are present in US data. Using the Inflation Psychology Survey, Bryan and Venkatu (2002a) show that reported inflation rates fall with rising income and education, the relationship between age and inflation is U-shaped, and women report higher values than men. In another paper, Bryan and Venkatu (2002b) report similar results for the University of Michigan consumer survey. Increasing income accompanies lower perceived and expected inflation, and women report higher inflation rates than men.

One obvious problem with these surveys is that the questions concern variables that are difficult to assess, or even understand. Inflation, for example, is a macro-variable measuring the aggregate price level, but as respondents' consumption baskets do not necessarily correspond to the one used for calculating the consumer price indices, the answers obtained with the surveys can differ substantially from the official inflation rates. This is often the case; many surveys show perceptions and expectations that differ from the official rates.

This chapter investigates [how and whether] incentives might explain the deviations between perceived and expected inflation and the official inflation rate. Since it is costly to gather and analyse data to predict inflation, only those people with strong incentives to do so will attain this information, and thus be able to give informative answers to the surveys. The Joint Harmonised EU Programme of Consumer Surveys has become a unique database, with information on respondents' views of past and future inflation, but it also contains information on respondents' likelihood to buy a new car, a house, and making major home improvements, activities that give strong incentives to form correct expectations on inflation.

As the dataset used is new, a substantial part of this chapter is devoted to presenting the data, analysing them, and comparing them to other measures of perceived and expected inflation from the same survey, as well as to the results of other surveys. The results will mainly focus on the euro-area aggregate.

The next section reviews the dataset. First the answers to the qualitative questions are studied to establish a benchmark for comparison with the quantitative answers. Second, the results from the quantitative answers, broken down by socioeconomic subgroups, are presented. Third, the results are compared with similar breakdowns from other datasets, to see if similar patterns arise in both the national surveys and in the euro-area aggregate. Finally, some preliminary results are given on the time series properties, which are compared with the qualitative data. Section 3 discusses the role of costly information, and how incentives to collect information matter for respondents when forming their expectations. The empirically obtained answer to the main hypothesis in this chapter, whether incentives to collect costly information improve respondents' inflation expectation, is given in Section 4. Finally, the last section concludes.

2 Data

The data employed in this chapter come from the Joint Harmonised EU Programme of Consumer Surveys. The surveys are conducted by national institutes in each of the 27 participating institutes. The harmonized questionnaire contains questions on the economic situation of the household and the country where respondents reside. It also contains information on income, occupation, education, age, and sex. There are also four questions on price developments: two inviting qualitative answers, and two requesting quantitative answers. The questionnaire also includes questions about how likely the respondent is to buy a new car, or a house, or make home improvements. A more comprehensive description of the harmonized EU survey programme can be found in *European Economy* (1997 no. 6).

The questions asking for a qualitative answer (the *qualitative* questions) regarding price developments are implemented in all participating surveys, and most of the data dates back to the beginning of 1985. The two questions where respondents are asked to put a real number on their perceived or expected change in the price level were introduced on a voluntary and experimental basis in 2003 (the *quantitative* questions).

The quantitative formulation of the price questions are currently implemented in 25 of 27 national questionnaires. So almost all institutes carrying out the consumer survey have included the two new questions. In most cases the questions were introduced from May 2003, but some countries began in January 2003, or earlier. France and the United Kingdom included the questions from January 2004. The only two countries that do not include the questions are the Netherlands, which stopped asking the questions in July 2005, and Hungary, which have yet to include them in their survey.

The quantitative price questions (labelled Q51 and Q61 in the harmonized survey) are based on the individual responses to the qualitative price questions (labelled Q5 and Q6 in the harmonized survey). The formulation of these questions and their respective possible responses are as follows:

Q5 How do you think that consumer prices have developed over the last 12 months? They have…
++ 1   risen a lot
+   2   risen moderately
=   3   risen slightly
-   4   stayed about the same
−   5   fallen
N   9   don't know

Q51 If question 5 was answered by 1, 2, 3, or 5:
By how many percent do you think that consumer prices have gone up/down over the past 12 months? (Please give a single figure estimate). Consumer prices have increased by ......, ... %/decreased by ......, ... %.

Q6 By comparison with the past 12 months, how do you expect that consumer prices will develop in the next 12 months? They will...
++ 1 increase more rapidly
+ 2 increase at the same rate
= 3 increase at a slower rate
- 4 stay about the same
− 5 fall
N 9 don't know

Q61 If question 5 was answered by 1, 2, 3, or 5:
By how many percent do you expect consumer prices to go up/down in the next 12 months? (Please give a single figure estimate). Consumer prices will increase by ......, ... %/decrease by ......, ... %.

The data employed in this chapter form a subset of the 24 national surveys containing quantitative questions, and comprise the results from nine euro-area countries. The nine country-surveys are used to form inflation perceptions and expectations for an aggregate resembling the euro area. The included countries are: Austria, Belgium, Finland, France, Germany, Greece, Ireland, Luxembourg, and Spain. They make up 73 per cent of the euro area by GDP. Data from Italy, the Netherlands and Portugal are excluded from this study: Italy because of an eight-month period of missing data (at the time of writing), the Netherlands for ending the experiment with quantitative questions in July 2005, and Portugal because the data available was not in a usable state (at the time of writing). Since the results differ substantially between different countries, in terms of the level of inflation reported, the data from the former two countries distort the results if included.

For most countries the time series begin in May 2003 and continue to October 2005, comprising a total of 30 months. All inflation figures are presented as weighted averages,[1] and no adjustments have been made to take care of outliers. The euro-area inflation figures are calculated as the weighted average of the individual country averages. The country weights used are the same as those that are used for calculating the harmonized index of consumer prices (HICP). For the first eight months the euro-area average does not include all the member states, as France did not introduce the quantitative questions until January 2004.[2]

As this dataset of answers to the quantitative price questions is new, it is appropriate to present the data in detail and describe their properties. The answers to the survey questions using a quantitative formulation can be evaluated on several dimensions. One is to study the overall values of perceptions and expectations, and compare them with the target variable, the HICP inflation rate. Another would be to compare the answers to the quantitative questions to those of the qualitative questions; and a third would be to compare with other recognized datasets.

2.1 Qualitative price questions

The qualitative answers can serve as a benchmark for what can be expected from the quantitative answers. To make the comparison, the qualitative data have to be quantified in one way or other. Several methods can be employed.

Three different quantification methods are used in this chapter: (*a*) the balance statistic, (*b*) the Carlson–Parkin method with constant thresholds, and (*c*) the Anderson method. For a literature review on quantification methods see Nardo (2003). The balance statistic (*a*) is defined as the difference between the weighted proportions of answers that perceived (expected) an increase in the price level and the proportion of answers that perceived (expected) a decrease. The Carlson–Parkin method (*b*) is an example of the so called probability methodology, which is a set of methods that derives an estimate of quantitative expectations starting from the "increase" and "decrease" survey answers and the movements in the actual reference series, e.g. the HICP inflation rate. Its properties are discussed in detail by Batchelors's contribution to this volume. The Anderson method (*c*) is an example of the regression approach, which uses the relationship between the actual inflation rate and respondents' perceptions of past price developments as a yardstick for the quantification of respondents' expectations about future inflation developments. Supposing that the individual perceived inflation rate is a function of the change in the HICP, it is possible to derive an expression that relates inflation to the answers to questions about past price developments. Assuming that the relationship between the inflation rate and the respondents perceived prices changes also holds for expected changes, the estimated equation for perceptions can be used as an expression for approximating expected inflation by just replacing surveyed perceptions for surveyed expectations in the estimated equation.

Table 11.1 shows the most recent quantified inflation rates for the euro area using the Carlson–Parkin and the Anderson methods. The balance statistic is excluded from the table since it does not have the same unit of measure as inflation, and therefore cannot be used for a direct comparison. The actual inflation rate for the euro area, as measured by HICP, was 2.6 per cent over the period September 2004 to September 2005. Depending on the method used, the expected rate for this period was 1.9 per cent or 1.8 per cent, and at the end of the period the perceived rate for the period was 2.6 per cent or 2.7 per cent. The last line in the table shows the September 2005 expectation for the inflation rate over the following 12 months. The expectation is 1.9 per cent for both methods

Table 11.1 Quantified inflation rates of perceived and expected inflation in the euro area using qualitative answers from question 5 and 6

Question refer to, survey month	HICP	C–P	And
Past 12 months, September 2005	2.6	2.6	2.7
Next 12 months, September 2004		1.9	1.8
Next 12 months, September 2005		1.9	1.9

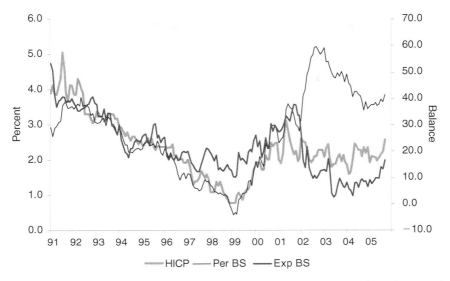

Figure 11.1 The Balance Statistic for perceived (Per BS) and 12 months lagged expected
inflation (Exp BS) in the euro area, and the actual rate of inflation.

used. These values could not be evaluated, at the time of this research, before the
HICP figures were released.

Figure 11.1 shows the time series of the year-on-year growth rate of the HICP
and the balances to the answers on perceived and expected inflation. Before the
introduction of the euro notes and coins, the balance series tracks the HICP fairly
well. The correlation between the balances and the HICP is around 0.85 for both
perceived and expected inflation. After the introduction of the euro, there is a
clear de-linkage between the time series. The correlation coefficient for expectations declines to 0.08, and for perceived inflation it even becomes negative.

Figure 11.2 presents the time series of the HICP inflation rate and the quantified perceived inflation rates over the past 12 months using the Carlson–Parkin
and the Anderson methods. The shift to a higher perceived inflation after the
introduction of the euro in January 2002 is also visible using the other two quantification methods. After the initial increase in the first half of 2002, perceived
inflation has been converging towards the actual rate as measured by the HICP.

Figure 11.3 plots the actual inflation rate and the quantified expected inflation
rate lagged 12 months. For example, the May 2003 expectation is compared with
the May 2004 outcome. Again there is a shift in expectations that starts in mid-
2001. Initially there is an increase in expected inflation for the coming 12-month
period, but as the date of the introduction of the euro approaches, expectations
decline. Inflation expectations fall to the extent that quantified expectations are
below the realized inflation rate.

For the total sample period, the correlations between the HICP inflation rate
and the balance statistic and the other quantification methods range from 0.22

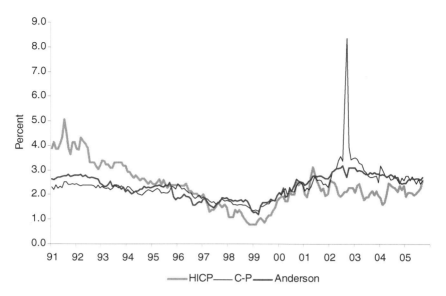

Figure 11.2 Perceived inflation rates for the euro area, quantified by using the Carlson–Parkin (C–P) and the Anderson methods, and the actual inflation rate.

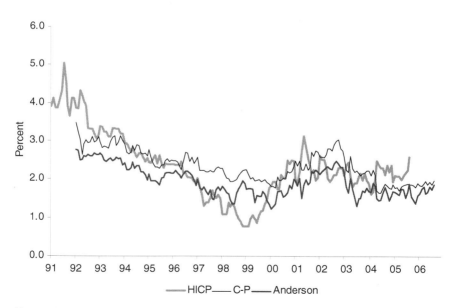

Figure 11.3 Expected inflation rates for the euro area lagged 12 months, quantified by using the Carlson–Parkin (C–P) and the Anderson methods, and the actual inflation rate.

with the Carlson–Parkin method to 0.55 with the Anderson approach. These figures are presented in Table 11.2. Splitting the sample in two, where the dividing date is 1 January 2002, the introduction of euro notes and coins, the correlations with HICP are very different. Before the euro introduction, the correlations range between 0.80 and 0.89 for perceptions and between 0.79 and 0.83 for expectations. After 1 January 2002, the correlations range between −0.19 and 0.03 for perceptions and between −0.03 and 0.20 for expectations. The breaks in perceptions and expectations are established to be significant by introducing a dummy variable into the Anderson methodology. Adjusting the estimated perceptions and expectations for this shift in the time series, the Anderson statistic presented in Figure 11.2 and Figure 11.3 changes, and looks like the series presented in Figure 11.4. In the figure the time series for perceptions and expectations, scaled by using the Anderson method including a dummy variable, are labelled "Exp And + Dum" and "Per And + Dum" respectively.

Table 11.3 presents the demographic properties of the qualitative data. The figures in the tables are averages of the balances over the period May 2003 to October 2005. In the Joint Harmonised EU Consumer Survey people are categorized according to five variables: income of the household (four categories), occupation (nine categories), education (three levels), age (four age groups), and sex (male or female). Excluding occupation, Table 11.3 shows clear patterns for how the answers are distributed depending on demography. Both inflation perceptions and expectations decline with increasing household income and increasing education. Perceived inflation seems to increase with age, but expectations

Table 11.2 Correlations between perceived and expected inflation and the actual euro-area inflation rate, for the total sample and two sub-samples split 1 January 2002, the introduction of the euro

Correlation between HICP rate of inflation	*Perceived inflation for the past 12 months*			
	BS	*C-P*	*And*	*And + Dum*
Jan 1991 to Sep 2005	0.48	0.22	0.55	0.55
Jan 1991 to Dec 2001	0.89	0.80	0.82	0.80
Jan 2002 to Sep 2005	−0.19	−0.05	0.01	0.03
Apr 2004 to Sep 2005	0.40	−0.17	0.24	0.25

Correlation between HICP rate of inflation	*Expected inflation for the next 12 months*			
	BS	*C-P*	*And*	*And + Dum*
Jan 1991 to Sep 2005	0.64	0.65	0.71	0.71
Jan 1991 to Dec 2001	0.83	0.80	0.80	0.79
Jan 2002 to Sep 2005	0.08	−0.03	0.15	0.20
Apr 2004 to Sep 2005	0.11	−0.09	0.04	0.06

Note
1 Expected inflation is lagged by 12 months.

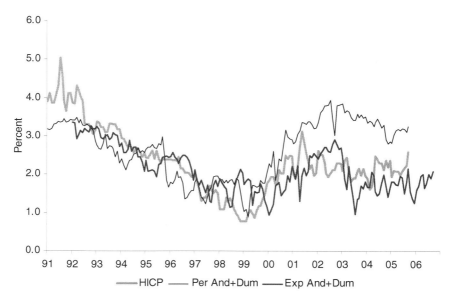

Figure 11.4 Perceived (Per And +Dum) and 12 month lagged expected (Exp And +Dum) inflation for the euro area, quantified by using the Anderson method adjusted for the structural break in 1 January 2002, and the actual inflation rate.

are hump-shaped. Furthermore, women have higher perceptions and expectations of inflation than men.

To summarize these results and to form a benchmark for what to expect from the answers to the quantitative questions Q51 and Q61, the stylized facts are presented in the conclusion.

2.2 Quantitative price questions

2.2.1 Comparison with the qualitative data

A first step to evaluate the new dataset is to compare the results from the quantitative survey questions to those of the qualitative questions. Table 11.4 shows the answers to the quantitative questions in the two columns labelled Q51 and Q61. The numbers in the two columns are inflation rates in per cent, and the demographic breakdown is the same as in Table 11.3. The first two columns show the balances from the answers to the qualitative questions.

Between May 2003 and October 2005, actual annual inflation averages 2.1 per cent, as against a perceived rate of 11.6 per cent. The average actual inflation rate for May 2004 to October 2005 is 2.2 per cent. These cover the 17 months that have been realized and overlap with the expectations formed since 2003, and thus can be compared to the expected rate of 6.1 per cent. Clearly, perceived

Table 11.3 Balance statistic for perceived and expected inflation in the euro area for different demographic groups

Euro area		Q5	Q6
Income of the household	1st quartile	46.3	11.1
	2nd quartile	43.3	9.2
	3rd quartile	41.1	8.9
	4th quartile	37.5	8.0
Occupation	Self-employed professionals	38.5	4.9
	Self employed farmers	36.6	4.8
	Clerical and office empl.	38.8	8.1
	Skilled manual workers	44.5	9.1
	Other manual workers	46.1	10.2
	Other occupations	42.3	7.2
	Unemployed	40.6	8.2
	Work full-time	44.1	9.3
	Work part-time	47.9	11.2
Education	Primary	46.2	8.8
	Secondary	41.7	8.0
	Further	35.9	8.1
Age	16–29	37.7	5.1
	30–49	42.5	8.4
	50–64	42.6	10.5
	65+	43.8	8.0
Gender	Male	39.5	8.5
	Female	45.3	8.1
Total		42.4	8.4

inflation is heavily overstated, while the difference is much less for expectations, although still very high. A similar effect can be seen in the qualitative data. The balances for perceptions are much higher than the balances for expectations, confirming the similarities in the summary at the end of this chapter.

Splitting the answers according to different demographic categories, several familiar patterns emerge from the quantitative answers. Perceived and expected inflation falls as income rises. Perceptions fall by as much as 2.8 per cent from the 25 per cent-lowest-income earners to the 25 per cent-highest earners. The difference for expectations is 1.3 per cent. The same pattern can be observed for education; inflation rates fall as education increases. The difference between people with primary schooling and those with an education that goes beyond secondary schooling is 2.9 per cent for perceptions and 1.2 per cent for expectations. Gender also matters. Women have higher perceptions and expectations than men. The differences are 2.0 per cent for perceptions and 0.7 per cent for expectations. Furthermore, answers sorted by occupation are also similar between the quantitative and qualitative datasets. These results confirm the similarities with the findings summarized in the conclusions.

Table 11.4 Quantitative perceived and expected inflation in the euro area and the balance statistic for different demographic groups (averages for May 2003 to October 2005)

Euro area		Q5	Q6	Q51	Q61
Income of the household	1st quartile	46.3	11.1	12.8	6.8
	2nd quartile	43.3	9.2	11.7	6.3
	3rd quartile	41.1	8.9	11.4	6.1
	4th quartile	37.5	8.0	10.0	5.5
Occupation	Self-employed professionals	38.5	4.9	11.5	5.6
	Self employed farmers	36.6	4.8	9.2	4.8
	Clerical and office empl.	38.8	8.1	10.6	5.7
	Skilled manual workers	44.5	9.1	12.1	6.4
	Other manual workers	46.1	10.2	12.3	6.9
	Other occupations	42.3	7.2	11.4	5.9
	Unemployed	40.6	8.2	14.0	7.6
	Work full-time	44.1	9.3	11.2	5.9
	Work part-time	47.9	11.2	12.5	6.6
Education	Primary	46.2	8.8	12.2	6.3
	Secondary	41.7	8.0	11.6	6.0
	Further	35.9	8.1	9.3	5.1
Age	16–29	37.7	5.1	11.8	6.3
	30–49	42.5	8.4	12.1	6.3
	50–64	42.6	10.5	11.3	6.0
	65+	43.8	8.0	10.7	5.4
Gender	Male	39.5	8.5	10.6	5.7
	Female	45.3	8.1	12.6	6.4
Total		42.4	8.4	11.6	6.1

2.2.2 Comparison with other studies

An alternative comparison is to use other datasets, similar to that of the Joint Harmonised EU Programme of Consumer Surveys, which are recognized and used both academically and in practice. For this purpose three surveys are mentioned: the University of Michigan consumer survey, the Inflation Psychology Survey conducted by the Ohio State University, and the Swedish Household Survey. The data from these surveys are not used directly in this chapter. Instead results reported by others, using these data sets, are cited in the introduction to this chapter. They can readily be compared with the ones presented here.

The properties described above of the quantified perceived and expected inflation rates are basically replicated by questions 51 and 61 in the harmonized EU consumer survey. For income, education, and gender the same results are obtained as with the other datasets, but there is very little dependence on age in the EU survey. If age matters at the EU level, the dependence is hump-shaped, not U-shaped.

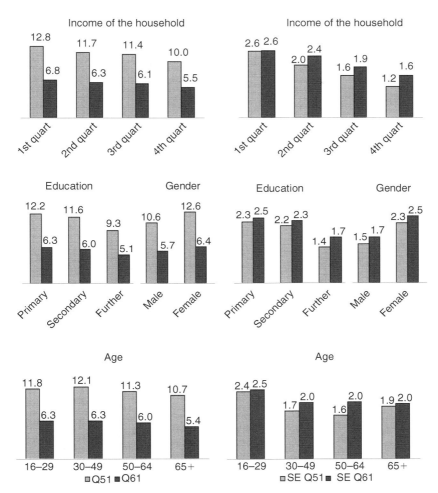

Figure 11.5 Quantitative perceived and expected inflation in the euro area (left) and Sweden (right) – depending on income of household, education, gender, and age.

2.2.3 Time-series analysis of quantitative price questions

Since the time series with quantitative answers are still rather short, only 30 observations, it is difficult to say anything conclusive about the time-series properties. The main focus must be on the perceptions, as these observations can be compared with the HICP inflation rate. For expectations, there are only 17 months with corresponding HICP observations (the HICP series ends in September 2005).

Figure 11.6 shows the time series for the HICP inflation rate, perceived inflation, and expected inflation. The expectations series is pushed forward 12

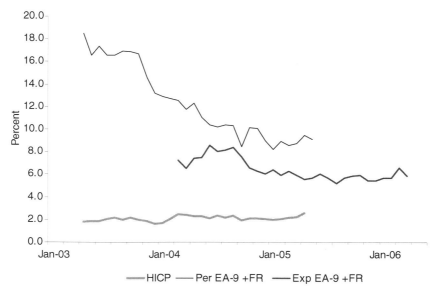

Figure 11.6 Quantitative perceived and 12 month lagged expected inflation rates for the euro area, and the actual inflation rate.

months. As expectations are forward looking, the expectations formed in May 2003 correspond to the outcome observed in May 2004. The graph shows that especially perceptions have so far very little to do with the HICP series. As the qualitative data show that there has been a de-linkage between perceptions and the HICP following the introduction to the euro, one cannot expect the answers to the quantitative questions to do any better. But the figure also shows that perceptions have been converging towards the actual rate of inflation, at least until the second quarter of 2005. This is similar to what can be observed for the qualitative data in Figures 11.1 and 11.4. It is difficult to say whether expectations are converging towards the HICP rate of inflation, but the trend is downward sloping and significant.

Table 11.5 presents the serial correlations between perceived and expected quantified inflation rates on one side, and the HICP rate of inflation and the different quantification techniques on the other. Perceptions, as measured by question 51, show a high correlation with the qualitative perceptions. With the balances, the correlation is as high as 0.91, but correlations are also high using the regression approach. Just as for the qualitative data, the quantitative data show low and negative correlation with the official inflation rate for the euro area. This result can be attributed to the convergence process towards the HICP rate of inflation.

The correlations for the quantitative expectations are in general low. This is true both for the correlations with the qualitative data as well as for the HICP rate of inflation. The highest correlation coefficient is obtained when the time

Table 11.5 Correlations between quantitative perceived and expected inflation and the actual euro-area inflation rate, and between quantitative perceived and expected inflation and the qualitative data

Correlation between	Q51	BS	Perceived inflation for the past 12 months (May 03–Sep 05)		
			CP	And	And + Dum
Perceived inflation Q51	1.00	0.91	0.58	0.78	0.74
HICP rate of inflation	−0.42	−0.43	−0.57	−0.33	−0.29

Correlation between	Q61	BS	Expected inflation for the next 12 months (May 03–Sep 05)		
			CP	And	And + Dum
Expected inflation Q61	1.00	−0.15	−0.14	0.04	0.06
HICP rate of inflation	−0.12	0.53	0.46	0.23	0.17
HICP rate of inflation (lag 6)	−0.03	0.01	0.01	0.11	0.11
HICP rate of inflation (lag 9)	0.39	0.51	0.49	0.09	0.01
HICP rate of inflation (lag 12)	0.35	−0.14	−0.30	−0.17	−0.13

series are lagged against each other. It turns out that expected inflation is forward looking with a lead of six months, with a correlation coefficient of 0.39.

3 Costly information and incentives to form expectations

If informational efficiency is defined as a situation where confidence indicators contain all available information at a particular point in time, can confidence indicators be informationally efficient, so that they give perfect information regarding, for example, expected inflation? Clearly not, if information is costly, people would have to spend resources on acquiring and processing information that would not necessarily be beneficial to them. Because information is costly, prices and other indicators that are the bearer of information cannot perfectly reflect all available information, since if they did, those who spent resources to obtain it would receive no compensation. There is a fundamental conflict between the efficiency with which markets spread information and the incentives to acquire information (Grossman and Stiglitz 1980).

For each question in the harmonized consumer survey, the amount of relevant information one respondent possesses depends on the relevance of the question and his incentive to obtain the necessary information. Most of the questions in the harmonized consumer survey ask respondents for their opinions about issues on which they have information, such as the economic situation of the household or saving intentions. For other questions it is less obvious to what extent consumers have the information necessary, or the incentives to acquire it, to form relevant opinions.

The four questions on price developments are of this kind. For example, respondents have different consumption baskets, which might not correspond to the one measured by the HICP. Furthermore, the general price level of a country is not a simple variable to forecast; it requires a vast amount of information and complex analysis. It also seems reasonable to assume that the more detailed the response demanded to a survey question, the more information is needed to answer it. It is therefore reasonable to assume that it is more costly to attain the information needed to assess general price developments, as compared to, for example, the household budget, about which a respondent would have almost full knowledge.

The poor performance of the survey questions in measuring inflation might be explained by the relatively weak incentives people face in their daily lives to gather information on inflation. Most of the answers to the surveys may be noisy signals. And at fairly low inflation rates, as the ones the euro area is experiencing now, it is not very important for people to have correct conjectures about future inflation on a daily basis. This is especially true when information is costly and has to be weighed against an alternative use of the available resources. On the other hand, there are instances when decisions have to be made where inflation becomes a very important variable in people's lives, e.g. when a major investment is going to be undertaken, like the purchase of a house.

The hypothesis investigated in this chapter is that incentives to form inflation expectations may explain the deviations between surveyed inflation expectations and the actual rate of inflation. Detailed questions in the harmonized consumer survey for the EU on household-purchasing plans of cars, houses, and home improvement, make it possible to study this issue. It is assumed that purchases of these assets are highly likely to induce respondents to take on new loans or cause them to rebalance their portfolios. That would increase the incentives to collect information on interest rates, the risk-premium, and inflation rates. Thus, the more likely the respondents are to spend large amounts of money, the closer the answers on inflation should be to the official rate.

4 Inflation expectations under incentives to gather information

Three questions are used to categorize respondents in terms of their likelihood to perform a major investment in the coming months. The hypothesis is that these investment plans are reasons to form better inflation projections, in order to make better informed investment decisions. The higher the likelihood to invest or spend, the closer the answers to the questions should be to the actual inflation rate. The formulation of these questions and their respective possible responses are as follows:

Q13 How likely are you to buy a car over the next 12 months?
     ++ 1 very likely
     + 2 fairly likely
     -   4 not likely
     − 5 not at all likely
     N 9 don't know

Q14 Are you planning to buy or build a home over the next 12 months (to live in yourself, for a member of your family, as a holiday home, to let etc.)?
     ++ 1 very likely
     + 2 fairly likely
     − 4 not likely
     − 5 not at all likely
     N 9 don't know

Q15 How likely are you to spend any large sum of money on home improvements or renovations over the next 12 months?
     ++ 1 very likely
     + 2 fairly likely
     -   4 not likely
     − 5 not at all likely
     N 9 don't know

In the following figures, the answers to these three questions are used to categorize the respondents' answers to the questions on price developments. Based on their likelihood of buying a car, a house, and spending a large sum of money on home improvement, average perceived and expected inflation rates have been

Figure 11.7 Perceived inflation rates depending on respondents' likelihood to buy a car, a house, or spend a large amount of money on home improvements.

Figure 11.8 Expected inflation rates depending on respondents' likelihood to buy a car, a house, or spend a large amount of money on home improvements.

calculated. Figure 11.7 shows the perceived inflation rates for the five different answers to the questions, and Figure 11.8 shows the expectations. The numbers above the bars are the average inflation rates, and these can be compared with the overall perceived (11.6 per cent) and expected (6.1 per cent) rates presented above in Table 11.4. Note that the vertical scales in the following graphs are adjusted to emphasize height differences. Furthermore, the differences between the bars in Figures 11.7 and 11.8 have not been formally tested for significance.

For perceived inflation, the bar-charts are U-shaped, but if one disregards the bars labelled "very likely", the bars in the charts increase as respondents become less likely to invest or spend large amounts of money. Respondents who are fairly likely to spend money perceive past inflation to be between 0.9 and 2.4 percentage points below those that are not at all likely to spend any money on cars and houses. The biggest differences are for those that are buying cars or houses.

For expected inflation, the bar-charts show a similar pattern. Disregarding the bars labelled "very likely" and "don't know", the expected inflation rates increase as respondents become less likely to invest or spend large amounts of money. The exception is the home-improvement chart, where the differences in expected inflation rates are small. The inflation expectations for those respondents that are fairly likely to buy a car or a house are almost 1 per cent lower than for those that are not at all likely to buy.

The figures also show that respondents that are very likely to spend money perceive and expect inflation to be higher than the overall average, and at least as high as respondents who are not so likely to spend money on cars and houses. One possible explanation for this result, which should be explored further, is if a respondent is in a minority thinking inflation is going to be very rapid that will make them keener to spend money now.

If it was not for the bars labelled "very likely", these results would show strong support for the hypothesis that incentives matter a lot for respondents to form their views on past and future inflation. The results presented in this chapter do not rely on any trimming of the data, all observations are included, and so far no consideration has been taken to outliers. Unfortunately there are many outliers, and some of them are very extreme, e.g. some respondents give inflation rates of as much as 400 per cent. There can be many sources to these extreme numbers, e.g. errors when entering data, or reluctance to answer to surveys. Regardless of the cause, the extreme values become an issue when selecting data based on respondents' likelihood to invest or spend, because there are relatively few observations for the category "very likely".

It turns out that the relatively high inflation rates obtained for the category "very likely" are mainly caused by the answers from the German survey. Since there are only around 450 respondents that answer "very likely" to questions 13, 14, and 15, compared to 2,200 in the French survey and 1,350 in the Austrian survey, the German results are more sensitive to extreme outliers. Furthermore the German results enter the euro-area aggregate with a much higher weight than the other countries, almost 40 per cent for Germany, as compared to 28 per cent for France and 4 per cent for Austria. The relatively bad German results for this particular category pass through to the euro-area aggregate.

To alleviate this problem of too few observations, an alternative measure of perceived and expected euro-area inflation is calculated. First, the very-likely and the fairly-likely respondents are grouped together into one category called "likely", and the not likely and the not at all likely are grouped into a second category called "not likely". This is done by averaging the results from the two respective categories. Since there are still relatively few respondents saying that they are very likely to invest, as compared to those that are only likely, the former group will be overrepresented in the new average labelled likely in Figure 11.9. Second, when calculating the euro-area averages, individual country results are weighted by the HICP-country weights and the number of observations for each category and survey. The alternative measure takes into account the differences in the number of observations between the national surveys.

When the answer categories are regrouped and the euro-area aggregates are adjusted for the country differences in sample size, the results show a strong support for the hypothesis that incentives matter when respondents form their views on inflation. In Figure 11.9 the results for perceived inflation are illustrated. All three questions show that the more likely respondents are to spend money, the better their perceptions are, i.e. the inflation rates obtained with the surveys are closer to the realized HICP rate of inflation. The biggest difference is found in the middle graph for house buyers, where the likely house buyers state an inflation rate that is 2.2 percentage points below that of those respondents who are not likely to buy. For the question on car purchases, the difference is 1.7 percentage points, and for the question concerning home improvements the difference is 1.5 percentage points. All these differences are statistically significant at conventional significance levels. The lowest level of 8.7 per cent is still far from the actual rate of 2.1 per cent.

Like for perceived inflation, expectations for future inflation rates are significantly lower when respondents are likely to buy a car or a house, or spend large sums on home improvement. The biggest difference is for house buyers, where likely house buyers report 1.8 percentage points lower inflation than non-likely-house buyers. It is also the house buyers that give the overall lowest inflation figure of 4.6 per cent. This might not be too surprising as the purchase of a house is probably the biggest investment a household makes, and usually it requires borrowing money for financing the purchase. This would give strong incentives to gather information on interest rates and future inflation. The two other questions, on the likelihood of purchasing a car and spending money on home improvements, show differences of 1 percentage point between the likely and not likely respondents.

Preliminary work shows that these results are robust considering the differences in income, education, age, and gender. The data show that, proportionally, richer, younger, and those with higher education are more likely to spend money

Figure 11.9 Perceived inflation rates depending on respondents' likelihood to buy a car, a house, or spend a large amount of money on home improvements. Individual country results are weighted by the sample size when calculating perceived euro-area inflation. The two "likely" answers are grouped into one category called "likely", and the two "not likely" answers are grouped into another category called "not likely".

Figure 11.10 Expected inflation rates depending on respondents' likelihood to buy a car, a house, or spend a large amount of money on home improvements. Individual country results are weighted by the sample size when calculating expected euro-area inflation. The two "likely" answers are grouped into one category called "likely", and the two "not likely" answers are grouped into another category called "not likely".

on the three investment categories, but the correlations are weak. Also low and middle income people buy houses; they just buy cheaper ones. Splitting the sample into the different socioeconomic categories (income, education, age, and sex) and recalculating the average perceived and expected inflation, the hypothesis still holds true.

The "don't know" answers, as presented in Figure 11.9 and Figure 11.10, cannot be used for anything purposeful. The "don't know" answers to the questions are used differently in the national surveys. For some countries the answer is not used at all, and for others it is an answer that is widely used. It turns out that in the Spanish survey a lot of people use the answer for "don't know" instead of, for example, the "not at all likely" answer. When weighting the results by the sample size, the Spanish inflation figures completely dominate the results; the weights are between 0.83 and 0.96.

The overall lowest expected inflation rate obtained with this sample is 4.3 per cent. The figure is obtained by weighting the country results by the country weights and the sample size, but without re-grouping the categories. It is respondents who report that they are very likely to make home improvements that state this figure. The corresponding expected inflation rate for house and car buyers are 4.4 per cent and 4.8 per cent. These numbers should be compared to the actual rate, which is 2.1 per cent. Just looking at respondents who have strong incentives to gather information on price developments improves the measurement of expected inflation from 6.1 per cent to 4.3 per cent, closing the gap to the official rate almost half the way.

5 Conclusions

There are two purposes of this chapter: first, to give a preliminary presentation of a new dataset on quantitative inflation perceptions and expectations, and second, to investigate whether incentives to form views on past and future inflation can explain the deviations usually found between surveyed inflation and the actual rate of inflation.

To address the issue, a new dataset is used, which has been developed within the framework of the Joint Harmonised EU Programme of Consumer Surveys, which is managed by the European Commission. Two new questions have been introduced into the questionnaires, explicitly asking respondents to quantify past (perceived) and future (expected) inflation. Included in the survey are three questions on respondents' likelihood to buy a car, a house, and spend a large amount of money on home improvement. These three questions are used as a device to group respondents in terms of the strength of the incentives they have to collect information on inflation. The hypothesis is that the more likely respondents are to spend money, the stronger incentives they have to collect costly information, and therefore they would produce better projections. The used time series starts in May 2003 and continues through October 2005, and the main focus is on the euro-area aggregate.

The main results show that stronger incentives to collect information on inflation induce respondents to state perceived and expected inflation rates that correspond better to the actual rate of inflation. Respondents who say they are likely to buy a house perceive inflation to be 2.2 percentage points lower than those that are not likely to buy a house, and they are 2.9 percentage points lower than the overall average. The results for the other two questions, likelihood of buying a car and making home improvements, are similar, but slightly less pronounced. Still, at around 9 per cent the perceived level of inflation is heavily overstated.

The question on expected inflation also supports the hypothesis that incentives to collect information matter when respondents form their views on future inflation. Respondents who are likely to buy a house expect inflation to be 1.8 percentage points lower than those that are not likely to buy a house, and they are 1.5 percentage points below the overall average. The results for the other two questions are similar, with differences of 1 percentage point. Again, the level of expected inflation is overstated as compared to the official rate, but the incentive-induced rate of 4.6 per cent for house buyers, almost cuts the distance between the HICP rate of inflation and the overall expected average in half.

This shows that it is important to ask questions that are relevant to respondents, in the sense that they should have readily available information on the issues they are asked to respond to. Furthermore, the results show that it is a valuable exercise to try to "cut" the data in different ways to reduce the noise introduced by respondents that have less information on a particular issue, this can potentially improve survey results in general and inflation projections in particular.

This chapter also presents an analysis of the data on the price questions 51 and 61 in the questionnaires that quantify inflation perceptions and expectations. Again, the focus is on the euro-area aggregate, and how the answers to the quantitative questions compare to the two qualitative questions 5 and 6 and to other similar datasets.

In general, the euro-area aggregate of the quantitative questions behaves in a similar way as the qualitative data. The main findings are:

- There is a structural shift in perceptions and expectations after 1 January 2002, the introduction of the euro notes and coins.
- Perceived inflation is overestimated after January 2002.
- There is a clear de-linkage between perceived inflation and the change in the HICP after January 2002. Correlations fall a lot after the introduction of the euro.
- Perceptions are converging towards the observed inflation rate.
- The level of expected inflation is more in line with the HICP inflation rate than perceived inflation after January 2002.
- Inflation perceptions and expectations fall as income increases.
- Inflation perceptions and expectations fall as education increases.
- Perceived inflation seems to increase with age, and expected inflation is hump-shaped.
- Women perceive and expect higher inflation than men.

One conclusion is, therefore, that the quantitative data exhibit similar strengths and weaknesses as the qualitative data. Furthermore, the quantitative data in the Harmonised EU Programme of Consumer Surveys for the euro area are able to replicate the results of other datasets.

This quantitative dataset is becoming unique in its richness, almost 400,000 observations just for the euro area. These vast amounts of data open up new possibilities for several studies of perceptions and expectations concerning inflation across EU member states. In terms of quality, the answers to these questions actually measure the variable of interest directly. This enables a direct interpretation of the level, as well as the change in the time series. Furthermore, the formulation of the new questions follows comparable methodologies of other country-surveys, which allows us to compare the developments of the euro area to other countries. Without methodological comparability this would be impossible.

Still, there are various problems regarding the homogeneity of the data on a country level, and there is a clear overestimation of inflation for the euro area, both regarding perceptions and expectations. Several hypotheses for this result can be put forward, e.g. that inflation perceptions of consumers are not directly related to the CPI. Bryan and Venkatu (2002b) tested this hypothesis by asking the respondents if they have heard of the consumer price index (CPI). The people who had heard of the CPI were also able to give a remarkably correct answer to what the rate of change had been during the past 12 months. Still, these people reported higher inflation rates than the CPI rate, on the general question on prices.

For the euro area there are two mitigating circumstances that should be taken into account when judging these data. First, inflation perceptions seem to be converging on the actual inflation rate, as measured by HICP. This is important when evaluating the results, since the effects of the structural breaks following the introduction of the euro still has not petered out. Second, the time series is very short, especially for evaluating the time series properties of expectations.

Even though the quantitative and qualitative data are similar, the qualitative data have one current advantage: they have a long time series. There are, however, also some drawbacks. The qualitative answers cannot answer questions regarding the level of the inflation rate. There are quantification methods that can be used to quantify the qualitative answers, but in most cases these methods just scale the qualitative data to the target variable, the inflation rate. This means that any information on too high or too low perceptions and expectations, potentially important for policy, are lost. Furthermore, some quantification methods smooth the data in such a way that any structural shifts in the resulting perceived and expected inflation rates are concealed.

Notes

1 At the country level, each individual response is weighted to correct for under or over representation in the sample. When aggregating across time, each monthly value is also weighted by the sample size for the respective month.
2 The exclusion of France in the beginning of the dataset over-estimates perceived euro-area inflation, as French perceptions are below the euro-area average. For expectations the difference is less pronounced.

References

Bryan, M.F. and Palmqvist, S. (2004), Testing near-rationality using detailed survey data, Sveriges Riksbank *Working Paper Series*, 183.

Bryan, M.F. and Venkatu, G. (2001a), The demographics of inflation opinion surveys, *Economic Commentary*, Federal Reserve Bank of Cleveland.

Bryan, M.F. and Venkatu, G. (2001b), The curiously different inflation perspectives of men and women, *Economic Commentary*, Federal Reserve Bank of Cleveland.

European Commission – Directorate-General for Economic and Financial Affairs (1997), The Joint Harmonised EU programme of Business and Consumer Surveys, *European Economy*, 6, Brussels.

Grossman, S.J. and Stigliz, J.E. (1980), On the impossibility of informationally efficient markets, *American Economic Review*, 70 (3): 393–408.

Jonung, L. (1981), Perceived and expected rates of inflation in Sweden, *American Economic Review*, 71 (5): 961–968.

Nardo, M. (2003), The quantification of qualitative survey data: a critical assessment, *Journal of Economic Surveys*, 17 (5): 645–668.

Palmqvist, S. and Strömberg, L., (2004), Households' inflation opinions – a tale of two surveys, *Economic Review* 4, Sveriges Riksbank.

12   Finding the optimal method of quantifying inflation expectations on the basis of qualitative survey data

Fabien Curto Millet[1]

Introduction

The importance of expectations is a central tenet of modern economics.[2] Expectations are seen as essential to the transmission mechanism of monetary policy and are key to inflation targeting frameworks.[3] For empirical economists, this has generated the fundamental challenge of seeking ways to measure these "animal spirits", in the words of Keynes. Simply assuming rational expectations is indefensible in empirical work. The hypothesis has been rejected by data directly (see *inter alia* Roberts 1997; Bakhshi and Yates 1998; Łyziak 2003) and indirectly (Ericsson and Irons 1995).[4]

Direct measures of expectations are therefore particularly valuable. A first such approach infers expectations from the prices of financial instruments (e.g. Bank of Canada 1998). Comparing the prices of nominal and index-linked bonds with identical characteristics (risk, maturity and liquidity) can yield a measure of expected inflation but extra assumptions are often needed (Berk 1999). Yet they reflect the expectations of actors in financial markets only,[5] and may involve additional complications (e.g. herding behaviour, time-varying risk premia, regulatory requirements[6]).

A second approach uses survey data. This chapter looks at the inflation perceptions and expectations of consumers in the European Union, and aims to find the best way of quantifying them. The approaches in competition are presented in the next section, and their predictive ability contrasted in the following one. We use quantitative data for the United Kingdom and Sweden (pp. 225–228) as benchmarks for the output of different quantification techniques (pp. 229–233). These outputs are then further contrasted in the estimation of wage equations for the eight European countries that we consider.

Quantification methods for qualitative expectations data

We primarily use the European Commission's Consumer Survey to derive a numerical measure of inflation expectations. We consider a number of alternative approaches to proceed to the necessary quantification (Table 12.1).

The various approaches fall into three broad traditions in the literature[7]:

Table 12.1 Expectations measures selected for comparison

	Measure	Description
Carlson–Parkin tradition	EXPINFLA	Past inflation perceived correctly
	EXPINFLPCP	Trichotomous quantification of inflation perceptions
	EXPINFLPBIS	Trichotomous perceptions, with threshold adjustment
	EXPINFLPBO1	Pentachomous perceptions, moderate rate is full sample inflation mean
	EXPINFLPBO2	Pentachomous perceptions, moderate rate from linear interpolation
	EXPINFLPBO3	Pentachomous perceptions, moderate rate is running average of inflation
Pesaran tradition	EXPINFLAPES	Pesaran's regression approach
Seitz tradition	EXPINFLASEITZ	Time-varying stochastic parameter model for thresholds

1 The Carlson–Parkin or probability approach[8]

This method relies on assuming a shape for the aggregate distribution function of inflation expectations. Interpreting the shares of respondents in each survey category as maximum likelihood estimates of areas under the aggregate density function of inflation expectations allows for the derivation of the mean of the distribution, which is the quantified measure of inflation expectations. The formulation of the questions on inflation perceptions and expectations in the European Commission's Consumer Survey creates an intrinsic link between them. The six variants of the Carlson–Parkin methodology considered differ in their assumptions on the amount of information that can be extracted from the question on inflation perceptions, and on the way in which this is implemented. See Curto Millet (2007) for details.

2 The Pesaran or regression approach[9]

This method relies on estimating a relationship between inflation realizations and survey data on inflation perceptions. The estimated relationship can then be applied to survey data on inflation expectations to derive a quantified measure of inflation expectations.

3 The Seitz or stochastic time-varying parameters approach[10]

This method extends the Carlson–Parkin approach by allowing the underlying "threshold" parameters to vary through time according to the Stochastic Parameter Variation model of Cooley and Prescott (1976).

The following sections now set out the results of a number of horse races between these methods.

Comparing methods on the basis of predictive ability

Researchers often contrast different quantification methods on the basis of their forecasting performance (e.g. Dasgupta and Lahiri 1992; Smith and McAleer 1995; Clavería González 2003; Nolte and Pohlmeier 2004), as shown by the Root Mean Squared Error (RMSE), and the proportion of correct turning points predicted.

We shall now do this, but stress that predictive ability would give a scientific basis for choosing the quantification method that most accurately *represents* the actual underlying expectations *only* in a world of rational expectations.

We first provide the RMSE as a measure of the accuracy of the eight competing expectations measures. This exercise uses the full sample of *monthly* expectations observations for each country, with sample starting points in January 1980 for Germany and later for the other countries. Inflation expectations data are available for all countries until July 2005.

The performance of each indicator in terms of ranking varies widely across countries. Table 12.3 summarizes. It provides the average country rank computed from Table 12.2 as well as the overall average RMSE and its associated ranking and standard deviation.

The table shows that the Carlson–Parkin indicator EXPINFLPBIS is the overall leader in predictive ability among the competing methodologies. Nevertheless, it just underperforms the naïve benchmark. The standard deviation of the RMSEs is roughly comparable across indicators, except in the case of EXPINFLPBO3, although this finding is largely driven by its poor performance in Spain and Italy.

The Mean Squared Error (MSE) can be split into three components, as noted in Clavería González (2003). Let y denote inflation; bars placed over variables indicate averages, whereas hats ^ indicate the prediction of the variable for the relevant period. Hence, the expectation error in period t can be written as $e_t = (y_t - \hat{y}_t)$ and we have:

$$MSE = \frac{1}{T}\sum_{t=1}^{T} e_t^2 = (\bar{\hat{y}} - \bar{y})^2 + (\hat{\sigma} - r_{y\hat{y}}\sigma)^2 + (1 - r^2_{y\hat{y}})\sigma^2 \tag{1}$$

Where $r_{y\hat{y}}$ denotes the correlation coefficient between predicted and actual values, while $\hat{\sigma}$ and σ correspond to the standard deviations of predictions and observations, respectively. The three components on the right hand side can be expressed as percentages by dividing through by the MSE: $1 = U1 + U2 + U3$. U1 refers to the *proportion of MSE imputable to bias*, the square of the difference between the mean of predicted values and actual values. Since U2 depends on the difference between the standard deviations of predictions and actual values, it reflects the *proportion of MSE due to dispersion* ("regression error"). Finally, U3 arises from the lack of correlation between predictions and actual

Table12. 2 RMSE results for predicting actual inflation

Measure	France		Spain		Belgium		Germany	
	RMSE	Rank	RMSE	Rank	RMSE	Rank	RMSE	Rank
EXPINFLA	0.0092	5	0.0160	4	0.0112	8	0.0118	2
EXPINFLPCP	0.0101	7	0.0202	7	0.0103	6	0.0127	7
EXPINFLPBIS	0.0088	4	0.0180	5	0.0103	5	0.0119	3
EXPINFLPBO1	0.0127	9	0.0221	8	0.0100	2	0.0138	9
EXPINFLPBO2	0.0121	8	0.0199	6	0.0101	4	0.0126	6
EXPINFLPBO3	0.0093	6	0.0366	9	0.0117	9	0.0124	4
EXPINFLAPES	0.0078	3	0.0124	2	0.0107	7	0.0117	1
EXPSEITZ	0.0076	2	0.0116	1	0.0100	1	0.0128	8
NAÏVE	0.0070	1	0.0127	3	0.0101	3	0.0124	5
Period	1987m4–2005m8		1987m6–2005m8		1986m10–2005m9		1981m10–2005m8	

Measure	Italy		United Kingdom		Sweden		Netherlands	
	RMSE	Rank	RMSE	Rank	RMSE	Rank	RMSE	Rank
EXPINFLA	0.0202	6	0.0202	7	0.0118	3	0.0099	4
EXPINFLPCP	0.0153	3	0.0163	2	0.0105	1	0.0101	5
EXPINFLPBIS	0.0164	4	0.0161	1	0.0107	2	0.0096	3
EXPINFLPBO1	0.0164	4	0.0214	9	0.0127	6	0.0117	8
EXPINFLPBO2	0.0122	1	0.0197	5	0.0126	5	0.0117	7
EXPINFLPBO3	0.0490	9	0.0180	3	0.0139	7	0.0145	9
EXPINFLAPES	0.0261	8	0.0182	4	0.0163	9	0.0091	1
EXPSEITZ	0.0247	7	0.0202	6	0.0155	8	0.0101	6
NAÏVE	0.0148	2	0.0205	8	0.0125	4	0.0092	2
Period	1983m1–2005m9		1982m11–2005m8		1997m1–2005m8		1987m4–2005m8	

Table 12.3 Average rank and RMSE for predictive success

Measure	Avg. Cty Rank	Avg. RMSE	Rank	RMSE Std
EXPINFLA	5	0.0138	4	0.0044417
EXPINFLPCP	5	0.0132	3	0.0037507
EXPINFLPBIS	3	0.0127	2	0.0035566
EXPINFLPBO1	7	0.0151	8	0.0044705
EXPINFLPBO2	5	0.0139	5	0.0037511
EXPINFLPBO3	7	0.0207	9	0.0142651
EXPINFLAPES	4	0.0140	6	0.0059798
EXPSEITZ	5	0.0141	7	0.005786
NAÏVE	4	0.0124	1	0.0040757

values and represents the proportion of MSE due to all *factors unexplained or unaccounted for*.

The ideal outcome would be for the greatest weight to be achieved by the unexplained component of MSE, with a minimization of systematic (U1) and regression error (U2). This gives an extra criterion to assess our quantification measures. Table 12.4 makes clear that significant differences in the MSE decomposition arise across countries for any given measure. The average results are provided in Table 12.5. Measures such as EXPINFLPCP, EXPINFLPBIS, EXPINFLAPES and EXPSEITZ exhibit the most desirable properties in this respect.

Finally, how well can our expectations measures detect *turning points* in the actual inflation series? Is the direction of monthly changes in annual inflation reflected by changes in consumers' expectations? Table 12.6 provides the results on this.

The incidences of correctly predicted turning points are all in the region of 0.3–0.5. There is no case that beats a fair coin flip. In many cases, the measures significantly *underperform* chance according to binomial tests.[11] Table 12.7 summarises. On balance, EXPINFLPBIS, EXPINFLPCP and EXPINFLAPES do best.

Two points stand out from this analysis. First, the best predictors would be the most traditional – EXPINFLPCP, the Carlson–Parkin method as adapted by Batchelor and Orr (1988) and Berk (1999), or its close cousin EXPINFLPBIS suggested and used in Curto Millet (2004). Second, predictive ability is not the appropriate criterion, given the empirical rejection of rational expectations. The survey measures contrasted here actually *underperform* (in RMSE terms) the naïve indicator used for benchmarking.

Therefore, we benchmark our quantification methods with the two sources of comparable quantitative expectations data available in Europe, with the aim of making a sounder assessment on pages 229–233. These are presented next.

Table 12.4 MSE decomposition, details

Measure	France			Spain			Belgium			Germany		
	U1	U2	U3	U1	U2	U3	U1	U2	U3	U1	U2	U3
EXPINFLA	37.0	7.7	55.3	45.5	6.8	47.7	15.8	34.7	49.5	0.1	28.8	71.1
EXPINFLPCP	34.0	8.1	57.9	31.9	17.8	50.3	20.3	19.0	60.6	1.0	4.2	94.8
EXPINFLPBIS	44.5	2.2	53.3	39.5	9.8	50.8	16.6	22.5	60.9	0.5	7.6	91.9
EXPINFLPBO1	57.7	1.5	40.8	56.9	1.9	41.3	32.1	5.5	62.4	20.5	6.7	72.8
EXPINFLPBO2	65.6	0.5	33.9	66.5	0.2	33.4	29.9	9.0	61.1	23.6	12.4	64.0
EXPINFLPBO3	44.2	0.5	55.3	79.1	7.0	13.9	7.1	44.2	48.7	0.0	8.5	91.4
EXPINFLAPES	0.1	0.0	99.9	2.6	0.0	97.3	34.9	10.8	54.3	1.7	1.6	96.7
EXPSEITZ	0.3	14.9	84.9	9.7	1.3	89.0	13.0	24.0	63.0	8.8	0.4	90.8
NAÏVE	0.2	17.7	82.1	3.2	27.3	69.4	0.1	39.3	60.6	1.7	23.1	75.2

Measure	Italy			United Kingdom			Sweden			Netherlands		
	U1	U2	U3	U1	U2	U3	U1	U2	U3	U1	U2	U3
EXPINFLA	8.0	63.1	28.9	0.4	40.7	59.0	2.5	27.8	69.8	9.2	36.6	54.2
EXPINFLPCP	3.8	7.1	89.1	1.2	6.6	92.2	5.8	3.4	90.8	28.1	1.5	70.5
EXPINFLPBIS	8.5	36.1	55.4	1.6	9.8	88.6	7.3	6.1	86.6	26.1	0.2	73.7
EXPINFLPBO1	0.1	6.4	93.5	43.4	3.4	53.2	38.0	0.4	61.6	51.7	0.6	47.7
EXPINFLPBO2	4.3	10.9	84.8	44.3	1.1	54.6	37.9	0.1	62.0	49.8	0.0	50.1
EXPINFLPBO3	51.6	44.0	4.4	5.3	10.4	84.2	46.9	0.0	53.0	59.0	0.9	40.1
EXPINFLAPES	41.0	1.9	57.1	28.2	3.1	68.7	31.3	29.9	38.8	19.7	7.0	73.3
EXPSEITZ	34.0	5.4	60.6	7.5	29.9	62.6	24.0	35.2	40.7	0.5	38.6	60.9
NAÏVE	15.5	32.3	52.2	1.7	34.1	64.2	0.0	38.2	61.8	1.4	30.0	68.6

Table 12.5 MSE decomposition, averages by measure

Measure	Avg. U1	Avg. U2	Avg. U3
EXPINFLA	14.8	30.8	54.4
EXPINFLPCP	15.8	8.5	75.8
EXPINFLPBIS	18.1	11.8	70.1
EXPINFLPBO1	37.5	3.3	59.2
EXPINFLPBO2	40.2	4.3	55.5
EXPINFLPBO3	36.7	14.4	48.9
EXPINFLAPES	19.9	6.8	73.3
EXPSEITZ	12.2	18.7	69.1
NAÏVE	3.0	30.3	66.8

Quantitative survey data

United Kingdom: the Gallup survey

Social Surveys (Gallup Poll) Ltd carried out a monthly survey on a sample of employees in the United Kingdom continuously between January 1983 and January 1997. The results were published in the *Gallup Political Index* reports, later renamed *Gallup Political and Economic Index* reports. This survey's requested responses were *quantitative*. The question was: "Over the next twelve months, what do you think the rate of inflation will be?" The sample had some 500 individuals, with roughly 80 per cent addressing this question throughout the sample period. Gallup published the average survey response monthly, which is the series used in what follows. Plotting these inflation expectations for the coming 12 months *at the time they are surveyed* against inflation yields Figure 12.1.

One remarkable feature of this picture is how quickly increases in inflation feed into expectations, while it took longer for the lower inflation period of the 1990s to reduce them. The graph also makes it clear that expectations exhibit extremely important "adaptive" characteristics.

Sweden: the HIP survey

The Households Purchasing Plans survey (Hushållens Inköpsplaner in Swedish, or HIP) has included quantitative questions on inflation expectations and perceptions on a quarterly basis between 1979q1 and 1992q4, and monthly from January 1993. With Sweden's entry into the EU and the subsequent questionnaire harmonization that took place, the survey started to include the standard EC qualitative questions on inflation perceptions and expectations[12] (in addition to the quantitative ones) from January 1996. The quantitative questions in the HIP survey are shown in Table 12.8.[13]

Table 12.6 Correctly predicted turning points (%)

Measure	France		Spain		Germany		Belgium	
	%	Rank	%	Rank	%	Rank	%	Rank
EXPINFLA	33.6	8	40.8	7	35.0	9	33.0	9
EXPINFLPCP	38.6	5	47.2	3	43.4	3	47.6	1
EXPINFLPBIS	40.9	2	47.2	3	43.4	3	47.6	1
EXPINFLPBO1	36.8	6	41.3	6	40.2	6	41.9	4
EXPINFLPBO2	39.1	3	42.7	5	40.6	5	41.9	4
EXPINFLPBO3	39.1	3	40.4	8	40.2	6	41.4	6
EXPINFLAPES	41.4	1	49.1	1	46.9	1	42.3	3
EXPSEITZ	35.9	7	47.7	2	44.1	2	38.8	7
NAÏVE	33.6	8	39.9	9	38.1	8	35.2	8
No.observations	220		218		286		227	

Measure	Italy		United Kingdom		Sweden		Netherlands	
	%	Rank	%	Rank	%	Rank	%	Rank
EXPINFLA	44.6	7	36.6	9	36.9	8	39.1	8
EXPINFLPCP	43.3	9	43.6	5	47.6	1	46.4	3
EXPINFLPBIS	45.9	3	44.0	4	47.6	1	46.8	2
EXPINFLPBO1	45.5	4	45.1	3	44.7	6	40.0	7
EXPINFLPBO2	48.9	1	45.4	1	46.6	4	40.5	5
EXPINFLPBO3	48.1	2	45.4	1	45.6	5	40.5	5
EXPINFLAPES	43.8	8	40.7	6	47.6	1	45.5	4
EXPSEITZ	45.4	6	38.8	7	40.8	7	49.1	1
NAÏVE	45.4	5	37.0	8	33.0	9	35.5	9
No. observations	270		273		103		220	

Table 12.7 Average rank, success in turning point prediction

Measure	Avg. cty rank	Avg %	Rank
EXPINFLA	8	37.5	8
EXPINFLPCP	4	44.7	2
EXPINFLPBIS	2	45.4	1
EXPINFLPBO1	5	41.9	7
EXPINFLPBO2	4	43.2	4
EXPINFLPBO3	5	42.6	5
EXPINFLAPES	3	44.6	3
EXPSEITZ	5	42.6	6
NAÏVE	8	37.2	9

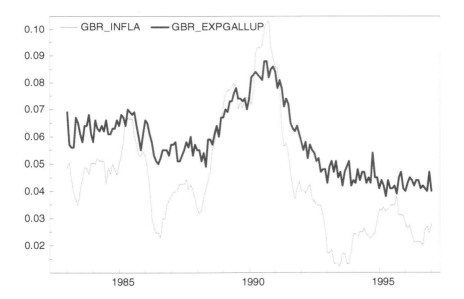

Figure 12.1 Quantitative Gallup data and actual CPI inflation, United Kingdom.

Table 12.8 HIP survey, quantitative questions

Concept	Question
Perceptions	Compared with 12 months ago, how much higher in percent do you think that prices are now?
Expectations	Compared with today, by what percentage do you think that prices will go up (i.e. the rate of inflation 12 months from now)?

Source: Konjunkturinstitutet, Hushållens Inköpsplaner – User Manual.

The survey has been conducted by Statistics Sweden (SCB) since 1973 and by GfK since 2002.[14] The next figures plot the quantitative HIP data on perceptions and expectations against CPI inflation for the whole sample period:

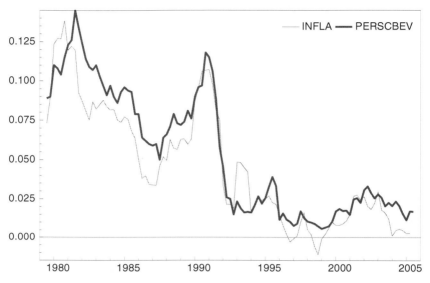

Figure 12.2 HIP perceptions versus actual inflation, Sweden, 1979q1–2005q3.

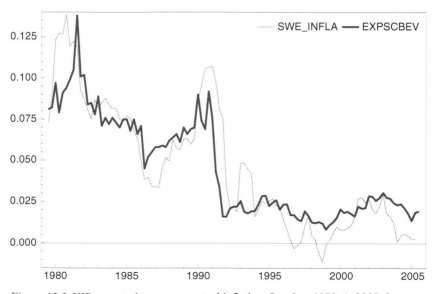

Figure 12.3 HIP expectations versus actual inflation, Sweden, 1979q1–2005q3.

Benchmarking EC qualitative data on quantitative data

Predictive performance statistics for the quantitative measures

We present for completeness the statistics on predictive performance used on pages 221–224 for our quantitative expectations series. The results are broadly comparable to the other measures.

Table 12.9 Predictive performance of quantitative measures

Country	Period	RMSE	U1%	U2%	U3%	% Correct Turning Points
United Kingdom	1984m1–1998m1	0.0230	37.8	0.3	61.9	42.26
Sweden	1994m1–2005m8	0.0142	36.3	10.2	53.6	46.04

Descriptive statistics

More interestingly, we contrast the quantified expectations from the EC Consumer Survey data with the quantitative data from Gallup surveys for the United Kingdom[15] as well as Swedish HIP data, the latter two being treated as an approximation of the "true" underlying expectations. This is a European exercise in the spirit of Batchelor's (1986) work on US data.

Table 12.10 shows simple correlations between our expectations measures and the quantitative ones. The ranking of measures differs in both countries. Why is unclear. The structure of expectations formation may differ, for instance in the behaviour of indifference thresholds. This still begs the question of what fundamental difference would lie behind this. The periods for which both quantitative and qualitative data are available for comparison (United Kingdom: 1983m1 – 1997m1; Sweden: 1996m1–2005m7) differ in inflation behaviour – low and relatively stable for Sweden, and volatile, downward-trending in-sample for the United Kingdom. Different measures may display different comparative advantages depending on underlying inflation behaviour.

Table 12.11 gives the same statistics for this "matching" exercise as on pages 221–224, adding the mean error (ME) to indicate bias.

Table 12.10 Correlations with quantitative measures

Measure	UK Corr	UK Rank	SWE Corr	SWE Rank
EXPINFLA	0.8755	4	0.7451	8
EXPINFLPCP	0.7763	7	0.9078	1
EXPINFLPBIS	0.8171	5	0.8806	5
EXPINFLPBO1	0.7957	6	0.8855	4
EXPINFLPBO2	0.8841	3	0.8531	6
EXPINFLPBO3	0.9027	2	0.808	7
EXPINFLAPES	0.6262	8	0.9066	2
EXPSEITZ	0.9086	1	0.8868	3

Table 12.11 Ability to match quantitative data

| Measure | United Kingdom | | | | | Sweden | | | | | |
	ME	RMSE	U1	U2	U3	ME	RMSE	U1	U2	U3
EXPINFLA	0.0151	0.0215	68.5	26.5	5.0	0.0116	0.0129	81.8	8.9	9.3
EXPINFLPCP	0.0158	0.0184	83.5	6.8	9.8	0.0121	0.0124	93.7	2.3	3.9
EXPINFLPBIS	0.0153	0.0177	83.5	8.6	7.9	0.0123	0.0126	94.6	0.5	4.9
EXPINFLPBO1	0.0308	0.0318	95.4	0.2	4.4	0.0172	0.0179	92.0	5.6	2.3
EXPINFLPBO2	0.0281	0.0288	97.2	0.0	2.8	0.0171	0.0177	92.9	4.1	3.0
EXPINFLPBO3	0.0192	0.0199	91.8	4.2	4.0	0.0188	0.0196	92.2	4.6	3.1
EXPINFLAPES	0.0042	0.0129	45.3	23.8	30.9	0.0011	0.0045	6.3	63.6	30.1
EXPSEITZ	0.0097	0.0154	61.7	31.3	7.0	0.0024	0.0069	11.6	73.2	15.2
NAÏVE	0.0132	0.0173	67.9	26.1	5.9	0.0097	0.0122	63.5	24.0	12.5
Period	1983m1–1997m1					1996m1–2005m7					

The best performers in RMSE and the MSE decomposition are EXPINFLA-PES and EXPSEITZ. This is in large part due to a considerably lower bias of these measures. EXPINFLAPES (and EXPINFLPBO) perform well in correctly indicating the direction of changes in the quantitative series.

For the United Kingdom, none of the measures is significantly superior to chance in predicting the direction of changes in the quantitative Gallup data (in fact, EXPIN-FLPCP and EXPINFLPBIS here are marginally significantly inferior at the 5 per cent level in a binomial test). This would seem to reinforce the case against the popular claim that tendency surveys are more useful at indicating the *direction* of changes rather than levels or magnitudes. It is consistent with past findings by Batchelor (1986) for monthly US SRC data over the period 1977–1984 and by Defris and Williams (1979) for a series of quarterly Australian data over 1973–1977.

However, the Swedish data present a very different picture. Here, almost all measures perform *significantly* better than chance at the 0.1 per cent level in capturing the direction of the underlying changes in the quantitative variable.[16] Possible explanations for this might point to the difference in the respondent bases of the EC survey and the Gallup one (respectively, consumers and employees) or to particularities of the relatively short Swedish sample with low and stable inflation.

This analysis is informative but cannot ultimately answer the question of which quantification method is to be preferred for control purposes in regression equations (where mean biases are corrected for by the constant in the equation, for instance). This question is the focus of the remainder of this chapter.

Non-nested testing of quantification methods

We next regress the quantitative expectations data for the United Kingdom and Sweden on the quantified expectations series. The aim is to see how much these measures can help to explain what we assume to be the "true" underlying expectations.

Despite the strong collinearity of several of these series, we may tell which broad

Table 12.12 Correctly indicated turning points (%)

Measure	United Kingdom		Sweden	
	%	Rank	%	Rank
EXPINFLA	48.81	5	63.16	8
EXPINFLPCP	42.86	8	81.58	1
EXPINFLPBIS	42.86	8	81.58	1
EXPINFLPBO1	51.19	3	78.95	3
EXPINFLPBO2	51.19	3	75.44	5
EXPINFLPBO3	52.38	1	75.44	5
EXPINFLAPES	52.38	1	78.07	4
EXPSEITZ	45.83	6	74.56	7
NAÏVE	45.83	6	53.51	9
No. observations	168		114	

"tradition" (Carlson–Parkin, Pesaran or Seitz) performs best here. In the regression for Sweden the sample begins in 1996, after which inflation was quite low and stable. The more varied UK data may therefore yield more informative results.

The data are monthly. The following tables present the results obtained after dropping insignificant and wrongly-signed variables:

Several findings stand out. First, the regressions perform badly in specifica-

Table 12.13 Non-nested testing results, United Kingdom

Modelling GBR_EXPGLP; Estimation sample: 1983m1–1997m1

	Coefficient	*Std.Error*	*t-value*	*t-prob*	*Part.R^2*
Constant	0.0236163	0.001598	14.8	0.000	0.5681
GBR_EXPINFLPBO3	0.527728	0.07259	7.27	0.000	0.2415
GBR_EXPSEITZ	0.287384	0.03438	8.36	0.000	0.2962

sigma	0.00453826	RSS		0.0034188974	
R^2	0.867681	F(2,166) =		544.3 [0.000]**	
log-likelihood	673.504	DW		1.1	
no. of observations	169	no. of parameters		3	
mean(GBR_EXPGLP)	0.058213	var(GBR_EXPGLP)		0.00015289	

Specification tests
AR 1–7 test: $F(7,159) = 6.9588 \ [0.0000]**$
ARCH 1–7 test: $F(7,152) = 3.7945 \ [0.0008]**$
Normality test: $Chi^2(2) = 4.9277 \ [0.0851]$
hetero test: $F(4,161) = 1.7482 \ [0.1420]$
hetero-X test: $F(5,160) = 1.5044 \ [0.1913]$
RESET test: $F(1,165) = 8.9499 \ [0.0032]**$

Table 12.14 Non-nested testing results, Sweden

Modelling SWE_EXPSCBEV; Estimation sample: 1996m1–2005m7

	Coefficient	*Std.Error*	*t-value*	*t-prob*	*Part.R^2*
Constant	0.00881046	0.0004257	20.7	0.000	0.7942
SWE_EXPINFLPBIS	0.460251	0.08247	5.58	0.000	0.2191
SWE_EXPINFLAPES	0.291735	0.04274	6.83	0.000	0.2956
SWE_EXPSEITZ	0.116332	0.03700	3.14	0.002	0.0818

sigma	0.00194931	RSS		0.000421777819	
R^2	0.893355	F(3,111) =		309.9 [0.000]**	
log-likelihood	556.49	DW		0.882	
no. of observations	115	no. of parameters		4	
mean(SWE_EXPSCBEV) 0.0193617		var(SWE_EXPSCBEV) 3.43911e-005			

Specification tests
AR 1–7 test: $F(7,104) = 11.704 \ [0.0000]**$
ARCH 1–7 test: $F(7,97) = 4.2134 \ [0.0004]**$
Normality test: $Chi^2(2) = 7.8746 \ [0.0195]*$
hetero test: $F(6,104) = 2.2495 \ [0.0442]*$
hetero-X test: $F(9,101) = 7.1888 \ [0.0000]**$
RESET test: $F(1,110) = 28.131 \ [0.0000]**$

tion statistics. This would be serious if we had tried to *model* the quantitative expectations data. Still, our quantified measures miss some information present in the quantitative series. Second, the constant is significant, again pointing to some bias, but not disqualifying the measures as controls in regression equations. Third, both regressions retain measures from two traditions – three for Sweden. Each method may capture information missed by the others. Finally, only measures in the Carlson–Parkin and Seitz traditions are retained in *both* equations, with a significantly larger coefficient on the former.

The quantitative data available permit no general claims on what combinations of measures would work best. If a choice is to be made, the results so far provide a nudge in the direction of a method in the Carlson–Parkin tradition. So does practical data analysis support this?

Inflation expectations measures in wage equations

The modelling of wages is a key application for inflation expectations measures. A good method should generate sensible wage equations, relative to theoretical sign priors. This is the test in this section.

Our proposed equation is presented first along with our sign priors. The next two subsections clarify the construction of the data and the econometric approach. The results are presented on and from page 237.

Model specification and sign priors

The equilibrium correction structure proposed in Curto Millet (2004) has a long-run solution that can be derived from a Nash bargaining model (Moghadam and

Table 12.15 Wage equation structure

$$\Delta \ln COMPTH_t = \alpha + a_1 INFLEXP_{t,t+4} + a_2 INFLEXP_{t-1,t+3} + a_3 INFLEXP_{t-2,t+2}$$
$$+ a_4 INFLEXP_{t-3,t+1} + a_5 INFLEXP_{t-4,t}$$
$$+ b_1 \Delta lCPI_t + b_2 \Delta lCPI_{t-1} + b_3 \Delta lCPI_{t-2} + b_4 \Delta lCPI_{t-3}$$
$$+ c_1 \Delta \ln COMPTH_{t-1} + c_2 \Delta \ln COMPTH_{t-2} + c_3 \Delta \ln COMPTH_{t-3}$$
$$+ c_4 \Delta \ln COMPTH_{t-4} + d_1 \Delta \ln U_t \tag{2}$$

$$+ e_1 \left[\ln \left(\frac{COMPTH}{P_c} \right)_{t-1} - f_1 \ln PRODIT_{t-1} \right.$$

$$- h_1 \ln(1 - ITAX)_{t-1} - i_1 \ln(1 + CTAX)_{t-1}$$
$$- j_1 \ln U_{t-1} - k_1 \ln BRR_{t-1} - l_1 ACOV_{t-1} - m_1 \ln EPL_{t-1}$$
$$- n_1 \ln UDENS_{t-1} - o_1 \ln BD_{t-1} - p_1 lRELPMPC_{t-1} - q_1 lCOORD_{t-1}]$$

COMPTH:	Hourly compensation of workers	BD:	Benefit duration index
INFLEXP:	Inflation expectations	ACOV:	Collective bargaining
PRODIT:	Trend productivity		coverage index
ITAX:	Income/direct taxation	UDENS:	Net union density
CTAX:	Consumption/indirect taxation	EPL:	Employment Protection
U:	Unemployment		Legislation index
P_c:	CPI, All items	RELPMPC:	Ratio of import to
BRR:	Benefit replacement ratio		consumer prices (Pm/Pc)
		COORD:	Bargaining coordination
			index

Wren-Lewis 1994), with short-run dynamics consistent with the staggered contracts approach. Full details of this are available in Curto Millet (2007).

We do not impose dynamic homogeneity *ex ante*, as workers will hardly adjust wages to price changes in full in the short-run. Homogeneity is imposed on the long-run equilibrium. The resulting wage equation is presented below; Table 12.16 lists our sign priors.

Some explanatory notes on our data[19]

General variables

The dependent variable is the hourly compensation of *workers* based on aggregate compensation of employees from the OECD's *Economic Outlook 77*, adjusted for self-employed workers following Batini *et al.* (2000). Total hours worked in the economy can be extracted from the OECD Productivity Database. The dependent variable is derived by dividing the aggregate compensation measure by the total hours worked.

Short-term variations in productivity should not greatly affect wage bargains, so productivity trends are more relevant. Our productivity measure is obtained by applying a Hodrick Prescott filter with lambda parameter 1600[20] to a productivity index provided by the OECD.

Tax variables

We adopt the definitions used in Bell and Dryden (1996), Nickell (2003) and Nickell and Nunziata (2001) to quantify the components of the tax wedge. Our data here extend the CEP–OECD dataset. The underlying data are from the OECD's *Revenue Statistics and Economic Outlook*.

The direct tax rate is:

$$ITAX = \frac{WC + IT}{HCR} \tag{3}$$

and depends on employees' social security contributions (WC), income taxes (IT) and household current receipts (H). The indirect tax rate is:

$$CTAX = \frac{TX - SB}{CC} \tag{4}$$

or indirect taxes (TX) minus subsidies (SB) divided by private final consumption expenditure (CC).

Institutional variables

The benefit replacement rate (BRR) is computed from data on the first year of unemployment benefits, averaged over family types of recipient (single earner/dependent spouse/spouse at work) (Nickell and Nunziata 2001).

Table 12.16 Empirical wage equation, sign priors

Core variables	
$a_i \geqslant 0$ for all i	Higher inflation expectations should raise wages. The magnitude of the coefficients should also be in line with the dynamics of the dependent variable.
$b_i \geqslant 0$ for all i	More inflation in the recent past should lead to a compensating adjustment of nominal wages, unless reflected in the previous wage contract.
$c_i \leqslant 0$ or $\geqslant 0$ for all i (variable)	Equation (2) is constructed in first differences rather than the fourth difference $\Delta_4 W_t$. Given that our measure of inflation expectations has a yearly horizon, if the data were best described by a fourth order difference, we would have: $\Delta_4 W_t = f(x_t) \Leftrightarrow \Delta W_t = -\Delta W_{t-1} - \Delta W_{t-2} - \Delta W_{t-3} + f(x_t)$ With x_t the vector of explanatory variables. In this case, $c_i \leqslant 0$. This argument does not go through if we choose to express the dependent variable as $\Delta_4 W_t$, or if the dynamics are genuinely quarterly. In such cases, positive coefficients should be expected, as higher previous settlements could boost present ones to preserve relativities. We let the modelling process determine the appropriate order of differencing.
$d_i \leqslant 0, j_i \leqslant 0$	Higher unemployment should lead to wage moderation.
$e_i \leqslant 0$	The EqCM coefficient should be negative, showing adjustment to long-run equilibrium of the model, and significant to demonstrate cointegration.
$f_i \geqslant 0$	Higher trend productivity should raise real wages; plausibly one for one.
Wedge variables	
$h_i \leqslant 0$	Direct/income taxes make workers demand higher wages, as they target the post-tax wage[17]. Here we expect a negative sign.
$i_i \leqslant 0$	Indirect/consumption tax rate increases widen the gap between producer and consumer wages[18]. Here we expect a negative sign.
$p_i \leqslant 0$	The net price received by the firm is lowered by higher import prices of inputs.
Institutional variables	
$k_i \geqslant 0 \ o_i \geqslant 0$	Higher benefit replacement rates and duration lead to tougher union bargaining.
$l_i \geqslant 0$	Higher bargaining coverage of unions implies a smaller competitive part of the economy and higher wages through tougher bargaining.
$m_i \geqslant 0$	Employment protection legislation reinforces union bargaining power.
$n_i \geqslant 0$	Higher net union density reinforces union bargaining power.
$q_i \leqslant 0$	Higher coordination leads in the end to wage moderation due to internalisation of externalities (c.f. Calmfors and Driffill, 1988).

The index for benefit duration is a weighted average of the following benefit replacement rates (Nickell and Nunziata 2001):

$$BD = \alpha \frac{BRR_2}{BRR_1} + (1 - \alpha)\frac{BRR_4}{BRR_1} \tag{5}$$

BRR1 is the unemployment benefit replacement rate received during the first year of unemployment, BRR2 is the replacement rate received during the second and third years of unemployment and BRR4 is the replacement rate received during the fourth and fifth years of unemployment. More weight is given to the first ratio ($\alpha = 0.6$).

The union density variable (UDENS) measures active union membership (excluding pensioners and students) as a share of the gainfully employed wage and salary earners (excluding the unemployed).

The bargaining coverage variable (ACOV) is *adjusted* so as to refer the number of employees covered by a collective agreement as a percentage of employees *equipped with the right to bargain* (Traxler 1994).

Bargaining coordination (COORD) extends an index compiled by Ochel (2000). The index has three dimensions, measured on the scales in parentheses:

- Centralization (1–3)
- Coordination (1–3)
- Capacity for implementation (1–2)

Indices are computed for each of the above categories, the (subjectively weighted) average of which yields the summary index, with scale (1–3).

The Employment Protection Legislation (EPL) indicator chains a multidimensional index from the OECD *Employment Outlook 2004* with data on severance pay from Lazear (1990) before 1985.

Econometric approach

We adopt Hendry's general-to-specific (*Gets*) modelling strategy. Behind this lies the theory of reduction, which describes conditions under which the actual (and complicated) Data Generating Process (DGP) can be represented by a (transformed) subset of the original variables with no information loss. This way we seek to recover the *Local* Data Generating Process (LDGP).

The *Gets* approach formulates a General Unrestricted Model (GUM). This is the most general model that can be postulated initially, using the current sample of data, previous empirical research and theoretical, institutional and measurement information. The GUM should contain as a special case the parsimonious representation at which the modelling exercise aims. The GUM must be *congruent*, matching the data in all measured respects, which is checked by testing for misspecification. A process of simplification is then applied, checking for congruence at every step.

We take the model presented in equation (2) to be the GUM.[21] We select our model with an informal Bayesian approach, in the manner of Aron *et al.* (2004).

Emphasis is placed on the long-run solution providing sensible results, leading us to impose the restrictions suggested by economic theory as needed.

The lag structure of the model is data-determined. The temporal position of the ECM is informed by the short-term inflation dynamics. We watch for the possibility of restrictions that would suggest fourth difference effects in the dynamics. For instance, $b_1 = b_2 = b_3 = b_4$ would suggest a $\Delta_4 lCPI_t$ formulation. Such effects may be interpretable as the consideration of inflationary changes since the last negotiations in a framework of yearly bargaining, for example.

The nature of certain variables in the equilibrium correction term makes them clearly integrated; for standard inference to hold we need them to cointegrate. This will be signalled by a significant coefficient for the speed of adjustment term e_1, whose distribution is non-standard but relatively close to a Student t-distribution (Hendry and Juselius 2000).

Results

We carried out a total of 64 general-to-specific model selection procedures.[22] All the equations obtained that result are congruent unless stated to the contrary. We comment on the summary results, then discuss specific results for each country.

Table 12.17 indicates the retained lags of the expectations variable (if any) and their significance. Several general features stand out.

First, France yielded no evidence of expectations affecting the wage equation. Perhaps, in certain countries, strong unions can recover the losses from any inflation within the contract period *ex post*, and bargain as if these were irrelevant in a forward-looking manner. A similar result was found by Aron *et al.* (2004) for South Africa. Other more plausible reasons in this instance are discussed later.

Second, there was sometimes significant collinearity between the inflation dynamics and the inflation expectations variables. This complicates the interpretation of some equations. The retained inflation expectations for Germany are lagged four quarters, which would seem a rather long lag, given that it is isolated and not part of a lag structure for expectations. Could this variable be proxying for lagged annual inflation? Augmenting the model for that possibility did not change the modelling outcome, however. The other possibility is that other lags in expectations which would have eased interpretation were dropped due to collinearity.

Third, there are some instances in which several lags of expectations are retained. This might imply contract staggering or "inattentive" agents only updating expectations periodically or taking decisions on outdated expectations, as in Mankiw *et al.* (2003). The issue of multicollinearity may mask this. Lags in expectations and other variables could also arise because negotiations between unions and employers take time to complete, yet reflect information when bargaining began.

Finally, the measures based on the Pesaran and Seitz traditions tend to be dropped when others are retained. This arouses suspicion but does not justify their exclusion as it could reflect the unimportance of the "true" expectations in

Table 12.17 Wage equations, retained lags of expectations

	FRA	ESP	BEL	DEU	GBR	SWE	ITA	NLD
EXPINFLA	X	(0***)	(0*, 2**)	X	(0,3***)	–	(0***, 2**)	X
EXPINFLPCP	X	(0***,4**)	(2***)	(4**)	(3***)	–	(0**)	(3**)
EXPINFLPBIS	X	(3***)	(2**)	(4***)	(3***)	–	(0**)	(3**)
EXPINFLPBO1	X	(4**)	(2**)	(4)	(3***)	–	X	(0***,4)
EXPINFLPBO2	X	(4**)	(2***)	(4**)	(3***)	–	(0**)	(0***,4*)
EXPINFLPBO3	X	(0***)	(2**)	(4)	(3***)	–	(0**)	(0***,4***)
EXPINFLAPES	X	X	(3**)	X	X	–	X	(0***)
EXPSEITZ	X	X	(1**)	(4)	(0***,3*)	–	X	(0***)
EXPGLP	–	–	–	–	(0*,3***)	–	–	–
EXPSCBEV	–	–	–	–	–	(0**)	–	–

Notes
X denotes the absence of expectations in the estimated wage equation; – indicates that the regression was not or could not be estimated; *, **,*** denote significance at the 10 per cent, 5 per cent and 1 per cent levels, respectively. Retained lags and their significance in brackets.

the wage process whilst other measures are retained as proxies for inflation dynamics, for instance. This issue will be resolved below.

The individual country results follow. The Swedish specification is shown next to aid intuition on our specification. For brevity, the remaining results are given descriptively; the finalized and selected models are offered in full detail in Curto Millet (2007).

Sweden

The wage equation for Sweden has an especially interesting dynamic structure. The dependent variable is the three-year change in the hourly compensation of workers, D12lCOMPTH, so the equilibrium term is lagged by three years. This

Table 12.18 Results from the Swedish wage equation

Modelling SWE_D12lCOMPTH; Estimation sample: 1983q1–2005q1

	Coefficient	Std.Error	t-value	t-prob	Part.R^2
Constant	− 13.4651	2.200	−6.12	0.000	0.3391
SWE_D4lCOMPTH_1	0.301122	0.06065	4.97	0.000	0.2525
SWE_EXPSCBEV	0.288568	0.1191	2.42	0.018	0.0744
SWE_D4lCPI	0.466969	0.09037	5.17	0.000	0.2678
SWE_D4lCPI_4	0.830359	0.07022	11.8	0.000	0.6570
SWE_D4lCPI_8	0.802234	0.09408	8.53	0.000	0.4990
SWE_D4lU	−0.0157295	0.009014	−1.74	0.085	0.0400
SWE_D4lU_4	−0.0281434	0.01090	−2.58	0.012	0.0837
SWE_D4lU_8	−0.0737631	0.007703	−9.58	0.000	0.5568
I1999	−0.0221632	0.004721	−4.69	0.000	0.2319
I1995:1	−0.0225431	0.008142	−2.77	0.007	0.0950
I2002:1	0.0235681	0.007949	2.96	0.004	0.1075
SWE_lRCOMPTH_12	−0.701336	0.04742	−14.8	0.000	0.7497
SWE_lPRODIT_12	0.514141	0.07215	7.13	0.000	0.4102
SWE_lU_12	−0.0710404	0.009310	−7.63	0.000	0.4437
SWE_lACOV_12	2.54092	0.5211	4.88	0.000	0.2457

sigma	0.0075778	RSS		0.00419188561
R^2	0.987712	F(15,73) =	391.2	[0.000]**
log-likelihood	317.079	DW	1.8	
no. of observations	89	no. of parameters	16	
mean(SWE_D12lCOMPTH)	0.166093	var(SWE_D12lCOMPTH)		0.00383307

Specification tests
AR 1–5 test:	$F(5,68) = 1.6675 \ [0.1543]$
ARCH 1–4 test:	$F(4,65) = 0.66158 \ [0.6209]$
Normality test:	$Chi^2(2) = 3.2054 \ [0.2014]$
hetero test:	$F(27,45) = 0.75711 \ [0.7774]$
RESET test:	$F(1,72) = 0.14568 \ [0.7038]$

is unique among the countries in our sample and reflects highly idiosyncratic features of the Swedish labour market.

Sweden and Denmark (possibly with Cyprus) have the longest usual duration of collective agreements in the European Union (three years) (European Commission 2004). Fregert and Jonung (1998) examine historical data on the average length of blue-collar worker collective agreements in Sweden. There were a number of major two-year agreements in the 1980s, with some three-year agreements apparently already in existence (Swedish Institute 2005). Fregert and Jonung (1998) locate the shift to mainly three-year agreements in 1995.[23]

The equation has a sensible long-run solution, with strongly significant productivity and unemployment effects. The speed of adjustment coefficient is 70 per cent. Long-run homogeneity for productivity cannot quite be imposed. Of the institutional variables, only bargaining coverage could be retained.[24]

Unemployment dynamics over the previous three years are highly significant. The inflation dynamics are equally strong in this equation and the coefficients for inflation in the previous two years could (almost) be restricted to one, and remain high for changes in the previous year. This might suggest a bargaining framework in which expectations do not matter *ex ante* – because, for instance, unions are strong enough or otherwise confident to obtain compensation *ex post*. Nevertheless, the equation also displays a forward-looking component: contemporaneous inflation expectations are significant.

The dummy variable for 1999 picks up a trough in the series for the growth of hourly compensation of workers. This was a quiet year between bargaining periods, with most of the public and private sectors covered by the 1998 negotiations. It reveals controlled wage increases with only marginal examples of wage drift. The four new collective pay agreements negotiated at the sectoral level in 1999 all followed the 3 per cent pay increase norm for 1999 that was set in the 1998 bargaining round (EIRO 1999). The moderation in hourly compensation growth observed in 1999 was also influenced by a cut in employers' social contributions.[25] This is set against the background of a new pension system in 1999 (Swedish Institute 2004).

The specification tests show the model is congruent in all aspects, with an excellent fit (sigma of 0.76 per cent). There is no significant autocorrelation when modelling a three-year change in compensation over the period of the last 20 years. A battery of stability tests (including 1-step, breakpoint and forecast Chow tests) confirms the stability of the model over the entire period examined. Individual recursive estimates of the coefficients reveal no break, further confirming the appropriateness of the model.

As stated earlier, the remaining set of results are presented descriptively, but can be found in their entirety in Curto Millet (2007).

United Kingdom

The wage equation for the United Kingdom models the yearly change in hourly compensation, with an equilibrium correction term lagged four quarters.

The model with quantitative expectations EXPGLP is estimated over 1984q1 – 1996q4. Institutional variables are absent from the long-run solution, which includes productivity, unemployment and the relative price of imports to CPI. There are significant unemployment and inflation dynamics. Expectations enter the model at two different lags – zero and three, although the former is only significant at 10 per cent. This is a finding that is impossible to reproduce when using our quantified measures for modelling purposes on this reduced sample. The closest equations to that of EXPGLP over this sample use EXPINFLPBIS, EXPINFLPCP and EXPINFLPBO1,2,3 – all of which have a matching long-run equilibrium and expectations at a lag of three.

The qualitative data are available over the longer sample 1983q1–2005q1. The long-run structure is identical to that of the model for EXPGLP, with the addition of a significant coefficient for either employment protection legislation or bargaining coverage depending on the equation. The great similarity in structure between the equations gives little ground for preferring one measure over another (except for rejecting EXPINFLAPES, which drops out).

France

The French wage equation captures the quarterly change in hourly compensation, with an equilibrium correction term lagged three quarters; the model is estimated over 1986q1–2005q2. The French specification includes a significant effect for changes in working hours in the dynamics of the equation as suggested in Curto Millet (2004).

The remarkable feature of the selected French models is the absence of inflation expectations. Yet all models are congruent with the data, and all specification tests are passed with ease. We asked earlier if strong unions might recover the losses from any inflation occurring within the contract period *ex post*, and therefore bargain as if this was irrelevant in a forward-looking manner. This seems unlikely to be the full story for France. Although inflation dynamics have a highly significant role, that is even truer of Sweden, which *does* exhibit a significant role for expectations. Furthermore, there are good reasons to expect backward-looking behaviour in France (e.g. indexation of the *SMIC* minimum wage; see Curto Millet 2007), but these are not exceptional in our sample nor could they blanket the entire labour market in such a way as to completely discard a role for expectations. A different interpretation may be relevant.

Could French unions set a premium that insulates them partly from prevailing economic conditions? The model for France includes highly significant effects for *both* benefit duration and the benefit replacement rate – unique in our sample of countries. However, the unemployment coefficient is also strongly significant, so bargaining is not completely insensitive to the economic situation.

More straightforwardly, the inflation expectations data may be significantly worse than in other European countries given measurement issues arising from the phrasing of the French questionnaire.[26] This would explain why France is such an exception, and suggests that special care should be taken using these French data.

Spain

The Spanish model regresses the yearly change in hourly compensation, with a long-run equilibrium term lagged four quarters. The model is estimated over 1987q3–2005q2.

Productivity data for Spain are only available at a half-yearly frequency – coarser than in the other countries. This makes for imprecise estimates in *some* of the equations and calls for a constraint of long-run homogeneity (easily accepted statistically by the data) to obtain a sensible outcome of the modelling process. The outcomes of the selection process are reasonably close in all cases, except for the drop of the EXPINFLAPES and EXPSEITZ variables. The retention of EXPINFLA is dubious due to the associated absence of any inflation dynamics.

The long-run typically includes significant effects for unemployment, employment protection legislation and the relative price of imports to the CPI. The most sensible equations from an economic perspective are EXPINFLPCP, EXPINFLPBIS and EXPINFLPBO2. The equation for EXPINFLPCP displays an interesting lag structure of inflation expectations, without reducing the inflation dynamics. Its long-run solution uniquely includes the benefit replacement rate but suspiciously drops lagged unemployment. The equations for EXPIN-FLPBIS and EXPINFLPBO2 are similar and have a more conventional long-run (including unemployment) but simpler expectations dynamics. The EXPINFLP-BIS model seems to do best overall, as the four quarter-lagged expectations of EXPINFLPBO2 are long.

Belgium

The Belgian wage equation regresses the two-year change in hourly compensation, and the equilibrium correction term is lagged eight quarters. The estimation is made over 1986q1–2005q2. This is consistent with the finding that the usual duration of collective agreements in Belgium is two years (European Commission 2004).

The resulting parsimonious equations display only minor differences in the inflation and expectations dynamics. The long-run solution invariably involves unemployment, the benefit replacement rate, union density and the relative price of imports to the CPI. In all cases, long-run homogeneity for productivity can be imposed. All the expectations measures perform adequately. EXPINFLA leads to the retention of two lags of expectations, unlike the other measures.

The Netherlands

The Dutch wage equation models yearly changes in the hourly compensation of workers over 1974q3–2005q2, with an equilibrium correction term lagged four quarters. The long sample available poses particular challenges given the economic volatility in the 1970s. This appears in the Dutch equation through the significance of a volatility index, both as a differenced variable and as part of the long-run solution. The rationale for its presence is that in a volatile environment, inflation surprises can hurt workers' real compensation during the contract period, and they may therefore seek to insure against that possibility *ex ante*. Volatility is captured by the following moving average measure:

$$MA[abs(D4/CPI - D4/CPI\_4)]$$

The equations have largely similar long-run solutions. The models of EXPIN-FLPBO1/2/3, EXPINFLAPES, EXPINFLPCP and EXPINFLPBIS all seem reasonable, although more or less significant heteroscedasticity often proved hard to eliminate, unsurprisingly given the sample period.

The models for EXPINFLPBO3 and EXPINFLPBIS stand out in the completeness of the equilibrium correction term. In both, long-run homogeneity can be imposed for productivity, and both tax terms are retained. Homogeneity can also be imposed for indirect taxation, making producer prices the relevant price concept in equilibrium. The models also include significant unemployment, coordination and volatility EqCM effects, as well as a benefit replacement rate or benefit duration term. EXPINFLPBO3 has a more interesting lag structure of expectations, although this comes suspiciously at the expense of actual inflation dynamics, which can be retained in the EXPINFLPBIS equation (which seems overall a more preferable choice).

Italy

The Italian wage equation is modelled over 1974q1–2005q2 for the two-year change in hourly compensation, with the long-run equilibrium lagged eight quarters. This is consistent with a usual duration for collective agreements of two years, as recorded by the European Commission (2004). Unlike the Dutch wage equation, controls for inflation volatility were unnecessary.

Three models give especially sensible long-run solutions: EXPINFLPCP, EXPINFLPBIS and EXPINFLPBO1. Long-run homogeneity can be imposed for productivity; the direct taxation variable coefficient is not negligible but insignificant at 10 per cent. The equation for EXPINFLPBIS is best: it gives significant roles to unemployment and bargaining coordination. Although all the models agree that adjustment is very slow, the coefficient is often implausibly low. The equation for EXPINFLPBIS provides a more reasonable (but still low) estimate of 15 per cent.[27]

In dynamic terms, the wage equation displays highly significant inflation and unemployment dynamics. The EXPINFLPBIS term itself is highly significant, although rather small (around 4 per cent).

Germany

We model the half-yearly change in hourly compensation with an EqCM term lagged by two quarters over the period 1991q3–2005q2.

The selected models have a similar structure, even in the two cases where the expectations variable is dropped (EXPINFLAPES and EXPINFLA), and all satisfy specification tests with ease. The long-run shows roles for the benefit replacement rate and bargaining coverage, and very strong effects from both taxation variables. Unemployment has an insignificant long-run effect but (modestly) affects the dynamic structure of the equation.

Despite great similarity in outcomes, the wage equation for the measures EXPINFLPBIS and EXPINFLPBO2 with their highly significant productivity effects and faster adjustment appear especially sensible, given a usual duration of collective agreements of 1–2 years (European Commission 2004). The equation for EXPINFLPBIS in addition displays a marginally insignificant union density variable at 10 per cent, absent from other equations.

Conclusion

This chapter presents a range of competing quantification methods for qualitative survey data on inflation expectations, with the aim of determining the optimal approach to this problem. These methods arose from three distinct traditions in the literature, identified respectively with Carlson–Parkin, Pesaran and Seitz. As none is free of theoretical weaknesses, an empirical examination is needed to help select the optimal method.

The methods were compared in terms of their ability to reproduce the quantitative data available for the United Kingdom and Sweden. EXPINFLAPES and EXPSEITZ performed better than the other measures in RMSE terms due to relatively low bias. The picture was less clear in ability to indicate the direction of change of the underlying variables, as the EXPINFLPBO measures also performed well here. Non-nested tests selected for both countries a combination of measures which included one in the Carlson–Parkin tradition and one in the Seitz tradition, with the Pesaran measure also being retained in the case of Sweden. This suggests that each tradition captures pieces of complementary information, although the largest coefficients were attached to information from the Carlson–Parkin approach.

We investigated the results of using these measures in practical econometric modelling in the economically critical context of wage equations. This selection criterion was much more decisive, with the measure EXPINFLPBIS demonstrating the best performance consistently and EXPINFLPBO2 also offering sensible outcomes overall relative to our sign priors, especially for the long-run equilibrium. Both measures are modifications of the Carlson–Parkin tradition suggested here, the former from Curto Millet (2004).

There was one country – France – where inflation expectations did not seem to matter. Potential institutional explanations were considered for this. Measurement error caused by the difference in wording of the French questionnaire probably bears significant responsibility. Apparently sound equations in terms of the specification tests were also found in other cases where the expectations terms were dropped, suggesting that these are not "critical" to a modelling exercise in this respect. Their importance is more subtle, however, as the equations including inflation expectations terms often had greater economic interpretability and the presence of such terms helped to give a more complete description of the long-run equilibrium.

This study supports the use of measures in the Carlson–Parkin/Batchelor and Orr tradition that use information on perceptions in the quantification. It points to gains from allowing for long-run trend changes in the underlying thresholds. Further investigation of more appropriate structural alternatives in the Seitz tradition may also be profitable, as would further empirical exercises contrasting these measures in other contexts.

This chapter also highlights the need for economists to notice the maturity of survey-based expectations measures, both in terms of the quantification procedures and their usability due to the sample sizes now available. These measures could make momentous contributions to econometric modelling and more generally to economic debates – including, but not limited to, that surrounding the mantra of rational expectations and credibility theory.

Notes

1 NERA Economic Consulting. E-mail Fabien.Curto.Millet@nera.com. I am greatly indebted to John Muellbauer for truly exceptional support and inspiration throughout this research. Peter Sinclair was instrumental in editing this chapter. I am very grateful for comments and help from: James Forder, David Vines, Roy Batchelor, Neil Shephard, Mark Williams, Jerzy Mycielski, Takamitsu Kurita, Samuel W. Malone, Cédric Viguié, Antonio Fuso, Luca Nunziata, Glenda Quintini, Wolfgang Ochel, Radhika Rathinasabapathy and Daniel Curto Millet. All remaining errors are my own, as are the views expressed in this chapter. In particular, they should not be taken to reflect the views of NERA Economic Consulting, nor of the European Commission.
2 For a historical overview, see Evans and Honkapohja (2001).
3 For instance, the Bank of England considers both survey and market-based measures of inflation expectations in its Inflation Reports, the former being derived from the Bank of England/NOP survey. See Bank of England (2005), for instance, and chapter 3 in Curto Millet (2007).
4 Further discussion and evidence is provided in chapter 3 of Curto Millet (2007).
5 This is likely given the findings in Bryan and Venkatu (2001) and Carroll (2003).
6 For instance, in the United Kingdom, regulatory requirements force institutional investors such as pension funds to invest in index-linked bonds to some extent, thereby artificially depressing their yield. Expectations computed on this basis would exaggerate the "true" underlying inflation expectations.
7 Please refer to Curto Millet (2007) for a detailed discussion of each approach.
8 Please refer to Theil (1952); Carlson and Parkin (1975); Batchelor and Orr (1988); Reckwerth (1997); Berk (1999, 2000).
9 Please refer to Anderson (1952) and Pesaran (1984, 1987).
10 Please refer to Seitz (1988).
11 As a benchmark, the critical percentage of correct turning points at the 5 per cent level for 220 observations is roughly 44 per cent.

12 See Table 7.1 in Chapter 7 of this volume.
13 See Palmqvist and Strömberg (2004) for further details on the practical implementation of the survey.
14 See GfK (2003), Consumer Survey 2003.
15 The Gallup data surveys employees. Batchelor and Dua (1987) remark that a sample of employees need not be equivalent to one of consumers. Indeed, employees may be relatively more rational in their assessments of inflation given their incentives to gather information for wage bargaining. We shall nonetheless use these data as a benchmark to assess the output of quantification techniques as a reasonable approximation.
16 The critical percentage of correctly predicted points at the 0.1 per cent level is roughly 64.5 per cent.
17 This shifts the Bargained Real Wage (BRW) curve up in the Carlin and Soskice (1990) framework.
18 This shifts the Price Determined Real Wage Curve (PRW) down in the Carlin and Soskice (1990) framework.
19 Refer to Curto Millet (2007) for a full explanation.
20 This is standard for a quarterly frequency.
21 Arguably, the model presented in the previous section could be further generalized, notably through additional delta effects. Further such lags were considered in the modelling process (e.g. for unemployment). Other delta effects (e.g. for institutional variables) are less plausible and appear to be more naturally features of the equilibrium rather than short-run influences on the wage bargain.
22 Of these, 17 concern the United Kingdom, as the process was carried out both for the full sample and the sub-sample over which quantitative data is available.
23 Although – as noted in EIRO (2004) – the current formalized system of three-year pay agreements in both the private and public sectors was initiated with the 1998 bargaining round.
24 It is however estimated imprecisely given the limited variation typical of this series (in this case, a single continuous increase over the years 1990–1995).
25 These fell by close to 10 per cent according to the OECD Revenue Statistics Database, mainly on account of reductions in employer contributions to certain pension categories.
26 Prior to harmonization in January 2004, the French questionnaire elicited inflation expectations from respondents by specifying an indeterminate time horizon covering "the coming months" instead of the "next 12 months" requested in other questionnaires. Inflation perceptions were also elicited for the period of the previous six months, rather than the previous 12 months in other questionnaires.
27 This issue is discussed further in Curto Millet (2007).

References

Aron, J., J. Muellbauer (2004), Modelling the inflation process in South Africa: keynote address, *Eighth Annual Conference on Econometric Modelling for Africa*, Stellenbosch University, South Africa.

Bakhshi, H. and A. Yates (1998), Are UK inflation expectations rational?, *Bank of England Working Paper*, 81.

Bank of Canada (1998), *Information in Financial Asset Prices*, Conference, Ottawa, Bank of Canada.

Bank of England (2005), *Inflation Report*, November.

Batchelor, R.A. (1986), Quantitative v. qualitative measures of inflation expectations, *Oxford Bulletin of Economics and Statistics*, 48 (2): 99–120.

Batchelor, R.A. and P. Dua (1987), The accuracy and rationality of UK inflation expectations: some quantitative evidence, *Applied Economics*, 19: 819–828.

Batchelor, R.A. and A.B. Orr (1988), Inflation expectations revisited, *Economica*, 55: 317–331.

Batini, N., B. Jackson, and S. Nickell (2000), Inflation dynamics and the labour share in the UK, *External MPC Unit Discussion Paper*, 2.

Baum, C.F. (2004), *SUGUK 2004 Invited Lecture: Topics in Time Series Modeling with Stata*.

Bell, B. and N. Dryden (1996), *The CEP–OECD Data Set (1950–1992)*, London: Centre for Economic Performance (CEP), London School of Economics.

Berk, J.M. (1999), Measuring inflation expectations: a survey data approach, *Applied Economics*, 31: 1467–1480.

Berk, J.M. (2000), Consumers' inflation expectations and monetary policy in Europe, *Research Memorandum*, Vrije Universiteit, Amsterdam, 2000-20, June.

Bowdler, C. and E.S. Jansen (2004), Testing for a time-varying price-cost markup in the Euro area inflation process, *Nuffield College Economics Working Paper*, 2004-W10.

Bryan, M.F. and S. Palmqvist (2005), Testing near-rationality using detailed survey data, *European Economy* (228).

Bryan, M.F. and G. Venkatu (2001), The demographics of household inflation surveys, *Economic Commentary*, Federal Reserve Bank of Cleveland.

Carlin, W. and D. Soskice (1990), *Macroeconomics and the Wage Bargain*, Oxford: Oxford University Press.

Carlson, J.A. and M. Parkin (1975), Inflation expectations, *Economica*, 42 (May): 123–138.

Carroll, C.D. (2003), Macroeconomic expectations of households and professional forecasters, *Quarterly Journal of Economics*, (February).

Clavería González, O. (2003), Cuantificación de las Expectativas de Precios a Partir de la Encuesta Industrial de la UE, *Tesis Doctoral*, Departamento de Econometría, Estadística y Economía Española de la Universidad de Barcelona.

Clemente, J., A. Montañés, and M. Reyes (1998), Testing for a unit root in variables with a double change in the mean, *Economics Letters*, 59: 175–182.

Clements, M.P. and D.F. Hendry (1999), *Forecasting Non-stationary Economic Time Series*, Cambridge, UK: Cambridge University Press.

Cooley, T.F. and E.C. Prescott (1973), Varying parameter regression: a theory and some applications, *Annals of Economic and Social Measurement*, 2: 463–473.

Cooley, T.F. and E.C. Prescott (1976), Estimation in the presence of stochastic parameter variation, *Econometrica*, 44: 167–184.

Curto Millet, F. (2004), The impact of EMU on the flexibility of European labour markets – structural break or "business as usual"?, University of Oxford MPhil Thesis.

Curto Millet, F. (2007), Inflation expectations, labour markets and EMU, University of Oxford DPhil Thesis.

Dasgupta, S. and K. Lahiri (1992), A comparative study of alternative methods of quantifying qualitative survey responses using NAPM data, *Journal of Business and Economic Statistics*, 10 (4): 391–400.

DG ECFIN (European Commission) (2004), *The Joint Harmonised EU Programme of Business and Consumer Surveys, User Guide*, Brussels: European Commission

EIRO (1997–2004), *EIRO National Reports*, (various countries): European Industrial Relations Observatory.

Ericsson, N.R. and J.S. Irons (1995) The Lucas critique in practice: theory without measurement, in K.D. Hoover, *Macroeconometrics: Developments, Tensions and Prospects*, Dordrecht: Kluwer Academic Press.

European Commission (2004), *Industrial Relations in Europe 2004*, Brussels: European Commission.

Evans, G.W. and S. Honkapohja (2001), *Learning and Expectations in Macroeconomics*, Princeton, NJ: Princeton University Press.

Forder, J. (2000), Could reputation-bias be a bigger problem than inflation-bias?, Oxford University, *Department of Economics Working Paper*, 22.

Fregert, K. and L. Jonung (1998), Monetary regimes and endogenous wage contracts: Sweden 1908–1995, *Working Paper*, 1998-3, Department of Economics, Lund University, Sweden.

Gerberding, C. (2001), The information content of survey data on expected price developments for monetary policy, *Deutsche Bundesbank ERC Discussion Paper*, 9/01.

GfK (2003), *Consumer Survey 2003*, Sverige AB: GfK.

Harvey, A.C. (1989), *Forecasting, Structural Time Series Models and the Kalman Filter*, Cambridge, UK: Cambridge University Press.

Hendry, D.F. (1995), *Dynamic Econometrics*, Oxford: Oxford University Press.

Hendry, D.F. (2001), Modelling UK inflation 1875–1991, *Journal of Applied Econometrics*, 16: 255–275.

Hendry, D.F. and J.A. Doornik (2001), *Empirical Econometric Modelling Using PcGive*, London: Timberlake Consultants Press.

Hendry, D.F. and K. Juselius (2000), Explaining cointegration analysis: part 1, *Energy Journal*, 21 (1): 1–42.

INSEE (2004), Enquête Mensuelle de Conjoncture Auprès des Ménages, *Note Méthodologique*.

Konjunkturinstitutet Hushållens Inköpsplaner [Consumer Survey, User Manual] (no date) Stockholm: NIER.

Lazear, E. (1990), Job security provision and employment, *Quarterly Journal of Economics*.

Łyziak, T. (2003), Consumer inflation expectations in Poland, *ECB Working Paper*, 287.

Mankiw, N.G., R. Reis and J. Wolfers (2003), Disagreement about inflation expectations, *NBER Working Paper*, 9796.

Nickell, S. (2003), Employment and taxes, *Tax Policy and Employment Conference*, CESifo.

Nickell, S. and L. Nunziata (2001), Labour Market Institutions Database.

Nielsen, H. (2003a), Inflation expectations in the EU – results from survey data, *Discussion Paper*, 13/2003, Sonderforschungsbereich 373, Humboldt Universität zu Berlin.

Nolte, I. and W. Pohlmeier (2007), Using forecasts of forecasters to forecast, *International Journal of Forecasting*, 23: 15–28.

Ochel, W. (2000), *Collective Bargaining (Centralization and Co-ordination)*, Munich: Ifo Institute for Economic Research.

OECD (2004), *OECD Employment Outlook 2004*, Paris, France: OECD.

Osgood, C.E. (1953), *Method and Theory in Experimental Psychology*, New York: Oxford University Press.

Palmqvist, S. and L. Strömberg (2004), Households' inflation opinions – a tale of two surveys, *Sveriges Riksbank Economic Review*, 4: 23–42.

Papadia, F. and V. Basano (1981), EEC-DG II inflationary expectations. survey based inflationary expectations for the EEC countries, *DG ECFIN Economic Papers*.

Pesaran, M.H. (1984), Expectations formation and macroeconometric modelling, in P.

Malgrange and P.A. Muet, *Contemporary Macroeconomic Modelling*, Oxford: Basil Blackwell.

Pesaran, M.H. (1985), Formation of inflation expectations in British manufacturing industries, *Economic Journal*, 95 (December): 948–975.

Pesaran, M.H. (1987), *The Limits to Rational Expectations*, Oxford: Basil Blackwell.

Pesaran, M.H. and A. Timmermann (1990), A simple, non-parametric test of predictive performance, *Cambridge Working Papers in Economics*, 9021.

Reckwerth, J. (1997), Inflation and output in Germany: the role of inflation expectations, *Bundesbank Discussion Paper*, 5.

Roberts, J.M. (1997), Is inflation sticky?, *Journal of Monetary Economics*, 39: 173–196.

Seitz, H. (1988), The estimation of inflation forecasts from business survey data, *Applied Economics*, 20: 427–438.

Sekine, T. (2001), Modeling and forecasting inflation in Japan, *IMF Working Paper*, 01/82.

Smith, J. and M. McAleer (1995), Alternative procedures for converting qualitative response data to quantitative expectations: an application to Australian manufacturing, *Journal of Applied Econometrics*, 10: 165–185.

Social Surveys (Gallup Poll) Ltd (various), *Gallup Political and Economic Index*, Washington, DC: Gallup.

Social Surveys (Gallup Poll) Ltd (various), *Gallup Political Index*, Washington, DC: Gallup.

Swedish Institute (2005), *Labour Relations in Sweden*, Stockholm: Swedish Institute.

Theil, H. (1952), On the time shape of economic microvariables and the Munich business test, *Revue de l'Institut International de Statistique*, 20: 105–120.

Visco, I. (1984), *Price Expectations in Rising Inflation*, Amsterdam: North-Holland.

Index

actual inflation: and expected inflation 166–8, *202*; and perceived inflation 121–2, *164*
Adam, Klaus 88
adaptive expectations hypothesis 38–40
adaptive learning 67–9, 72
ADP (Akerlof–Dickens–Perry) model: nearly-rational inflation expectations 177–8
agents' inflation expectation 78
Akerlof, George A. 36, 177
Anderson method 200–3
Anderson, Oskar, Jr. 81
Ang, A. 2
anomalies: of bounded rationality studies 35
Aron, J. 236, 237
asymmetric impact: of information 52–3

backward-looking expectations 53–4, 112, 115
Bai-Perron (1998) break-points tests 182
Bakhshi, H. 160
balance statistic 16–17, 200, 201, *205*
Balcombe, K. 20
Batchelor and Orr model 20–1, 120, 223
Batchelor, R.A. 9, 10, 13, 18, 20, 120, 162, 229
Bayesian approach 236
Belgium 242
Bell, B. 234
Berk, J.M. 20, 102, 160, 161, 223
Bernanke, B.S. 1, 165
Bhalla, S.S. 162
bias: testing for 105–6; *see also* unbiasedness
Blanchard-Quah (1989) identification scheme 142
bounded rationality 35
break-points 182

Bryan, M.F. 197
business conditions *30*, 31, 32

Calvo model of price setting 76–7
Carlson and Parkin (1975) study 8, 17, 23, 120, 160
Carlson, J.A. 8, 18, 80, 120, 160
Carlson–Parkin models 8–9, 17, 20, 25, 27, 31, 160, 200–3, 220, 221, 223
Carrol, Christopher 37
causality: statistical concept 165
causality tests 163–4
CEE4 (Central European economies) 78–80
central banks: and credibility 37, 53, 158, 159, 165–6, 168; homogeneous expectations 73–4; and inflation rate 164; monetary policy 62–3, 70–2, 158; price stability 38
Central European economies (CEE4) *see* CEE4
Cheung, Y.W. 162
Chinn, M.D. 162
Cholesky decomposition 142, 144, 146
Clarida, R. 66
cointegration 108, 129–30, 161, 163, 164
Consensus Economics 118, 123–5, 125–6, 141, 151–2
Consumer Price Index (CPI) *see* CPI
consumers' inflation expectations: survey data 78–80
consumption models 36–7
convergence 86–7, 89
costs: of formation process 35–7, 49–51
CPI (Consumer Price Index) 21, 42, 182
credibility: central banks and 37, 53, 158, 159, 165–6, 168; and uncertainty 37
cross-section variation 43–4
Cukierman, A. 162
Curtin, R.E. 18

Czech Republic 78–80, *81*, 82–9, *91*, *92*, *94*, *95*

data reification 41–2
DeGroot, M.H. 12
demographic subgroups 49–51, 197, 203–4, 205, *206*
Denmark 169
determination: of inflation 148
Deutsche Bundesbank 172*n*2
digit preference 44–5
disagreements: in expectations 36
dispersion of expectations: and uncertainty 9
Doepke, J. 130
Döhring, B. 169
Driver, Rebecca L. 88
Dryden, N. 234
Dua, P. 9, 162
dynamic stochastic general equilibrium models 158
dynamics: of inflation expectations 128–32
Dziuda, W. 169

EC consumer survey 78–80, 101, 118, 119–23, 125–6, 160–2, 219, 229
ECB (European Central Bank) 159, 162, 169
ECM (error correction models) *see* error correction models
ECM-based test 163
econometric approach 236–7
"economic misery" 1
Economic Outlook 7 234
economic reporting 36
education: demographic subgroup 49; and inflation perceptions 197, 205
efficiency: informational 127–8
employment 158
error correction models (ECM) 40
EU data surveys *see* EC consumer survey
euro area: expectation measures 164; expected and actual inflation rates *202*; perceived and expected inflation *207*; predictive performance 102–5
euro area data *144*, *145*, *147*, *150*, *152*
euro introduction: effect on inflation 168–71
European Central Bank (ECB) *see* ECB
Eurosystem monetary policy 162–71
Evans, G. 162
expectations data: sources 140–1
expectations errors 183–6

expectations heterogeneity 62, 66, 70, 73–4
expectations trap 37–8
expected inflation: and actual inflation 166–8, *202*

Ferrero, G. 73
Figlewski, S. 162
financial instruments: expectation measures 219; prices of 158–9
financial positions *30*, 31, 32
Fishe, R. 12
focal points 45
forecast consistency 162
Forsells, Magnus 88
forward-looking information 39, 53–4, 112, 166
France: actual and perceived inflation *121*; consensus forecasts *124*, 125; data sample size 119; Granger-cause inflation expectations 132; measurement errors 122; national survey 199; output gap 135; survey results *126–8*, *130*, *133*; wage equation 237, 241
Friedman, Milton 34, 177
Fu, D. 2–3
Fuhrer, Jeffrey 77, 165

Galí, Jordi 77
Gallup survey 225, *227*, 229
game-theoretic problem 165
gender: and inflation perceptions 197
General Unrestricted Model (GUM) *see* GUM
Germany: actual and perceived inflation 121; affect of expectations 132; consensus forecasts *124*, 125; data sample size 119; expectation measures 164; expected inflation *122*; output gap 135; retained inflation expectations 237; survey results *126–8*, *130*, *133*; wage equation 244
Gertler, Mark 77
Gesellschaft für Konsumforschung (GfK) *see* GfK
Gets approach 236
GfK (Gesellschaft für Konsumforschung) 119
Giordani, P. 17
Goodhart, C.A.E. 159, 168
Gorter, Janko 88
Granger-causality tests 129, 131, 135, 163–4
Granger Causality (Block Exogeneity Wald) Tests 135

Great Moderation 1, 6*n*4
Greenspan, A. 159–60
Groeneveld, J.M. 163
Gulamani, R. 162
GUM (General Unrestricted Model) 236

Harmonised Index of Consumer Prices (HICP) 102, 200–1
Hendry, D.F. 236
Henzel, S. 15
heterogeneous expectations 62–3, 66, 73–4
HICP (Harmonised Index of Consumer Prices) *see* Harmonised Index of Consumer Prices
HIP survey 181, 196, 206, 225, *227*, 228, 229
Hodrick–Prescott variant 143
Holden, K. 127, 162
homogeneous expectations: central banks 73–4
Households Purchasing Plans (HIP) survey *see* HIP survey
Hungary 78–80, *81*, 82–9, *92*, *94*, *95*, 198
hybrid Phillips curves 5, 88, 101, 112, *113–14*

Idson, T.L. 12
IFO World Economic Survey 15
imperfect information 36
impulse responses 152–3
incentives: for information gathering 197, 210–15, 216
index-linked bonds 159, 219
inflation break-points 182
inflation expectation measures: usefulness of 82–3, *84*, *94–5*
inflation expectations: importance of 1–2
inflation expectations heterogeneity 62–3, 66
inflation forecast targeting 163
inflation indexes 42
Inflation Psychology Survey 197, 206; Federal Reserve Bank of Cleveland 196
inflation rate 164
inflation shocks 142, 151, 152
inflation targeting regimes 62, 141, 163
information: asymmetric impact of 52–3
information environment 10–13
information flows 36
information sources 41–2
informational efficiency 210
institutional variables 234–6
interest rates 2, 23, 25, 29
Ipsos survey 78–80

Ireland 164
Italy: actual and perceived inflation *121*; consensus forecasts *124*, 125; data sample size 119; EC Consumer Survey *123*; inflation expectations 132; output gap 135; survey results *126–8*, *131*, *134*; wage equation 243

Johansen method 129
Joint Harmonised EU Programme of Consumer Surveys: data set 198–210
Jonung, L. 197

Kenny, Geoff 88
Khan, Hashmat 37
Knöbl, Adalbert 80
Kremers, J.J.M. 163
Kuttner, K.N. 166

lagged changes 51–2, 77, 133–4
Lahiri, K. 18
Lazear, E. 236
Leeuw, F. de 162
Lelyveldt, I.P.P. van 168
Levin, A. 141
Livingston Survey of Professional Forecasters 179
Lovell, Michael C. 35
Lundborg, Per 180

McAleer, Michael 82
McCallum, B.T. 107
McKelvey, M.J. 162
macroeconomic efficiency 109–12
Madsen, J.B. 160, 162
Mankiw, N. Gregory 37, 78, 237
Mastrobuoni, G. 169
mean estimators: alternative *21–2*
Mean Squared Error (MSE) *see* MSE
measurement errors 48–9
Meltzer, A.H. 162
Menil, G. de 162
Michigan SRC surveys: application to data 21–8; as comparative study 206; demographic properties 197; expected inflation 179; frequency 9; qualitative questions 8; quantified expectations 27–8; quantitative data *18–19*; questions 10, *11*, 42, 181; sample size 10; survey responses 13–15
Mishkin, F. 2
model uncertainty 36
models of expectations 38–41
monetary policy: central banks and 158;

design of 154; effect of 70–2; and
   forecasts 165; implications 37–8
monetary policy analysis: Eurosystem
   162–71
monetary policy shock: effect on inflation
   168–71
money illusion 169
Moore, George 77, 165
Mordonu, A. 169
MSE (Mean Squared Error) 221–3, *224*,
   225
Muth, J.R. 12, 34, 126

Nash bargaining model 233–4
nearly-rational inflation expectations: ADP
   model 177–8; and survey data 181–92;
   testing the hypothesis 179–81
Neilsen, H. 20
the Netherlands 164, 169, 198, 242–3
New Keynesian models: of aggregate
   supply 132; of business cycles 62, 63–6;
   of price dynamics 112, 132
New Keynesian Phillips Curve (NKPC)
   see NKPC
news media 36
Nickell, S. 234
NKPC (New Keynesian Phillips Curve)
   76–7, 88, 133, 135, 142
nominal bonds 159, 219
non-inflation targeting regimes 141
non-nested testing 231–3
non-stationarity: of time series 143
Nunziata, L. 234

Ochel, W. 236
OECD data 141–2, *145*, *146*, 151–2
OECD Productivity Database 234
Orr, A.B. 10, 13, 20, 120
output gap 141
output shocks 152
output variance 151
output volatility 172n2

Padula, Mario 88
Palmqvist, S. 197
Paloviita, Maritta 88, 132–3
panel data 47–8
Papadia, F. 160
Parkin, Michael 8, 80, 120, 160
Pearce, D.K. 162
Peel, D.A. 127, 162
perceived and actual inflation 121–2, *202*
perceived and actual prices 159
perceived and expected inflation *203*

Pesando, J.E. 162
Pesaran approach 220, 237
Pesaran, Hashem M. 81, 162
Phelps, Edmund S. 177
Phillips curve 1, 37, 83–9, *97*, 140, 179
Plato 38
Poland 78–80, *81*, 82–9, *90*, *93*, *94*, *95*
policy shock: effect on inflation 168–71
predictive ability 221–5
predictive performance: of a quantitative
   indicator 102–5; quantitative measures
   229
predictive power: comparison 125–6
price development questions *119*
price stability 159–60
price stickiness models 158
private information 37
probabilistic approach 116n3
probability method 80–1, 89

qualitative data 32, 78–80, 119–20
qualitative price questions: Joint
   Harmonised EU Programme of
   Consumer Surveys 200–4
qualitative questions: surveys 8, 10
quantification 16–21
quantification methods 80–2, 219–20
quantification results 82–3
quantified expectations: Michigan SRC
   surveys 27–8
quantified mean expectations 9
quantitative data: and qualitative data
   benchmarking 229–33
quantitative evaluation 102–5, 120, 159
quantitative price questions: Joint
   Harmonised EU Programme of
   Consumer Surveys 198–200, 204–10,
   217
quantitative survey data 225–8
questions: Joint Harmonised EU
   Programme of Consumer Surveys
   198–200, 200–4, 204–10, 217; Michigan
   SRC surveys 8, 10, *11*, 42, 181; price
   development *119*; qualitative 8, 10

range responses 45
rational expectations hypothesis: appeal of
   40–1; costs and benefits 35–7; debate on
   35; expectational errors 109; key insight
   112; limitations 140; Michigan data
   54–8; restrictions of 101; tests of 34,
   38–9, 126–8; unbiasedness 83–5, 89
rational inattention 35
rationality 34, 35, 162

"realized" inflation expectations 140
regressional analysis 51–2, 81–2, 89, *95*, 200, 220
REH (Rational Expectations Hypothesis) *see* rational expectations hypothesis
reification: of economic data 41–2
Reis, Ricardo 37, 78
Relative Wage Model 77
reliability: subjectified measures 83
Rich, R.W. 17
RMSE (Root Mean Squared Error) 221, *222, 223*
rotating panel design 47–8

Sacklén, Hans 180
sample size: EC consumer survey 119
Seitz approach 220, 237
Seitz, H. 20
Shigehara, K. 163
Shimer, Robert J. 179
shocks 152, 162
Simmons, Peter 81, 160
Sims, Christopher 36, 78
Slovakia 78–80, *81*, 82–9, *93, 94, 95*
Smith, Jeremy 82
Soderlind, P. 17
Spain 119, 164, 242
staggered information hypothesis 48, 51–2, 55
staggered updating 36–7
standard deviations: alternative estimators *25–6*
sticky information 35, 37
sticky-information Phillips curve 78
sticky information theories 37
Stochastic Parameter Variation model 220
stochastic time-varying approach 220
Strömberg, L. 197
subjectified probability measures *95*
Survey of Professional Experts 118, 123–5, 125–6
surveys 2–4, 8, 196–7; *see also* individual surveys
Sweden 169, 180–92, *207*, 225, *227*, 228, 229, 239–40

tax variables 234
Taylor, Mark P. 80
Taylor Rule 2
Teigland, C. 18
Theil, Henri 80
theory-loaded implicit methods 137n3
Thomas, D.G. 162
threshold models 23, *24*

time series *144, 145*, 207–10
time-series variation 45–7
Traut-Mattausch, E. 169
turning points 223, *226, 227, 231*

unbiasedness 83–7, 126–8, 136, 141–2, *154*, 162
uncertainty 13, 28–31, 36
unemployment: ADP model 179–80; demand shocks 168; as determinant of consumer expectations 9; and inflation 1; nearly-rational inflation expectations 177–8; Sweden 180–1; and uncertainty 28
unemployment rate 21, 36
United Kingdom: actual and perceived inflation *121*, 122; affect of expectations 132; consensus forecasts *124*, 125; and the euro 169; expected inflation *123*; Gallup survey 225, *227*, 229; harmonized EU survey programme 198; output gap 135; sample size 119; survey results *126–9, 131, 134*; wage equation 240–1
United States of America 118, 181–92
University of Michigan consumer surveys *see* Michigan SRC surveys
US Survey of Professional Forecasters 17
US Treasury Bill yield 21
utility maximisation 34–5

VAR models 129–32, 141–55, 163
variance decompositions: comparisons *150*; euro area *150*; individual country data *151*; time horizons *149*
VEC system 129–32
VECMs (vector error correction models) 143, 163, 166, 167
Venkatu, G. 197
Virén, M. 132–3

Wachtel, P. 162
wage equations 233–44
Wald tests *154*
Walsh, C.E. 158
Weiserbs, Daniel 81, 160
Wollmershauser, T. 15
Woodford, Michael 38, 158, 165

Yates, A. 160

Zarkesh, F. 17
Zhu, Zhenhua 37